The Townshend Moment

꒯ꞷꞔ

THE LEWIS WALPOLE SERIES

IN EIGHTEENTH-CENTURY CULTURE AND HISTORY

The Lewis Walpole Series, published by Yale University
Press with the aid of the Annie Burr Lewis Fund, is dedicated
to the culture and history of the long eighteenth century (from
the Glorious Revolution to the accession of Queen Victoria). It
welcomes work in a variety of fields, including literature and
history, the visual arts, political philosophy, music, legal history,
and the history of science. In addition to original scholarly work,
the series publishes new editions and translations of writing from
the period, as well as reprints of major books that are currently
unavailable. Though the majority of books in the series will
probably concentrate on Great Britain and the Continent, the
range of our geographical interests is as wide as
Horace Walpole's.

The Townshend Moment

The Making of Empire and Revolution in the Eighteenth Century

Patrick Griffin

Yale

UNIVERSITY PRESS

NEW HAVEN AND LONDON

Published with assistance from the Annie Burr Lewis Fund and the Mary Cady Tew Memorial Fund.

Yale University Press books may be purchased in quantity for educational, business, or promotional use. For information, please e-mail sales.press@yale.edu (U.S. office) or sales@yaleup.co.uk (U.K. office).

Set in Fournier type by IDS Infotech Ltd., Chandigarh, India.
Printed in the United States of America.

ISBN 978-0-300-21897-8 (hardcover : alk. paper)
Library of Congress Control Number: 2017938433
A catalogue record for this book is available from the British Library.

This paper meets the requirements of ANSI/NISO Z39.48-1992 (Permanence of Paper).

10 9 8 7 6 5 4 3 2 1

For Tim Breen, Nicholas Canny,
Peter Onuf, Tom Bartlett,
and the late Drew Cayton

Men make their own history,
but they do not make it as they please.
—Karl Marx, *The Eighteenth Brumaire of Louis Bonaparte* (1852)

Contents

Acknowledgments

As you will soon see when you begin reading this book, I am fascinated by the way contingency, providence, or good fortune—call it what you will—shapes broad dynamics. The writing of this book became a laboratory of sorts for how this mysterious process works. So many people shaped how I saw the themes the book explores, sometimes in ways they probably don't even remember. But I remember! And I recount my many debts fondly. Bit by bit, their insights, at critical moments, helped me see things in new ways. The many people listed below informed this book by talking to me, listening to my ideas, challenging my half-baked notions, and supporting my research. They even did it by visiting castles with me, letting me know of sources, or giving me their dissertations to hold on to. Each of them did so generously, so much so that a few are listed a number of times.

It is a great pleasure to thank all the scholars who helped me with the many moving parts of the book as they were being designed. Through numerous talks I refined what I was doing, focusing on different aspects of my argument with each new talk I gave. These scholars include colleagues and friends at the following institutions and venues: Aberystwyth University, the Huntington Library, the Early Modern Seminar at the University of Southern California, the Irish Seminar in Buenos Aires, the Global Seminar of the Institute of Historical Research in London, the University of Edinburgh, Bielefeld University, the Rothermere American Institute at the University of Oxford, the University of London, Notre Dame's Institute for Advanced Study, Notre Dame Law School, the Newberry Library, Northwestern University, Mississippi State University, Yale University, the Rocky Mountain Early American Seminar at the University of Utah, and Trinity College, Dublin. It was a treat and honor to have presented my work at all of these venues.

Unstintingly, archivists were extraordinarily helpful. I was privileged to work at the Beinecke Library at Yale; the Clements Library at the University of Michigan; the Huntington Library; the National Army Museum, Chelsea; the Public Record Office of Northern Ireland; the Oireachtas Library, Dublin; the National Archives at Kew; the Irish National Archives; the British Library; the Bodleian Library at the University of Oxford; the Westminster Abbey Archives; the Grolier Club of New York; Sir John Soane's Museum; and the Jefferson Library at Monticello. Similarly, a number of museums, galleries, and collections kindly allowed me to make use of the images that are so important for the book. These include the National Portrait Gallery, London; the Clements Library; Tate Gallery, London; Westminster Abbey; Mansion House, Dublin; the Osher Map Library; the Art Gallery of Ontario; Clare College, Cambridge; the McCord Museum, Montreal; and the National Archives and Records Administration in Washington, D.C.

More important, I have been the beneficiary of the help of so many individuals who shared their thoughts and time so freely over many a conversation. These interactions, some intense and others fleeting, had a profound effect on the shape of the book and how I came to appreciate how a "moment" works. These scholars include (in no particular order) Martyn Powell, David Dickson, Tom Bartlett, Andrew O'Shaughnessy, Ian McBride, Vincent Morley, Nicholas Canny, Ciaran Brady, Michael Brown, Joe Buttigieg, Declan Keiberd, Patrick Geoghegan, Philip Hamburger, Owen Dudley Edwards, Jan Stievermann, Jessica Roney, Richard Drayton, Ben Bankhurst, Will Hay, Steve Pincus, Eric Hinderaker, Neil Longley York, Chris Hodson, Sam Fisher, Jack Greene, Brian Schoen, Kevin Whelan, Jimmy Kelly, Rachel Banke, Diarmuid Ó Giolláin, Tim Shannon, Lige Gould, H. T. Dickinson, Richard Bourke, Andrew Mackillop, Mary Daly, Frank Cogliano, Pekka Hämäläinen, Barry McCrea, Brendan McConville, Andrew Beaumont, Macdara Dwyer, Justin du Rivage, Tom Cutterham, Peter Mancall, Jim Sheehan, Alex Barber, Max Edelson, and D. G. Rogers. One, Maurice Bric, even gave me the gift of a George Townshend caricature. As I look at this list, I am humbled by the many wonderful people I have been blessed to work with over the years.

I owe a special word of thanks to Lord Charles Townshend, who invited me into his house and shared what he knew of his family. I am deeply appreciative of the time he took with me to answer my questions. Also kind thanks for reading a draft of the Prologue, which I sent to him and in which he plays an important part.

At Notre Dame I am fortunate to have some great colleagues. The following from the history department were especially generous with their time and with their insights. Jim Smyth, Bob Sullivan, Kathleen Cummings, Tom Tweed, Jim Turner, Jon Coleman, Dan Graff, Felipe Fernandez-Armesto, Brad Gregory, Tom Kselman, John Deak, Ted Beatty, Margaret Meserve, Rory Rapple, Mark Noll, Alex Martin, and Evan Ragland were kind enough to offer their thoughts on various aspects of the project, in large and small ways. Jon Coleman was good enough to read a bit of the manuscript for me. I am fortunate to work for a university that has resources to help scholars accomplish what they set their minds to. My work has been supported by the generosity of our president, Fr. John Jenkins; our provost, Tom Burish; our dean, John McGreevy; and the director of the Keough-Naughton Institute, Chris Fox. I am not sure if anyone thanks Notre Dame's development team or its investment office when a book is published, but there is always a first time. If I did not thank Scott Malpass (and Paul Buser!) for all they do for scholars at our university, it would be churlish. I served as chair of the history department while I worked on this book, so there's no chair to thank. Then again, it is a thankless task. The department's chief admin, Lisa Gallagher, deserves a great deal of credit for helping me with the logistics of a great many things that went into the book. Another group of scholars and friends at ND also offered a great deal of guidance, support, and thoughtful responses to my ideas. These would be Neil Mac Donald, Catherine Bolten, Tom Cummings, Ian Kuijt, Brian Ó Conchubhair, Sebastian Rosato, Sean McGraw, Lisa Caulfield, and Rick Garnett.

Research assistants offered terrific help along the way. I am grateful to Aaron Willis, Sam Fisher, Johnjo Shanley, and Bry Martin. Aaron and Sam, especially, were magnificent.

Then there are those few people who shaped my broad approaches to the past over many years, usually over beers or whiskey (or both), and who weighed in on this project as if it were their own. I am delighted to recognize Peter Onuf, Tim Breen, Robert Ingram, Peter Thompson, and Elliott Visconsi. The book could not have happened without them.

I owe a special thanks to a number of historians who suffered through a rough first draft. Tim Breen, Tom Bartlett, Bob Sullivan, Martyn Powell, and Robert Ingram, I am sure, saved me from many a foolish mistake.

The good people who run the Lewis Walpole series at Yale University Press have been wonderful to work with. Chris Rogers was my first point of contact at the press. The book was then picked up by the very able and affable Erica Hanson. My thanks to her for the close reading of the manuscript and her fine work behind the scenes. The three outside reviewers offered wonderful reads of the manuscript. The book is much better for their time and effort. As luck would have it, I discovered the identity of two of the three after the fact. It would be unbecoming to name them here, as they were supposed to have been anonymous. They are listed in these acknowledgments, and they know how grateful I am for their insights.

Every one of my books could and should be dedicated to my family. All of my others have been. However—for a change—I have chosen five senior scholars who have played especially formative roles in my life's work. Each has served as a mentor and patron. Four now are dear friends. One, alas, has recently passed away. Honoring these historians serves also to thank the generation of scholars that came before me and transformed the ways we conceive of colonial America, early modern Ireland, and Britain's Atlantic empire. These five stand, in my mind, as the leading edge of that generation.

But I am the author of this book, and I will finish these acknowledgments with a second dedication. Here's to Mary Hope, Michael, Liam, Maggie, and Annie! This book is theirs as much as mine. Here my treasure lies.

The Townshend Moment

Prologue

Raynham Revisited

An American traveling in England can be all too easily impressed. I learned this basic lesson when I journeyed from London to Norfolk to visit an aristocratic house called Raynham Hall. I was going to Raynham because I was writing a book on two brothers who had lived there in the eighteenth century, the men who grace the jacket of this book. George and Charles Townshend, who figured in the histories of Britain, Ireland, and America during a tumultuous period, had spent a great deal of their childhoods at Raynham. Eventually George, the eldest, called it home after their father passed away.

My project began with nothing more than a hunch. One brother featured in America's history, the other in Ireland's. They did so at the very same moment. In 1767, Charles Townshend began his work in earnest as Britain's Chancellor of the Exchequer, charged with overseeing an empire's fiscal affairs and revenue, and devised those duties that bear his name, which we know led to concerted resistance in America to Britain's Parliament. In that same year George Townshend assumed the position of Lord Lieutenant of Ireland, the king's chief official in the kingdom, and worked to tighten the bonds between Britain and Ireland and to undermine Ireland's autonomy. Could the two stories be related? No one had suggested as much before. If they were, would this linkage prove more than coincidental, and what would such a tale tell us of the period in which the brothers lived?

Eager to see Raynham and to put my hunch to the test, I contacted the present occupant, Lord Charles Townshend, and sent a rather impertinent note, asking if I could view his home. He responded positively, invited me to lunch, and told me the train to catch.

The train from London's King's Cross station to King's Lynn takes about two hours. After Cambridge, it wends its way past a number of small towns and villages, and before too long London becomes some sort of distant memory. In fact, when I alighted from the train I entered some place lost in time, as I was picked up at the station by his lordship's butler. We made the forty-five-minute trip from the station to Raynham in a Land Cruiser through a gently rolling landscape of small farms, discussing the family's history, the state of the estate, and the plans for my visit. Mile by mile, I was being drawn into a different world.

When I arrived, the place looked just like it did in the photos, and I felt like Charles Ryder must have when he first set eyes on Brideshead. Raynham, in many ways, typifies the eighteenth-century great country house in that there is nothing typical about it. Like other such structures, it dominates the surrounding landscape and casts an imposing and impressive shadow. The house lies at the end of a lane up from a small river and just past a picturesque little church, no doubt also belonging to the Townshends. Raynham is built in a style Americans call Georgian. It is, as most of these sorts of buildings are, beautifully proportioned and pleasing to the eye. Its brick facade, which seemed to me inspired by baroque churches in Rome, distinguished it from others I had seen, as did the Dutch-style gables, what the Irish in Dublin refer to as "Dutch Billy's." Large, stately, and singular, Raynham projects power.

I was escorted into a side door and asked to wait for his lordship. The place apparently had been haunted by a ghost known as "the Lady in Brown." Sitting and waiting, I focused on other things. An American can become quite self-conscious during moments like these, especially an Irish-American whose father had harbored intense republican sympathies. I could have considered myself ambivalent; in fact, I was anxious, wondering if I was dressed appropriately.

At that moment, Lord Charles Townshend, the eighth marquess, bounded into the room, dressed in the same khakis and white button-down I was wearing. His easy manner disarmed me. And what happened in the very first room we visited seemed to confirm why I had made the journey. Before the tour began, Lord Townshend sat me down in the library to discuss my project and what I hoped to learn. As we recounted what I knew of his ancestors, I was looking at shelves, now only partially filled and numbered by some indecipherable

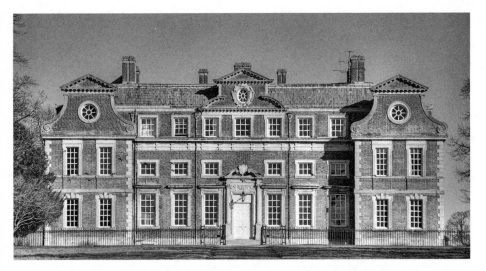

1. Raynham Hall (Photograph by Adrian Turner)

system. I told his lordship that, as luck would have it, I knew what lay in the library in 1764, as well as the exact location of any book. Incredulous, he asked me how. I then told him a story of how just a few months earlier I had had a chance visit with a scholar from Columbia University. Here is how it unfolded. When the visitor asked me what I was working on and I told him, his eyes grew large, and he went on to explain how decades earlier as a child he had held an inventory for the library for Raynham Hall in 1764. He explained that his father had worked as a rare book dealer and when they were visiting London in the 1970s, they had viewed the manuscript. I asked if I could see it. Alas, he said, his father did not buy it. But it existed somewhere! I started digging, and eventually I learned that a small research library in New York called the Grolier Club held such a manuscript. I then flew to New York to view the document.

I shared photos I took with his lordship. We were able to view the contents of this very library from an inventory taken in 1764 and could see how the numbers on the shelves corresponded to where the books were placed in the inventory. Lord Townshend was clearly delighted. So was I. At that moment in the library, before the tour even started, I began to sense I was not here by chance. And I thought my hunch was being confirmed. The brothers, I was growing sure, had come to power at the same time, and their ascent in tandem somehow changed the fortunes of two of the provinces of empire in conjoined fashion. That they rose together could not have been a coincidence and demanded explanation. That I held the key to the contents of their library seemed to mean that I was the one destined to do the explaining.

I had good reason to think as much during my visit. Lord Townshend takes pride in Raynham because it is an impressive place. The interior astonishes. The sight lines struck me as ingenious, and one could view the whole length and width of the house from each corner, seeing the intervening rooms telescoping before one's eyes. The harder I looked, the more enamored I became. The furnishings, those not on loan for an exhibition to the Victoria and Albert Museum, were exquisite. Whoever devised the interior did magnificent work. The paintings caught my eye more than anything. The walls were covered with portraits of family members, including a few by their favorite painter, Sir Joshua Reynolds, the greatest artist of his day. Here I saw a portrait of George that I had never seen before, and viewed a famous full-length portrait of Charles, a copy of which I had just seen days before in Cambridge. We ended the tour of the main floor by spending some time in the front hall, mainly by looking up at the intricate plasterwork of the ceiling emblazoned with the family crest. One afternoon in Raynham confirmed that George and Charles were powerful men of their age.

After we finished with the upstairs, Lord Townshend took me downstairs. Here where the servants would have worked in times past I found two archivists under desk lamps cataloguing the wealth of material the family held, acquired through generations of public service and many adventures, proof positive of the family's stature throughout Britain's history and the present occupant's reverence for the family's past. We glanced at a few documents before making our way to the dining room for lunch.

We were joined by her ladyship for a simple but elegant meal of partridge and claret. Now came the time to discuss what I knew of the Townshends. Did I realize their mother was called "Naughty Audrey"? I did. Had I learned how their brother Roger was killed? I had not. What did I think of the feud between James Wolfe and George Townshend? I suggested that I took the side of George. His Lordship was pleased. Apparently, he told me, a group of people calling themselves the "Wolfe Society" still met to toast the great things General Wolfe had done at the time of the Seven Years' War, and one of its members informed his lordship that some still impugned the memory of George. More than two hundred and fifty years later!

Therefore, the past still endured at Raynham, certainly in Lord Townshend's mind. Indeed, it is fair to say that he sees his legacy and charge as making that past manifest in the present and of protecting it for the future. He and this place suggested that once Raynham betokened power and mastery. It was this that Lord Townshend took pride in. To him, Charles and George still mattered, almost as if the eighteenth century were not a world away but just yesterday. Places such as Raynham, my visit was confirming, still existed not merely as relics of the eighteenth century but to sustain a link between the past and the present. There was nothing nostalgic about Raynham then or now, however much we could hear only echoes of a bygone age.

After about another hour, the visit ended. The butler then took me back to the station, stopping on the way for me to go inside and see the interior of the lovely little church, called St. Mary's, to view where my brothers, as I took to calling them, lay buried.

As I traveled back to London, I was convinced I understood what my project was about. The book would explore how two men, exceptional in their age by virtue of upbringing and experience, had transformed their world and helped bring our world into being. Like their house in which they were raised, they were extraordinary men who had a sense that they were destined to lead at a momentous time. The themes of the book took shape on the trip back to London. "The Townshend Moment," as I would call the book, would explore how two men in the eighteenth century triggered an age of revolution. It would chart how the two brothers from Raynham, both largely forgotten today, had a defining hand in one of the great events in world history—the reform of empire in the eighteenth century—and how what they did reshaped the provinces of that empire.

It all seemed so clear on the train back to London, as all of my reading and work mingled with the magic of the visit. I came to believe that although the world has largely forgotten the two Townshends and contemporaries underestimated them, they were convinced they could manage history's patterns and control contingencies, or those little things that occur often construed as accidental, unintended, providential, lucky, or unlucky. They thought, in fact, they were living during a critical moment, a window of time when past met present and that could shape the future, requiring urgent action by those rare few who could stand above history's patterns and make sense of them. This sensibility sustained their vision of empire, and this is how they hoped to reshape the world around them. Of course, it all fell apart, as such plans do. Such is the nature of drama, and such is what their story seemed to present to me as I left Raynham.

ꝋ⅏Ꝁ

I should have known better. On sober reflection, I should have realized that appearances can deceive, even for a gob-smacked American. It was all there to see on the visit had I not been so gullible, so sucked in by illusion. Raynham itself offered all sorts of signs. A clearer eye would have noted the place was a bit down on its heel. Some rooms were in need of a great deal of attention, and the present occupant has had to pour his income into trying to make them habitable once more. I cannot imagine how much this will cost, but I reckon millions when all is said and done, if doing so is even feasible. Charles Townshend spoke of the expense of upkeep and of refurbishing a great deal of what had not been sold off in earlier generations. The plasterwork, however elegant, was in disrepair. The plumbing did not work. The roof leaked. One bed, a gift of Queen Anne to the family for services rendered to the state, would cost in excess of a hundred thousand dollars to bring back to its original condition. In fact, Lord and Lady Townshend had to live in a house in the nearby town.

This story is unexceptional for England. Many of these houses have languished or fallen into ruin because of the massive upkeep required to keep them habitable. Estates have shrunken. Raynham once controlled forty thousand acres; now the total is five thousand. While farming has changed dramatically, taxes must be paid, even without tenants. The present occupant, therefore, spends much of his time figuring out how to raise money from the estate, its documents, and the historic charm of Raynham. There is a catch. Historic trusts promise help, but signing on with them makes for a Faustian bargain. Owners have to renovate according to the trusts' costly rules, and such a house quickly becomes a ward of the state. Moreover, few want to purchase documents, however important they may seem. Lord Townshend had undertaken a herculean task, a fight against time to preserve the past, one that he would have to struggle to win. His task is complicated because Raynham does not cater to the tourist trade like some of the great houses. Upon further reflection, I saw reality for what it was. Beneath the surface, things appeared more complicated.[1]

By the time I revisited my trip to Raynham with a mind cleared of illusion, I had learned that the Townshend brothers and their moment were complicated as well. What I had come to discover is that the brothers were not exceptional at all. No doubt they wanted the world to believe this was the case, and they thought so themselves. Nonetheless, many of their peers also believed that they were living during a critical period. They, too, thought they could understand history's patterns and so reshape the world. The particulars of plans different actors championed may have varied, but this heady conceit of distinctiveness and singularity intoxicated most, as did the impulse to act urgently, the sense that time was of the essence and the window of possibilities would close. The brothers and their peers believed they were exceptional, and this belief made them all remarkably alike.

Events conspired to inculcate a notion that the brothers were distinctive and destined to lead. Although they believed that they could control the little things, the contingencies of their world, they came to power by a series of good strokes. The fortune or misfortune of the brothers was that fate, or whatever we would call it, placed them on the stage when it did just as they had developed a heightened sense that only they could rule and reform the whole empire. Fate had given them, as opposed to some others, the ability to act. The accidents of history, then, created an open window for two men convinced that the world was made of windows.

The impulse to shape empire stemmed from the idea that they were living during a critical moment as they stepped into the conversation that dominated the age. It also shaped the contours of what that empire would look like, in that the belief that the brothers were almost predestined to rule would, of course, have unforeseen implications. In other words, that they came to power when they did, how they did, and with the ideas they did mattered to empire. Most critically, by believing they could control the little things by discerning history's patterns, they unleashed the furies in those places they thought they could manage. They tried to reform an ancien régime; instead, they accelerated its demise.

The two places the brothers fixed their plans on, Ireland and America, were transformed through their actions. Indeed, revolution in America and legislative independence for Ireland stemmed from their conceit of control. These eventualities also arose as men and women on the margins began to believe that they too lived during a watershed moment. Provincial elites contested what the Townshends proposed. This we know, although we do not fully appreciate the rival models the Irish and Americans devised in response to the Townshends, or the distinctive binds in which the brothers' actions placed provincials. More critically, those at the very margins of provincial societies became politicized actors at this time. They too began to pattern the past, present, and future in exactly the same way the Townshends had done, taking the contingent events of their lives and drawing them together into a meaningful narrative of the inevitable. They too did so through a deep engagement with their own troubled histories. The year 1767, then, proved a watershed moment because people on both sides of the ocean made it so.

The term "moment" can and does mean many things. At the most basic level, it denotes a period, an impulse, and a tipping point.[2] For the brothers it was a time that presented challenges to empire that they thought they could remedy by harnessing the patterns of history. Those living in the period just after the Seven Years' War believed they were engaged in one of history's great projects and in the great question of the age: how to map imperial sovereignty onto a dynamically changing and increasingly competitive Atlantic world. The period and the task at hand signaled a belief that in this brief critical window, actors could shape broad processes. The Townshends thought that if they could manage the vicissitudes of a system, then they could reform empire, and virtue would be the result at this singular time, so long as they acted with vision. As one scholar puts it, a moment could be a period when men and women confronted "a problem grown crucial."[3] The term, therefore, also represents a way of thinking and of considering the relationship between past, present, and future. A moment determines when people begin to change in fundamental ways how they engage the world. Above all, it is the most unexceptional of human constructions. We could say that the urge to think in this way, to imagine historically by pinning meaning on a time, is embedded in our imaginations. A moment suggests singularity, destiny, and urgency, the sense that reality can be transcended and that only the exceptional or virtuous can manage the period's tensions and reorder the world, even if it is a mind-set commonly shared.[4]

Yet, the Townshend brothers were not the only ones to display this sensibility. Even those on the margins—on the peripheries—embraced this way of thinking. To appreciate "moment," and how and why actors adopt this way of engaging the world, is to understand what happens at the time of imperial reform and for provincial revolution. The term explains how one leads to the other. It also suggests how even common men and women, believing they were living during a critical period, could become actors with a sense of agency and even destiny. Even the most marginalized—slaves in America and poor Catholics in Ireland—embraced this way of thinking, potentially imperiling the rule of elites in each society and placing them in difficult predicaments as they tried to negotiate an imperial crisis.

Through this process, this "moment" when reform tipped to revolution, the role of the Townshends would be forgotten. They would vanish from a world now engulfed in revolution. The reason why is simple. They changed the world in ways that transformed the ways people thought, convincing all that a system's inevitabilities—and not men—were to blame. For this, the Townshends were lost to memory. Each of the societies they touched would then be haunted by the ghosts of its past.

This book offers a meditation on revolution, a case study of sorts, but one focusing on an earlier "Age of Revolution."[5] It explores why such interconnected, transnational episodes happen. It also offers a view of the broader Atlantic processes that led people to create imperial and revolutionary moments. But it focuses more on "how," particularly how people pattern events, and, in so doing, how some make empire and others revolution out of the same materials, getting us back to the critical importance and mysterious nature of contingency.[6] Of course, men and women grapple with broad forces that can tend to overwhelm, such as, for example, globalization, and they also try their best in often difficult circumstances to bring interpretive order to the changes engulfing them. Patterns are what people create, but these often hinge on the little things. Yet even if it is made of contingent materials, in a "moment" people craft narratives of inevitability, of rise and of fall. Empires and revolutions are born through this dynamic. In other words, those caught up in this dynamic do not appear in a drama, written by someone else, in which they play prescribed roles; they create the drama. Few, however, have the influence, the opportunity, and the capacity—agency, in other words—to apply their ideas and to believe they can manage the chaos around them. The Townshends did. Only for a brief moment. And that contingent moment would change their world.

The story of the brothers and their moment takes us back to Raynham Hall and its library, when it was more than a relic of a bygone age, when it bespoke power, when it was filled with the books that informed the brothers' understandings of the world. The story moves to London, to the proverbial corridors of power where Charles learned to master the trade of an ocean, and to battlefields far removed, where George practiced his craft. It spells out in great detail how they came to view themselves as distinctive men who could master their times, as well as the "moment" they confronted and created in that fateful year of 1767. It also examines the moment in the provinces, its tangled and multilayered legacy in America and Ireland, and nature of the world the Townshends and provincials bequeathed to posterity.

Therefore, in 1767, these two brothers had to believe they could change the world. As luck would have it, the world cooperated with this conceit. For a time, this "imperial moment," when officials in the center embraced the idea that they were living during a critical period of time, became the "Townshend moment." Empire was shaped by this shift and the ability of the brothers to enact their vision. And this subtle change in appearances ensured a "revolutionary moment," in which provincials reordered their understandings of their own pasts and for which the brothers were lost to history. In this transatlantic drama, all conspired to transform an age into a moment. All struggled to understand if they and their period were exceptional. All tried to comprehend small events and to see how they fit into broad patterns. In doing so, some, like the Townshend brothers, made empire. Others, like the provincials, made revolution. What follows is this complex story, in five acts.

ACT I

Making Empire

Family Matters

How does one gauge the distinctiveness of two men? Perhaps the simplest place to start is where George and Charles Townshend started and with what shaped them: their family and their background. Certainly, all others who have examined the brothers have begun there. And since the brothers' background provides a great deal of colorful material, they have tended to end there as well. On one hand, George and Charles enjoyed extraordinary opportunity and access to power. On the other hand, they struggled with a difficult childhood, one made so by two extraordinary, in every sense of the word, parents. Combined, these two facets of their lives—boundless possibilities and the limits imposed by neglect—would appear to make for a straightforward story of George, Charles, and their experiences in the world.

Their father, Charles, third Viscount Townshend, came from one of the great families of the realm and should have been a great man. He was the son of a diplomat and political heavyweight known as "Turnip" Townshend, himself directly descended from one of William the Conqueror's lieutenants, a "Noble Norman" named Lodavie, who took the name Townshend.[1] Noted for his schemes of rural improvement, Turnip ruled Britain in his day in conjunction with the great personage of the early eighteenth century, Sir Robert Walpole, until Walpole deposed him. While in power, he and Walpole had worked to keep Britain out of war, to avoid the trap of debt, and to orient British policy away from the Atlantic and toward the Continent. The third viscount followed in these estimable footsteps. He held some important posts in government and had cut a figure as an expert in economic affairs. He

did all the things a great country gentleman and lord of the realm was supposed to do. He sat in Parliament, first in the Commons and then in the
Lords, served as a local leader in many capacities in Norfolk, and styled himself a national statesman. In an elite world defined by status, patronage, and
connections, he was well placed.

Yet, he could not rise above his own smallness. He held fast to fixed and
stubborn ideas of which his prudent father would have approved. In 1751, he
published a well-received pamphlet entitled *National Thoughts, Recommended to the Serious Attention of the Public*. In it, he displayed what we could
anachronistically call an almost Scrooge-like understanding of wealth and
the poor. Trade generated income, he believed, which in turn propelled
industry, which begat more trade, all of which sustained national greatness.
In such a scheme, poverty equaled idleness, and the poor had no one to blame
but themselves for their plight. In some ways, he remained firmly and
inflexibly a man of his times; in other ways, he seemed out of step with
eighteenth-century England. In a world that revolved around the idea of
loyalty, loyalty meant little to him. In Parliament he proved as able as he was
trustworthy. Accordingly, he could only go so far in political life.[2]

Viscount Townshend at times treated his children as hindrances, especially when they did not fulfill his orders to the letter. He could be unsteady,
unpredictable, and manipulative. He would on occasion offer to help and
support his children, while at another juncture, turn a deaf ear. He made,
moreover, a dreadful husband. No sooner had he married than he took up
with a maidservant, who would be his constant companion throughout the
rest of his life and with whom he would father three children.[3]

One senses that the children knew they were players in a parental
drama. Young Charles, writing at the age of ten and signing off as "your
most obedient son," asked his father if he could "have the pleasure of seeing
you all down here if you have any time to spare." He asked only for "a suit
of cloes for we want some badly." The boys' father could also be whimsically rigid, at one point, for instance, upbraiding Charles for wasting his
time playing tennis, even if for exercise. Charles treated him obsequiously
but appealed to his no-nonsense sensibilities. At one point, as a means of
trying to gain his father's favor in his career, he observed: "Your present
allowance to me is a very large one, larger not only than what I as your
younger son could have asked, but than your encumbered estate [can] con-
veniently pay." George's correspondence betrayed a stilted formality where

his father was concerned. In one letter George spoke of the "shade of Silence and the Cloud of Awe" that governed their relationship. In another letter, written with clumsy discomfort, he disclosed "a deeper concern, or a more fearful alarm at the incertitude of what was so worldly essential to him," meaning his father's health.[4] Whether he meant what he said we will never know.

Their mother, born Etheldreda Harrison, but known as Audrey, presented a different set of challenges for the brothers. Although she could dote on her children, she cared a great deal more about herself than about them. Most conspicuously—and throughout her life she remained nothing if not conspicuous—she did not concern herself with her reputation, at a time when reputation determined a family's standing. In 1742, to give just one telling example, she received a coded letter from a suitor or lover, complaining of the "miscarriage" of a lost letter that amounted to an "abortion." The writer spoke of "flirtation" and "violent passion," which presumably must have been requited. "Are you not surprised, Madam," he asked, "how I came to learn these technical words?" In another letter, he suggests an answer. He wrote he was delighted "for your Indulgence in receiving." What was given and received left little to the imagination: "I am very sensible when you allow the Copy a Place in your House, you confer an Honour upon it, equal to the Pleasure you give the Original, when you admit him there." To his credit, no one else called Lord Townshend an "original."[5] To add to the intrigue, the man in question, George Hervey, was the son of a political opponent of Turnip.

In 1740, Lady Townshend separated from her husband and took up with a series of powerful men. Her behavior was regarded at the time as scandalous. Two years later, she was consorting with a leading politician named Thomas Winnington. In 1746, her attentions fixed on a dashing Scot named William Boyd, a supporter of the interests of the descendants of the exiled King James II, who had lost his throne during the Glorious Revolution. She then also supported what was called the Jacobite cause. Once Boyd had left the picture, she pursued other prominent men and kept an apartment on St. James Street in Westminster, where she held legendary entertainments.[6]

She was, as one gossip put it, "a frolicksome dame," sleeping with some of the great personages of the age. He added that her adventures explained the virtues of her children:

Charles, thanks to the Lady his mother, has wit,
Has Winnington's Honest, William's Fire,
Some others perhaps might contribute a bit:
But George, Peerless Peer, if full son of Sire.

At least George came by his virtues honestly. The word "frolicksome" only begins to capture her spirit. In one letter General John Campbell, later the fourth Duke of Argyll, swears himself "under your wing as my Queen," calling her later "my princess." As if this is not enough, he playfully scolds her for "spoil[ing] [his son] Frederick." Little did he know (or perhaps he did) that Frederick would also likely become her lover. A woman of great wit and extraordinary energy, Lady Townshend would serve as the inspiration for the character Lady Bellaston in Henry Fielding's *Tom Jones*.[7]

George was born 28 February 1724 in London. Charles followed on 27 August 1725 at Twickenham in Essex.[8] Audrey had three other children with the viscount before they separated. Edward died of smallpox at a young age. A daughter named Audrey would later prove nearly as naughty as the mother, eloping against the family's wishes. A son Roger set his heart on a life at sea.

The brothers were raised in the Norfolk countryside in Raynham Hall. Built in the seventeenth century in the style of the renowned architect Inigo Jones, Raynham sat on the hill immediately above the Wensum River, which was connected to the house by a wide tree-lined avenue. The parish church, St. Mary's, nestled close by. Perched behind a wall on which sat large Grecian urns, Raynham was built of brick. Later, a builder added columns to one of the entranceways to give the house a more suitably classical air. The family subscribed to the sorts of architectural design books, such as *Vitruvius Britannicus*, that lionized classical lines, and the layout of the building would have met with the approval of eighteenth-century English eyes.[9] Jones followed the ideas of proportion and symmetry laid out by the Italian architect Andrea Palladio. Measurements had to be exact, and complex mathematical ratios determined the distances between elements. Raynham Hall, with its symmetrical facade and proportionally presented vertical and horizontal lines, offers a model of the Anglo-Palladian sensibility.[10] Although not large, certainly not as grand as some of the great homes going up in the eighteenth century, it did command—literally and figuratively—its surroundings. Raynham Hall reminded the locals in Norfolk that the Townshends served as their natural leaders.

The grandfather of George and Charles, the second viscount, tried to amplify the family's reach through a renovation of the house in the 1720s. He hired the most famous designer of the day, William Kent, to redesign the interior. And what Kent produced astonished. Young George and Charles grew up in a home with some of the finest furnishings money could buy, amid portraits of their forebears by some of the best painters of their day, and surrounded by plasterwork a king would envy. The entrance hall serves as the perfect example. Here the designers laid out, above a chessboard marble floor, a ceiling emblazoned with the family's crest in deeply cut stucco. The Townshend coat of arms included greyhounds and stags as heraldic supporters, and in its plaster rendering the deer appears to be leaping from the ceiling. True to his tastes, Kent brought in an expert named Isaac Mansfield and hired some of the best plaster workers from Italy to complete the elaborate detail.[11]

The interior, reflecting some of the Italianate tastes that defined Georgian Britain, now announced that the Townshends had designs far larger than Norfolk. They redesigned Raynham to impress men of national stature. And befitting the Townshends' status in the eighteenth century, the leading lights of Britain's political firmament visited and dined in the room that Kent designed. The designs also suggest that the second viscount, who had hired Kent, intended to display his pedigree boldly but tastefully.[12] The Townshends could claim to live in a "temple of the arts" built to the very latest tastes, a place that suggested their family was destined to rule.[13]

The house presented a facade in more ways than one. It could not conceal the fact that the brothers' parents could not live together. After the marriage failed, George and Charles went their separate ways, George to his mother and Charles to his father. Charles's relationship with his father verged ever on the tempestuous. George's relations with his mother remained as warm as they could have been, though as he became older she became emotionally dependent on others.

Their own journeys continued at the University of Cambridge. George lived at St. John's, Charles at Clare College. Both would stay connected to the university and their colleges, and, appropriately, the internal politics of a very political place. In fact, England's political conflicts played out at the university perhaps just as intensely as at Westminster. St. John's, one of the largest colleges, rivaled the other behemoth, Trinity, and they were renowned for their distinctive sets of patrons. Clare, where Charles studied, had close connections to the Norfolk gentry and its most influential patron, Thomas Pelham-Holles, the Duke of Newcastle. The brothers knew Newcastle as their uncle, though in actual fact he was a great-uncle, a brother to their grandmother. Along with his brother, another political titan, named Henry Pelham, Newcastle would hold the reins of government after the reign of Sir Robert Walpole and come to define the age. To this day, paintings of its two famous sons Charles and Newcastle grace the dining hall of Clare. George, too, remained close to his connections in Cambridge, and he too involved himself with its high politics. Unlike at, say, the universities of Edinburgh and Glasgow, at Cambridge members of England's political elite made the connections they would use thereafter in a world that depended on connections. Cambridge offered a beginning tutorial on how to rule, as well as to negotiate the world of networking and politicking each of them entered next.[14]

The sons, no doubt, bore the scars of a troubled childhood, of a cruel father and a narcissistic mother. And to understand them we should perhaps psychoanalyze them. That is certainly what one of the most famous gossips of the eighteenth century did. Horace Walpole, a member of Parliament and close associate of the brothers, saw their childhood as fundamentally shaping the brothers in strange and twisted ways. The son of Robert Walpole, Horace took delight in trying to figure out what made others tick. And as targets for his pen, the Townshend brothers made simple sport. He portrayed Charles as a man of great talent and profound weakness. He was a "weather cock," a fickle man who could not decide what political faction to back and who refused to be pinned down. Walpole described Charles this way: "A young man of unbounded ambition, of exceeding application, and, as it now appeared, of abilities capable of satisfying that ambition, and of not wanting that application." Nevertheless, the barbs always came after such praise: "To such parts and such industry he was fond of associating all the little arts and falsehoods that always depreciate, though so often thought necessary by, a genius." With a loud voice and loud laugh, Charles was consumed with "vanity," especially vexing because it forced him to court the opinions of others.[15] He was a paradox, but one fatally flawed, in other words.

George, Walpole argued, being more like the father, made enemy after enemy for his pig-headed ways. As Walpole put it, George was "a very particular young man . . . with much oddness, some humour, no knowledge, great fickleness, greater want of judgment, and with still more disposition to ridicule." Nonetheless, as Walpole conceded, he "had once or twice promised to make a good speaker." George would prove himself throughout his career "brave, clever, and not devoid of good feeling," but he could be "impatient of authority, and possessed in a singular degree the faculty of detecting and exaggerating the faults of his superiors." He, therefore, made "hasty and striking judgments." Pride made George rigid in the very same way vanity made Charles ambivalent. Decision making, even at times to spite himself, never proved a problem for George. He was, beyond doubt, a dashing character, "manly in person, demeanor, and sentiment," and "agreeable to his friends and formidable to those he disliked."[16]

The brothers could not change, for better or for worse, certain aspects of their inheritance. On the plus side of the ledger, and as their portraits testify, both George and Charles were "fair and handsome men." Charles, the more studious of the two, who by his own admission was always reading, became a man both "satirical and facetious." He loved to be in the company of friends late into the night. One acquaintance from his college days recalled Charles "has wonderful parts, [and] equivocal Honesty." He was talented but enigmatic. Those who knew him later would echo these sentiments, speaking of "his transcendent parts, his good qualitys, and his great failings." Charles struggled with physical ailments, including headaches—presumably migraines—and "bowel" issues, as well as, more than likely, epilepsy. It would appear he suffered from anxiety too, but like many who do, he denied this was the case. "My want of health," he argued, "arises I believe more from natural infirmities than any uneasiness of mind . . . but I am convinced I often suffer illnesses which have no other source, than a constitutional weakness." George, by contrast, was a model of fitness. The more adventurous brother, he seemed destined to develop into a natural leader. As contemporaries noted, he certainly could be stubborn to a fault. He also possessed hidden talents. He had, for example, an extraordinary gift for caricature and could sketch a reasonable likeness of someone in seconds. He, too, was outgoing and bright. Yet, as one critic alleged, George was "a man of more ability than sound judgment."[17]

We could take such portrayals with a grain of salt. Horace Walpole, ever waspish, could be accused of writing more about his own conflicted sense of self and warped sense of perspective than about his many subjects. He also regularly took digs at his family's political enemies, and with the Turnip-Walpole falling out and the rivalry to be the chief family in Norfolk,

Horace Walpole was choosing promising targets. Moreover, the characterizations come off as simplistic, almost of a one-dimensional quality. One brother, for instance, in Walpole's estimation, wanted to make friends too much, the other too little. They resembled perfectly the flawed people who raised them. The only twist on this story is that though Charles as a child spent more time with his father, he ended up more like his mother, cursed by vanity. And George came to resemble his father in his pride, though he lived with his mother. We could, therefore, simply agree with Walpole's observation that behavior followed the fact that each was "not loved by either of his parents" and say the case is closed.[18]

Despite its limitations, Walpole's interpretation has lived on. Sir Lewis Namier, a leading expert on eighteenth-century political culture during the mid-twentieth century, wrote a penetrating study of Charles's life and a shorter treatment of George. In both, he argued that the behavior and political stances of each could be fixed to their troubled backgrounds. For Charles, when it came to the duties that bear his name, Namier writes, "there was a strong emotional colouring to that programme, derived from his early impressions of family life." These were not the cheeriest. "Fear seeking relief in mockery" is how he summed up Charles, and that penchant for humbling others through wit was for Namier "a weapon of the intelligent under oppression." Charles balanced his abilities with "inordinate vanity, and poverty of heart," all of which explains his vacillation. George was in for similar treatment. Namier follows Walpole's line and explains that George "was governed" by his mother. His George, cribbed from his Charles, is "warm hearted, sensitive and capable of enthusiasms, but unsteady and odd, intermittently ambitious, often disgruntled, quarrelsome, lacking in judgment, and burdened with an insuperable urge to ridicule, the resort of the intelligent under oppression."[19]

Namier casts a long shadow both over the Townshends and over the eighteenth century more generally, exerting, as one scholar argues, "a magnetic pull" on other historians of the period. At the hands of subsequent historians, Charles always plays the role of "shuttlecock" with a "propensity to fluctuate," and the actions of George stem from his "inflexibility" and "sense of duty," all of which are attributable to background.[20] Their ideas matter naught. In this way, they resemble the Namierite understanding of the nature of eighteenth-century politics in Britain, a place in time defined by venality and the most local of interests. However damaged, they became men that defined their age. And such a characterization causes grave difficulties if we are to consider the brothers' imperial visions. By definition, they could not have harbored any.[21]

We may finally be moving out of Namier's shadow. Scholars are increasingly taking the ideas and principles that informed eighteenth-century British political culture more seriously and peering beyond what one historian refers to as "displays of ambition cloaked in a show of morals."[22] After all, making inheritance, which leads to twisted ambitions and hypocrisy, the stuff of destiny all sounds too neat. Does a life unfold almost inevitably from the way it begins? Family, and the other accidents of history, matter. But so, too, do a great many other things, including ideas and context.[23] No doubt, the Janus-faced inheritance of the brothers made deep behavioral traits or ruts that they would fall into time and time again. For George, pride and stubbornness were traits that confounded him. For Charles, extraordinary flexibility and concern for the opinion of others compromised his abilities. But these same vulnerabilities went hand in hand with great strengths. Charles had fine political skills; George possessed an iron will.

More critically, who the brothers were and how they understood the world shifted with the many circumstances, difficulties, and opportunities that they confronted throughout the years when they were trying to carve out their reputations. Who they became also reflected how effectively they could or could not confront the issues that bedeviled them. And this gets us beyond biography to how they gave the world and its contingencies meaning. Alone, they struggled. Together, however, each challenged the other to grow. The sum total of their lives reflected the templates of their past, the contexts they negotiated, and their ability and inability to see themselves honestly. In grappling with these entangled variables, they crafted the narratives of their lives, gave the vicissitudes of life meaning, and imposed order on a messy social reality. This process, more than their varied pasts, would drive them.

Much more interesting and informative than trying to figure out how the brothers' shortcomings stemmed from their parents in an almost Freudian manner is to place them in the world they moved through and to try to see how they created narratives of order. What emerges when one reads that record of how they brought meaning to the events and tensions of their lives is not only their foibles but also their staggering talents, distinctive to be sure and perhaps a bit paradoxical if taken separately, but complementary if viewed together. And that is the way to consider them: as two halves. As they matured they became their own men, each confident but reliant, in an admirable way, on the other. In fact, little did either of the parents realize that their sons, together, would help create the world that they moved through, one dynamically changing and one on which Britain through trade and arms would leave an indelible stamp. They would do so by trying to make sense of that world, of themselves, and of each other.[24]

Commerce and the Atlantic

What they chose to do reflected their inclinations and talents. That they enjoyed opportunities of course stemmed from the connections their name brought them; they happened to come from a connected family in a world defined by patronage. Their connections, in fact, were second to none. As well as being considered nephews to Newcastle, the brothers had been godsons to the king. Though an honorific relationship—George II did not attend their christenings—the honor spoke to the influence of the family. The brothers had an easier entry than most into a life of opportunity that would allow them to make the most of their talents. They would each for a few critical years ply this world of patronage separately, learning how the political, military, and commercial worlds worked through practical experience. They would do so in two distinct ways.

Charles at first—and not for the first or last time—disappointed his never-to-be-pleased father. He had a promising start. He opted for a career in the law, studying for an M.A. in Roman law at Leiden. This did not amount to the standard Grand Tour. Charles's father would not sponsor one. Nonetheless, after his trip to the Netherlands, Charles continued with the law, residing for a year in Lincoln's Inn before gaining admittance to the bar. No sooner had he done so than he set his training aside, to his father's chagrin, for a life in politics. In 1747, he was elected to Parliament in a constituency his family controlled, and settled for a post with a body called the Board of Trade. He had hoped for the Admiralty, but in this he met with disappointment. His ambition, at this point, outstripped his experience. He would have to learn how the state ran before he could have a hand in running it. With time, however, he became a great defender of the board and at times "panegyrized" it.[25]

Though created long before and ostensibly designed to offer counsel to the government on trade in the empire, the Lords and Commissioners of

The Honourable *CHARLES TOWNSHEND.*

2. Charles Townshend, line engraving by Miller after unknown artist, circa 1750 (© National Portrait Gallery, London)

Trade and Plantations, to use its proper title, to this point had little voice in the state's affairs. That changed with the appointment of Lord Halifax as president of the board in 1748. Halifax breathed life into the board, transforming it from a deliberative and consultative body into one that designed policy for the empire. Moreover, he was one of a rising generation who believed that Parliament should assert more control over colonial affairs. Convinced of the supremacy of Parliament in Britain, he believed that any assertion of its authority over the colonies and their assemblies need not create a constitutional crisis. The board under Halifax assumed this to be the case. Nearly all of the board's policy was geared to trade. The prevailing theory of commerce held that colonies existed for the mother country's benefit and that all trade had to be geared to amassing wealth in the metropole. What came in and what went out of a nation, therefore, transfixed officials and required a studied expertise. Halifax also believed the board should work to bring some semblance of order to colonial-metropolitan relations. He aimed to turn the board into the body that would enable him to achieve both of these goals. What Halifax needed more than anything was someone who had a passion for the arcane details of a commercial empire and the intricacies of the mercantilist system of trade. He found this in the bright and hard-working Charles Townshend. Even though Halifax was not completely successful in empowering the board, Charles's great fortune was to serve his apprenticeship with the visionary Halifax, a man ahead of his time.[26]

At the Board of Trade, a dizzying array of issues crossed Charles's desk, all of which honed his abilities into expertise. Charles's papers show a man who had to know a great deal about fisheries, tobacco, the making of iron, and manufacturing in and shipping from Manchester. Charles dealt with furs from Hudson Bay, the fisheries off Newfoundland, and the manufacture of beaver hats in Britain. He knew the officers who superintended Indian affairs, as well as their deputies. He read papers on coffee. He could tell the difference between any sort of cloth, where it came from, and where it would go. He appreciated how and why cambrics were smuggled. He knew the sorts of ships that would travel from the Middle Colonies of Britain's American holdings to ports in the north of Ireland laden with the flaxseed that would eventually become the linen that would sail back to America, along with migrants, in those very same ships. He also could tell how much that trade accounted for.[27]

While at the board, Charles kept lists, composed time lines, readied notes for debates, sketched brief histories, and categorized the role and function of each of the colonies within the whole. He was a rigorous and systematic thinker. For instance, he composed hypothetical exercises to explore currency valuation and its effect on domestic and international trade. "Suppose . . ." case after case started. He concerned himself with wines, oils, and fruits from places like Portugal and how they should be transshipped to the colonies. He had to understand how distilleries worked, as well as the illicit trade that flowed from them, and how spirits distilled in the colonies would compete with British manufacturers. White and green glass, red and white lead—for ships' bottoms—paper, china, capers, olives, vinegar, cork, oranges, and lemons: all fell under his purview.[28]

At the board, Charles did more than read. He synthesized the information coming from the colonies. The board members judged petitions and solicited reports from colonial agents and merchants on the state of each colony. Charles, the other members, and their staffs then drafted their own reports to the ministry distilling the vital issues governors were struggling with. Many such reports bear his signature. They tended to focus on balance of payments, budgets, the composition of the population, production that should be encouraged, relations with France and Spain, Indians, and security from threats without and within. The reports betray a detailed understanding of the many issues individual colonies struggled with, as well as the comparative advantages each enjoyed. All Charles and other members did was designed to benefit the whole and to promote trade throughout the empire. Accordingly, in the House of Commons, he resolved to take "some part in every matter of finance or commerce which has occur'd."[29]

The movement of goods he was facilitating was, in part, helping to turn the Atlantic from an assemblage of regions and societies into a coherent and consolidated system. Yes, it was first and foremost an ocean—a barrier to be crossed—and in the seventeenth century it was plied by all sorts of Puritans and adventurers who hoped to settle in and exploit a New World. These places then developed not so much in isolation from one another as along parallel but not heavily entangled lines.[30] The colonies were bound to the center by sovereign claims, of course, but different sorts of political arrangements tied distinctive colonies and plantations with varied histories to England, and in truth they all enjoyed a great deal of autonomy. Management, even under the earlier Board of Trade, did not amount to much. The Crown's demands on those across the ocean were not heavy.

The world was changing dramatically. And by the time Charles began his apprenticeship as a statesman responsible for foreign policy and imperial affairs, he was dealing with the management of a commercial empire in an Atlantic world increasingly defined by imperial competition.[31] By the eighteenth century, the period of conquest and colonization largely by English men and women had come to an end. From Massachusetts to the Caribbean, the colonies and plantations were becoming more settled societies. As they became so, trade began to accelerate, hastened by a consumer revolution in Britain, the development of homegrown industries that manufactured more and more goods, and the rise of a class of enlightened and ambitious merchants in London intent on improving Britain's fortunes by opening up greater avenues of trade with America. At the same time, with the growth of trade, thousands of men and women from the peripheral regions of Europe

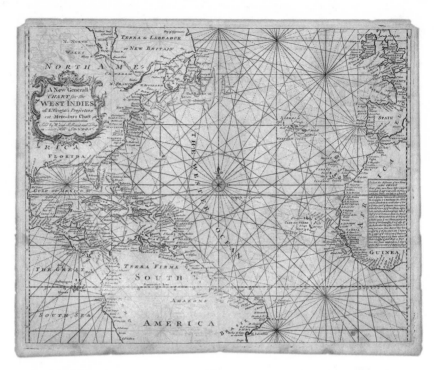

3. A Map of the Atlantic World, 1761 (Courtesy of the Osher Map Library, University of Southern Maine)

and the British Isles—the very margins of the Atlantic—were drawn into the emerging system and burgeoning community, as they sought to leave a labor-saturated and land-poor Old World for a labor-starved and land-rich New World.[32]

By the time Charles was on the board, center and metropole were increasingly tied together by dense networks of movement and trade, making for a more consolidated and mature system.[33] And he, for instance, had to know about the movement of Germans across the ocean and what sort of work they hoped to do, as well as whether they could fight for the Crown if need be. It was his charge to try to understand, facilitate, and manage this movement for the state. Ideally, Charles would foster its growth and learn how to harness its potential to a state that had been focused on the archipelago and the Continent but that now harbored greater ambitions.[34]

Even with the development of a system, he still had to understand the particulars of each colony, its laws, its distinctive relationship to Britain, and its history. He had to know the quitrent rates of each colony, and he asked his clerks to provide outlines of the legal precedents—again, different for each colony—that had been passed during the seventeenth century determining why rates differed.[35] He perused abstracts of acts of Parliament that had been passed for each colony. The empire resembled a rabbit warren of differing arrangements passed under different monarchs all for different reasons to address different problems. Such laws confronted him with a thicket of contradictory and distinctive arrangements for Britain.[36] Bounties and regulations, all passed by Parliament and supported by colonial assemblies, had to be understood more urgently as the new levels of trade began to eclipse older institutional apparatuses. In part, the board was beginning to assume the role of that apparatus.

The Atlantic represented one part, but the one most integrated, of a broader global system of trade. And the board operated under such global assumptions and aspirations. Charles tried to open up greater trade with the Levant and Turkey. He did a great deal of work on the East India Company, that giant trading concern that sent all the goods of the Orient to Britain and its colonies. Tea, of course, was the most precious cargo. But the company dealt with much more than that. It also had sovereign control of small sections of India, really factories or outlets of trade in some coastal regions on the subcontinent. Better considered a "company-state," to use the term of a historian, the East India Company tied the Atlantic economy and British consumption to global patterns of trade.[37]

Charles also had a great say and a growing expertise in perhaps the most important commodity in the eighteenth century: slaves. Slaves created the British Atlantic system, in terms of their inherent value as trade "goods," the commodities they produced, such as sugar, and what their labor allowed the wealthy to purchase. The British state also benefited enormously, and the commercial empire that Charles was learning to navigate grew hand in glove with the exploitation of Africans. In fact, by the time he was coming of age, Britain dominated the sale and exploitation of slaves throughout the Atlantic. The trade in humans transformed the Atlantic, just as it lay at the heart of the British Empire in the eighteenth century. With the phenomenal growth of the slave trade in the years Charles was coming of age, the Atlantic grew to be more sophisticated, requiring new levels of expertise for competing states.[38]

Charles became one of these experts. His papers testify to the critical importance of the West Indies and their plantations for the whole system and increasingly for the British state. He had to concern himself with the ins and outs of the production of sugar, distillation of rum, and management of plantations. He knew the strengths and weaknesses of the Royal Africa Company, the joint-stock company that had been created to buy, sell, and transport men and women from Africa to New World holdings. Although no longer enjoying a monopoly of that trade, the company—and its many competitors—now fell under the board's purview.[39]

Charles's work on slavery ranged from the general to the particular. Charles and his office worked, for instance, on the redemption of a slave in Barbados who was the son of an important African partner of the Royal Africa Company in Annamabo. On another occasion, all for the good of the slave trade, his office paid a bill for the board, lodging, and clothing of two black "princes." He did the same for a number of "Black Boys." The board also managed or oversaw the disbursements in Barbadian currency for "an African Gentleman," who presumably helped the slave trade function. Everything he, the other members of the board, and its staff did was geared to making the burgeoning system work. He also acquired a keen appreciation of the different regions in West Africa that provided slaves, the goods that had to be sent to each. His office facilitated the movement of the trade goods sent to slaving factories such as Bonny and Calibar, as well as to regions such as Angola, the Gambia, and the Gold Coast. Here, he knew, traders sold pants, shirts, iron, guns, powder, brandy, rum, and pewter.[40]

The issues at stake had immense significance for Britain. Because the slave trade grew to its full extent in this period not only for the British but for all European powers, deciding how that trade would be managed mattered if Britain was to compete in the Atlantic and if some of the profits from sugar-producing plantations would fill the Treasury's coffers. Charles's office, therefore, had to count "Negroes exported in foreign bottoms" as well as the duties on those "imported to be drawn back on Exportation to our own colonies." The fortunes of places like Jamaica rose or fell on such considerations, and Britain's future, he sensed, rose or fell with the islands and those who toiled on them.[41]

Charles's interventions did not end there. He read of the trade in slaves to almost all the territories the British possessed, including the sale of a boy named Cupid for debt in Bridgetown in 1747. While he served, the board ensured money would be paid to "castle slaves" in Africa, those people who worked in slaving factories along the coast, which British merchants visited, to keep the flow of trade open.[42] He also had a hand in turning the colony of Georgia into what we could call a "slave society." The colony, the most recent on the mainland to be chartered, had from its origins been free of slaves. It served as a buffer to Spanish holdings in Florida and was not supposed to be tainted with the institution of slavery. Such plans, amid the economic pressures to make profits on plantations, did not last. Within a generation of its founding, it followed the example of the slave-majority model to the north—the colony of South Carolina—and became a society defined by the institution of slavery.[43] In August 1751, Charles signed a report considering whether the colony of Georgia should permit slavery. His report went through the benefits point by point. It argued that certain conditions had to be in place from the very beginning if Georgia was to function properly, especially because of its proximity to Spanish Florida. "In almost every colony where the use of slaves has been introduced," the report stated, "Laws have been passed for the well ordering and governing them." Laws differed colony by colony; nonetheless, certain patterns held: "The sole Principle of all of them is, to guard against the Mischief which may happen from the rebellious and vindictive Temper of Negroes, and for preventing Offences committed by them." The report went on to say that slaves could not possess firearms unless defending the colony. They would have to carry "tickets" to move about beyond their plantations. For capital offenses, they could be tried without a jury. Masters had to follow South Carolinian convention when it came to work hours, clothing, and feeding of slaves. Charles, therefore, knew about slavery in a less than abstract sense.[44]

With increased movement of people, both free and unfree, and goods across the ocean, competition inevitably grew. Therefore, Charles understood what the Spanish, French, Dutch, and Portuguese were trading in. His papers noted, for instance, how the price of French spirits on the coast of Africa undercut what colonial producers in New England could sell their rum for. "A Hogshead of Rum on the Coast of Guinea," he read, "purchases a Slave, which the New England Man after having made that Voyage returns to the West Indies, and sells to the French and Spanish." This arrangement had to stand, but how it would, as the stakes for trade in the Atlantic grew, was anyone's guess. One thing was certain: Britain could not turn its back on the changing Atlantic. "Besides employing a number of Hands in Navigating his vessel and distilling the Rum, there remains a clear Profit to his Country," Charles was learning. Understandably, as his papers attest, he and others worried how "the price of French spirits upon the Africa coast, against at which our rum is to be sold," could imperil Britain's ability to trade for slaves.[45]

Increased imperial competition forced Charles to learn about regions far west of the Atlantic. Though geographically removed from the ocean, even the frontier regions of America made up part of the system and an arena for imperial competition, and accordingly, mastering the frontier became part of his remit. The issue of land settlement in America consumed much of the board's time and energy. Charles read reports on the construction of forts, including the width of their walls, their placement, and the troops that manned them. He also kept notes on the history of French "encroachments" along the borders of each of the colonies. The board formulated all sorts of policy for the interior of America, even producing reports on the possibility of arming ships in the Great Lakes. Charles kept tables of the distances of portages to rivers in the American interior, including even a place called "Cheiagou," one of the Indian settlements that yoked the Great Lakes to the Mississippi system by a small body of water we know today as the Chicago River.[46]

Similarly, colonial relations with American Indians captured his attention. Should the Iroquois, as the most powerful native group in the eastern woodlands, be accorded special status? Should the arrangements between individual colonies and the Iroquois, the so-called covenant chain, be extended to encompass the British as well?[47] And who would pay for such arrangements? Charles also had a say in the appointment of superintendents of Indian affairs, men who would act as go-betweens between the British state and the many tribes that lived in America. Although plans had not as yet been developed for changing Indian ways, increasingly the British realized that they had to reckon with Indians as they tried to figure out what America meant to the empire. As the Atlantic became integrated, as competition between powers grew, the lands in the West represented the future and could become a site of conflict. While Britain was clearly sovereign, what that sovereignty meant was not yet clearly articulated.

Charles also worked to make fiscal policy mesh with prevailing understandings of political economy. What sort of currency should colonies use? How would the ministry deal with depreciation? The lines of fiscal authority involved more than duties on imports and exports, and Charles became the master of both trade and fiscal matters for colonies ranging from "Georgia to Nova Scotia," each of which had a different line of authority to Britain.[48] He read many papers on the theory of trade. He participated in discussions about how Nova Scotia should be incorporated into the colonial structure in the early 1750s, acquiring a mastery of the "charges for maintaining the settlement" of subjects there. The Board of Trade would devise the notion that settlement should be directed there rather than to the North American interior to better link such regions to the center and to ensure these provinces served the interests of the mother country. How many settlers should be sent to Nova Scotia, and should they be "foreign Protestants"? How much would it cost? Just as critically, how many troops from Ireland would have to be dispatched to protect the settlers should the French try to regain the island? Charles was involved with the board in the first attempts to try to see if or how the state should manage what it in theory possessed. The mistakes of the past, it was imagined, through which the perplexing complexities of the American colonial world had come into being, would not ruin Nova Scotia.[49]

In just one year, say, 1750, Charles was present for the lion's share of meetings at Whitehall. They were held in a cockpit over the Treasury and staffed by a number of officers who spent long hours preparing reports and readying agendas. In January of the year, the board spent much of its time working on the slave trade between Africa and the Americas and how or if the state should support it. Meetings in March brought reports on New Jersey, as well as laws passed in Pennsylvania and North Carolina. The board members wondered, for instance, if French Huguenots in New Jersey should be sent to Nova Scotia, the implications being that they would contribute to economic development there. In April the emphasis shifted to affairs in the Caribbean and trade, security, and settlement there. The meetings for the rest of the year ran the gamut, culminating with discussions on 18 December to consider council minutes in Nevis and the conducts of officers in Nova Scotia.[50]

These were more than just academic concerns. While trade networks helped to turn England into a "polite and commercial" nation, they did not yet fully bind all the colonies.[51] Englishmen had addressed such questions before. A series of measures known as the Navigation Acts, passed in the mid-seventeenth century during a period of war and tension with the Dutch, stipulated that the import and export of goods could only proceed along lines laid out by Parliament. Goods had to be shipped in "English bottoms," and anything coming to and from the European continent or its colonies had to travel through English ports. There were exceptions. But trade had to benefit the mother country. Mercantilist policy dictated as much.

Once again, in a period of heightened imperial competition, men at the center were suggesting that the board reorder the arrangements tying colonies to Britain. They were doing so in a period and in a place in which states had grown more powerful and in which networks of trade were more developed than in the seventeenth century. The British did not yet have a "system" for addressing these concerns, Charles lamented.[52] And that is just what he was developing. Throughout his stint on the board he was struggling to appreciate the parameters and imperatives of a broader system emerging before his eyes. These questions were becoming more pressing with Atlantic consolidation.

Charles's work reflected a view of the Atlantic, Britain, and the world in which trade played a critical role in the process of civilizing empire. The acquisitiveness that trade occasioned could corrupt. Many of the books he had read at Cambridge, especially Roman histories, suggested as much. But the flow of goods, and their manufacture and consumption, as leading theorists of the day were arguing, could civilize, first Britain and then the peripheries. The centrality of commerce set Britons apart from those on the Continent. It underscored the liberty that they also claimed as distinctively theirs and dovetailed with polite Protestantism. As a man consumed by trade and as a proud Briton, Charles made civility his watchword.[53]

His views on Scotland, where many of these theorists lived and worked, suggest as much. Charles did not embrace his mother's Jacobitism—far from it, as he was a proponent of the radical reform of the Highlands. The Jacobite Rising of 1745, which saw some Highland clans rally to the cause of putting a Stuart back on the throne by force of arms, had stemmed, he believed, from "Barbarous Rapine and Violence." Now in Parliament he strove to bring civility to backward regions, especially to estates that had been forfeited after the suppression of the Rising in 1746. Scotland could be reformed and brought in line with more civilized places. In this spirit, Charles worked on a bill to bring industry and security of property to the Highlands.[54] Some Highlanders were still mired in what was regarded as superstitious Catholicism, a pastoral economy, and clan structure. But reform of customs, beginning with outlawing of Scottish emblems and artifacts, such as the kilt, the clearance of land to reform agriculture in the region and replace people with sheep, and evangelization of remote areas were part and parcel of a process of reform to bring British civility. And it was working.

Charles made good on his Scotophile sensibilities. In 1755, he married Lady Caroline Scott, a widow formerly married to the third Duke of Buccleuch, an Anglicized Scottish nobleman. Caroline was the eldest daughter of one of Scotland's great lairds and the titular head of Clan Campbell. Her father, John Campbell, the second Duke of Argyll, owned vast estates in Scotland. But he personified the sort of Scot Charles and many English elites could feel at ease with. Argyll also held land in England and had an address in London. Caroline, in fact, had spent most of her childhood in the South. She counted the Campbells, whom Charles's mother, Audrey, befriended, as cousins, and Audrey could not find fault with Caroline. Charles's father, it should be noted, did not approve of the match, observing, caustically, "From what I have experienced from your constant and uniform conduct towards me . . . nothing I can offer on this occasion to dissuade you from your present scheme will or can have any effect." The viscount could not have been further off the mark. The match proved providential for Charles. It brought him a country estate in Oxfordshire and a great house in Scotland.[55] With the marriage, he also had means, meaning financial independence from his father.

In fact, his happy marriage almost represents the relationship between the two kingdoms writ small. If his marriage is any indication, Charles had a sense of the inclusive nature of Britishness. He saw the Scots as full partners in empire. Soon after his marriage, he even thought of declaring himself a candidate for a constituency in Edinburgh. It is safe to say that he was enamored of the Scots and of Scotland. "The women," he found, "are lively, the men are learned, and both are well bred."[56]

On his first visit to Scotland, Charles became acquainted with Adam Smith in Glasgow, a philosopher whose writings he admired. He seemed excited by Scotland's intellectual vitality and impressed by how the kingdom seemed on the cusp of dramatic change. While there, Charles also began plans for making improvements on his vast estate, and in so doing introduced what could be called methods of enlightened improvement to Scotland by bringing in a few estate managers from Norfolk for guidance. For Charles, the intrigues of the seventeenth century and the violence and uncertainty that had defined relations between England and Scotland were a thing of the past with the dawning of this new Atlantic age, one defined by commerce and improvement, even for hitherto backward regions like much of Scotland.[57] Charles, it seems, could leave the ghosts of the past behind.

He was avowedly a man of his times. In the House of Commons, he demonstrated at least a veneer of having principles solidly rooted in eighteenth-century British culture. He castigated his opponents for supporting "prerogative" as opposed to "revolution principles," meaning the power of the Crown versus the rights won by Parliament at the time of the Glorious Revolution. In other words, he professed to be a good Whig. Then again, who did not? The ideas he espoused represented a commonplace in the eighteenth century. His avowal of Whiggish principles also ran concurrent with his bid for higher office and his pursuit of place and position, another eighteenth-century theme in British politics. "He never meaned ambition nor courted popularity," Walpole declared, "but looked upon himself as an executor of those who had planned the Revolution." The recourse to such principles did not make Charles a hypocrite. In fact, they made him a politician, and this was now his craft.[58]

In certain ways, therefore, Charles emerges as an astute statesman, a man far more mature than his age would suggest. As a politician, he was clearly destined for high office and had the ambition, skills, and connections to take him there. Horace Walpole, for instance, observed how Charles from time to time "had displayed such abilities as had not appeared since that House was a House." As the Irish-born member of Parliament Edmund Burke among others would testify, Charles could hold a room when speaking. And Burke, an extraordinary talent in the House, went so far as to declare him "a prodigy." Just as impressively, Charles had acquired expertise in a critical aspect of British economic, political, and cultural life. Through his apprenticeship, he had become, a contemporary remarked, "a perfect master on West Indian affairs and history." He was the board's America expert, a title that required mastery of a great many trades.[59]

He struggled, however, with limitations he could not quite see. And it seems in this regard the diarist Walpole did hit the mark with a few observations. Walpole alleged that "Charles Townshend astonished; but was too severe to persuade, and too bold to convince." However mature, Charles still needed seasoning. At this point in his career, and this view was corroborated by others, he did not care "whether himself or others were in the right, [but] only spoke to show how well he could adorn a bad cause, or demolish a good one." As another critic charged, Charles could be "vain and imprudent," and these tendencies along with "ambitious views" motivated him. He still worked though "duplicity," Walpole charged. But the talent, he conceded, was staggering, and from time to time, the judgment could be reliable.[60]

Coercion and the Continent

Charles contributed to the creation of a British Atlantic commercial system, effectively doing so from a desk in London and from his study in the growing development called Mayfair on Grosvenor Square. George, too, participated in the century's epic events. But he did so in a different way, spending little time behind a desk and serving an apprenticeship—and a first master—very different from Charles's. George chose the army as his profession. On leaving Cambridge, he took the Grand Tour, also without much support from his father, and ended up joining the army in Flanders as a volunteer. The military became a career. By 1745, George was serving as a captain in a regiment of dragoons. Through his connections, he also became aide-de-camp to General Lord Dunmore.[61]

The army became his vehicle for making a name for himself and continuing in the tradition of a family known for its service to the state. He soon caught the attention of the most important man in the army, the Duke of Cumberland. A huge man in every sense of the word and son to the king, Cumberland would cast a large shadow over George's life and career, proving as significant for George's fortunes as Halifax did for Charles's. George's star rose quickly once Cumberland assumed control of the army on the Continent during the War of Austrian Succession.[62]

"Succession" is the right word in more ways than one for this and other wars of the eighteenth century. While they ostensibly centered on dynastic contests over succession and their political implications, these struggles invariably involved Britain, which historically had played the role of balancing Europe's many powers. Focused intently on the Continent, certainly more so than on the Atlantic at this juncture, Britons found themselves fighting a series or succession of wars in Europe in alliance with different nations but always against France. In some ways, the wars influenced imperial competition, the sort that Charles was trying to comprehend as the Atlantic was consolidating, but they stemmed from Continental power struggles. They also emerged from the heightened ambition of European states, growing as a result of a more integrated Atlantic.[63] This perspective, of course, was not lost on George, nor was the significance of the Continent for Britain's future.

GEORGE MARQUIS TOWNSHEND.
IN THE POSSESSION OF THE FAMILY.
London,1836. Hodgson & Graves, 6, Pall Mall.

4. George Townshend, mezzotint by Samuel William Reynolds after Joshua Reynolds, 1759–1761 (© National Portrait Gallery, London)

George enjoyed varied experiences in the army, all of which shaped him. He reckoned with a great deal of the routine, including courts-martial and boredom in camp, punctuated by battles and spectacular episodes of violence. He recounted, for instance, how he had seen a German colonel split in two before his very eyes by a cannonball during a skirmish. He also deepened his appreciation for the other peoples in the British Isles and their participation in empire. From his initial service with Dunmore, George "had a Company conferr'd on him by the Duke of Cumberland" in 1746. No sooner had he become aide-de-camp than he suggested that a brigade of Irish soldiers be led by an Irishman. He took issue with the fact that so many of the Irish opted for French service, when such manpower could and should be put to British use. He knew most of them did so because they were Catholics, and as such did not enjoy political privileges in Ireland; nor were they eligible to serve—officially, that is—in the British army. Unfortunately for George, a Scot used his influence to win command.[64] The army, therefore, expanded his horizons. He saw the world with fresh eyes and understood that Britain, though an island, was enmeshed with Europe. In the service, he visited Paris and Amsterdam, fought in German hamlets, and tramped through any number of countries.

Most significantly, his experiences in the army impressed on George the importance of discipline, as well as the need to root out what he took to be corrupt practices. Throughout his career, he despised what he regarded as small-mindedness and had a difficult time relating to people who placed parochial interests above the greater good. As a junior officer, he hated those in higher authority to lord it over him, and he made it his mission to ensure that civility, not arbitrary authority, ruled relations between officers, whatever their rank. Commanders who abused their powers earned his scorn, especially those who had "oppressed and despoiled" their inferiors. George championed virtue even when it proved politically inexpedient. One erstwhile ally complained how George raised questions which "comprehended the civil and military behavior" of prominent officers in a way that could "embarrass the ministry." He was, as he put it, "astonish'd at his [George's] ignorance."[65]

Like Charles, George had a hand in extending civility in the service of the British state. But his methods involved militarization and coercion. George participated, for instance, in the reduction of the Highlands in the wake of the Rising. This desperate and romantic episode that attracted the attention of people like his mother, was cause for great concern as far as the state was concerned. For centuries, England had had an uneasy relationship with its less-than-civil borders, or "Celtic fringe." Ireland had proved an unending challenge to stability in the archipelago. In the mid-eighteenth century, though, Scotland posed an even greater threat. Highland clans had a long history, admittedly by this time lost in the mists of myth and history, of alliance with France. Moreover, those clans that had not taken the Anglicization route of, say, the Campbells, resisted what the union of the two kingdoms meant and rejected English standards of religion and civility. The cause of the Stuarts presented a challenge to the hard-fought stability that had consigned the uncertainty of the seventeenth century to memory. The thought of a Stuart on the throne again—Bonnie Prince Charlie, the Young

Pretender, descendant of the beheaded Charles I and his exiled son James II—promised yet more chaos, and potentially the fracturing of the 1707 union between England and Scotland. When the clans rose to depose the House of Hanover, now in the person of the reigning George II, the state spared no expense to put down what it called "treason." Like thousands of other soldiers, George Townshend was brought back home to advance the civilizing mission once more. He would engage the enemy at the Battle of Culloden on 16 April 1746. He would later use the words "disgrace and distraction" to refer to the Rising.[66]

George recounted how he left the Continent to join his regiment in Scotland. The Twentieth Regiment of Foot saw action in the battle but lost only one man, with sixteen wounded. Compared to what the Highlanders endured, the numbers amounted to nothing. More than twenty-five hundred Highlanders lost their lives. Claymores proved no match for bullet and bayonets, never mind disciplined troops just over from battle on the Continent.[67] George never shared what happened, or more critically revealed his hand in it, but ended his diary entry simply with: "After the defeat of the Rebels at Culloden he embark'd with Lord Albemarle for Ostend." What he recorded, in other words, was the simple tale of a soldier following orders.[68]

This brief and enigmatic entry glides over incidents of profound violence visited on Highlanders by British forces. In the aftermath of Culloden, the British, under the command of the Duke of Cumberland, laid waste to Highland forces and their homes. Showing no mercy and granting no quarter, the army fought to ensure that the clans would never rise again. Doing so was critical for union, English security, the economy, and the sovereignty of the Crown. Rising meant treason, and "rebels," a charged term, had to be put down ruthlessly. Cumberland, remembered later as a "butcher," put thousands of the Highlanders to the sword. No one's hands were clean, presumably not even George's.[69]

For all of his silence about his role in the massacres, George had a relationship to Scotland that proved more complex than Charles's, no doubt because of the nature of the brothers' apprenticeships and because this period had become such a formative time for his self-understanding. In a long letter to a close friend, George discussed what he thought of Edinburgh, where he was stationed waiting for orders, and of himself after the rebellion had been put down. "My time here passes as disagreeably as you can possibly imagine," he complained, "and I suffer as much as a person must do, who has once kept good company, and is afterwards involved in a set, very few of which have either a good education or any natural parts." He differed from his fellow officers and, as he put it, found "our acquaintance [like a] society without any friendship." He began, he wrote, "to shut myself up in my own quarters, and have recourse to books . . . but the worst of all is, that I cannot get a soul to laugh with me." He thrilled to his role of leadership. "If I delighted in power," he boasted, "I might indeed be happy, for I am, in a manner, king over seventy men, by whom I may be worshipped if I please. The captain is a title, and character tres redoutable; particularly in these times."[70]

Boredom led to reflection. "There is not a woman in this part of the island, of any rank, handsome enough to engage one's attention," George assured his friend, and "those that are tolerable, are so disaffected that they have shut themselves up ever since that day so fatal to their ambitious hopes." And here we get to the dilemma he faced and all Britons confronted in the wake of Culloden. "They look upon the militaires with abhorrence," he wrote, "as we have had so good a share in slaughtering so many of their husbands, brothers, and lovers, who were, as I am since informed, a heap of the finest, robust, brawny corpuses that ever were seen." He worried about the implications of rebellion, "for I assure you," as he put it, "the spirit and strength of rebellion is yet sufficient to furnish you more entertainment on Tower Hill before your time is out. There are peers enough yet left, and enthusiasts enough, to declare for so rash a cause, whenever occasion presents itself." George summed up his views of Scotland in this way: "The disaffection which still remains is too apparent to all, and I wish it was still less latent, that the land might be more effectively purged at once, and the lenity of the government less exposed." He ended his letter by mentioning the fate of Lord Lovat, one of the leaders of the rebellion who would be executed, "and of the ladies we have in Edinburgh Castle: I mean the squadron of the Pretender's Amazonians, some of whom I know." He was referring, of course, to bekilted Highlanders, who hatched the plan with Lovat. He concluded by telling his friend, "I hear my brother is to go soon to Lincoln's Inn; let me know if you see him."[71]

George showed two faces to the peoples of the margins, as his account of the Irish unit and of Culloden would suggest. On the one hand, recalcitrant uncivilized peoples—those opposed to the professed ideals of Britons— could be regarded as rebels. If they did not embrace the ideas that made Britons distinctive—an identity and notion of civility rooted in Protestantism, commerce, and liberty—they forfeited their rights as subjects and would not enjoy the protection of the Crown. This ideology bound British peoples from both Britain and Ireland together, tying together different nations, ethnic affiliations, and histories. It had served as the sole means of bringing the tumult and uncertainty of the seventeenth century to an end. Highlanders and Irish Catholics, then, in theory lived beyond the bounds of this identity, and as such, especially as the Jacobite threat loomed, they posed a threat to the very being of Britain. On the other hand, once people beyond the pale of civility had made their peace with the status quo, even if they did not embrace it, they could provide a service to the state, particularly to the military, which was perpetually starved of fighting men and was regularly engaged on the Continent. To give just one example, Lord Lovat's son, Simon Fraser, within a few years would serve by George's side in the army. Scots, in fact, came to see great opportunities for advancement within the empire, even if their primary role was to provide manpower for the army.[72]

George first gave voice to this Janus-faced understanding of the provinces at the time of the famous—or for Britons, infamous—Battle of Fontenoy in the War of Austrian Succession. Fighting in present-day Belgium, the famed Irish Brigade in the service of France would break the British lines and win the day. George credited the French with a brilliant battle plan, but he also noted how a Highlander division had stood in the way of the Irish. Why, he would later ask, should the Irish fight for the sworn enemy of Britain when Highlanders fought for the British even just a few years after the "Scotch Rebellion?"[73]

By 1748, after the suppression of the Highlands and the War of Austrian Succession, George had become aide-de-camp to Cumberland and had risen to the rank of lieutenant-colonel. At the end of the war, he returned home, taking up lodgings in Craven Street, the same road on which Benjamin Franklin would live. He was still in the good graces of Cumberland, even buying him a few greyhounds so fast that, George wrote, "he desired me to secure him another brace." Once home, he stood for election to the House of Commons for Norfolk, which he won, apparently against the wishes of his father.[74] George proved as single-minded in Parliament as in the army. In fact, in civil life, his two lives intertwined, and he made military affairs the focus of his time in Parliament. His special mission, as he saw it, involved reforming what he took to be corrupt and abusive practices. In Parliament, he focused on rooting out corruption in the army and ensuring that the military would be prepared for any future conflict in Europe. It would be fair to say he became transfixed by these causes.

In pursuing public-spirited policy, George did not stand alone. One of George's greatest influences was Lord Bute, the well-connected confidant of and tutor to the future king. George described him as "the first friend I ever met with in public life." Bute reciprocated. Although often vilified, Bute publicly stood for a set of values that set him apart from George's more natural patron, the Duke of Newcastle, and George's mentor, Cumberland. Bute believed that factionalism and party spirit would undermine all British virtue. The Scot Bute, like Charles's new parents-in-law, epitomized the polite notion of British civility that should in theory tie the union, and one hoped the empire, together. Only those who had developed virtuous habits of service, even as they courted patrons and harbored ambitions, could develop the disinterestedness necessary to lead and to overcome factionalism.[75]

Despite the connections he enjoyed and the good sense underscoring his initiatives, in prosecuting his reformist agenda George faced vigorous, even wearying, opposition. Most conspicuously, his vocal support for reform of the army "incurred the disgust of the Commander in Chief," Cumberland the butcher, that is. George had come to vilify Cumberland. Perhaps, as some have argued, they came to hate each other because George took issue with his treatment of a subordinate officer.[76] Or, less likely, he came to despise him because his mother abhorred Cumberland. More than likely, hers was the hatred of a spurned lover. Rumors abounded of how she had been bedded by the duke while having an affair with a Scottish laird during the '45. Whatever the cause, George met bile with bile. As a diarist at the time put it, George "took all opportunities of opposing any of the Duke's measures, and ridiculing him . . . which he did with much humour."[77] George would feel disgust for his former patron from this point on.

He took aim at Cumberland with his pen. With this target, he produced some of his finest work. Over and over again, he sketched caricatures of the duke, always accentuating his substantial girth. In all of the drawings, Cumberland appears with perfect uniform, medals and sash on his chest, but no face. George has him facing away, or if he is shown in profile, without distinguishing features, almost as if George has drawn an egg with a wig on top of it. He appears as a "lump of fat," like what one scholar calls an almost faceless doughnut. Doing so was prudent. Lampooning facelessness would not open George up to charges of libel. George, though, showed little reluctance in drawing other faces, including even King George II. George suggested, in many ways, that Cumberland had larger-than-life qualities but was a nonentity. The whole image of Cumberland leaves the impression of his massive presence and his lack of distinction as a personage—a faceless monstrosity, like a corrupted institution, be it a faction-ridden ministry or the army.[78]

In Parliament, George supported measures that he knew would humble Cumberland, such as new regulations dictating that capital punishments should be determined by courts-martial and not by arbitrary commanders. He also wrote a pamphlet in 1751 that criticized Cumberland's leadership during the recent war. In it, he declared that "the **** ** ********** [Duke of Cumberland]," who had ensured "victory at C_ll____n," had mismanaged the Continental war, leading to some striking defeats, such as at Fontenoy, and some missed opportunities for the British. As George put it, "Dreams

5. Caricature of William Augustus, Duke of Cumberland, by George Townshend (© National Portrait Gallery, London)

of glory vanished" once Cumberland had taken command of the army. George had no choice to serve with him because, he argued, "the **** ** ********** must be employed." Cumberland's sinecure as head of the army, and subsequent "Blunders," cost the British a great deal, George alleged. Party factionalism and poor generalship had lulled Britons into believing "*England* has nothing at all to do with the *Continent*." The expense of the war, the failures, the predictable growth of French ambitions again had left Britain complacent and not focused on the Continent as it should have been. Instead, some grew fixated with a "blue water" vision of Britain's future. George predicted he would soon again be engaged in a war of "self-preservation" against France, even if his countrymen wanted to delude themselves that the Continent mattered naught.[79]

However salient his points about Cumberland's character and Britain's retreat from Europe, George had taken on someone he had no business fighting. And he soon learned the hard lesson that what patronage created, patronage could destroy. Cumberland did what he could to undermine George. He even tried to have him arrested, unsuccessfully as it turns out, on spurious charges. He let George know that "he must consider himself a Mark'd person." Desperate, George asked his father for help. "I would not ask any favour of you," he opened, "if I did not wish you well." He acknowledged the "check he would receive in his majesty's service" for his actions. He had no choice but to confront Cumberland because, as he put it, "neither my Conduct therein deserved as a soldier nor my character as an Englishman would admit of" any other course. But, as the rather strained letter suggests, his father could not help fight one of the heavyweights of the age.[80] George, therefore, had no recourse but to resign his commission.

The experience did indeed mark George, and arguably he never shook it off. In his notes for his memoirs, he takes special care to point out 1748 as a pivotal year in his life and career. It was the year "he quitted the Service on being put under Arrest." Even if he exaggerated, this slight he would remember. Cumberland came to stand for the vice and corruption he thought undermined any organization, be it the army or the state.[81] In his drawings and in his actions, George demonstrated a vindictive and an idealistic streak, and tried to use all of his talents both to pillory the man who was wrecking his career and to do all in his power to press for what he thought the British state at this juncture needed. He also showed his inability to abide, especially in his superiors, anything he considered corrupt. He could not countenance the sorts of compromises that men in Cumberland's position had to make and did make without hesitation.

George retired, for a while, to politics and to London. By 1753, he had taken up residence close to Charles in fashionable Mayfair at South Audley Square. Audley Square was a more appropriate address than Craven Street for a man of eminence. The brothers' two homes, in the latest development of London, sat less than a quarter mile apart, separated only by Grosvenor Church and a few residences of the political and military elite of Britain, such as Lord Bute. Like Charles, George had married well. In 1751, he wed Lady Charlotte Compton, who held the title Lady de Ferrers. She was the daughter of a wealthy and well-connected grandee from Northhampton. The marriage, again like Charles's, allowed George to live in a station he had grown accustomed to, perhaps better, without having to rely on his father. He then focused on his seat in Parliament for Norfolk, but he did so as a man whose future did not appear as bright as it had before. His apprenticeship had not gone as well as Charles's. He had gained a great many skills and had made a name for himself, but not always in the ideal way. George bore some scars from the Cumberland affair, and he styled himself a man concerned, perhaps obsessed, with corruption, especially when men placed status and ambition above virtue and the needs of the state. He also pressed other military issues, particularly the need to have sufficient numbers of troops at home, more than the three regiments in the mid-1750s, to defend England.[82]

Brothers in Arms

With the Cumberland imbroglio and George's becoming a "marked" man whose fortunes seemed uncertain, the brothers rediscovered each other. They both knew of the other's accomplishments and setbacks. But separate upbringings, divergent career paths, and sheer geographic distance meant they had never before had an opportunity to work with and for each other. They could, no doubt, trade stories about their father; however, the union of the brothers grew into a bond, not so much over a common enemy as because of mutual affection. Charles suggested his rediscovery of George marked his life. "Wherever he goes," he predicted to his mother during George's dark stretch of the 1750s, "fame and confidence will attend his steps and dignify his retreat and alleviate his disappointments."[83]

As he grew closer to George in his period of political exile, Charles saw in him inflexibility but greatness as well. "Why is he for ever to be the sport of men, but the occasional mimics of his steady integrity," he asked. "Will experience never give him either caution or indifference? Must he always derive uneasiness from his virtue," he wondered, concluding with a rhetorical question: "Who could expect either happiness or greatness if George can not?"[84] George, it seemed, needed some of the flexibility Charles had in abundance.

Warfare, once again with France, served as the catalyst that would bring the brothers together. While George was living in Norfolk and London, and Charles was getting ready to marry, the French and British were on the verge of war in the American wilderness. Eventually, these powers would fight on every known continent in the epic imperial struggle of the century. Justifiably, Winston Churchill called the conflict the "first world war." The term "the Great War for the Empire," as it was christened by the historian Lawrence Henry Gipson, speaks more fittingly to what was at stake, why it started, and what it would mean than Churchill's label, the more prosaic "Seven Years' War," and the even more misleading "French and Indian War." The last name, one used by Americans, suggests how they understood things from their vantage point on the other side of the Atlantic. The penultimate reflects the formal duration of a war fought between European powers that was declared in 1756 and ended with the Treaty of Paris in 1763. Whatever its title, it became for George, Charles, and their generation the formative moment of their lives.[85]

The war combined the tensions that the brothers had been grappling with singly during their apprenticeships: old Continental rivalries and rising militarization, Atlantic trade and competition, and the very nature of Britishness. It began with imperial competition in North America and soon engulfed Europe and preoccupied all Britons. The world that Charles helped shape through commerce had heightened imperial rivalry. With the productive capacity of America and Africa tied to Europe through the movement of goods and bodies, what happened in faraway places affected the center as never before. Competition over the Ohio River valley, a land for future settlement and where hostilities began, represented a logical extension of this dynamic. The Caribbean had become the engine room of imperial ambitions, as sugar had become an indispensable commodity in the life of Europeans. Merchants had grown rich, whole industries had been created,

shipbuilding had boomed, and vistas had been enlarged as networks bound
New World to Old World as never before. The war then destabilized the alliance system in Europe once more, pitting nation against nation and forcing
the British to send troops to the Continent to fight alongside Prussian allies.
Reformed Highland Scots and Irishmen, some clandestinely Catholic, made
up a large proportion of the troops venturing across the English Channel and
across the Atlantic. Through war, the commercial and the coercive were now
being conjoined by a state with a vital interest in such a union. This was the
emergence of what one scholar calls "militarized capitalism."[86]

Charles, not George, would make the first contribution to the war
effort. In 1753, as tensions were rising in America and war appeared immi-
nent, officials at the center and at the margins of empire hoped to devise a
plan to coordinate imperial and colonial efforts at defense. Charles made the
first gesture toward rethinking relations in the empire when he drafted instructions to the governor of New York, telling him to order the assembly
there to make proper provisions for paying Crown officials. He instructed
the New Yorkers to establish "a permanent and fixed revenue" for salaries.
He hoped the governor and other officials could be made independent of the
whims and wishes of a popularly elected body, which could raise and lower
salaries, or refuse to pay them, and so strengthen Crown authority in that
most recalcitrant of colonies. It struck him that with tensions rising, anach-
ronisms of governance had to be addressed.[87]

Two other plans emerged that would capture Charles's attention. In
May 1754, hostilities erupted on the American frontier. A young Virginian
named George Washington and his party had clashed with and been defeated
by French forces as he was marching toward Fort Duquesne on the Forks of
the Ohio to lay claim to the region for British Virginia. With the terrors of a
frontier war looming, colonists assembled in Albany at the behest of the
Board of Trade to discuss plans for union in the face of a common threat.
Facing a growing crisis and working with a sense of urgency, these provincials were pressing for some sort of imperial structure that could govern the
whole and effectively protect the colonies. The printer, scientist, and diplomat Benjamin Franklin led the way. On the table was a plan that would create
almost a commonwealth understanding of empire, one in which the colonies
would be bound together in an American provincial legislature with a representative from the Crown, in effect a viceroy, acting as executive. The model
appeared a great deal like the Irish relationship to Britain, but in this case, the

American legislature would only address common concerns, such as Indian affairs and defense on the frontier. The plan came to nothing, as the colonists could not move beyond their individual concerns and squabbles over land on the frontier proved intractable. Corruption and interest clouded all.[88]

Meanwhile, the Board of Trade was also scrambling to come up with a scheme for governing the colonies beyond the ad hoc array of relationships and arrangements that defined the whole. Halifax drew up the plan. It would adopt a model strikingly similar to the one put in the dustbin in Albany, with a provincial assembly and a Crown representative in an executive capacity. The plan reflected the views of Charles's mentor, initiated by the center and styled as more of a partnership. Any plan, as Halifax argued, required the support of provincials in America. The planners had to tread carefully in devising something efficacious but at the same time suggesting that power would be negotiated.[89]

Charles thought both the plan put forward in Albany and the one drafted by Halifax fatally flawed, largely because they were out of step with history. Halifax's plan, as well as that of the colonists, he wrote, "begins a great work in a wrong manner." Fundamentals mattered, and neither plan attended to them. In what he called his thoughts on the "Plan for a General Concert," Charles laid out his developing vision to Newcastle. These sorts of things, he argued, had been tried before, and he listed a 1710 bill in Parliament designed "for raising a permanent revenue in America by the act of the British legislature" as a fitting "precedent." At that time, New Yorkers were refusing to pay what officials regarded as their fair share to defend empire, but as soon as this bill was threatened, they relented. He foresaw the same sort of imperial dance now. The colonies, he surmised, "have been engaged in a settled design of drawing to themselves the ancient and established prerogatives widely preserved in the crown as the only means of supporting and continuing the super intendancy of the mother country." The inevitable centrifugal forces of a decentralized system would work against any sort of arrangement. Parliament, he insisted, had to draw up any plan, and taxation had to be governed by the metropole. Furthermore, so long as the basic relationship was not reformed, any plan would be tainted by corruption.[90]

Moreover, Charles thought these sorts of plans ill considered from the perspective of political economy. Now he spoke to Newcastle as an expert. "The articles of Trade" specified in these kinds of plans "were ill chosen because it is certainly bad policy to incumber with duties those exports which facilitate and extend our American commerce." Nonetheless, these plans arose from a proper impulse: "to regulate a disordered colony . . . by the authority and necessary super intendancy of the mother country."

Charles then listed his objections point by point. He thought it madness to have the colonies offering their own idea of union. Given their histories, their different populations and wealth, their position on the continent, and their distinctive constitutional relations to the center, he could not see meaningful cooperation even over the simplest matters. Take forts, for instance. Why would one colony not affected by raids make sacrifices for another? How would the colonies agree on a proper "supply" for such an arrangement? Charles suggested the whole arrangement was "impracticable," as he put it, "damned" because of "local prejudices." The individual provinces, riven by "jealousy," would never be able to obtain useful information. Only those at the center, men like him at the Board of Trade, could do that and had the expertise to act upon it. All flowed from the hubs to the spokes. Authority had to work this way. Charles knew of and lamented the historic "Inactivity of the Colonies" when it came to looking after their own defense. Even when push came to shove, they demonstrated a "Reluctance" to "enlist in any but their own corps." This had been clear since "the defeat of Washington" in the American wilderness. Americans had to be led.[91]

Before any scheme could be implemented, as a set of instructions to the governor of New York made clear, certain things needed to be done. Assemblies still determined the salary of officials charged with executive powers in America. The effects were as lamentable as they were predictable. Such actions "dispossessed the Crown of almost every degree of executive power ever lodged in it." This would not do.[92] Any plan had to start at the center and radiate outward.

All of the plans, as well as Charles's critique of them and his instructions to the New Yorkers, just drifted away amid the welter of more pressing organizational concerns, such as winning a war against France.[93] The first few years of hostilities, especially before formal declaration of war, entailed survival, certainly according to Charles. In 1755, he made some dazzling speeches in Parliament, calling for an end to all dithering over France. At issue was Britain's Atlantic future. He charged that Britain had to put an end to "moderation" with France because of the basic threat of "trade to America." Earlier treaties, he argued, had allowed the French and the Spanish to plunder shipping and construct forts while Britain was tied up in negotiation. In 1754,

British troops should have made a "bold and vigorous push" to keep the French from supplying Canada. War would be declared, and so Britain needed to prepare fully, he asserted. Citing Roman historians and Hugo Grotius, the great Dutch jurist and theorist of trade, he said: "A wise nation will always . . . make the first attack as sudden and vigorous as possible." Doing so would "bring us quickly to a state of open war or honorable peace; and even the former is more eligible than the middle state in which we are at present."[94]

As the British sat in an uncomfortable middle ground between peace and war while the colonies were engaged in open conflict with French troops and their Indian allies, Charles lamented how "every body had defended only their part; nobody the system. Who would defend the melancholy state of America?" He also asked why the plan he helped draft, "so singular," was "not supported." In fact, not even he had the measure of the "system" and what it would look like and what it would do. No one had. In the meantime, he chastised the administration officials "for their tame and negligent administration of the Plantations."[95]

From his perspective, factionalism and the jockeying for position paralyzed government. "Sober and thinking men," Charles observed, "admit that this Country has ran its race; that, as in other past monarchys, the genius of our people has undergone a change." The early years of the war seemed to bear out this concern. "We are," Charles feared, "no longer capable of being successful thro' our own councils or arms."[96] The system that Charles through trade and George through coercion had helped bring into being was now imperiled. The incompetence and shifting uncertainty of the government stymied any prescription for saving the whole.

Charles observed the tragedy from the outside looking in. He could, no doubt, be intemperate in what he had to say, castigating the ministry for making what he regarded as missteps for the wrong reasons. Tellingly, however, he focused on the theme of the need for bold leadership to save Britain, which he portrayed as "upon the brink of further confusion." Shut out in 1754 when Newcastle took over, he now settled for the Admiralty Board, even though he had asked for a position on the Treasury Board. Meanwhile, the war did not go well for the British early on. As the French were enjoying victory after victory in North America, William Pitt took control of the government. Alas, with a change in leadership, it did not appear Charles would have an opportunity for a cabinet-level post. As soon as Pitt accepted the reins of government, following protocol, Charles proffered his resignation, hoping for a more influential post. Pitt refused the resignation.[97]

Charles believed he had earned the right to enter the ranks of cabinet ministers, and at key points throughout the war, as a contemporary noted, he "firmly engaged" himself to Pitt. His name, however, continued to be overlooked. What is clear from these years is that the brothers, Charles in particular, yearned for those things other politicians did, even as Charles preached the virtues of virtue. The two did not conflict. Charles aimed for a position his training and upbringing had, in his mind, prepared him for, the higher the better. With Pitt's accession, both brothers were "professing support and attachment" to him, yet Charles made "a determination not to accept any office . . . that is not an office of business," in other words, one he regarded as beneath him. A correspondent wrote to Pitt of Charles, "[He] does not like his situation in the arrangement; is determined his brother shall not like it, either for him or for himself." It was all academic, though. Charles was "convinced" nothing of the sort would be on offer.[98]

In a long letter to his brother, Charles poured out his heart. Before the brothers could ever hope to serve, someone had to launch "a free perfect and impartial enquiry into the causes and after the author of our late dishonor and public calamities." The author he had in mind was Cumberland. The word "our" was no mistake. Now yoked together, what had befallen George also befell Charles. He admitted his ambition. It was "warm and active." Charles wished "for office with rank as any man." But the proper opportunity was not presenting itself. Charles argued, "I do not wish to take any office after the stand we have made, upon doubtful or uncertain ground of public measures." He knew the brothers had a patron in Pitt, but even he could only do so much. In the meantime, he said, they would have to tread carefully "the real grounds we are to go upon . . . and the influence" of lurking enemies.[99] The war years thus bound the brothers together in confounding ways. Even though they had rediscovered each other, Charles sensed he would rise or fall with George, and if he was to achieve his ambitions, someone would have to clear George of the black mark against him.

Frustratingly, he found himself, as he reported to George, "neutral, quiet, retired, and independent." He exerted his energies in Parliament on showing up those who acted corruptly, such as those who did not make good on government contracts for victualing troops in America. Political enemies could be attacked under such cover. And Charles took aim at the members of a failing ministry, which in his mind "have either secreted or misapplied the strength of this nation in every part of the globe."[100] George, too, lived in a virtual exile, though one of his own making. He was, through his penchant for making enemies, "dragging his brother Charles into opposition to their uncle the Duke of Newcastle" merely because of Newcastle's connection to the hated rival. This did not make for good politics, but it pointed out how some in Parliament saw "the Two Townshends" acting together.[101]

One of George's obsessions, however, proved to be the key issue that brought them together in a political partnership. George made it his mission in Parliament to see to the passage of a militia bill. His idea was simple. Britain, now stretched at home and abroad, needed a reliable stock of troops to provide protection. The question had preoccupied George from the moment he took up his commission in Flanders. British troops manned barracks in Ireland and Scotland—the two margins of the British state that had to be garrisoned for stability—and had been at war with France more often than not since the 1690s. With a new war under way, Britain needed, in George's estimation, a reliable number of men that could be sent to protect the interests of the state and the burgeoning empire, as well as deal with any home-grown insurrections. If local men could be organized into militias for domestic service, especially to protect England from potential invasion, regular troops could be freed up to do the critical work overseas armies had to do. As George would put it later, Britain had to "establish so numerous and permanent a force as may enable it all times to act with superiority abroad, without endangering its own safety or liberties at home." At issue was manpower. He recalled, in particular, the Jacobite Rising, how he and his comrades were stretched between the Highlands and the Continent while they worried about the colonies overseas. A national militia, not just independent units locally organized, seemed imperative and could only be opposed by those animated by what he would call "pride and envy."[102]

To his mind, this lay beyond debate. "In vain," George reminded his colleagues in Parliament, "have the enemys of the revolution endeavoured to wrest from you by violence and treason the blessings you enjoy under the present constitution." Such enemies now opposed a militia bill. In truth, the politicians who stood against the measure tended to because of the difficulty of forcing men to muster. They feared riots. George and other supporters countered by tapping into patriotic sentiments. Much like his brother, George stood behind the Whiggish conventions of the day, attaching himself as any good politician would to the legacy of the Glorious Revolution. But he also rejected the "mock" patriots, those of the old ruling establishment who, too, claimed the Glorious Revolution as theirs, men like Newcastle. He considered himself, like Charles, a patriot Whig. "Faction," George argued, which was to blame for the obstacles the militia bill faced, acted as the silent solvent that worked on both order and liberty. "Chameleon like," such factionalism "took the stain of every passion, every fear and was better calculated to alarm and to deceive." George then went into a detailed history of England, how monarchs and elites had abused their privileges and how William, at the time of the Glorious Revolution—almost Christ-like—had redeemed the nation. Salvation, however, he cautioned, was "imperfect." Corrupt ministers, intent on breeding the factionalism that threatened his militia bill, had to be thwarted at every turn.[103]

George had Charles challenge all in the House who took issue with the militia. Charles "broke out in a vehemence of passion" if confronted over George's plan. "The Townshends clamoured" together. But at least one critic suggested something less than principle was at stake. The brothers seemed no different from any of the politicians he saw at work in the House. Place fixated them. "The Townshends," Horace Walpole charged, "pretended to be managers against the Ministers," doing all they could to stymie their opponents. In general, he continued, the brothers represented an unholy alliance of Charles's ambition and George's contempt to achieve a position in government.[104]

The brothers explained things differently. In 1757, in the midst of the militia business, William Pitt finally approached them about a position in his administration. George reported how he and Charles together met with Pitt "and to our Astonishment heard him avow the ridiculous and dishonest Arrangement of Men which is now to take place." They did not like the composition of the cabinet Pitt proposed, even if he shared George's enthusiasm for the militia scheme. More to the point, they did not see a plan for good government. They berated Pitt's failure to adopt "any Publick System of Measures." One was not "even hinted at" by Pitt. "Upon this occasion," George wrote, "I without hesitation declared my resolution to be no part of it—my Brother did the same." No system meant no cooperation.[105]

The brothers went a step further in their intransigence. One insider reported that, astonishingly, Pitt met with an insolent George to say "he was going to the King; asked George Townshend if he might name him to his

Majesty for any employment, and hoped things had his approbation." George answered "he would take nothing, that he had a *friend or two*, by whom he would make his sentiments known to his Majesty." Pitt then turned to Charles and asked him about his plans. Charles said, apparently coolly, that "he should not go to Court on Monday with the new administration, but retire into Norfolk to-morrow with his brother."[106]

Claiming principled independence, George pressed Pitt to push for the militia scheme and to shepherd it through the House of Lords, where it had been quashed the previous year. George argued that sponsoring a militia, though seemingly old-fashioned and out of step with Cumberland's ideas for the army, was a "constitutional" means of defending the realm, one that he regarded as "this essential and indeed almost only remaining effort in defence of our liberties and ability as a nation." Pitt claimed to be doing all he could to support the measure but he too faced opposition, both from Cumberland's party and from country gentlemen who did not want the bother. Charles then lent his talents to the cause. Ultimately, the measure was, George reported, "supported by several respectable and independent Characters." And it earned a hearing "in spite of the prejudice and tumults, who were excited against it." It did so with Charles's help and shrewd management. Charles courted the right patrons; he also appeared "offended" if bills bearing on the military did not include provisions for the militia.[107] He provided the institutional channel for George's beliefs.

George offered Charles just as much. George advised his brother to "divest" his mind of the political effects from George's fall from grace and of Charles's inability to find a ministerial post. He conceded to Charles, "[You are] more prepared for an Event of this nature than myself." They just had to outmaneuver or outwait the corrupt opposition to fulfill Charles's ambitions. George seethed because of what was happening to him, to his bill, to Charles, and to the nation as whole. "The Sovereign Contempt I feel for those who have flung away so fine a game—and what is more, abandon'd their Duty to their Country, when their Efforts every Hour were attended with an Increase of Honour and prosperity" motivated him like little else. "My contempt for them is too great to permit me to feel any shame." George told himself, "[That I am] disparaged from them is sufficient Comfort to me in any personal disappointment." Because of factionalism and petty politics, the country had been "injured." "I had rather be a Baker at Windsor at this moment than the Great W[*illiam*] P[*itt*]," George informed his brother. "It is upon this [virtue]," he argued, "and not upon the false Patriots of [the] Day that we must maintain our Liberties if we mean to be free."[108]

As he put it, they lived "at a time when our situation . . . directs us to maintain an immediate and constant Correspondence." The trust grew, as well as the transparency, as they struggled through their difficulties and disappointments. The state of the nation, the state of the brothers' fortunes, and the state of politics all pointed to a need for virtue. "The desertion of others from the publick Cause," George believed, "can only Conform and fortify me in my adherence to Principles founded upon the promotion of my Country's Good." This sentiment would not or could not shift with "the Variations of every week or every day." The present political constellation could not address the challenges they all faced. They needed a "more just, impartial and manly System." The men of faction, George declared, "dread an Experiment of this kind." The militia bill represented George's salvo, the only one he was capable of firing at this moment.[109]

George plied public opinion as best he could, working out of doors and in so doing bringing a new voice into the halls of Parliament. He did so most visibly through his use of caricature, a "new species" of satire, as Horace Walpole argued. What George produced, he added, "had amazing vent," lampooning his political enemies, including his uncle Newcastle, in much the same way George had pilloried Cumberland. He presented card-sized caricatures to his friends and allies highlighting the visibly distorting effects of corruption. He pinned up his drawings on "the shutters, walls, and napkins of every tavern in Pall Mall." As a newspaper put it, "He has dealt his grotesque cards from house to house, and circulated his defamatory Pictures from Towns-end to Towns-end." Ultimately, exaggerating the flaws and foibles of his enemies, and his friends, did not win him many admirers—and the famous artist William Hogarth hated George's caricatures in terms of both intent and craft—but his producing them did suggest that George was becoming a man of fixed and uncompromising principles.[110]

George worked out of doors in other innovative ways. To create and sustain support for the militia bill, he drafted a circular letter, sending it to boroughs and corporations. In it, he asked voters to instruct their representatives what to do. For the son of a landowner who sat in Parliament through his status as a gentry leader, this tactic posed all sorts of potential pitfalls. It represented politics of a different order altogether, encouraging freemen to exercise their own judgment and to make those who had been their betters their deputies. Instructing representatives represented the height of "impropriety," as Horace Walpole asserted, smacking of "dictatorial authority." It met "with the contempt it deserved."[111]

The tactics George used occasioned more than anger. In fact, his stubbornness and pride almost led to a duel with an aging nobleman named Lord Leicester. When Leicester said what George regarded as scandalous things about the militia bill and about him, suggesting that George's motives were not as pure as they seemed, George sent a scathing letter requesting satisfaction. George castigated Leicester as "a malignant, mercenary, pensioned Renegade Peer" who sought to "obstruct the Public Service, and to blacken the Character of a Set of Gentlemen, who devote themselves from Principle." This was for him a point of honor and, of course, virtue. Leicester stammered that he was sorry if he had offended George and could not consent to a duel, as he "never hit a barn door with a Gun" and never wore a sword anymore. George relented.[112]

George had boasted, "[I] recollect no appearance that I gave and give of any attachment or Connection whatever with the Great Men of the Helm." He went further: "I am no more fascinated by Mr. Pitt's Name than I was with the Sound of Sir Robert Walpole." He reported to his brother, from whom he had nothing to hide, "I am as little liable to prejudge Events as think I have shewn myself incapable of any servile and interested attachment to Men." In other words, he prided himself on his independence in exile. Charles, whom he now referred to as his "affectionate brother and ever faithful friend," encouraged him not to lose sight of how to accomplish lofty goals even if in exile. George could be uncompromising, even with his brother. At one key juncture, Charles apologized to George for his less than perfect attention to the movement of the bill through the House. "I am sorry my best endeavours are so unsatisfactory to you," he wrote. He promised that he would rededicate himself to the cause. "I will *tomorrow*," he underlined, "move the Bill."[113]

The experience of working together began to shape Charles in some fundamental ways. The so-called shuttlecock was not so much flitting from side to political side as steering clear of any entangling alliances. Upset by the way some challenged George's militia scheme, Charles lamented: "We live in a paltry age; incapable of anything great; and every sentiment of public spirit and genuine freedom that ought to animate the breast of man is lost in self-interest." At the same time he promised to be more attentive to

George's wishes, he also laid out his vision of politics. "It is my firm resolution," he declared, "to act the part of a man of business and a man of honour; to be decided by things and not men; to have no party; to *follow* no leader, and to be governed absolutely by my own judgment." He would, like George, he might have added, "preserve that which I sincerely value above either the lustre of popularity or the reward of subservience." Nothing would make him side with George's enemies. He would, he said, henceforth "show I am determined and *not inconstant*."[114]

The bond worked. Charles managed the House and the tactics. George, as Charles discovered, did not have a head for detail; he could, in the wrong hands, be an "honest instrument of the deceit and . . . success of other men."[115] George provided a great deal of the moral energy of the partnership, as well as the single-mindedness. His sense of aggrievement allowed him to style himself a patriot with moral credibility. Charles added adaptability. The ideas belonged to both. At times, tensions ruled the relationship. George could overwhelm Charles, almost to the point of bullying, which Charles at times resented.[116] But these episodes proved the exception, not the rule. The brothers loved and respected each other. More to the point, the talents and sensibilities of each made up for the limitations of the other. In no small part through their efforts and coordination, the militia act passed in 1757. No doubt, George's pride and stubbornness and Charles's adaptability and penchant for appeasing may speak to their troubled childhoods. But as the militia business demonstrated, in another context, together these strengths and weaknesses could prove a potent combination. That moment, though, had not come.

George's Redemption

The Seven Years' War also offered George a new opportunity. No matter what Cumberland thought of him, George had, of course, proven himself as a commander and had gained valuable experience on the Continent. More important, in the early years of the war Cumberland disgraced himself. In 1757, while serving as commander of British forces on the Continent, he virtually capitulated to the French in a bid to protect Hanover, deserted his Prussian allies as he did so, and created a diplomatic and military mess for the ministry to clean up. He was recalled, and then retired to private life. With Cumberland gone, George could resurrect his career. As Charles put it, "The retreat of his formidable and abdicated Enemy; the disreputation of almost all the senior officers hitherto employed," as well as the hope for restored honor "unite in indulging and inflaming his [George's] original Genius and uncommon Talents for the army."[117]

Charles had another good reason to hope. George, Charles observed, seemed "to be not a little urged and accelerated by the quick rise and very promising prospect of preferment and command now opening to Roger." After trying his hand at sea, their brother Roger sought his fame and fortune in the army. Like thousands of English, Irish, and Scottish younger sons, Roger traveled to North America to fight the French. Early on, he would meet with disappointments, as potential patrons would not make his path an easy one. But war allows talent to rise, and after a while, he began swiftly moving through the ranks. He was eventually named a Colonel of Foot and "Deputy Adjutant of the Forces in North America." War clearly suited him. Before a siege campaign in the Hudson River valley, he declared: "We appear to feel bold and I really believe the Dragon is in us"; "we shall drub them."[118]

Like Roger, George saw opportunities, and he asked Charles to help him secure a commission. He also sent a note to Pitt, declaring, "I own I am anxious for service." George claimed that Pitt's leadership had inspired confidence and swayed him to request a letter of recommendation. "Glory and every solid advantage to this country" that British arms had won, he told Pitt, "is a national spirit, in a great measure of your own raising." With a war ongoing, procuring a position would not prove difficult. Rank posed the greater question. In 1758, George read the new promotions and swore some of those who were now colonels "[I] cannot possibly serve under." To do so would be humiliating. "I ask only to be where I should have been according to my Rank of Lieutenant Colonel," he pleaded with a prospective patron, "and see with Pleasure those who have been passed over me by American commands." No doubt influenced by Charles's approach to political matters—and a commission for George was a political matter—he also asked for the names of more potential sponsors.[119]

He succeeded. In 1759, the war now having raged for a number of years, he was appointed brigadier general in North America. This was more than he could reasonably have hoped for, placing him in a rank that he would have achieved had he never been marked by Cumberland. He owed it in part to his brother's cooperation. Ultimately, however, it was "the all-powerful patronage of Pitt" that extricated him from his purgatory. The appointment came with a catch. George would serve under Generals James Wolfe and Robert Monckton, men "who had been his Juniors" earlier in his army career. It seems he still took issue with authority and with what he regarded as infringements of ideal or principle.[120] He did, however, have his commission.

Although one friend suggested that he look beyond his injured pride and spoke to him of the "glory you will obtain," George met with difficulties in America. He did have his brother Roger to rely on, and one of his fellow officers suggested to him that Roger "will inform you of everything that passes here." Roger promised George's wife that he would look after George on his arrival in the New World. He sent him vegetables after the sea journey and tried his best to serve with him. Roger hoped George would "receive the praises due to him from his K[in]g and Country." America meant redemption. But redemption comes with cost. The ever-skeptical Horace Walpole judged the situation correctly. Writing in early 1759, he predicted a storm once George met his superior. "Ambition, activity, industry, passion for the service, were conspicuous in Wolfe," he found. "He seemed," as he put it, "to breathe for nothing but fame." George was made of different stuff. His "proud, and sullen, and contemptuous temper never suffered him to wait for thwarting his superiors till risen to a level with them."[121]

Moving toward Quebec, where George would make a name for himself, became a journey into his own heart of darkness. On 18 February 1759, his ship, the *Neptune*, lay at anchor off Plymouth in the West of England, waiting to sail. On 15 May he arrived at the great fortress of Louisburg, the "Gibraltar of the New World." The French had surrendered Louisburg in two successive wars to the British. Now the British held it, and, perched along the St. Lawrence, it protected the approaches to the interior of North America. George noted a stripped-down culture and untamed wilderness as he sailed up the river. Small settlements amid seas of rye grass and wild berries lay next to "Indian wigwams." George saw the land as barely touched, just punctuated by scattered French settlements. Now able to employ his skills as a limner, he drew a number of prospects of the New World he saw. They appear bleak: not forbidding, just devoid of humanity.[122]

The first encounter of George with his new superior, James Wolfe, confirmed his worst fears. Townshend saw Wolfe as petty and vindictive. As he confided to his wife, Wolfe's "Health is but very bad. His Generalship in my poor opinion—is not a bit better." Over and over again, George characterized Wolfe as an ass. The general, it seems, critiqued George and did little else.

Wolfe, according to George, chastised him for placing his men in the wrong positions. At other times he upbraided him for being "dilatory." At yet other times he scoffed that George took too much initiative or made a position almost too impregnable, not allowing nimble movement of his forces. George bore the arbitrary criticisms silently. But he seethed in his journals. He wrote of how thirteen rangers, troops developed for irregular warfare in America against Indians, had been scalped and how if he had not carefully shored up his positions, he would have exposed even more men to sacrifice at the hands of the "savages." Wolfe, he complained, "must have had an uncommon disposition to find fault with me." He soon learned of "the futility of objections and the partiality of his judgment." Moreover, Wolfe "laughed" at serious threats to the safety of his troops and, as George acidly put it, took important affairs "lightly." Others apparently shared George's judgment. Another of the brigadiers, the Scot James Murray, thought "his orders throughout the campaign show[ed] little stability, stratagem or fixed resolution."[123]

Once again George turned to caricature. One of the best renderings we have of Wolfe was done by George's hand. In it, Wolfe looks like a young, relatively handsome officer. But this is the exception. George usually portrayed Wolfe as a chinless fool and martinet. To be fair, Wolfe had a receding chin. George fastened on this feature and made it his most pronounced trait. The small-minded, incompetent officer is the one who emerges in the images. In a number of drawings, he treats the French around Quebec unfairly and with an arbitrary and haughty demeanor. The images did not lie. Charles had learned, for instance, that Wolfe believed the "country should be ruined and destroyed."[124] George, most provocatively, compared Wolfe to Oliver Cromwell, the infamous tyrant and commander of an army from the previous century. That George would liken Wolfe to the famous regicide is telling. Men like Wolfe, he thought, would bring the empire low through their corrupting pride and unchecked self-regard.

Thus in America George had his share of difficulties to deal with. The most debilitating demon he confronted was Roger's death. Roger's fate was, as a witness put it, to be "kild by a Cannon Ball" on 25 July 1759—just days after sensing the "Dragon" within him and his men—during siege operations at Fort Ticonderoga in the Hudson River valley. Roger was, as the story goes, one of a small number of casualties as British engineers began digging trenches for the siege, a plan ultimately aborted.[125] George blamed the war, one he was only just involved in, and the place where Roger was

6. "Shade of Cromwell—Has England then come to this," a caricature by George Townshend of James Wolfe (McCord Museum M19856)

killed. "Accursed be this American tomb," he cried, "so fatal to all those who have too much Honour to refuse the Service of their Country in all Climates."[126] The death haunted him. Writing to his wife, he "reproved" himself, as he put it, "for not consulting my own nature more, when I ask'd you to [let me] return to the Army." He found himself in "a Scene of Ambition, Confusion, and Misery." The "War of the worst Shape," as he called it, only compounded his suffering. "I never served so disagreeable a Campaign as this. Our unequal Force has reduced our Operations to a Scene of Skirmishing Cruelty and Devastation." It was Culloden again.[127]

The war revealed a darkness in George, one he in all likelihood would have exhibited at Culloden as well. He drew a number of images of the Indians he came across. They look forbidding, barely human creatures that show only the most depraved symbols of incivility: the scalps of Europeans they have killed. They lived, much like the Highlanders a generation earlier, beyond the pale of civility. George, however, had all about him in the ranks and even in the officer corps living testaments to the possibilities of reform. As he saw it, after the conquest at Culloden the hitherto barbarous people now fought with George and with the late Roger against savagery in the New World. George, then, inhabited a conceptual world that bridged conquest and reform, civility and barbarism.

George's war in America ended, surprisingly, on such an ambivalent note. The year 1759 would prove an annus mirabilis for the British. They had known defeat and stalemate up to this point, but at last they experienced unfettered success in the war. George's diary provides a clue to how and why

7. "An Indian War chief completely equipped with a scalp in his hand," a caricature by George Townshend (© National Portrait Gallery, London)

this happened: his ship had sailed unmolested to Louisburg and then up the St. Lawrence River. Pitt had seized on a strategy of squeezing the French on the seas. By preventing French goods and supplies from reaching the interior, British forces ensured that the French could not supply their men, forts, or Indian allies. Whereas earlier strategy had focused on the interior of the colony of Pennsylvania and the Hudson River valley, where Roger had been killed, the new strategy centered on supremacy on the seas and inevitable attrition in the field. Only then, once fundamentals had been attended to, could commanders prepare a daring attack against the very capital of New France, Quebec. By the time of George's arrival, the British were now poised to strike.

The battle that took Quebec is well known. The city sat atop a bluff overlooking the St. Lawrence. And on paper, or in one of George's sketches, it looked impregnable. The French commander, the marquis de Montcalm, had secured all the approaches to the city save one, a steep incline running up from the river to the rear of the French lines. British commanders decided to approach the town from that exposed side. The plan proved a brilliant stroke. Under cover of darkness British troops, led by the other brigadiers, Monckton and Murray, and the Scot Simon Fraser, made their way silently down the river to the base of the incline. Ranger units followed by regular troops climbed up the hillside until by dawn the British had effectively outflanked the French. Wolfe then formed the main line. Caught between Britons on the front and at their undefended rear, the French had little hope, and the battle that took place on the Plains of Abraham turned into a resounding British victory.

George secured the left on the northern edge of the plains, what would have been the most exposed flank. "Tho I was not in the warmest part of the action," George recounted immediately after the battle, "yet I had more shots near me than in any other action I've seen." In fact, he saw heated action. He struggled to stem bold strikes by Canadians and their Indian allies and led a decisive counterstrike. As one historian argues, if the center of the battle had not been so central for victory, George's clashes "might have entered history as a military epic." What is clear is that he had participated in an epochal defeat of the French. Victory stemmed from a bold and brilliant plan, pulled off by disciplined and committed troops. "We have at last struck a very decisive stroke in this Country," George gushed.[128]

How the British came up with the plan remains a bit hazy. Was it Wolfe, whom everyone assumed drew it up? Charles's letters from the period suggest that the brigadiers proposed the idea of scaling the heights to Wolfe.

Wolfe, in Charles's rendition, appears a bit cautious, even dithering. George provided a more enigmatic answer. As he put it in a dispatch to Pitt after the battle had been won, "It being determined to carry the operations above the town," the British had proved victorious. "It being determined": those words would come to haunt George. And he continued to discuss the planning in these passive terms, even if he did add, "We lost poor General Wolfe who fell in the warmest part of the engagement."[129]

In the immediate aftermath of the battle, that death and that passive-voice construction turned out to have long-lasting consequences for George's life. More immediately, Monckton, the next in command, was incapacitated, and in their stead George left the northern flank and "repaired to the centre." He halted the pursuit of the French, reformed the lines, and ensured that the French did not mount a counterattack. He had acted with what one historian calls "prudence and presence of mind." He then initiated a siege of the city, though he had little experience coordinating naval and land forces, that led in a mere matter of days to the ultimate French surrender. George, as commander of the forces and of the conquered city, signed the articles of capitulation. The inhabitants would not be plundered, and they would be free to exercise their religion. Even the Catholic bishop could do his work unmolested. George oversaw a kinder, gentler occupation than the one he and Charles suggested Wolfe would have instituted.[130]

Troops solemnly escorted Wolfe's embalmed remains to a ship that set sail for England.[131] George for his part, as second in command, took care of mopping-up duties. To be sure, he could have pressed the advantage and broken the French army. He decided, however, no doubt wisely, that holding the capital of New France with its strategic and symbolic place in France's New World enterprise could not be jeopardized. In any event, with Quebec secure, the St. Lawrence dominated by the British navy, and with the French now hemorrhaging Indian allies, the future was not hard to predict. Nor was it difficult to foresee how Wolfe, the man George characterized as an incompetent micromanager, would be portrayed in Britain.

The End of Apprenticeship

They lit bonfires for George at Raynham. When news spread to the tenants, the common people of Norfolk roasted a brace of sheep. On Beacon Hill, locals feasted on a bullock. And one night they cracked open twelve barrels of ale. "A prodigious Joy in all the Villages," a local minister reported, with each "striving who shall out do Each other; in Market Towns they illuminate." And why shouldn't they have? The brother was returning covered in glory after his pride had led him to be disgraced. It appeared he was now redeemed. One writer, who lamented the loss of Wolfe, exclaimed to Pitt, "Townshend still remains, and many a gallant officer, animated by your spirit, and by you brought forward into action." Charles and the family now basked in the glow of a brother who had seemingly come back from political death. Charles rejoiced at the prospect of "the safe return of my Brother Townshend."[132]

After the battle, and with North America now won, George stayed on in Quebec for a while as the British secured the region. Here he was doing the mundane stuff of garrison command: maintaining discipline, presiding over courts-martial, ensuring the troops did not take advantage of the French in their midst, and procuring the help of local blacksmiths. He did everything from arranging for church services in an old Ursuline convent in the town to regulating the drinking of the troops. He sailed for England on 18 October, after the fleet had fired a twenty-one-gun salute to the departing conquerors.[133] He then was ordered to travel to the Continent, where battles seemingly awaited. The remainder of George's war proved to be denouement. America for the first time had served as the central theater of war. The Continent from this point began to recede in the imagination of Britons, as the Atlantic loomed larger than ever before. In part, Charles's work in crafting networks had seen to that.

In Portugal, George performed the routine duties of commanding a garrison. He tried to keep his men out of "tippling houses" and keep women from "strolling" about camp. Any women "infected with the foul disease," he ordered at one point, had to be seen by a surgeon. If any concealed their condition, they would "be drumm'd out of the Regt." George also learned a great deal about provincial politics and manpower. England, Scotland, and Ireland had different relationships to the army, and as a commander, he could appreciate the implications of difference. From Portugal, he complained that "the Irish Regts. Excuse their want of Camp Implements from their being fitted out so in Ireland." The Irish Parliament was supposed to support troops raised in Ireland, but it often did so grudgingly. George discovered "how little a Military commander has to do with the army there" and "consequently, how much the service suffers." The regiments were keen for "reforming" but unable to do so through "the disadvantages . . . [they] laboured under."[134]

Charles also had some new duties as the war came to an end. He assumed what looks on paper to be a critical position: secretary at war. He owed this position to Lord Bute's influence over the new king, George III. With most large-scale operations over, the post consumed Charles with the sorts of things he had done when he served on the Board of Trade: ensuring goods and people headed where they had to go. He sent troops to places like Portugal, where George was stationed. He determined where prisoners of war would be dispatched to. He saw to the shipment of waistcoats as well. He even learned in his post, and undoubtedly to his delight, of the places the Norfolk militia was marching.[135] His was the world of finding commissions and promotions for sons and friends of men worth befriending.[136] Charles would not allow great sums to be sent to America to treat with Indians, even if these were requested by Sir William Johnson, the Irish-born superintendent of Indian affairs and a hero of the war.[137] He could not escape what he had mastered under Halifax.

Charles remained "the great master of our West Indian affairs" and knew "of our neglects in that quarter of the world" better even than Pitt. He still plied the vast Atlantic from his desk, in other words, and he used his knowledge of "American affairs" and even alleged "American grievances" to castigate his political adversaries, especially if they pretended to have insight they did not in fact possess. He still longed for higher office, and by 1762, as one friend wrote, he "disliked the War Office" and planned on something else. More troublingly, even as Bute and then the king worked hard to convince him that a lasting government was being formed, he worried "this system had not taken place."[138]

As the brothers assumed new duties, the rest of the war belonged to Britain. By the time of the triumph at Quebec, British troops were gaining control of the interior of America. In late 1758, they had taken Fort Duquesne, where only years earlier their comrades had been slaughtered by the French and their Indian allies. They now secured the Hudson River valley, that key dividing line in the east of the continent, whereas earlier it had been the graveyard of Roger and many others. Pitt's strategy had worked beautifully, and for the rest of the war, with North America won, victory followed victory in all four corners of the world. Charles was not alone in pronouncing Pitt's plan "divine," for it had brought a victory that could not be considered anything other than providential.[139] Fittingly, as soon as Duquesne was taken, British engineers rebuilt a fort of masonry and named it in Pitt's honor. The massive and imposing Fort Pitt loomed over the landscape, announcing to all that America belonged to Britain.

The war, then, brought opportunity, frustration, and heartbreak. It also cemented the relationship between George and Charles. Even the king learned as much. In November 1761, Charles attacked the administration for a failure to address George's Militia Act, which was due to expire. On the face of it, the move proved foolish, and the king chastised Charles for trying to discredit an administration that he had spent a great deal of time and effort trying to construct. Charles, though, was only acting the part of his brother's keeper.[140]

Roger's Tomb

The story of George and Charles Townshend and the making of empire does not finish with the end of their apprenticeships at all; it ends with their younger brother, Roger. When the family received word of Roger's death, they were shocked and saddened by the seeming meaninglessness and profound misfortune of his passing. Because of ill fate in the form of a cannonball, George carried a deep sorrow for some time, and after arriving home as a victor, tried to make sense of it in this way: "What a Bouquet this had been a year or two hence for poor Roger . . . I assure you I return thoroughly wounded from America. I loved him sincerely." Victory brought sense to the senselessness of his death. Charles tried to console his mother, Audrey, inviting her to stay at his townhouse in London. They were trying to come to terms with what he called "our late unhappy common loss," but he conceded he "was not able to bear the reflexions they bring with them." He was still searching for a way to comprehend it. Even the father talked of the "severe calamity lately befalling me."[141]

The family hoped to bring the body back home. At least the father did. Upset by "the loss of so valuable a Branch of the Family," Lord Townshend "wished poor Roger might be laid at Rainham where his family lie." He discovered, however, "that for certain reasons it is not practicable to have it brought over." He mourned alone, plagued by what he termed "the headach disorder on my nerves and with grief for the loss of poor Roger." America would be Roger's tomb. To console herself and preserve Roger's memory, and to give his sacrifice proper meaning, the mother arranged for a monument in Westminster Abbey, erected, as it would read, "by the disconsolate Parent, The Lady Viscountess Townshend." For her son, her favorite, only the best would do.[142]

Lady Townshend contacted one of Britain's leading architects and interior designers, a Scot named Robert Adam, to design the monument. Charles counted Adam as a friend, and Adam reciprocated. "Be good to him," a Scottish acquaintance counseled Charles, "for you have not a more sincere admirer" than Adam. Adam's great public works epitomized the hold the neoclassical had on the British imagination. Buildings he designed would include such iconic structures as the beautifully proportioned Shelburne House on Berkeley Square and eventually the imposing new main building for the University of Edinburgh and its New Town development.[143] Adam had a keen interest in the war and in its memorialization. He had, for instance, drafted and sent in a proposal for a monument for a much more famous Englishman who died in the war, none other than the new national hero General James Wolfe. He did not win the commission, but when Lady Townshend called, he now had something on hand he could use for Roger's.

Roger Townshend was no Wolfe; nonetheless, the memory of Wolfe dominates Roger's monument.[144] Adam's earliest sketches include renderings of the Theban general Epaminondas, who had fallen while trying to protect his people, and who for eighteenth-century Britons represented the pinnacle of martial virtue. His sacrifice had ensured victory in the classical world, every bit as much as Wolfe's did in the eighteenth century. As such Wolfe was memorialized, usually at the moment he expired.[145] In his first sketches, Adam jotted down the words "Quebec" near a castle in the background and "St. Lawrence River" next to a stream running by it. Roger, of course, had been nowhere near either. In one rendering, Adam has the dying hero handing a baton of command to his next-in-line. Ironically, that would have been Roger's older brother George, who assumed command at Quebec after Wolfe expired. Adam, however, settled for a subsequent drawing he had made, one in which the hero is gesturing toward the battlefield, held aloft by his comrades, as he expires. Whether the family knew that the original renderings were intended for a Wolfe monument is unknown.[146]

Nonetheless, the dying Epaminondas/Wolfe would repose in marble in the middle of Roger's monument with older brother George nowhere in sight. Adam planned to stage the relief in statuary marble—expensive and pure white—on an elaborate sarcophagus. The sarcophagus would be flanked by Roman military standards, and it would be borne aloft by sculptures of two Roman boys. The boys would form part of the architectural structure of the memorial. They would also signal something that resonated deeply in the eighteenth century. For examples of virtue, one had to look to classical Rome. Somehow Britain now, as an empire, was taking up Rome's

8. Roger Townshend Memorial, Westminster Abbey (Copyright Dean and Chapter of Westminster)

mantle. It did so through virtuous sacrifice of men such as Roger and, of course, Wolfe.[147]

Ultimately, for the human pillars Adam chose something more appropriate for a monument of a man who had fallen in America: two Indians. Simply dressed and ornamented, they would more than likely be Iroquois, most probably Mohawk. Some Mohawks fought alongside the British at Quebec. Though they were late entrants into the war, they could be counted as allies nonetheless—and one of Britain's few Indian allies. Britons did know of American Indians, largely through the intermittent visits of Indians to Britain. The most famous, a Mohawk called Hendrick, became a symbol of Indian loyalty to the British cause—and a real Mohawk named Hendrick, often confused with the earlier visitor, also had died during the war in the Hudson River valley. Even if Adam knew this, and it is doubtful he did, Hendrick also served as a stock image of "Indian-ness," and by extension America, for a generation of British artists.[148]

We could view the Indians as two stoic and noble savages holding up the coffin of a fallen hero who had redeemed an empire of virtue now extending to America. The entablature suggests as much. Also done on statuary marble, the tablet records how Roger's sacrifice "enroll[ed] him with the Names of Those Immortal Statesmen and Commanders, whose Wisdom and Intrepidity . . . Have extended the Commerce, Enlarged the Dominion, and upheld the Majesty of these Kingdoms, beyond the Idea of any former Age."

On this monument, we begin to see the narrative emerge that allowed a family to make sense of the senseless. Indians, though exoticized in the eighteenth century by Britons, had literally sustained the war effort in the way they supported Roger Townshend's monument. The war had indeed won what was claimed on the tablet, the dominion and commerce that George and Charles in their apprenticeships had extended. It would be America— symbolized by Indians—that would benefit from the sacrifice of men like Roger and would now presumably have to do its part to support empire. The monument, then, combined the classical motifs that all Britons at the time would have appreciated—they were now, after all, heirs to Rome. But it did so by adding an American twist. Roger bequeathed all this to the world.

The monument was first sculpted in terra cotta by Luc-François Breton on the Continent and put into marble in 1761 by John Ekstein, who contrasted the white statuary with the more colorful Siena.[149] Lady Townshend, according to Adam, was "charmed with it." Such monuments cost a small fortune, but they had become the rage of the day for families that could pay. Comparable monuments about this time went for between £1,400 and £3,000. The family paid £41 to Westminster Abbey to have the monument placed there. Half of that amount paid the "fine," or the fee for the space in the abbey. The other half went to pay for funeral expenses, even though Roger was not entombed in the abbey.[150]

Far away from Poets' Corner or other places tourists visit, the monument to Roger would seem to have little place amid the heroes of the British nation, titans all, enshrined in Westminster Abbey. It sits, after all, only yards from Newton's monument. It stands among this and other, more famous memorials admirably. As Robert Adam exclaimed, it was and perhaps still is "superior to anything in the abbey."[151] However striking, it jumbles images and allusions, juxtaposing the naturalness of the Indians with the Greek-inspired relief on an Egyptian sarcophagus topped with an obelisk-styled apex and adorned with Roman standards. But it is the sentiment on the tablet that deserves a place in the abbey. Roger died for an empire unlike any that had come before it, in a war that for Britons became the defining moment of the eighteenth century.

Just as the war brought the brothers together, it also tied the visions of empire each personified. With battles on either side of an ocean, the commercial and the coercive, the Atlantic and the Continental, coalesced. These seeming opposites, then, were not diametrically opposed. War had made for a confluence.[152] Virtue, the sort demonstrated by Roger, could keep them yoked. The period after the war would decide if they would or would not remain tethered, whether the liberty one underscored could remain reconciled with the imperium the other ensured.[153] Both Charles and George would be heirs to such a moment, and they too would see their lives as memorials to all that Roger's sacrifice represented and all that the entablature promised. They were not exceptional in this regard.

In the wake of Roger's memorialization, a more significant change occurred for both brothers, almost as a coda to a period that saw them create names for themselves and forge bonds with each other. This change, no doubt, also exorcized a few demons. In 1764, their father died. He left George the estate. He had little choice. It was entailed, and as such it went to the oldest son. George also now assumed the title. Henceforth he would be George Viscount Townshend. Charles received £8,000, a little more than his sister. To be more precise, he had received this amount when he married, when "you," as his father put it, "called upon me for your fortune and told me you must have it directly." A few years before his death, the father had let this prodigal son know he would receive nothing more upon his death. Charles had his eyes on some family land newly purchased in Hertfordshire, but Lord Townshend would not let him have an acre of it or any of its income. Gallingly, Charles had recently even helped his father with some furniture designs for Raynham, while George would not speak to him.[154] Now George inherited the lot. Fortunately for Charles, he had married very well.

In 1759, as George was reaping glory, Charles wrote to his mother and told her that though her sons were separated, they were not divided. Roger was mourned, to be sure, but her two remaining sons were on the rise. Charles declared, "Lady Townshend! you bred us up together as one child from our cradles!" He assured her that "when our different ranks in life separated us, they separated but not divided us: when we met again in life, we met, as we parted, with the same affection." In the meantime, "many and very dear connexions have since made us more one and the same person than habits could do in our infancy."[155] Thus connected, they would now work as one. They were now their own men. And as they had become so, their world had changed profoundly, in no small part through their attempts to make their way through it.

ACT 2

Britain's Imperial Reckonings

Wolfe's Revenge

In hating a national martyr, George made a grave mistake. An even greater one involved letting it be known. George, as was his wont, spoke his mind when it came to Wolfe, and on his return to Britain suggested it was he, not Wolfe, who had devised the plan to take the Plains of Abraham. Because of his indiscretion and, more to the point, the Wolfe mania that followed George's return home, his thoughts became widely known. Horace Walpole charged that George and his friends "attempted to ravish the honour of conquest from Wolfe."[1] Once rumor of his opinion spread, George was damned if he defended himself and damned if he did not. After all, the battle pitted a fallen martyr to the cause of Britishness against a seeming malcontent who had a history of conflict with superiors.

George, however, would not relent. One story illustrates the depths of his tenacity and injured pride. In 1760, George challenged the Earl of Albemarle to a duel after a pamphlet appeared contesting the story George was propounding about Quebec. He assumed his old nemesis, the Duke of Cumberland, was behind it, and he vented his spleen on Cumberland's "favorite." George suspected Albemarle of writing a pamphlet titled "Letter to an Honourable Brigadier General." The piece pilloried George. It accused him of "violat[ing] the rules of war in an appetite for glory." George had "received into his protection the capital of an Empire, larger than half the Roman conquests," yet, as the piece accused, "though you had formally entered your protest against attacking the place, you alone enjoyed the honours of its being taken." The writer, whether Albemarle or not, lambasted George for erecting "a lying monument of fame to the living," not the dead Wolfe. The pamphlet even alleged that he was "thrice happy for the Scots in their rebellion" and that victory at Culloden was achieved despite his "natural antipathy to a northern campaign." Surprisingly, considering the tone of the pamphlet, the duel never came off.[2]

These attacks on George upset the family. Lady Townshend, a friend found, was "very low-spirited." In a letter to his mother when the scandal first broke, largely to assuage her worries, Charles had said: "The world seems to lament, not blame George's absence from Quebec." With the publication of the piece, Charles grew enraged. "I lately received a Pamphlet addressed to my Brother," he snorted, "the malice of which provokes me." He considered it libelous. Most infuriatingly, it downplayed George's prior service, charged him for "an actual protest against the Expedition He succeeded in execution of," and insinuated that "he signed the Capitulation surreptitiously."[3]

George struck back. He described the piece as written by a writer with "a mind full fraught of the most rancorous." He reminded the writer that his brother Roger had made the supreme sacrifice and that he, George, had fought willingly. He defended his admiration for Scots, particularly those who fought for Britain. "The *Scots* have long rendered themselves conspicuous at the bar, in the army, and all branches of literature: they are a respectable people," and Highlanders, in particular, "had done great service before *Quebec* that day." He claimed he acted as he did on assuming command to avoid "any further fatigue and unnecessary effusion of blood." As for the charge that George had opposed Wolfe's plan, he moved beyond the protection of the passive voice that "he did not protest against the scheme which reduced *Quebec*, but quite the reverse." He had proposed it. He then produced evidence in the form of letters to prove his points. The damage, however, was done, and there was little he could do to salvage his reputation.[4]

The insults kept coming. To George's undoubted chagrin, images of Wolfe appeared everywhere, on statuettes, jugs, and saucers, as did national monuments and statues extolling his glory.[5] He would be immortalized in stone and bronze throughout the three kingdoms and even in America. Most conspicuously, Wolfe was memorialized in Westminster Abbey, in the wake of the competition that Robert Adam lost. The monument does not differ much from Adam's design. In it, figures tend to the fallen hero. George, of course, is not one of them.

The slights did not end there. In a perverse twist, one almost too cruel to be believed, one of the leading history paintings of the period, *The Death of General Wolfe* by the American artist Benjamin West, excluded Townshend in an image of the fallen hero and his brigadiers. One of the three brigadiers is depicted. Another brigadier, who also hated Wolfe but proved more discreet than George, declined to sit for the painting. George, apparently, was the only one never asked. The painting is so well known because in it the fallen Wolfe stands for the glories of Britain, as he is held by three men close to him who represent the three constituent kingdoms of the British state: England, Scotland, and Ireland. On the left side of the nationalist pietà or deposition from the cross, West has assembled a group of those present (and a few who were not) to tell a tale of how even Americans—seen in the person of the Indian eerily like the columns supporting Roger's memorial—belonged in the empire and would soon be the equals of those in the center. Included was Simon Fraser, the son of the traitor Lord Lovat, whose fate George had discussed after Culloden. Fraser, in his tartan, was now part of empire and of the image West presents.

But note the image of Wolfe. It exactly mimics in gesture and in composition the image of Roger in the Adam composition. The similarities are

9. Benjamin West, *The Death of General Wolfe* (Clements Library, University of Michigan)

eerie, and West must have based his Wolfe on Adam's Roger Townshend.[6] In the painting, the hand that should be passing the baton to George Townshend vaguely points to space in exactly the same manner as Roger's memorial. George, again, is nowhere to be found. George III hailed the George-less painting based on Roger's monument as a masterpiece. And in this regard he was right.

In other words, George could not have chosen a more formidable and tenacious enemy than the memory of Wolfe. Charles counseled a cooling-off period for George, until the whole affair blew over. In the meantime, George would find himself in the political wilderness. So he retired to Raynham Hall in Norfolk. He still dreamed of a larger stage, and his time in Norfolk suggested a bit of wanderlust. One prominent neighbor complained that George "ever avoided entering into any engagements relative to the affairs of Norfolk."[7] George apparently had a great deal of time to begin to appreciate a simple lesson he should have learned already: some, such as Wolfe, were beyond reproach. Charles now suffered much the same fate. His star hitched to his brother's, he also faced an uncertain and isolated future.

The Costs of Victory

The sort of uncertainty that George and Charles faced in the wake of the Wolfe scandal now confronted all Britons. Victory brought euphoria and confidence but also confusion and anxiety. The Treaty of Paris in 1763 following the Seven Years' War confirmed as much. The treaty gave Britain the greatest territorial empire the world had seen. Aside from a few small islands in the North Atlantic on which to dry their catches of fish, the French surrendered all of America. The British now had sovereign control over the region west of the Appalachians, where the war had been touched off, what had been French Canada, the Maritimes, and Grenada in the Caribbean. The empire in the New World stretched from the Arctic Circle to the Gulf of Mexico, and from the Atlantic to the Mississippi. It did not end there. In India, the British controlled whole sections of the subcontinent with the defeat of the Nawab of Bengal and his French allies at Plassey in 1757. The triumph was really a victory for the army of the East India Company: this company-state now ruled, or at least had some sort of claim over, the lives of millions. Our image of the pink covering nineteenth-century world maps dates from this moment. It could be said, without hyperbole or irony, that the sun never set on Britain's agglomeration of colonies, provinces, protectorates, company territories, and kingdoms.[8]

Charles supported the treaty, even if some considered it somewhat ill designed. He appreciated what the treaty did and did not accomplish. What would Britons substantively gain by adding millions of square miles to their holdings in North America? The French before them had struggled to construct a profitable empire there, and much of the territory remained unsettled by Europeans. On the map, the additions looked impressive, but a few more tiny islands in the Caribbean would have meant a great deal more for Britain than all of Canada, which now had to be protected.[9] Charles squashed these concerns as, ever astute, he was "dreading to differ with Mr. Pitt when the latter was likely to exert all his powers."[10]

Even if Charles realized the symbolic weight of the new acquisitions, he also tallied the costs, which staggered the imagination. On balance, he could not say if the benefits outweighed potential losses. His ambivalence captured perfectly what was at stake. He ended up "defending the peace as well as it could be defended, burned incense on the altar of prerogative, and sang almost hosannahs to the praise of the King." Pitt, for his part, recognized how important Charles's help was in figuring "how to wind up the war." He singled out Charles on "his moderation and clear method of stating the question" of what was at stake.[11]

The question officials confronted, which they could not dodge, was how to rule this empire. This vexing issue consumed statesmen—and in some cases, their careers—for the next few years. For a start, the populations to be integrated were extraordinarily diverse. The king's new subjects included Muslims and Hindus on the subcontinent, wealthy Catholic planters in the Caribbean, poor Francophone Catholics in Quebec, a mixed multitude of Native Americans, and a larger number of Africans and Afro-Caribbeans. Britons had inherited not only the Atlantic world but also the world's human diversity. Previously the English had struggled to incorporate Irish Catholics and Scottish Highlanders. Now that complexity would be amplified. Diversity, however, was the least of Britain's worries. Officials also had to figure out how to manage space. The new territories had to be secured in some fashion, as policy makers considered it only a matter of time before they would be fighting the French to hold on to these areas. That could well entail troops.

Finally, and most pressingly, there was the issue of debt. Britain had incurred a massive debt by war's end, which stood at a staggering £146 million, as well as yearly interest payments amounting to more than £500,000. The Crown's income would not exceed, many believed, £8 million per year.[12] These figures fixated officials, including, of course, the financially adept Charles.

Empire posed new questions for the British, in the form of both problems and possibilities. Dilemmas did not arise because the war had created a new set of conditions; rather, victory and the euphoria surrounding it, as one scholar argues, crystallized imperatives.[13] To be sure, Britain had ruled over the kingdoms of the British Isles and over the colonies in North America and the Caribbean. But as Charles's experiences on the Board of Trade had suggested, the arrangements binding the center to the periphery varied from place to place and certainly did not stem from any systematic vision. And as George's experiences made clear, the force of holding rebellious regions in check preceded any sort of integration. Britons embraced the notion, in theory, that they were a people "Protestant, commercial, maritime, and free," as a historian argues.[14] But beyond this ideology that tied the peripheries to the center, what else bound them? Parliament, to be sure, had emerged from the tumult of the seventeenth century as sovereign in Britain and Ireland. But could or should that institution rule an empire? Or would the Crown alone suffice? At home, Britons had rejected such an idea. Prerogative could not sustain the complexities of governance in an ethnically and religiously diverse multiple kingdom. Only Parliament could.

Most critically, therefore, officials confronted the question of how peoples and places were to be managed. Previously, the question did not matter, except for times of profound stress, such as in 1676 in Virginia, or in regions where a military presence was crucial, like, say, the slave societies of the Caribbean. So long as the colonies remained quiet, few cared about issues of governance. It would be wrong, however, to assert that such presence betokened a form of garrison government. Nor does the phrase "salutary neglect," coined by Edmund Burke, quite capture the cultural or ideological attachment linking center to periphery. Americans and Caribbean planters considered themselves British. No doubt still provincials, they lived in societies geographically separated from but culturally and economically bound to Great Britain. If, however, Burke's term fails to capture certain types of bonds, it works well to define the institutional and governmental connections, or lack thereof. The task officials now faced was to devise a means to manage a diverse array of people while in debt without the benefits of useful blueprints or precedents.[15]

Complicating the task were the institutions that men like the Townshends would have to work with. The ruling elite was chosen to govern through family connections and nepotism. The system encouraged some to think that they were predestined to lead, and at times it could produce virtuosos, who through their charisma and confidence could motivate others to follow a certain path. Robert Walpole had been one. Turnip had very nearly been another. It could also produce ineffectual rulers. There was no "party" system as such. Very nearly all who believed they should rule considered themselves good Whigs who swore allegiance to a Glorious Revolution settlement. The ways things worked, then, depended on personality and connection, as well as the constant jockeying necessary to hold any coalition of egos together, even for those who considered themselves "patriotic." At one turn, a grandee could be in government; at another, he could be a member of the opposition. Alternatively, if he did not play by the rules of the system, he could find himself out altogether. Britain, therefore, faced a postwar world with institutional structures and approaches that were almost medieval.

What the British confronted, however novel, was not unique. The issues they grappled with came to preoccupy all European powers in the latter part of the eighteenth century. All struggled in their own ways to transform what one historian calls the porous "fabric" of imperial sovereignty, almost stringlike in composition, into something cohesive and uniform. The British, though, had to deal with this reality more pressingly at this moment because of the costs of victory. Composite states, the sort of loose arrangements used for governing before, would not be up to the task.[16]

The period after the war, therefore, taxed not only treasuries; it also taxed imaginations. No longer a space defined by commercial empire bound together by an ideology, the postwar Atlantic demanded the state's attention. Those who hoped to govern, or to map sovereignty on to, the integrated Atlantic had to ask what sort of power was required, how it would be administered, and where it would reside. The state had a newfound capacity after fighting a global war; however, how would that power translate into an ability to govern? This issue would bedevil and break successive ministries. The fruits of success for the British created more problems than they could solve. What was won gave the conceit that elites could do what they were ill prepared to take on.

The stresses and strains, the drama of figuring what to do, and the perils of debt entranced the Townshends as they did other officials. Charles feared, even though he defended the Treaty of Paris, that "we should sink from a dream of ambition to a state of bankruptcy." This was, as Charles and George believed, a critical time, both for them and for the empire. "The times are delicate," and their "rank in business and character in public life are now in suspense: God guide us for the best," Charles declared to George. The time seemed like no other. It was what one historian calls "a moment of singular promise" in the minds of Britons. "We had," Burke would argue, "humbled every power which we dreaded," and now could establish "a New kind of Empire upon Earth." He was hardly alone in believing as much.[17]

With the victory over Catholic France, the war became a defining feature of British identity and of the idea that sustained empire. Most concretely, the war encouraged a new fascination with the idea of empire—the urge to look west for Britain's future—at the expense of the Continent to the east and Britain's traditional commitments there.[18] And the treaty seemed to suggest that a moment of great import was at hand, one during which empires could rise or fall, a period of some momentous possibility and peril. As an official named Thomas Pownall would put it, and he had a great deal of experience working as a colonial governor, "The several changes in interests and territories . . . have created a general impression of some new state of things arising." He intuited "some general idea of some revolution of events, beyond the ordinary course of things; some general apprehension, of something new arising in the world."[19] The final, most vexing part of the postwar conundrum, or what for many was now taking the cast of an "imperial moment," was the growing belief that the many issues arising from the fruits of victory had to be addressed urgently.

Into the Woods

The times posed untold challenges, but British leadership was not up to those challenges. After a long period of one-party rule and the stability born of patronage, like-minded officials, and a politically quiescent populace, the 1760s ushered in a time of flux. The first leader to try to work his way through the period's complexities was the brothers' erstwhile patron Lord

Bute. He was the favorite of the new king, an ardent defender of virtue, and a foe of corruption, but the nation regarded Bute as "anathema," mainly because of his coziness with the young king. As he put it in a letter to "my Dear George," Bute protested "I have hardly met with anything but cruel abuse and base ingratitude. If this is a tribute necessary to be paid by those who hold the Helm, I will never envy the Man that succeeds me." Nonetheless, he helped secure the peace and hoped to manage imperial holdings in the wake of the war by appointing a like-minded group of governors, largely military men.[20]

All leaders found themselves in a wilderness of sorts. Bute could not form a stable ministry, by and large because of the fact that he had risen to high office solely on account of his relationship with the king. He had also fallen out with the popular Pitt. In 1763, for what he regarded as the best interests of the state, he resigned and handed over the reins to a former protégé, with whom he also had a falling-out, George Grenville. Bute took this course from necessity, so as to avoid more bitter enemies securing power, most especially Pitt. From this point forward, Bute would be seen and feared as an éminence grise far too close to the Crown for any good Whig to trust, a shadow behind the throne. Grenville would, from the outset, not fare much better for many of the same reasons, dogged as he was by fears that Bute lay lurking in the wings, that the king did not trust and support him, and that any alliances he formed could not withstand a crisis.[21]

The brief ascendancy Bute enjoyed did little for the brothers, and his fall from grace made securing political roles even more difficult. He still cultivated a connection to George, promising to secure a position for him when he resigned and Grenville took office. But this is beside the point. The Townshends had little substantive to do at this juncture because George once more found himself in a political wilderness. While he spent his time drawing and entertaining and attending to his beloved militia, he may have been slipping into what can only be called depression. In late 1763, Charles observed: "My brother himself writes calmly, and seems unhappy where he is." Charles tried everything he could to reach George. "I have touched on every point that could animate, alarm, or satisfy him," he wrote, "and I should hope he will gradually return to a better way of thinking, and his own natural and wisest situation and party." Alas, a month later, little had changed. Charles was having a difficult time contacting his brother, worried because "he left London in ill-humour." George spent a great deal of time at Raynham. "I am at too great a Distance and am in all respects too remote," he told Charles, "to know much of what is passing in the world."[22]

Charles, too, stood on the outside looking in. In December 1762, he approached his old mentor and patron, the Earl of Halifax, asking to obtain the king's permission that, he said, "I may lay my Commission, as Secretary at War, at His Feet." Charles argued that his request was "imposed upon me by circumstances not arising from myself." Halifax agreed. "It was," Halifax found, "a painful Task to an old Friend who heartily wishes you every agreeable Circumstance in Life." In 1763, with the treaty ending the war signed, Charles became president of the Board of Trade. His status as the expert on all things Atlantic and American had won him the place. Yet, despite the vaunted title, his office did not offer him a real leadership position. While he had assumed his mentor's former job, he did not join the cabinet.

Charles was of two minds. He decried the marginal roles he had to play, yet he understood why, and accepted his lot. "For after all that within these 8 years has happened to me," he wrote after he was "forced" to accept the Board of Trade, "and all the lengths I have gone with others against interest and from attachment, I can not persuade myself to reason upon practical views with the least expectation or confidence." He seemed, as Horace Walpole suggested, to slip through the fingers of all "at every turn, and could not be held down to no decision." But Charles could see the failing nature of administrations in these years, one of which was, as he put it, "a pretty lustering administration, which would do very well for a summer wear."[23] As others jockeyed for position and schemed to craft alliances to rule or to enter into opposition, Charles demurred.

On the one hand, according to some, he refused to countenance possibilities to join any coalition because he appeared to be "stuck to Mr. Pitt." He professed, as he put it, a "sincere and grateful sense" of Pitt's "partiality, generosity, and friendship towards me." On the other hand, others suggested that the failure of any group to propose any plan for the period and its momentous issues explained Charles's standoffish behavior. Though out in the cold, Charles portrayed himself "determined, and not inconstant." He would "act the part of a Man of Business and a Man of Honor." He would refuse to enter government, "not from a want of ambition, but from a love of *Consistency*," declaring: "I will not be the obedient instrument of any Sett of Men."[24]

The brothers regarded the bonds that had united them during the early years of the war, when George endured his first period of political exile, as growing even stronger with this second period in the wilderness. "I wait for you, and am happy to have an opportunity of proving to you, by deeds, not words, how much I prefer your advice and our union to all friends and all motives," Charles reassured George in 1763. He trusted none more than George. "I have not opened my unguarded lips to a soul," he assured him; "they shall be sealed till I see you." Charles would show George "dutifull deference." George felt such sentiments just as deeply. He confessed, "I own my Heart is hurt (and it would not be so if I wanted affection to you) at seeing my Brother, with whom I have pass'd thro life, and who is possessed of perhaps the most uncommon nay commanding Talents" when Charles was struggling to find a role. "As an Individual or as part of a System, you may Unquestionably be the head of any thing you please," George told him. All Charles needed was "patience and Confidence" and he would be "in the first Rank of power and estimation in this country." If they both bided their time, all who aspired to power would, George wrote to Charles, "wish for your heights, trust your motives, and form under your Ability." He summed up his estimation of his brother in this way: "You my Dear Charles if you will lead mankind, must make such men [as Pitt] follow you." He ended by saying, "I love you sincerely."[25]

Therefore, both brothers pinned their independent stances on the political confusion of the times; and their exile, which they were convinced sprang from pettiness and corruption, was a symptom of this larger problem. "The ministry is mixed," meaning unable to unite and fix on a plan, Charles told George at one point immediately after the war. "Things continue as they were in general," he sighed to George, "unless you think it be a farther discovery of the real bottom of the present imperfect ministry." Because of "sudden changes in our Parliamentary climate, violent heat and extreme cold alternately," Charles believed he had little choice but to act "honestly, independently, and therefore wisely." The corrupt British Whig establishment, of which admittedly the brothers were a part, still rose and fell with connections, alliances, and patronage. On the outside looking in, the two came to believe that the Whig status quo, which could work under normal circumstances, was not suitable for the bewildering times. Charles noted the "numberless ills which embarrass every man and surround this Kingdom" in a letter to George, adding: "I agree with you in thinking that He is no man who, of either side, is overcome by the fear of the storm." He predicted "the winds will blow hard from all quarters, and every man at sea will have occasion for watchfulness, resolution, skill and strong tackle."[26]

What the brothers effectively did, as they had done before, was to turn a necessity of exile into a virtue of independence, but this sensibility was magnified by what they perceived to be the critical nature of the moment. They convinced themselves that the political world was whirring around them at a momentous juncture as they held fast. In 1764, pressed once more by the Duke of Newcastle to join the government, Charles wrote a long letter to Newcastle. "Speaking my Sentiments fully" he said, "[my] mind is full both of matter and anxiety." But he demonstrated an extraordinary sense of confidence in what he and his brother were doing, or in this case, not doing. "I have not found reason," he argued, "to change the Idea I lately expressed to you of the temper, character and deadness of the Time we live in." He meant deadness in two ways: the present ministry, and the broader difficulties Britain faced. The "national temper" appeared "subdued," and "indifference and distrust are become habitual and general," affecting the ways that the nation responded to the crisis it confronted. "I wish any degree of Spirit, Care or Attention were able to reform this Error, or to awaken Men to a Sense of Danger, but I expect it not, and, I should disguise, if I did not frankly confess to you that I despair of any such Revolution." The government and the nation were sleepwalking.[27]

Charles did not apologize for his own actions or inactions. He stood condemned, he wrote to Newcastle, by those "who have no right to circumscribe any one Sentiment or direct any one Action of my political conduct: in whose Plans I had originally no participation, whose Systems I am not bound to adopt, and to whom I stand, in no Sense, nor any degree accountable." He added, "My Idea goes farther." He wanted "in this critical Minute," he continued, to "open my Mind freely." The "critical Minute" brought politics and context together. At this juncture, if the terms were right, he would "bring things to a decision" so long as he was "at liberty to act as his judgment advises." He would "wait for the communication of such a systematical and probable Plan as may induce and justice those who shall again embark." At this point, the ministry looked as bankrupt as the state. The only hope revolved around a strengthened minority, "if it can be done upon proper Terms, by a connexion with Lord Bute, or with Lord Holland, or by reconciling Lord Temple and Mr. Pitt and Mr. Grenville." Only such a constellation of leaders could stand against "an Age of extravagance, indigence, immorality, and indifference."[28]

Even though the formation of such a leadership group was an impossibility, given intractable differences and hatreds, this was a powerful

manifesto. What emerges is a clear sense that Charles was using the correspondence to Newcastle as an opportunity to plant his flag behind the idea of
"Evidence of real concert, consistent Plan, and solid Grounds of strength."
He was convinced, of course, as was George, that he could lead, that he had
the ideas and the abilities to design a plan that could bring harmony to the
whole. Prospects did not, however, seem bright in the immediate wake of the
Treaty of Paris. Not for him, and not for the nation. Charles preferred one
name above all others that could work at the moment, the name sure to cata-
pult him as well. "Let me add," he ended his note to Newcastle, "the generous manner in which Mr. Pitt behaved to the whole Party last year. His name,
His Weight, His Talents all make his concurrence a necessary part of any
Union." Charles went on to conclude that he "should very much fear any
plan would be ineffectual" without Pitt's accession to it.[29]

George, in effect, rationalized his marginalization by fetishizing virtue
and by justifying his exclusion from the political world not on the basis of his
own missteps but through the idea that he and Charles possessed sensibilities
that others at this critical juncture, without their scruples, did not. He considered "the Distress of the Poor in this Country" a "Disgrace," one abetted by
"the most radical National Imbecility." The potential costs of imbecility
were immense. "If I am not mistaken," he wrote in 1766, "the American
Colonies have in 25 Years doubled the Number of their Inhabitants." Yet, he
exclaimed, "How many have starved here, that might have worked there! Or
at home!" No one, he alleged, was conceiving of such costs and benefits and
how the whole empire should function as a unit. Just the opposite was occurring. "Luxury among one part and Misery with the Other," as he put it, "is
daily expelling our Inhabitants by Thousands and then we are surprised that
our Empire should be moving?"[30]

From their disengaged perch, the brothers saw how the rot also affected the provinces. George learned of a "variety of Disputes" in Ireland.
A group of discontents calling themselves "the Patriots" were clamoring for
some sort of reform. They had some laudable goals, chief among these challenging a corrupt band of elites that controlled patronage in the kingdom.
Though the Patriots numbered only a handful or so, their power increased
and grew alarming, as George understood, when constitutional issues arose.
Some suggested that the nature of the link between Ireland and Britain was
to blame for Ireland's misfortunes. George learned that some Irish, especially an "able" leader of the Patriots, Henry Flood, styled themselves "great

asserters of liberty." This was not the sort of reform, he believed, that could address the challenges Britons faced. It would, in fact, exacerbate problems.[31]

In London, Charles wrestled with similar concerns oceans away. Holding North America, he knew from the ministerial papers he perused, cost £317,282, 13 shillings, and 7 pence annually for troops alone. That amount, he learned, was "exclusive of the Civil Establishments of Georgia, Nova Scotia, and East and West Florida," which together added nearly £20,000 and which would have to be supplied by the Exchequer. He also knew of plans for frontier forts, and whether they should be kept up or abandoned for another more expedient plan. In the mid-1760s, Thomas Gage, the British commander for North America, was "propos[ing], as the present Forts fall into Ruin, to build them on smaller scales."[32] America's concerns did not mirror Ireland's, at this point in any event. But unless certain anomalies could be addressed, problems would grow.

Uncertainty and Sovereignty

The problems, as the brothers sensed, were growing not into *a* crisis but perhaps *the* crisis of the age. At its most basic level, that crisis began with debt, or better, how to manage it in the immediate aftermath of war. Like most momentous events, however, this one had inauspicious beginnings and took shape in unforeseen ways. Unsurprisingly, it led to a period defined by muddled debate. It also took on its tenor from the ways different voices, each equally confident in its prescriptions for empire, responded to the debt crisis. Each of these voices participated in the debate with a similar set of assumptions about sovereignty, though they differed on how it should be realized in the new imperial world that all confronted. The same goes for the brothers. George had decided opinions, though he would not stand out in the debates in the House of Lords when after his father's death he took his seat. Charles, in the Commons where responses were heated and varied, would demonstrate a fine-grained and sophisticated understanding of the many questions involved as Britons first struggled to devise an ideal of sovereignty that could address the costs of victory.

In 1764, to try to confront the debt by raising revenue from trade, Parliament passed what is called the Sugar Act. The act was meant to enforce old laws on the books designed to regulate trade. In this case it laid a duty on the importation of foreign molasses into the colonies. The first stab at reform, a revenue measure, then, was devised to address the debt issue. Americans complained, especially merchants. Some suggested that Parliament was overstepping its bounds. Then again, any protester had to know that the 1764 act was passed merely to put teeth into laws already on the statute books, laws that essentially stemmed in the first place from the Navigation Acts. Few in Britain believed that Parliament could not act to regulate colonial affairs.[33]

What followed saw tensions grow to new heights. In 1764 George Grenville, the new prime minister, argued that Americans had an obligation at least to pay for the troops that were to be garrisoned for their defense in North America. Simply put, this stance defines how Grenville responded to the crisis. Britons would manage the debt, but Americans, or so it was believed, had enough wealth to sustain the new demands of empire and shoulder the burdens of garrisoning empire in America, a responsibility that had grown with the acquisition of former French territories and forts. Grenville had a clear, uncomplicated sense of how empire should work. We could appreciate this approach in two ways. One historian puts it like this: Grenville had a "narrow, cramped outlook." He had "no vision, no grasp of the wider problems of Empire." Another believes Grenville advocated a well-thought-out policy of "extraction and austerity," one that emulated Continental European methods of ruling empire and that represented a profound and conscious volte-face on earlier Whiggish conceptions of political economy. Whichever view we subscribe to, the end result was the same: Grenville showed little compunction in dictating how empire should work.[34]

This characterization may be a bit uncharitable; however, it does hit on some essential truths. For Grenville, Parliament enjoyed supremacy and Parliament could legislate simply because it was supreme. He epitomized an understanding of rule premised on what we could call "imperial grandeur." He assumed that Parliament's status in the empire should mirror its role in the British Isles. Sovereignty struck Grenville as self-evident, in much the same way Continental rulers held to centralized understandings of rule. No system of thought or thought of system was necessary. Considerations of how the colonies could contribute to prosperity for empire over the long haul or how a government could use its power to encourage production and consumption paled in comparison to using the state to take what colonists owed it. Grenville believed that colonists could and should pay taxes; he knew Parliament could legislate for the colonies.[35]

At this early juncture, Charles seemed to agree. As soon as Grenville uttered his first words on America, Charles gave the first firm indication of how power and authority had to be centralized for the empire to function. The colonies in America, in his estimation, "were not to be emancipated." Charles did not take issue with taxes or revenues. One of the members of the Commons shot back that the colonies "are more free than Ireland, for America had not been conquered: on the contrary, it was inhabited by the conquerors." Charles told his colleague that he should not be alarmed, that he only meant that "the Colonies were not to be emancipated from their dependence on the supremacy of this country." What supremacy and dependency entailed was never mentioned. But Charles soon would make his mind known.[36]

Grenville then prepared a bill proposing a Stamp Act, stipulating that Americans, like subjects in the British Isles, should pay a modest stamp duty on paper goods, especially the paper used for documents that were issued for legal purposes. Paper shipped from Britain would be stamped or embossed with a seal, stored in warehouses in American cities, then sold to retailers, and even newspapermen, who then passed the tax burden on to consumers. The plan was simple and seemed uncontestable. Britain had fought for empire in America, and Americans had benefited more than any other group from the war. The French had left, and colonists enjoyed great security. Americans seemed wealthy, or at least well off, to the British. And Americans, like other provincials, were subjects, and Parliament was supreme. Once again, Grenville showed little tolerance for any discussion of any of these points, so cocksure he was of the justice of his cause and the principles at stake. For him, revenue was the rationale. As the act would read, "certain stamp duties" would be used "towards further defraying the expences of defending, protecting, and securing" Britain's colonies. He assumed Parliament had the power to raise such revenue. "We have," he declared as he proposed his scheme, "expended much in America. Let us now avail ourselves of the fruits of that expence."[37]

The initial American response mirrored Grenville's initiative. It, too, proved just as insistent. Francis Bernard, the British-born governor of the Massachusetts Bay Colony, captured the essence of that response when he catalogued what he saw as a "mob" ransacking the town of Boston. The "Temper of the People" was crazed. "It is difficult," he wrote, "to conceive the fury which at present possesses the People of Boston of all Orders and degrees of Men." While such activity also relied on assumptions about what it meant to be British, it tapped into deep emotions and wells of provincial history, just as Grenville's ideas sprang from metropolitan history. Most Americans looked to their own pasts and their English heritage to make their voices heard about the Stamp Act. Most famously, Bostonians adapted older celebrations for the new crisis. "Pope's Day," as it was called in New England, recalled the occasion when Guy Fawkes had tried to blow up the Houses of Parliament in 1605. Bostonians, in particular, had made the fifth of November their own, a day of raucous celebration when they announced to one another their identity as English Protestant provincials. When word reached Boston about what Parliament was planning, common men and women took to the streets and used the symbols and ceremony of Pope's Day celebrations to declare, through word and deed, that they too possessed the rights of Britons. New Yorkers followed suit. As did others up and down the coast. Only in those regions in which slaves predominated, such as South Carolina and the Caribbean, did cooler heads prevail. Contesting Parliament's presumption to control a subject people, as Bostonians were doing, could unleash slave rebellion, and elites in slave societies feared this more than any parliamentary innovation.[38]

We are all too conditioned to see the Stamp Act crisis as the first act of an inevitable drama about home rule or who was to rule at home. Insurmountable tensions emerged between center and periphery or between classes of subjects. Or so the story goes. But if we look around the British world and to the American past, a different picture comes into focus. Rioting as a response to what authorities tried to do was nothing unusual. Men and women commonly took to the streets in England, Scotland, and Ireland to protest the measures that governments took, especially when such measures impinged on their abilities to get ahead or to keep body and soul together. Indeed, Parliament had warmed to the idea of taxing Americans, in part, because English men and women had raised a furor over a proposed cider tax. Bostonians, in particular, had a long and distinguished history of rioting, defining who they were, their status, and their credentials as good British subjects by taking it out on each other.[39] Moreover, anything touching on constitutional issues could set provincials to rioting. In the British Isles, men and women also threatened violence if the constitutional status of each was to be changed, as the Irish and the Scots, for instance, did when a rumor spread in 1759 that the Act of Union would be extended to incorporate the Irish or even earlier in Edinburgh when the Act of Union had been passed for the Scots in 1707.

Therefore, Americans were not so much acting the part of revolutionaries as being conventional provincials. As such, they employed basic British
ideas to contest what they regarded as an unjust measure. The Stamp Act crisis, as it came to be called, did not only initiate a visceral response; it also led
some colonists to grapple with basic issues of rights that challenged what
Grenville hoped to accomplish. A Bostonian named James Otis published a
few pamphlets contesting the measure. Others followed suit. In essence, the
responses of the Americans, those who took issue with the Stamp Act in any
event, fastened on their rights as Britons to argue that Parliament had no
right to do what it was doing. The notion of "no taxation without representation," that old right that Americans and other provincials held fast to, was
all the principle they needed. Older privileges and agreements, the stuff of
the arrangements that had animated empire up to this point, were premised
on the simple assumption that Americans, and again by extension other provincials, such as Irish Protestants and Lowland Scots, did not surrender the
rights of metropolitans because they lived on the margins. Fittingly, when
they fastened on one figure to take issue with, it was Lord Bute, the bête
noire of all Whiggish-minded subjects who supported the Glorious Revolution settlement in the British world. Interestingly, they focused more on him
and the abstract idea of "enlightened despotism" he seemed to represent
than even the one person responsible for the Stamp Act: George Grenville.[40]

For the most part, the Townshend brothers did not take a vocal part in
the debate, though they had definite thoughts on it. Now in the Lords,
George did not participate in the drafting of the bill or in debates in the
House over the principles and practicalities involved in enforcing it. We do
know that he supported both the idea of the Stamp Act and its enforcement.
After all, it was in keeping with his developing philosophy of empire. He
even recommended a "distributor of the Stamps in Jamaica," a friend he had
served with in Germany and Portugal who had fallen on hard times. Most
critically, he sensed the Stamp Act coalescing with other issues of the day like
the failure to create a stable ministry "in one noble Political Mass," but he
could not predict, he wrote to Charles, "how it will ferment."[41]

Charles's thoughts bespoke principled ambivalence. Charles supported
the passage of the Stamp Act, though he had not participated in the debates,
claiming to be ill. No doubt, he supported the thrust of the measure. In fact,
"he asserted with vehemence his approbation of the Stamp Act, and was for
enforcing it." But in some respects, he thought the act a foolish measure, one

passed by a ministry that could not enforce it. He agreed with George's observations about fermentation. What he regarded as the rickety nature of the present establishment did not give him confidence in the measure, either in the government's ability to follow through or, more pointedly, the lack of principle that necessarily underscored the measure.[42]

For Charles, unlike for Grenville, sovereignty could not be assumed. It had to be made manifest if taxation were ever to work. In February 1765, as members of the Commons first began grappling with the principles involved with the Stamp Act duty and the nature of the American response, Charles laid down his thoughts on the matter. "He has heard," he said in the House, "with great pleasure the right of taxing America asserted and not disputed." If it had been disputed, the word "colony" could no longer be applied to the American settlements, "for that implies subordination." And they were and should be subordinate. He harbored no doubts about this. What of their ability to pay? As an expert on this issue, "he judged the ability of the colonies from their trade and other circumstances which are the best pulses of their health and vigour, and thinks they can bear it perfectly well." He did not think taxing them implied a "servile connexion." As he put it, "If America looks to Great Britain for protection, she must enable her to protect her. If she expects our fleets, she must assist our revenue."[43] The colonists, like all Britons, were subjects and subject to the state.

In many ways, then, Charles found himself sympathizing with Grenville. He suggested that Americans were "children planted by our care and nourished by our indulgence." With time they would, he believed, grow "to a degree of strength and opulence." Would they, he wondered, after being protected by British might, "grudge their mite to relieve us from the heavy weight of that burden which we lie under?" At this point, support for the Stamp Act revolved around basic justice and the needs of the state during a critical time. Isaac Barré, an Irishman who had served with George at Quebec and who—unlike George—had appeared in West's painting, berated Charles "severely" in debate, especially for characterizing the Americans as being "planted by our care."[44] The two had a history of clashing in the House. But on this point, Charles would not be persuaded.[45] Charles, therefore, had no issue with asking Americans to pay for empire. He did not scruple with duties on molasses or taxes on stamps in theory.

What bothered him was process, or lack thereof. And this gets us to principles and practicalities. When Grenville first aired his thoughts about the budget in 1764 and extracting revenue from America, Charles expressed "great surprise at the precipitation." The hows and whys of raising revenue had not been properly considered. Nor had Grenville raised the issue of a systematic plan. Charles let him know that he "would find the very profession of precipitation is not the prudent way of gaining dispatch."[46]

Moreover, he differed from Grenville on what subordination entailed. It did not mean humiliation or treating Americans like rebels. With the Stamp Act riots, Grenville maintained that "the Provinces were in Rebellion, and compared it to the Rebellion of 1745." He argued that some Americans, like the Jacobite Highlanders before them, had taken a British fort in New York "by storm, sword in hand." He may have been referring to a frontier disturbance on Sideling Hill on the borders of Maryland and Pennsylvania during which western insurgents burned goods going to Indians farther west and besieged a British frontier post. Charles took the view that, no matter the provocation, Americans were not Jacobites, and he "spoke exceedingly well; & In the fullest handsomest & strongest manner against" what Grenville had asserted.[47]

Whatever the impetus behind early British postwar plans for America, the provincial response generated a metropolitan response. With the crisis, officials struggled to understand how sovereignty had to work, even if most assumed Parliament was the seat of that sovereignty. Sensibilities, as much as anything else, defined responses, and because of this, they differed. Those who stood for "imperial grandeur" were forced to marshal meaningful arguments to confront an opposition that did not espouse such principles. Little could be assumed.[48] One such pro-grandeur voice belonged to Francis Bernard. By the summer of 1764, he was drafting "Principles, upon which it seems to me it would be most advisable to reform and resettle the American Provinces." What he had in mind echoed the sorts of things Charles and the Board of Trade had aired a decade earlier. A year later, he pressed for firmer measures. "The first thing to be done in America," he wrote an official at the board, "was to regulate support and strengthen the Governments, so that their Authority might in no way be dependent on the humours of the People." Authority, he believed, had to be clarified before any taxes could be collected. Whatever the prescription, he had a clear idea of the malady that had to be treated. "It is my Opinion that all the Political Evils in America arise from the Want of ascertaining the Relation between Great Britain and the American Colonies." Perhaps Ireland, a fully subordinate kingdom, could serve as a model.[49] Others disagreed. Another veteran of colonial administration, Thomas Pownall, called for more lenient treatment, even going so far as, eventually, to call for American representation in a British imperial Parliament. He did so, and changed tack a number of times in the mid- to late 1760s, as debates raged over how to imagine an empire.[50]

In other words, where there had been ambiguity, or a salutary neglect, the response on the part of Americans compelled statesmen to begin to grope toward how the whole should function. And grope they did, however confidently each official aired his theories of how sovereignty had to work. In fact, they had few workable templates to address such a large empire, one that stretched across an ocean and covered continents, a situation that, as one scholar argues, pushed prevailing wisdom "to the breaking point."[51]

As the range of visions between Bernard and Pownall suggests, different, sometimes contradictory, approaches took shape in these early days. Some critics of Grenville lambasted his administration and kept the debate focused on the primacy of rights. Barré responded by declaring that Americans were true "sons of liberty," coining a term that was avidly adopted by colonists. His observation made essentially the same point that Otis and the rioters were making: Americans, too, were entitled to the rights of Britons. The Crown certainly did have authority. But perhaps not Parliament in the way some argued. Barré subscribed to Parliament's sovereignty for the whole, even if he seemed to soft-pedal that authority. Ultimately, he did not think it proper to "bridle" the colonists.[52] This view, premised on the state encouraging commercial development by discouraging parliamentary taxation, proved the exception for British officialdom at this juncture.[53]

Others, under the pressure of events, stood on a middle constitutional ground. William Pitt famously asked his colleagues if Americans were "the bastard sons" of England even if they lived an ocean away. He thought not, and because of their birthright, they too were entitled to basic British protections. Yet, Pitt did not quibble over the fact that Parliament was sovereign. The question he faced was what that sovereignty meant or how it would be applied. For him, Parliament could legislate for America, but it could not or should not tax, for the simple reason that Americans were not represented in Parliament. But what Pitt perceived to be the illegality of taxation did not diminish Parliament's role as the chief legislature not only of the British Isles but also of empire. It seemed Parliament could regulate for the whole, but what that power entailed was not clear. In fairness to Pitt, Barré, and even

Grenville, vagueness and uncertainty defined these days, but it was the uncertainty born of men leveling their contending certainties at one another. Indeed, debates were only beginning in earnest after the Stamp Act, and parameters structuring those debates were just being laid out, even if Charles was also showing glimmers of a coherent, albeit unconventional, approach.[54]

With time, the vying certainties led both, on the one hand, to more refined positions and, on the other, to imperial cacophony. As Pitt's quip about alleged illegitimacy suggested, the British had moved onto terra incognita, or at least a spot of land that had not been explored since the time of the Glorious Revolution. Although most did not articulate the problem quite this way, they were trying to impose sovereignty on a dynamic Atlantic system, one in which the stakes were growing higher.[55] In Parliament, nearly all agreed with the great jurist Sir Edward Coke that sovereignty could not be divided. But what did sovereignty mean in an empire that was more an assemblage of places with distinctive relationships to the center? And in the wake of the Stamp Act, members of Parliament paraded contending theories of how sovereignty should be applied to the problems Britons faced in what was generally considered a critical period in world history.

What was happening in Parliament was closely followed throughout the empire. In fact, the debate over what to do with America resonated far and wide, as provincials from other places began to consider their plight and status in light of American demands and British responses to them. In Ireland, most noisily, the small but vocal group of Patriots, led by a Dubliner named Charles Lucas, had been arguing for changes to Britain's Irish administration and for an end to corrupt practices. They saw the disturbances over the Stamp Act in America through an Irish prism. Patriots like Lucas paid great attention to the transatlantic drama, as they, much like Otis, hoped for recognition of their rights as subjects equal to any other. Indeed, they targeted laws on the books, such as the Declaratory Act of 1720 for Ireland that stipulated Britain's Parliament could legislate for Irish affairs "in all cases whatsoever."

The Stamp Act and the ensuing debates struck a chord in Ireland. Part of the empire, part of the state, semiautonomous in theory, dependent in fact, Ireland's status had not been debated for some time. Lucas was the exception. He had for years harangued his readers in Dublin about the corruption that underscored the provincial-metropolitan relationship, corruption that stemmed from Britain's not-so-salutary neglect of Ireland. He decried in particular the unusual arrangements that had emerged since the time of

Swift to ensure British business would be undertaken in Ireland with as little fuss and trouble as possible, an approach that was premised on patronage and corruption. Lucas thought that what was called the "undertaker system," in which local politicians did Britain's bidding, was rotten to the core and would not allow virtue to flourish in Protestant Ireland. Moreover, the issue of elections also bedeviled him. In Ireland, as opposed to Britain, general elections to the Irish Parliament took place only on the death of one monarch and the accession of another, something that allowed practices like undertaking to take root. "The practice of *keeping one and the same Parlement so long on foot,*" Lucas wrote in 1765, corrupted the kingdom.[56]

With the Stamp Act crisis, the Patriots discerned striking parallels between the American and Irish cases. Perhaps they could, in Lucas's words, "join in the Common Cry." Lucas had no concrete solutions, but he could note problems. He rejected the notion that the colonies were "were virtually represented" in Parliament. His newspaper, the *Freeman's Journal,* printed resolutions supporting the Americans as they rioted. The editors of the paper even took bets to see if and when the Stamp Act would be repealed. In early 1766, the odds at one public house favored repeal 240 to 133. Events in America, and official responses to them, held up a looking glass to Ireland for radicals like Lucas.[57]

As provincials, the Irish and the Americans both had grievances. They both labored under a series of arrangements that encouraged corruption to take root. At issue for Lucas were what he regarded as ancient privileges the Irish possessed as inhabitants of a kingdom and their legacy as the descendants of English men and women in a kingdom they helped conquer. Although he developed a bogus history to sustain his vision, his interpretation meant the descendants of English settlers did not surrender rights because they lived across the Irish Sea. Lucas began to see, or at least to give voice to the possibility of, a provincial interest, a possibility that only increased the complexity of the task Britain's Parliament was struggling to comprehend.

Brothers' Keepers

When protests continued and Grenville argued that Americans should be considered "in open rebellion," Charles declared: "[I am] strong for the supremacy of Parliament, yet we and the colonies [are] mutually dependent." He thought Grenville's idea both wrong-headed and likely to inflame tensions. He certainly advocated some sort of declaration of Parliament's authority, but he wanted this issue disentangled from the fortunes of the Stamp Act. For him, something else was at stake, something most in the Commons had missed. "He thinks," it was reported in February 1766, "if some proper plan is not formed for governing as well as quieting them at present and for the future, it will be extremely dangerous." The nature of the empire, its looseness, troubled him. "The magistrates at present," Charles found, "in many colonies [were] elective, the judges dependent on the assemblies for their salaries." Measures like the Stamp Act were all well and good, as were strong words. But how could they be enforced? "We are now without forts or troops. Our magistrates without inclinations and without power," he argued. "Would you raise this temper while you are most unable to resist it?" The plan of government in North America, he believed, had to be "altered."[58]

The Stamp Act, then, proposed taxation without effective sovereignty. It was doomed to fail. Certainly, the sort of thoroughgoing system Charles and George espoused and hoped for was not reflected in the act, which had the look of a blunt instrument. Charles still dodged the issue of repeal, however. Principle again concerned him. He told the House "he could not repeal the act on account of the right, whereby it was imposed, nor on account of the violence that had been used against it." Repeal could only be premised "on the impracticability, or inexpediency of it."[59]

Balance, therefore, proved a precious commodity at this juncture. And the brothers could not find it, even if they, like others, stood secure in their ideas about the crisis. The years 1765 and 1766 witnessed a frenzied scramble for power and over ideas. Grenville was flailing, and other aspirants were vying to lead, each scurrying to find members of Parliament who could put together a viable coalition. The Townshend brothers had their opportunities. Indeed, they flirted with suitors. George saw possibilities in joining Grenville, agreeing with the ends he proposed, and he even assumed the minor role of lord lieutenant of the ordnance in his administration. As one of Grenville's allies put it in a note to the prime minister, "You love Lord Townshend" and should be pleased to know "his good heart and his attachment to the Government appear in full colours." Looks, though, could be deceiving. George discussed with Charles whether Grenville merited support. Charles had a problem with Grenville's plans, and he had clashed publicly with him, though he regretted it, and "did not like the rest of the Administration." To Charles, Grenville meant "proclamation of whim and firmness, internal jealousy and apprehension. No plan for our colonies." He vetoed the move. Throughout Grenville's time in charge, Charles cultivated what might be called a benign neutrality. He promised to "give all possible assistance to Government," as he applauded some of its aims even if he dismissed its methods. Although he would not join the opposition, he could not bring himself to cast his lot with Grenville.[60] George did not push the matter and also remained supportive but neutral.

Charles saw more possibilities with Lord Rockingham, who as a neighbor at Grosvenor Square had become a friend. He was also growing close to Rockingham's secretary, Edmund Burke. Charles may have disagreed about some of their visions, but these were, like him, thoughtful men. George, however, would have nothing to do with Rockingham, as his archnemesis, Cumberland, supported Rockingham's bid to form a government. And Charles did not insist with George. They then did nothing, not even engage the opposition. "I have walked strait upon the line we drew," Charles assured George in the midst of the debates.[61]

Both sets of suitors came to appreciate the strength of fraternal bonds. As Grenville was struggling to figure out what would happen in the wake of the Stamp Act, and it appeared as though Rockingham might form a new ministry, he reported that Charles was to be asked to become Chancellor of the Exchequer or, if he refused the post, secretary of state for North America. Burke also inquired about his health to probe his willingness. Both positions would be ministerial posts, the sorts of leadership positions he craved. When Charles demurred, Grenville knew he would have to work on George. When it came time to discuss "the new System that would be formed," George met with officials "to speak both for himself and Mr. C. Townshend." In effect, George had traveled down from Norfolk to act as Charles's agent, "having expressed his resolution to act in concert with his Brother." George told Grenville that "he could not engage to act with or support those whom he came into the King's Government to oppose nor would he advise his Brother to do what he did not think right to do himself." Grenville went on to explain that he thought "it likely that Mr. C. Townshend will be spoken to himself." Of course, he was wrong. Grenville was not alone. When Rockingham approached Charles without George's blessing, he left the meeting "*re infecta*," that is, with nothing accomplished.[62]

In the summer of 1765, both brothers even refused the king to his face. George III knew that he could only approach Charles through George. In

July 1765, he wrote: "I have just seen Ld Townshend who seems cooler & to set his Brother at Liberty to take the part He thinks fitting, I shall now see Charles, & therefore hope to gain him." Going from one brother to the next—"to get his Brother's leave to accept"—humiliated the king, but he realized that no other approach would prove successful. "What does not these horrid times," he complained, "make me stoop to." George III, as the Earl of Sandwich reported, "used every fair as well as every fallacious argument to engage him [George] to accept some office himself, and to prevail on his brother to accept the seals as Secretary of State." George refused. "The King," as the earl put it, "was not satisfied with this, but sent for Charles Townshend; but that audience had no other effect than a confirmation of what his brother had said in both their names."[63]

The brothers would not go it alone at this critical but unstable juncture. As George put it to the king, he would "refuse both on his brother's account and his own, declaring strongly his disapprobation of the new Ministry, and his firm adherence to his former opinions." He went on to tell the king that "he could never act in contradiction to them, nor persuade his brother to [do] what he could not do himself." He could not "disgrace himself" by supporting those who were aspiring to form a government.[64]

One observer believed that Charles did what he did out of "a firm adherence to Mr. Pitt." Others saw something more elemental at work. As their great-uncle the Duke of Newcastle explained, the answer to why Charles refused was quite simple. Charles declared "his own inclination to accept, but that his brother . . . would not permit him to do it." The power of the filial bond, which appeared to overawe ambition, must have perplexed one of the eighteenth century's great political animals. Only an explanation rooted in self-interest and intimidation could suffice to make sense of such behavior.[65]

The brothers themselves had a different explanation. They resolved that one did not move without the other because of the ends they hoped to achieve and how they aspired to achieve them. At this point, Charles could declare: "My entire union with Lord Townshend . . . gives me perfect satisfaction and new strength."[66] In rejecting all suitors, Charles pleaded principle. "Surely, in these times, with a little common sense, I might have been dependent if I had pleased," he noted. Charles, like George, had opinions that were deeply and passionately held. But he judged neither Grenville nor Rockingham the man to enter government with. Rockingham was, Charles believed, "a stranger to his own voice in the Senate, and not of a temperament to bear fatigues or blows of his station." Grenville had "lost his weight within doors and without, at court and abroad. He is become peevish, obstinate and offensive." Neither could manage the difficulties of the day. Their ministries, Charles wagered, would not stand, quite apart from the lack of a systematic plan. Because of this, he assured George, "I now see no body; I keep a clear plain direct road; firm and resigned; ready to serve my King, if he enables me, and resolved to serve my country in all stations."[67]

They could decide the proper moment together. Charles wrote to George to say he would not consider a position in government until his brother was properly placed. He considered George the man "with whom I shd act entirely." And he "would not be [Chancellor of the Exchequer] to any man living." They had "to settle the part we are to take, for the manner of it will be delicate, and must be unexceptionable." Charles claimed—and here we see that history has a sense of irony—that the Exchequer would not do for him, "nor the reported Ld L[ieutenancy] of Ireland" for George. Charles's head still reeled with the times. "It is very difficult to form any judgment in the present state of confusion," Charles wrote to George, but "it is necessary to form an opinion, to be prepared for the day of application to us both and to have some consultation about the part we are to take." When the time was right, he argued, they would have to act, but would have to do so in concert with one another.[68]

George concurred, but he saw hope in how history turned. "My opinion is that by every Change, Government and Power must naturally devolve from the Weak and Ineffectual, to the able and Effective." He told Charles not to worry. "It should never give me an anxious moment," he counseled, "nay scarcely my Dr Charles, excite my attention, were it not the Connected and affect[ionate] Light I stand in with respect to you." In this context, history would find them both. "Passions and the variety of events," George argued, "will from time to time detect the fictitious Characters which amuse the Publick. The King's Business and Publick Confidence must ultimately rest upon those who are most able and consistent." Only such men would "be able to distinguish where a good Navigation and anchorage lies."[69]

The critical question they confronted was one hinging on a "permanent" system. As Charles declared numerous times in the midst of the crisis in 1766, "the [present] system would never do." He was right. Grenville was in fact eventually followed by Rockingham. Rockingham repealed the Stamp Act, a move Charles reluctantly supported. Prudence dictated such a course, even if it set a terrible precedent. Nonetheless, it eased tensions almost immediately. As Bernard noted, upon repeal of the act, Boston fell into "a tolerable state of tranquillity."[70]

Rockingham also passed a declaratory act for the colonies that was based entirely on Ireland's. Parliament could legislate for the colonies "in all cases whatsoever," even if it chose not to exercise that right. The impulse to take this course was Burke's, though it was shared by others in Rockingham's cabinet. In Burke's estimation, Parliament had to be supreme, as it was the only institution, and a progressive one at that, that could safeguard liberty and oppose unfettered prerogative—hence the need for the Declaratory Act. But even if Parliament could act and legislate, it did not mean it was prudent to do so, nor did it follow that passing such a measure would help the empire's economy—hence the repeal of the Stamp Act. The issues for Burke revolved around consent and authority. Both, he believed, had to be recognized. He also argued that Rockingham had to craft a more durable vision of empire at the time, a "compleat revision" that would be premised as much as possible on free trade. The Stamp Act failed in terms both of consent and of free trade.[71]

Rockingham, however, had built a ministry on shaky foundations. While the impulse to develop some grand plan made sense, the political "system," to use the term the brothers relied on, could not sustain such an attempt. The ministry was sure to collapse, and even if it did not, it could not support the construction of a system for the whole to address the pressing issues of the day.

The brothers still lamented the instability and the dithering. How could the peripheries of empire be reformed, the whole made into system, if the center remained corrupted? "In the meantime," Charles worried, "America calls for all out talents, skill, discretion and firmness." And how could he and George have a voice in these critical debates, ones that they were intellectually prepared for, if they still inhabited the political wilderness? In the midst of the crisis over the Stamp Act, Charles wrote George a note of solidarity and of lament. "How entirely our sentiments have agreed upon the subject of the late political negotiations," he remarked. But they could not find their way amid the turmoil of the times. They had walked through "many dark passages . . . in the last mysterious months." Charles did not seem sanguine about the prospects of finding their way through the difficulties they faced. "In what Distress is this King," he observed," and "in what Condition are these Kingdoms in such a dilemma in the History of any time?" He claimed to "seek no power." He believed he and George were just the men for the times. "Surely," he asked rhetorically, "things hasten in this embarrassed country to some sudden revolution." As far as he was concerned, "all the world was in motion." The brothers struggled to find a center while those about them shifted. Nonetheless, even though in 1766 Charles told George, "Every thing seems to be at sea," he assured him that they would stay united. "I wish to remain as I am," he suggested, "and see you situated as you like."[72]

The Reformers' Library

The explanation for the sense of confidence the brothers had in their ideas, as well as the stances they took over the Stamp Act crisis, can be traced not only to their political exile, when they were "attached to nobody, and trusted by nobody," but also to what they were reading.[73] Once we enter their libraries and untangle their intellectual associations, it becomes apparent that they were developing what they believed to be a distinctive understanding of the tensions that were coming to define the period. They did not hold to such a conceit because they embraced uncommon ideas. In many ways, they were ordering their world and coming to terms with the crisis with unremarkable ideas about empire, liberty, and progress, the same ideas all of their Whiggish-minded colleagues and rivals subscribed to. The ways they assembled the ideas and, more critically, the urgency to apply them stemmed, in their minds, from the contingencies that had led them into the wilderness and placed them outside the mainstream.

Reconstructing the mental universe of two men who lived centuries ago is a tricky business. How does one get inside their heads? Fortunately, the Townshends left a trail we can follow. The brothers were fortunate enough to have been raised in a house with many books. At Raynham, the library, just off the main entrance hall as one entered, was organized meticulously according to section and shelf. And by anyone's estimation it contained a treasure trove. When George and Charles's father died, an inventory was taken of what the library at Raynham contained. The same would happen much later when George died and was buried at Raynham. We also have lists of some of the family's books kept in other places.

It is clear the brothers read the books. Charles discussed, as he phrased it, "how much benefit I have found from translations" of great classical texts.

"[I have prepared] short speeches upon such incidents in history as have struck me and seemed analogous to events likely to occur in our own kingdom." He went on to list how one should read Cicero, Tacitus, and Demosthenes. He also lauded English writers he favored, including John Locke, James Harrington, and John Milton. George could quote from such texts and had a solid grounding in history in particular.[74]

The books contained in the library at Raynham would have been the kind found in any great house owned by members of the Whig establishment. The collection focused on history, both recent and classical. The Townshends owned many volumes of writings from the classical age. They also had, again befitting their station, a great many books that explored politics, political theory, various aspects of religion, and economics. Breaking down the collection this way, however, does not do justice to the sum total of what it contained and what this library was designed to do. It was meant to create informed and knowledgeable leaders. The classics and history did not merely edify. They offered keys to the present and blueprints to the future.[75]

At its most basic, the library at Raynham held the standard and fundamental texts of the Whig Enlightenment, that is, books on political theory and history that had been written during the tumultuous seventeenth century in England and that would contain the ideas that sustained the post–Glorious Revolution British state. Notions, for instance, of individual rights, the critical role of Parliament in protecting liberties, and the idea of the consent of the governed found their clearest expression in such texts. Whether fully realized or not, the ideas undergirded the Whig oligarchy of the period and demonstrated the bona fides of rulers by tying them to the values and virtues associated with the Glorious Revolution. The brothers subscribed to these ideas, and the library had all of those books that made them, literally in the case of Raynham Hall, household words. We find on the shelves the works of Locke, Harrington, Algernon Sidney, Thomas Hobbes, and Lord Bolingbroke, who though a Tory took some of these ideas to great heights. The library also contained works of John Trenchard and Thomas Gordon, the Irishman and the Scot who jointly wrote a series of celebrated essays that characterized corruption as antithetical to the legacy of the revolution, later compiled into what would be called *Cato's Letters*.

The Townshends also owned the works of some of the leading non-English political theorists of the day, who had a great influence on British political thinking, such as Samuel Pufendorf, Jean-Jacques Burlamaqui, and

Hugo Grotius. The library abounded as well in what could be called French Enlightenment thinkers, such as Montesquieu, Rousseau, and Voltaire, and, of course, the great Florentine political theorist Niccolò Machiavelli, who more than any of those listed above laid out the nature of the historical struggle between virtue and corruption that so exercised George and Charles.[76]

Beyond standard Whig ideas and associations, the library points to the brothers' engagements in one of the great British Enlightenment projects of the day: reconciling newer ideas emerging from places like Scotland with the older inheritance of classical Rome shared by all Europeans within the distinctive contours of British history. In fact, the brothers, like their contemporaries, interwove these three strands. The strands demand a little unpacking. Fortunately, the contents of the brothers' libraries offer a clue as to how to do so.

One strand is easy enough to understand because it harkened back to the apprenticeships of Charles and George. Most clearly, they had at their disposal templates for rule and political development that went back to the British Isles in the seventeenth century, to the process of integrating the peripheries into the state. This set of ideas grew out of both the more consensual process of the Union with Scotland and the passage of the Declaratory Act for Ireland, as well as George's coercive pattern of state formation. On one hand, integrating the kingdoms on the periphery into the state depended on a belief in the power of "improvement," that through commerce, politeness, and Protestantism backward regions could become civilized. This dynamic defined the ways members of the Church of Ireland and Lowlanders conceived of their relationship to the center.[77] On the other hand, in both Ireland and Scotland peoples deemed beyond the pale were conquered, after which officials sought to reform their manners. Conquest in both instances was made complete by attempts to remake the landscape and the ways of the people, to civilize them.

The shelves contained books on Ireland and Scotland, ranging from mundane histories to celebrated Whiggish volumes, such as William Molyneux's *The Case of Ireland Being Bound by Acts of Parliament, Stated.* Molyneux considered Locke a friend and tutor, and he applied the simple notions that had animated Locke's "Second Treatise of Government" to the Irish cause after the Glorious Revolution. The brothers had all the works of Jonathan Swift, edited by Thomas Sheridan, who in many ways took up Molyneux's Whiggish mantle in the early eighteenth century. George read and could quote from Swift, who famously would level his intelligence and pen at what he regarded as the uneven ways in which British rights were extended to Ireland. He and Charles had read discourses and reports on the Union with Scotland, as well as *Memoirs of the Scots Wars* that had migrated to Raynham from Charles's library in Grosvenor Square. What the library contained ranged from the works of Oliver Goldsmith to James Macpherson's *Ossian* saga. The latter, a fraudulent epic tale of Ireland and Scotland that romanticized the Gaelic pasts of each, was widely read across the British Isles and across Europe.[78] The library at Raynham also included histories and official documents that shaped what was then the present state of affairs, such as reports on land forfeitures in the seventeenth century in each place.

From the experience of state formation in the British Isles had emerged the notion, championed especially by Charles, that even the Irish and the Scots could be and should be partners in the British state. That is, once they were reformed. Not only did an idea of "reform" emerge as a powerful tool to governance; Parliament emerged as the vehicle for reform. In other words, the institution that had become the site of sovereignty for the three kingdoms, and the institution that bound them together became the body ideally suited to governing a complex state, more so than, say, the Crown. Perhaps some had scruples concerning the powers Britain's Parliament applied to the near provinces. The Irish did, but less so the Scots, who were yoked more completely to the center. The Irish had their own parliament in Dublin, but this functioned, the brothers knew, in a less than ideal fashion.[79]

History, they learned, had chosen Parliament to govern. In theory, Parliament stood as the touchstone of virtue, as it had played a role in curbing the potential and real abuses of prerogative. Corruption, in other words, had thrived under outmoded forms of governance; it had also flourished when provinces were incompletely tied to the center and in those places beyond the reach of sovereign power. And given Britain's history—or the fact that Britain was an answer to a problem of establishing efficacious rule throughout the British Isles—only Parliament could serve as the chief vehicle for reform and undo corrupting influences. Such was Whig orthodoxy.

The second set of ideas the brothers relied on to understand the world emerged from a common European belief in the ideals of the classical world, as well as the classical understanding of how history worked.[80] Charles in particular was attracted to the study of Greek and Roman history, devoting his studies at Cambridge to this topic. Yet, George also demonstrated a fine-grained understanding Roman writers and of the Roman past. He could argue that those who exhibited military virtue, like Scipio, deserved more esteem than others.[81]

Roman history served as a template for Britons to understand the present time. At this moment, those in the circles of officialdom, like the Townshends, struggled with a problem that confronted all concerned with imperial rule: maintaining virtue even if the state took on the form of an empire. Writers of the classical canon wrestled with the vexed question of how or if liberty could coexist with imperium. And this issue, for those thinking about global empire, was far from academic. It had great practical implications, especially for a people who up to this point had no well-formed imperial vision.[82]

The books that the brothers had access to on this score ranged from popularizations of great works from antiquity, such as Dryden's translation of Virgil to Plutarch's *Lives* and Melmoth's *Cicero*. They also included works by Petrarch.[83] The 1764 catalogue, or list of books the brothers were raised with, includes an astonishing array of works from the classical period. The library contained, unsurprisingly, plenty of Virgil and six sets of Caesar's *Commentaries*. These must have delighted and enthralled the young George, who could still sketch the battle lines described in them when he was venturing to Quebec. The library contained the work of Juvenal, Livy—in three languages—five sets of Pliny, and nearly as many of Sallust. Horace and Cicero were also given pride of place on the shelves, as the family owned six sets of the latter's work. But it was the works of Tacitus, more than any other, that the Townshends seemed to have a mania for. As well as numerous commentaries and collections of paraphrases on his work, they owned nine multivolume sets of his writings in four languages: Latin, English, French, and Spanish. Tacitus's works laid out most simply and clearly the tensions between a republic and an empire, between liberty and power.

In fact, the simple ideas of writers like Tacitus formed the chief template for understanding how government, society, and the world worked and most clearly paralleled the preoccupations of Whiggish Britons at the time. Eighteenth-century Britons feared that they would become an empire in the classical sense and lose all virtue. They believed that not only were they heirs to Rome but also could succeed where Rome failed. The controversy surrounding Benjamin West's decision to clothe the subjects in his *Death of General Wolfe*—excepting, of course, George—in contemporary not classical garb is a case in point. Sir Joshua Reynolds believed that the classical world offered the best examples of universal virtues and the surest means to elevate taste, especially for a Britain that had inherited the civilizing mantle of the Romans, and that contemporary subjects or settings obscured the ways virtue worked and also confounded taste.[84]

The urge to refer back to the classical world to address present concerns should not surprise us. The categories of republic and empire and the tense relationship between imperium and libertas preoccupied Britons. Like their forebears, but perhaps in a heightened way because of the very real implications of empire after 1763, political culture was suffused with this sensibility, and Rome became the ultimate historical model.[85] It rested on what one scholar calls "cosmopolitan history," in that historians in the British eighteenth century drew from common understandings of the classical world to make an argument for a common European past that was informing the present.[86]

Prominent historians of the eighteenth century argued that the classical transition from republic to empire could be used to address time and historical process, and they advocated fixed notions of unitary sovereignty to guarantee liberty in an empire and to keep corruption at bay. This belief emerges especially powerfully in the work of two most celebrated historians of the day: David Hume and William Robertson. Whatever the fears or the conceits of Britons, sovereignty offered a means to negotiate a transitioning wider world. After all, Britons had done so in the past within the British Isles through a unified understanding of sovereignty.[87]

The third set of ideas emerged in Scotland, as the names Hume and Robertson suggest. These Scots were two of Britain's most celebrated thinkers. By the eighteenth century, it had become a commonplace to explain the differences in the manners of peoples by the stages of development their societies had achieved, a belief rooted in a set of ideas known as stadial theory or conjectural history. The Scots had developed these notions as, to use Edmund Burke's phrase, "they unrolled the great map of mankind." "Stadial" refers to Scottish ideas about the ways in which societies moved from hunter-gathering savagery, through barbarous pastoralism, to more civilized agrarianism and then commercial respectability—stages that also reflected the manners and ways of a people. Hume, Robertson, and Adam Smith all subscribed to these ideas.[88]

The library at Raynham was filled with works by these scholars. In fact, the Townshends owned multiple copies of Hume, who seems to have been a favorite of the family. The same goes for Smith.[89] In 1759, Smith learned that Charles had been presented with a copy of his *Theory of Moral Sentiments,* which elaborated on an idea first made by the Irish-born philosopher Francis Hutcheson that men and women possessed a "moral sense" that inclined them to sociability. George's library had Hutcheson's seminal work. Smith's breakthrough was to link this sensibility to the natural proclivity of people to take joy and solace in the good deeds of others, which then became for Smith the engine that drove cultural and social maturation in societies. Hume's *History of England* pulsed and shifted with the ideas of sociability and cultural stages that animated Smith. The same goes for Robertson. If Hume represented one Townshend favorite, Robertson would be the other.[90]

The upshot is that during the eighteenth century as Britons struggled to understand their place in the world, they also looked back to the classical past and came up with approaches to governing that drew from Britain's long engagement with the archipelago and the globe, and that suggested men could "reform" or reshape history. Eighteenth-century Britons combined what we would call stadial beliefs with an idea that actors could interject themselves into natural, historical processes and reform them, channel them, or even stem them. On the one hand, these beliefs led to an idea that officials could reform the relationship between center and periphery, that they could extinguish the most corrupting aspects of these relationships, and in so doing, could safeguard virtue. On the other hand, this sensibility suggested that one could master history's stages and help shift society from one stage to the next with sovereign power and control.

Through mapping the Scottish ideals onto the other strands, a progressive understanding in history amended an older cyclical notion. Virtue and vice, imperium and libertas remained powerfully evocative categories; however, now they could be laid out on time lines that mandated how society progressed. One could have an empire of politeness and commerce. That is, so long as the guardian of liberty—Parliament—was at its head. At moments of transition the three strands intersected most compellingly, and the experience of state formation within the British Isles merged with a conjectural past and the neoclassical idea of how history hinged on critical moments to convince officials they would and could act. The stadial assumptions that went hand in hand with Britain's history animated this notion of the tension between libertas and imperium and pointed toward Parliament as the institution that could shape history, achieve balance for society and for empire, and safeguard virtue.[91]

The brothers took such ideas seriously because they read them closely. Charles, for instance, left handwritten notes about some of what he read, including bits and pieces of Hume's *History of England*. The book became standard fare for the eighteenth century, detailing how England rose as a power from its origins in the Middle Ages until its apogee after the Glorious Revolution. But what is particularly interesting is Charles's interpretation of Hume's method. In his notes on the *History of England*, Charles fastened on key turning points Hume employed to explain change over time, when virtue was at stake and vice had to be held at bay. When it came to the Norman conquest, for instance, a moment that Hume regarded as fundamentally transforming English politics, Charles saw a period eerily similar to his own. "The Normans," Hume wrote and Charles noted, "indeed were in an Age so Violent and licentious" that they could have been "pronounced in[capable] of any true or regular liberty." As Charles reported, times such as these "require[d] such a refinement of laws and institutions, such a comprehension of views, such a sentiment of honour, such a spirit of obedience, and such a sacrifice of private interests and connexion to public order, as can only be the Result of great reflexion and experience." Charles, no doubt, believed he was writing autobiography, explaining his predicament and his beliefs. Such "reflexion and experience," he argued, ventriloquizing Hume, "must grow to perfection during several ages of a settled and established government." In his notes, he suggested that such periods "cannot be determined by particular studies as by studies of history."[92]

Hume, as much as any other writer in the eighteenth century, combined the three strands in his work, with all the implications about turning points and leadership that so enthralled Charles. In Hume's reading, institutions and law were needed to reform corruption. Sacrifice was also necessary. At watershed moments, events could propel the polity forward along a virtuous path or backward on the path of corruption and vice.

The Townshends did more than read. They patronized history writers. And, more critically, they rubbed shoulders with some of these titans. Ironically, Hume himself thought Charles read his work too closely. He learned that Charles had pored over his work and was "extolling me and decrying me alternately." Hume conceded to Adam Smith in a letter that "Charles

Townshend passes for the cleverest fellow in England." He also pointed out that Charles could be the most critical. "Three years ago when I was in London," Hume remembered, "I was told by a friend, that Mr. Townshend said, that my History of the Stuarts . . . was full of gross blunders in the facts." Charles had gone back to read the journals of the House of Commons. Hume was "surprised and alarmed" at Charles's fastidiousness. Nonetheless, he wrote to a friend in Paris that Charles "passes for a man of worth and honour." He reckoned "his wit" would succeed in Paris.[93]

So perfectly did the brothers' thinking map onto Hume's that some could mistake Hume for George and Charles. In 1761, a friend from Scotland wrote to Charles about the progress Hume was making on his latest work. Hume had, he reported, finished about a fourth of his "history from the conquest." He told Charles how Hume was making use of stadial theory and was writing of a time when "manners [were] so extremely different from those we can see in more polished ages." It would in his estimation "be a most valuable archive for the history of the humane mind." Hume had written the work, but, as the writer put it, "other people give it to you and your brother for no other reason but because they know none other clever enough to write it."[94]

Adam Smith and Charles enjoyed an even more cordial relationship. Charles referred to him once as "my friend Smith." Smith served as tutor to Charles's stepson, the Duke of Buccleuch. Indeed, as his stepson's guardian, Charles hoped Smith's tutelage would, he wrote, "mould these excellent materials into a settled character, [and] I make no doubt but he will return to his family and country the very man our fondest hopes have fancied him." So close was the association that Smith could, as a friend, call Charles to account for not writing as often as he should. For instance, when Buccleuch was recovering from a fever, Smith the tutor upbraided Charles: "We are all astonished that we have not heard from you. Whatever be the reason of it?"[95]

Charles even counseled Smith on what reading to assign his stepson. He wanted him to understand the rudiments of political economy, in particular how the French seventeenth-century experience compared to that of the British eighteenth century. Charles instructed his stepson to pay special attention to Hume's *History of England*, in particular the tempestuous seventeenth century. In essence, he saw the present moment in similar ways. Such reading had to remind young Buccleuch that the age was "idle, ignorant, extravagant, and vain" and that he had to remember that, Charles wrote, "your own country is, and will be for some time, in distress, confusion and danger." A Scot like Smith, Charles believed, could train his stepson for a career in public affairs through a judicious study of the past and of the current state of the world.[96]

Charles similarly enjoyed a close relationship with Robertson, who was a professor at Edinburgh and Scotland's historiographer royal. From the correspondence, it is clear that Charles had read his work, including the influential study of Charles V. He was also apprised of Robertson's progress with the study by an acquaintance in Scotland. Letters illustrate that Robertson knew of George's doings, too.[97]

What these Scots wrote had dramatic implications for how leaders thought of their roles at key turning points in history. Within this sense of a narrative structure laid out by Hume and Robertson, it was clear that some individuals helped propel history from one stage of development to the next. Leaders acted, literally, as paradigm shifters, in that they moved history from state to state, much as societies and manners shifted.[98] Human agency entered the equation as the virtuous or depraved acted, channeling history upward or downward and obviating what Machiavelli called "fortuna." Certain men could master chance, but they could do so in virtuous ways or corrupt ways. The notion that chance could be avoided represented a new way of conceiving history, both in terms of writing it and in terms of applying it to the real world.[99]

Charles saw that such a dynamic happened at key moments. Reading Hume's *History of England*, he pointed to two instances in the seventeenth century when challenges between authority and liberty "called forth, created, and improved the Talents of men beyond any other period in History ancient or modern." Only when this occurred could "liberty of the People" be sustained for Britain as much "as the imperfection of all civil government, the wickedness of man, and the Empire of Chance will ever permit."[100]

Contingency, then, could be overcome at certain moments through virtuous leadership. As Hume argued and as Charles agreed, the Glorious Revolution, which inaugurated a golden age after the faltering moment, represented one such moment. The revolution did not herald a return to some imagined time of liberty, even if it betokened a dramatic change, brought stability, and balanced order with liberty. Nor did it arise inevitably. It need not have happened, save for the work of a few people at key moments. Robertson saw the same. Society stood on an edge between the virtues of Parliament and William III and the vice epitomized by James II and Scotland's past, and the moment proved transformative, ushering in a new period of liberty. As Robertson suggested, the Glorious Revolution heralded a period of politeness that Scotland too was now party to. Union, Robertson reckoned, had made Scotland the nation it had become and allowed it to graduate through history's stages to a moment of refinement. Under the arrangement of 1603, he suggested, stagnation had occurred. Constitutional ambiguity had heightened corruption, particularly of Scotland's elites. Greater forms of virtue, education, refinement, and enlightenment—what we could call "improvement"—stemmed from political union and the ending of constitutional ambiguities. Scotland could escape history and enter the linear path of progression so long as sovereignty was unified in Parliament and so long as leaders acted to make it so.[101]

Together the three strands—stadial theory, classical antiquity, and the history of England on the margins—produced a compelling blueprint for the brothers in the years after the war. Past was prologue. After 1763, as was clear to George and Charles, Britons confronted another critical period akin to the ones Hume and Robertson studied, as the brothers testified to time and time again, one on a global scale that harkened back to the earlier watershed within the British Isles. This, too, represented a period on which history hinged and one that could lead to progress or regress. The window of time during which the virtuous could work with history's ebb and flow would not stay open for long. The history George and Charles read taught as much.[102]

Much of the formative work they read did not set them apart from others. During their lifetimes, the reading of history among the leisured classes surpassed the reading of all other genres. "History," Burke argued, "is a preceptor of prudence." The ruling elite at this time, which included the brothers, held this maxim to be true, and the study of history prepared men to lead. Robertson became the most popular author of the day. His *History of the Reign of the Emperor Charles V* and *History of Scotland* were read more than other comparable works. The same holds true for David Hume.[103] The rivals and patrons of the brothers also knew of these ideas, just as they believed all Britons were standing at a crossroads of history after the war.

Moreover, in struggling with the tensions they did, the Townshends, or the British for that matter, were not exceptional. Other Europeans were engaged in the same exercise in the postwar period. Hapsburg Austria, Prussia, and Russia initiated domestic reforms in these years. The same held true for

Atlantic imperial powers. The Spanish and also the French reacted to the Atlantic crisis by drawing upon Enlightenment principles and their older traditions to reshape the relationships between center and peripheries. Their responses emerged from European-wide discourses leavened by their distinctive histories. For the brothers, engaged in the same task but with a different history, only Parliament could address the moment, the seeming rabbit warren of imperial arrangements, and the problem of bringing stability to the whole after mythic victory. That was the British leaven to the imperial/Atlantic conundrum. The beliefs, then, that the brothers had embraced through readings, varied experiences, and years in the political wilderness represented a British variation on a common European imperial theme.[104]

The lessons of the library were clear. The liberty that defined Britain could be extended to empire under the right circumstances at the proper moment only by the virtuous. Empire was not intrinsically evil but could serve a positive good in that it could order the international system and the regions of the tumultuous Atlantic that were now consolidated. It could act as an agent of reform. Institutions such as Parliament could ensure liberty coexisted with empire, so long as its reach was extended.[105] The virtuous could shape or channel history's processes for the benefit of the whole. Such an idea was not as far-fetched as it seemed. Although pilloried by some as a Jacobite, Lord Bute believed that postwar Britain needed virtuous officials and a government that was not run by a corrupt cadre intent on enriching themselves and their cronies. George, in particular, was attracted to this sensibility, though the brothers believed that reform had to come through Parliament. The virtuous working in and through Parliament had to act. In a letter to Bute, George recognized the moment in which he lived as a "Period when the Power of Faction, Trampling upon all Reverence to Principles and Characters, assails every Rampart of our Constitution." Quoting Sallust, he explained how the time to act was urgent, even though the level of corruption was so daunting.[106]

All who styled themselves reformers found much to subscribe to in the brothers' library. Up to this point, though, as officials struggled to comprehend the shape of the crisis and to formulate ideas to address it, no one had been able to apply the idea that virtue was needed to meet the moment. Certainly not Bute, who could not win a parliamentary majority and championed Crown prerogative as opposed to Parliament as the reform vehicle. And certainly not the brothers, so long as they remained out of office.

Nonetheless, the ideas that so excited Charles and George made for compelling blueprints with which to understand the postwar crisis of empire, as they mapped onto the imperial moment and their own fortunes so perfectly. The brothers, then, were armed to understand and potentially act upon a crisis involving sovereignty that called, in their eyes, for an unambiguous understanding of how it would work. Yet, all would be academic as long as they were out of power.

The Fruits of Defeat

Edmund Burke lamented the refusal by the brothers to lead. Their position "has drawn tears of indignation and grief from me, to see the manner in which they proceed," he confessed to a friend. He believed this owed to George's hope—despite his protestations to the contrary—to become lord lieutenant of Ireland, a position of real influence, and how this goal would fit with Charles's aspirations.[107] Burke had a point. The brothers certainly were driven by their interests. And they could not if they wished disentangle themselves from a political system that functioned as a network of connected elites with its own arcane rituals. They worked in a system defined by the competition for place and by patronage. This reality proved as commonplace as the ideas they espoused.

The brothers, though, did not see themselves in this light. In fact, they construed themselves—largely through failures, exile, and crisis—as something scholars such as Lewis Namier would claim they had no business becoming in eighteenth-century Britain: principled men intent on reform and driven by ideas. Like others as well, George and Charles professed to be animated by virtue and to be concerned with the common good. As one of their allies, Lord Holland, observed, Charles had become a more polished version of George. Holland considered Charles a genius and thought "his heart is often penetrated with the love of virtue." This defined him, as did his habits. "He has," Holland continued, "studied everything, [and] he cannot but perceive the beauty of truth and the primary virtue of a social being is to promote the happiness of the community."[108]

For the brothers, political exile sharpened and refined commonplace understandings of the need to act in certain ways at critical times, giving them a political edge and compelling purchase. Wolfe's revenge, then, had unforeseen implications for the brothers. It amplified a sense of their distinctiveness. Others could tell similar tales and interpret their pasts in similar ways, but few turned the realities of political marginalization into a political philosophy as insistently as the Townshends did. In the world of the unexceptional, a belief in exceptionalism was the norm. This sensibility was heightened for the brothers, and their tale of woe perfectly tied into what they were reading. The great processes that drove history could, they believed, be harnessed only by the virtuous at specific times. What set them apart in their own minds was their shared belief of how the contingencies of their lives had exiled them and made them men for the moment. What they read only confirmed the independent course they were setting to justify their political circumstances.

Prevailing views of the period as a watershed encouraged such thinking. Shifting contexts, varied responses of those sure they had the proper prescriptions, and the flow of events had created a period of time difficult to define but certainly significant and one likely to overwhelm the prevailing way of doing things. Through these dynamics, "Government had become," Charles observed, "what he himself had often been called, a Weather-Cock."[109] A series of missteps and miscalculations had brought him and George together at the same time they found themselves out in the cold. They were, no doubt, rationalizing this period of isolation as they were trying to justify the sort of political gamesmanship they would have to play to move out of it. Withdrawal to a fixed set of ideas, stubbornly held and resolutely defended, addressed both personal and imperial concerns.

The world the brothers and their fellow Britons inherited cried for clarity and resolution, and the crisis of the mid-1760s stemmed from a cacophony of ideas. What had been tried, unsystematic and the result of political jockeying, would not and could not in their eyes address the profound problems and promise of the age. Staying aloof as they had done also positioned George and Charles as ideal candidates to step in and truly reform the system, armed as they now were with the ideas to do so. "I shall [not] change my system, nor in any thing act with any man without your perfect concurrence, satisfaction, approbation, and honour," Charles promised George in 1766. Deferring as always, he averred, "You will never wish me to humiliate this country and erect America into an independent kingdom." Brotherly unity would, according to Charles, enable "the Great work of the ages!" Only men such as them could do such work. "If His Majesty really [sought] an efficient government," he had to construct it "upon the plan of talents and character, without proscription or absolute empire in any man, upon an explained system of constitutional measures, with an equal regard to all men and family worth, and fame and service."[110]

In this letter to his brother, in which he discussed his vision for the times, Charles was testing George to see if he would deign to serve in government should Pitt form a ministry: "Mr. Pitt alone was the minister who could put His Majesty's affairs into an easy and solid state." In the letter, however, Charles also reasserted the virtues of independence and how it would inform their roles if and when they took the stage. "I speak in the dark," he conceded, "but no man speaks in the dark, who has light within himself." The time was coming. "I know you are free and independent. I am as much as you," he started. "I shall consult you; I shall respect your opinion; I shall place my happiness in affairs with you," he promised. He ended the long letter with a sentiment that summed up their hard experience and their attempt to find virtue in this world of exile. "God forbid," he wrote, "that, in the sad critical minute, we should either of us have any personal engagement or former connections to direct us." They had stayed free of obligation, so that when and if the moment came they could lead. "I will do nothing," he ended, "without your concurrence."[111]

As ministries rose and fell and no stable platform could be constructed, George was astonished by "all the various and most Wonderful Revolutions of late." He "remain'd like other serious Men in a state of Amazement unlikely to Terminate, as has been the case at similar Periods in which those who have more principle than ambition, in a State of Indifference." The government was still "bedeviled." After a series of letters in the midst of the crisis, Charles summed it up to George this way: "Thus you have a long gazette upon which you may depend. Take the map, consider well and when we meet we shall be the better prepar'd to judge, agree and act upon a plan which may be honourable and manly."[112]

By this time, however, signs were suggesting that at least one of their concerns was being addressed. In a letter to George, Grenville wrote that some of the things he imagined that people held against him were mere phantoms. When, for instance, George worried that the Duke of Bedford, another political kingmaker of Newcastle's stature, would thwart any attempt by George to gain office, Grenville suggested otherwise. "The Report which you have heard of his zeal against you," Grenville assured him, "is entirely without Foundation." Perhaps it was time for George to end the self-imposed rustication at Raynham. About this time, Charles sensed a different spirit in London. The Wolfe affair, in his mind, was drifting into the past as those at the center struggled with the implications of victory. He counseled George that perhaps the time had come for him to take up permanent residence again in London. "I wish you would pass thro' London," Charles chided his brother, "for I believe the difference of your seeming behaviour *now* . . . may also erase an impression never to be erased."[113]

In 1766, George began to see possibilities as well for resurrecting his career hopes. He still spoke to Pitt of his "too convincing proofs of the aversion of a particular party to this national establishment"; yet, he was suggesting to Pitt that the passage of such measures as a Militia Act gave him hope. This demonstrated that a government might "henceforth derive great stability, if it be blest with ministers who shall be wise and honest enough to prefer public and generous principles to party affections and the little jealousies for a court." Pitt was such a man, and maybe with him George could leave the wilderness. "I am now a full 40 years," he wrote to Charles, and had been successful in running affairs in Norfolk. "I have served amongst Men in Camps, and even a Campaign or two under the Great Mr. Pitt." Perhaps he could once again aspire to "some great office Military or Civil; and depend a little upon the Encouragement of a Dozen or more friends." He could not do so alone, even as he left his period of exile: "My Dear Charles, I may have had perhaps a third of your friends and a third of your experience of them."[114] He needed his brother. More important, perhaps he had outlived Wolfe after all.

ACT 3

Charles Townshend's America

The Townshends' Moment

The Townshends' moment came in 1767. It came not by design but through a turn of events. The first contingency involved Pitt. After the almost inevitable collapse of the Rockingham administration, all looked for some sort of stability. As one wit put it, the Rockinghams "were dead, and only lying in state; and Charles Townshend (who never spoke for them) was one of the mutes." Rockingham had tried to get Pitt to join his administration to shore it up, but to no avail. Although it initially appeared that Grenville in combination with another would take over the reins, the problems that had plagued him less than a year earlier meant that this plan was effectively off the table. George III would not countenance another Grenville administration, so deep was his dislike of the man.[1]

While he was loath to do so—for he had a strong distaste for Pitt as well—the king, upon advice from the leading players, asked Pitt to form a new government. It seemed the only plan that could work. For his efforts during the Seven Years' War and as an inducement to construct a lasting new ministry, Pitt was elevated to the peerage in mid-1766 as the Earl of Chatham. He could no longer be considered the "great commoner."[2]

He seemed at the time an inspired choice. No doubt, some still believed that Chatham had created the imperial crisis. His critics understood that the war had saddled Britain with a huge debt that had now necessitated reform. Yet despite the questions and uncertainty, many more adored the idea of Chatham at the helm. He had devised the bold strategy that had won the war. Whether loved or loathed, he seemed the only possible leader to form a government that could manage its way through a crisis that demanded some sort of stability, come up with an agenda for empire, and right the ship of state.

George and Charles participated in the intrigues that went into creating a workable political "system." Now it was becoming clear that the one person they had pinned their hopes on was about to assume leadership once more. "When I heard on Friday last," Charles exclaimed, "from an indifferent correspondent that Mr. Pitt had actually been sent for by His Majesty, I treated the rumour lightly." When the report turned out to be authentic, "my unbelief changed into astonishment." Charles now believed that "the result of this condescension on the part of the Crown may be productive of a permanent settlement." He had "grown impatient to see an administration formed in which the People will place Their confidence, men of superior talents and fair characters shall take their proper rank, and the Friends of the Crown have justice." His and George's rationale was simple and could be intuited even a year earlier: "Events every hour hasten that issue, in which Mr. Pitt's superior talents, his unrivalled weight with the nation, and his reputation in Europe, must give him the decision of every point in the reestablishment of this distracted and unhappy country."[3]

What the brothers had hoped for had come to pass. George had honed and shaped his abilities and worldview through periods of difficulty and exile, as well as by navigating an independent course in a tempestuous context. And no one could ignore Charles's abilities, least of all Chatham. On the advice of Augustus Henry FitzRoy, the Duke of Grafton, Chatham approached him. "Sir," he wrote to Charles in July 1766, "you are too great a magnitude not to be in a responsible place." If Chatham were to form a government, he would, he told Charles, "intend to propose you to the King to-morrow for Chancellor of the Exchequer." The first thing Chatham did was dispatch a messenger to Charles's brother to persuade him to accept. Charles, unsurprisingly, told Chatham he could not decide "without any communication with Lord Townshend and others with whom I act in friendship." George thought the time had come, and Charles formally accepted on July 26, 1766. "I relinquish my own natural inclination and evident interest," he wrote at the time, "to sacrifice, with chearfulness and from principle, all that men usually pursue."[4]

By 1767, when he began his work in earnest under Chatham, Charles would direct the finances and administration of empire and be charged with implementing a vision of political economy. He was joining, he argued, "a Ministry so popular, so able, and so sure of success" that division or opposition would be unconscionable. "It is," he summed it up, "mean to think of private situations when so general an interest is at stake." Lord Holland told Charles he would, in fact, be responsible for more. The move, he said, effectively "puts you at the Head of the House of Commons, and an Administration." Moreover, it appeared that this government would become "both creditable and lasting." Charles would, soon after agreeing to the appointment, join the cabinet as well. This and securing a peerage for his wife were two more self-serving aims he was after at this juncture.[5]

With time and through Charles's insistence, George would become lord lieutenant of Ireland, an executive post designed to ensure that the recalcitrant kingdom, essential to British might, contributed to the state and to the empire. However tarnished his image had been, George had emerged from the wilderness with bargaining power. He had said no to offers before and had made it clear the brothers would not be divided and would enter any arrangement together. Early on in 1767, George was asking the king for his portion of any settlement, and he signaled "himself much indebted to the King's favor for a promise of one of the first Governments of the highest class." Ireland would fit.[6] Ironically, what only a year before Charles had dismissed as a possibility—he for the Exchequer and George for Ireland—had come to pass.

With hindsight, some would see the ministry for what it was. Punning with the term "cabinet," Burke would later characterize it as "an administration so checkered and speckled . . . so grossly indented and whimsically dovetailed" that it would prove "a piece of diversified Mosaic."[7] But at this moment, it seemed to the brothers that stability had come at last. Although this ministry would ultimately stand on the same uncertain and fickle foundations as the last few, to the brothers the prospect of a Chatham ministry in 1767 promised to mark a new departure. The moment seemed propitious, certainly as promising as any they were likely to see in their lifetimes.

Chatham realized that his mandate was to reform: to achieve solvency and to address manpower problems in the largest empire the world had seen. To help him, the Townshends seemed inspired choices. Given their apprenticeships and their different experiences of empire, the posts of Ireland and the Exchequer suited their sensibilities and abilities perfectly. They were playing roles that in their minds they had prepared for their entire adult lives. As Chancellor of the Exchequer, Charles would oversee not only the Treasury but also all affairs relating to trade. With his expertise, all would bow to him when it came to American affairs. In a kingdom facing grave budgetary constraints, none could be better prepared than Charles. The same holds true for George. He had led armies and had championed the cause of manpower in the service of empire. He was now to manage a kingdom that had a large reserve of underutilized men.

And here we come again to the turn of events that placed Charles on the stage. For there would have been no Townshend moment without it, and the brothers would appear little more than footnotes to a less than interesting story of reform in the 1760s. The next twist of fate involved Chatham himself, of rather it involved his absence. First, as he was trying to form his government, his health was failing. He was visiting a physician at Hampstead, where he remained "indisposed," one of Charles's friends wrote, "and was blooded to prevent as ('tis rumoured) the danger of a fistula." Bouts of gout, headaches, and maladies we could associate with depression and anxiety, perhaps even bipolar disorder, had troubled Chatham during the war. They returned with a vengeance in early 1767. Second, ennobled and sitting in the Lords, Chatham could not preside in the Commons. He had to rely on others to pursue his agenda. Now he was forming a ministry during a crisis that some likened to the period of the Glorious Revolution, though he could not participate in any meaningful debates, only direct others from afar. For a man prone to anxiety in such a high-stakes moment, it is a wonder he could function at all.[8]

In fact, he barely did so. He spent much of early 1767 at his country estate suffering from various ailments, physical and emotional. "The Earl of Chatham is still at Bath," Grenville complained in January 1767, "and consequently the King's Administration has got the Gout and hobbles terribly." The result was that Chatham was often "absent and still in the Clouds" and that "Mr. Ch. Townshend indeed seems to wish to move a little more nimbly and to try to walk a little without crutches." Ministers came and went, as Chatham tried to dictate government business and to manage the Commons from afar. At other times, he was too ill to do much of anything. While he was indisposed, government had no "Appearance of Stability, Firmness and Unanimity," as Grenville argued.[9]

In Chatham's absence, Charles Townshend took control. Questions still cloud his ascent. One historian suggests that Chatham more or less knowingly allowed Charles to fix his own course. Chatham, or so the thinking goes, supported some sort of tax measures for the colonies, but as the darling of the patriotic colonists, he was more than happy to cede the floor to Charles and see him take responsibility for the inevitable difficulties that would arise. Chatham was, this historian argues, "a strange man," who, though he was "continually adverse to principles such as American taxation when out of power, he implicitly adopted them when in place." Whether Charles took over to shield Chatham or because he was ailing, it was clear a great deal of latitude was given to the person with the most well-developed plan for imperial reform. As one commentator noted, "Charles Townshend has now the sole management of the House of Commons; but how long he will be content to be only Lord Chatham's viceregent there, is a question which I will not pretend to decide." Ultimately, he gave himself "more ministerial airs than Lord Chatham will, I believe, approve of." Whatever Chatham's motives, and the label of "strange" seems to fit in this regard, he was not completely comfortable with the arrangement. Charles declared him "incurably jealous of me." But there was little the ill prime minster could do.[10] Charles, as the most able thinker and rhetorician, with all of his skill and experience, and now holding a position of highest rank in the cabinet, seized the moment, effectively gaining control of the ministry, and for a brief window of time made the House of Commons, and Britain, his.

Pretense for the Colonies

Some Americans welcomed Charles's appointment. A group of New York merchants sent him a note of congratulations, signed by more than forty of their number. In the note, they praised what they called the "independent and disinterested part" he had played in the repeal of the Stamp Act. They also lauded, as they put it, the "great Character you sustain in political and Commercial knowledge." The New Yorkers hoped that Charles's time in office would "bring on a reconsideration of the Commerce of this Country, and fixing it on a basis the most advantageous to Great Brittain and her Colonies." The "foundation" that they hoped Charles would support was attached in a petition that they had signed. Complaints, predictably, came disguised as congratulations. In particular, the merchants opposed a free port strategy that Rockingham had championed and Charles was favoring, one in which some ports in the West Indies would be able to import and export certain goods from European countries duty free. The petitioners worried they would not benefit from such a scheme. They also laid out the disadvantages that they suffered under because of trade restrictions. They asked for protection from foreign competition but wanted to revisit some of the tenets of the Navigation Acts. Like all others, they were certain their ideas of reform would benefit the whole.[11]

Writing the petition turned out to be a pointless exercise. For by the time it had arrived, Charles had already devised a plan that he hoped to implement, a plan that differed fundamentally from the more flexible approach that the government's leader, Chatham, seemed to subscribe to. Chatham objected, as Charles understood it, "to the *universality* of the last words" of the Declaratory Act of 1766. He "went out of his way to show that the subject is not in *all cases whatsoever* bound by Acts of Parliament." Charles also took issue with the Declaratory Act, albeit for different reasons. He wanted Parliament to be able to pass measures for all "matters," not only "cases," and he wanted it known that it could be done "*in common with the subjects of Great Britain.*" Sovereignty had to be unified, and Parliament had to have sweeping powers. Charles's plan emanated from this simple idea.[12]

By the time the New York petition arrived, Charles had assembled a working group, led by an able American aide named John Huske, to devise a plan of taxation for the colonies upon which he would mount his system. Part of the planning involved understanding how any measures would affect the whole as well as the constituent parts. Efficiency would, Charles hoped, overcome corrupt practices such as smuggling, which, like political vices, stemmed from the want of system. He then could determine the particulars of his plan, figuring out, for instance, exactly how much could be expected to be collected through duties on select items. He learned all this through studies he commissioned. In one of these, he figured £43,420 could be raised through modest duties on a range of goods produced outside the colonies.[13]

Charles, therefore, did intensive work leading up to the plan's implementation. This was not an affair, to quote a critic, of "rash and undigested measures," prompted by the insecurities and the "inconsiderate vanity of Charles Townshend." As Charles put it in April, he "had given [his plan] a fixed attention for many months." He read newspaper reports from various places in America, detailing their responses to the Stamp Act. He went back to older precedents in colonial rule, including the charter for Massachusetts Bay that was put in place just after the Glorious Revolution. He asked an American acquaintance "to keep up a constant and steady correspondence with him while in America, that he may be furnished with materials and all necessary measures to be taken for us."[14]

Charles studied how salaries of officials such as governors and judges were paid. A report he asked done noted how the governor of Massachusetts Bay was paid £1,300 "New England Money" or £1,000 sterling by a yearly "Act of Assembly." Charles explored military and naval costs in America, Indian affairs, questions of customs, the nature of colonial opposition to the Stamp Act and other measures, such as the Mutiny Act. He also commissioned careful studies of excise collected on various goods, ranging from chocolate and candles to malt and hops, during the war years, as well detailed analyses of the national debt, annuities charged, the salaries of customs officials at work in the colonies, and all revenue paid to the Exchequer through customs. His vision was comprehensive.[15]

Charles had invested time interviewing men in Britain who had a stake in the whole system. One such man was Henry Hulton, an official who had worked in Antigua to stop smuggling and to collect duties. Charles summoned him to discuss "what goods it might be proper [upon which] to lay a duty" for America. A savvy clerk with much experience, Hulton advised him with these words: "Sir, before you lay any fresh duties in America, it might be best to see those well collected that are already laid." As he saw it, "The authority of Government should be well established, before it is proposed to raise a Revenue from any people." On this, he and Charles agreed.[16]

Charles and the Board of Trade also questioned Brook Watson, a trader who had invested in tea. Watson had come from modest beginnings. He was orphaned, went to sea on a merchantman at an early age, and lost a leg to a shark attack in Cuba at the time of the war. In a short time, he had become a respected trader, a person tied to some of the principal trading families in places like Boston and the West Indies. In fact, he eventually became the subject of one of the best-known paintings of the day, *Watson and the Shark*, by the American painter John Singleton Copley. Charles's committee questioned him on trade between North America and the islands in the Caribbean. They also queried "sundry merchants" who specialized in molasses and rum.[17]

Charles relied on all available expertise to draw up the particulars, even employing his friend Adam Smith to help him devise strategy. In 1766, as soon as Charles was named chancellor, Smith became a frequent visitor to the Exchequer's office on Downing Street, poring over financial records and the history of what was called the "Sinking Fund." The fund had been created earlier in the century to help the state deal with the debts that were growing through international warfare with France. It offered, in theory, the flexibility to allow the state to incur debt, service it, and perhaps even pay it off, so long as ministries did not raid surplus funds as crises arose. Charles thought the fund could be shored up from a number of sources, including duties on goods imported or shipped to America, and he commissioned a number of studies on its use and history. Smith helped Charles determine if such a scheme could work.[18]

Charles would not make the mistakes Grenville had made with the Stamp Act duties. Charles thought that the act, though right-minded, had mistakenly imposed taxes without enforcement mechanisms. He would, ironically, use duties to achieve enforcement measures. For him, ends mattered, and while others had conflated means with ends, he would not do so. The innovation Charles introduced is what these duties would go to pay for: a British American establishment. The Stamp Act had been designed to pay for stationing troops on American soil and to help service the debt that had been incurred by the war with France. The act was, therefore, a revenue duty, something created to generate money. The duties that Charles envisioned would indeed raise money, but revenue from the acts would pay for Crown officials in the colonies. In essence, while the money they raised was almost incidental, it was nonetheless critical to the plan in that it served as a primum mobile for the system, ensuring that those charged with collection would have the ability to collect.

Charles suggested as much through what could only be called a pretense for proposing the measures. During the Stamp Act crisis, Parliament had famously summoned that best known of all Americans, Benjamin Franklin, who also served as an agent for a number of colonies in London, to discuss the American response to Grenville's measures. Charles asked Franklin a number of questions. He wanted to know the American view of Parliament's role, if Americans thought the late war had been fought to safeguard America, if strengthening the frontiers was in America's interests, and what sorts of taxes in their eyes Parliament could pass. Franklin did not appear pressured when Charles raised these points, and Charles did not follow up with more probing questions.[19]

When asked about American views on taxation, Franklin argued that Americans distinguished between "internal" and "external" taxation. Charles, in fact, questioned Franklin on this very issue.[20] By internal, Franklin meant those goods that were produced and consumed in the colonies. These, he contended, could be subject to taxation, but only if levied by local assemblies. The rationale revolved around justice, rights, and common sense. Colonists consented to those who would represent them. These representatives were the only ones who should be able to tax goods that circulated within the colonies. He went on to explain that colonists would not quibble with the taxation of those goods that were produced in Britain or the broader empire, or the "external," in other words. For generations Americans had, after all, more or less stayed quiet when Britain regulated imperial trade. In such instances, certainly since the passage of the Navigation Acts, Parliament had a critical and accepted role to play. Americans did not directly consent to those who sat in Parliament, but Franklin understood that Parliament oversaw not only British affairs but also imperial affairs when it came to trade. Parliament could regulate.

In parliamentary debates after Franklin's visit to the Commons, a number of others, including Chatham himself, had fastened on this distinction between the two; Charles did not do so. He considered any supposed difference an absurdity. In what was regarded as a speech "superior to almost any I ever heard," as one witness observed, Charles "spoke of the distinction between internal and external taxes as not founded on reason." Grenville expanded a bit on what Charles really thought of the distinction. Charles, according to Grenville, called it "absurd, nonsensical and ridiculous to the highest degree."[21] In making such sentiments known, Charles was asserting he would be led not by a prime minister but by his vision. Parliament, Charles believed, could do as it wished, as it had become over the course of the seventeenth century the chief guarantor of liberty for the British Isles and, he believed, for the Atlantic empire as well.

Yet, Charles took note of what Franklin provided and what others saw as a meaningful distinction. Indeed, he would eventually use it as a Trojan horse of sorts. As he put it, distinguishing between internal and external could still be "proper to be adopted in policy," even if it contradicted a fundamental tenet of sovereignty that he held fast to.[22] He stood behind the distinction, and in these early days did so publicly, so long as it enabled him to construct duties that would sustain a new establishment. In so doing, he would, or so he hoped, disarm provincials. As far as he was concerned, he was using provincial logic, however flawed in his estimation, to create something that would benefit the whole.

This modest pretense points to a remarkable aspect of Charles's behavior in 1767. No one doubted that Charles had the intelligence and the experience or even the vision to develop a systematic approach to empire. He never before, however, displayed the political acumen to pull off such a feat. Now he did. He displayed in these days "undoubted abilities." He was, even critics noted, "superior to rivals" in a number of ways. He made extraordinary speeches. He pandered and cajoled. He connived. He may even have feigned an accident and a "fit" to avoid certain debates or postpone proceedings until he had properly prepared the ground. No doubt, he was struggling with illness throughout the early part of 1767; nonetheless, he made what use he could of indisposition to ensure debates took place at fortuitous times. He demonstrated a keen ability to stage the unveiling of his system, moving step by step, preferring the practical to the theoretical as he did so. By such an approach, he was able to win over even his sternest critics to the broader principles he would invoke when he unveiled his system. He was, by anyone's estimation, magnificent. "I never felt myself so little as the moment he opened his mouth," Horace Walpole remembered. "Many men greatly exceeding me in talents," he wrote, "ought to have shrunk, too, into themselves, and felt their own futility when Charles Townshend was present."[23]

The second pretense, or better, pretext, involved New York. Charles had already made New York an example when his office responded to the petition from the New York merchants who were asking for the sort of reform that would benefit them. The response addressed and then demolished each point the petition raised. The rebuke also found the petition "a little strange" in that it asked for redress to novelties and at the same time took issue with the ways things had been done before. Moreover, the New Yorkers sought relief for any trade restrictions when they and other Americans had given "strong assurances" that they would be happy to comply in order to have the hated Stamp Act, with its focus on internal taxation, repealed. This was only one contradiction that Charles's office was happy to point out.[24]

But Charles went much further. He fastened on the intransigence of New Yorkers as an opportunity to lay the cornerstone of the system. Astutely, he reimagined the refusal of some to abide by the stipulations of what was called the Quartering Act as a strategic opening. Part of a measure called the Mutiny Act, the regulation on quartering mandated that locals pick up the cost of housing troops stationed in New York. Ostensibly, the troops remained there to protect British interests and provide security for provincials.

New Yorkers argued that they had not consented to the laws in question, and accordingly—echoing responses to the Stamp Act—they were not obligated to pay for the quartering of troops on their own soil. Only their assembly could pass such a law.[25] New Yorkers, then, were refusing on a point of principle, and in so doing, they gave Charles the opening he needed.[26]

In late April, as he began his move against New York, Charles framed his discussion by letting the House know that "he had formed his opinion for asserting the superiority of the Crown and endeavouring to lay a foundation for such a taxation as might in time save this country of a considerable part of the burthen for the colonies and he *trusted* government would agree." At this point, few could object to such a sentiment. A short time later, he began the discussion in earnest by declaring his subject "a matter of the utmost difficulty and importance." He pointed out problems with Massachusetts, with Rhode Island, with New Jersey, and with New York. He did not wish to consider all the colonies that had caused concern in London. He wanted to focus on New York, where the transgressions in question "seemed to him most particularly to desire the present attention and interposition of Parliament"; it was the colony that had proven "the most disobedient." He then hit on a theme he and George had dwelled on for quite some time. In America, in his mind, there were "in several of the Assemblies a set of factious men closely cemented together upon a fixed plan from motives of self interest to establish their popularity in their own country." The corrupt hoped to corrupt others, including the whole, as their plans were premised "upon the ruin of dependency of the colonies upon Great Britain."[27]

Charles did not want to consider principle. He wanted to discuss practical considerations. Nor did he wish to inflame "Mr. Otis" or even dignify the arguments of the rights he was claiming. Charles only hoped to propose resolutions dealing with New York. In so doing, he provided even those people likely to find fault with his system, particularly the Rockingham Whigs, with little room to maneuver. New York, in Charles's mind, stood accused of contesting the measure that had passed on Rockingham's watch: the Declaratory Act. He framed his condemnation around this simple point. And the time had come to act. The quarrel "must soon come to an issue," he told the House. "The superiority of the mother country can at no time be better exerted than now."[28]

And so, with New York in his sights, the House could see to the problem of sustaining Parliament's—not the Crown's—rights in America. "New

York," he was reported to have said, "had boldly and insolently bid defiance to its authority and threatened the whole legislative power of this country, obstinately, wickedly, and almost traitorously in an absolute denial of its authority." Using Barré's term to good effect, he charged that "those Sons of Liberty had acted quite the reverse from their bold and free ancestors." In his mind, "they went from the tyranny of prerogative," rogue kings of the past, in other words, "to hope for the protection of Parliament." Now "these men with violence" sought to escape the sovereignty of Parliament "for shelter under prerogative." They were staking out positions, Charles alleged, like some of the great historic losers in the war against Britishness and Parliament: the Royalists of the seventeenth century and the Jacobites of the eighteenth. With New York, he made the issue of reform both urgent and uncontestable. He had also laid the groundwork for the principles of his system. And the plan would be his. He would initiate it without the support of anyone in the cabinet, most members of which, especially Chatham, considered themselves to be friends of America.[29]

A Plan for America

When he accepted the post at the Exchequer, Charles declared to Chatham, "I shall be happy . . . if I shall be acknowledged by posterity to have in any degree contributed, under your protection, to facilitate the re-establishment of general confidence, real government and a permanent system of meas-ures." He meant what he said. His initiative was about system, not revenue. "He opened the whole state of America in a masterly manner," one observer noted. Charles argued that New York signaled something amiss that had to be corrected. Though he desired, as he put it, "to take some steps which by showing the Americans that this country would not tamely suffer her sover-eignty to be wrested out of her hands," and "to strike an awe into the factious and turbulent," he pushed for resolutions that would target New York's government.[30]

The first part of his plan was simple enough. On 13 May, the Commit-tee of the Whole in Parliament considered whether it should not allow New Yorkers to pass any law until they complied with the Mutiny Act and, more broadly, the Declaratory Act. Under the New York Restraining Act, the colony's assembly would not be permitted to meet until New Yorkers acqui-esced. At this juncture, as Charles argued, the House should distinguish between those colonies that resisted and those that did not. He did not make a case for general policy, at this stage at least. Nonetheless, Burke worried: "A standing army, Quarters enforced, Legislature suspended, Taxes laid on, Tests imposed." He feared Charles had much more in mind. Despite Burke's qualms, the Restraining Act passed by a comfortable margin after eight hours of debate and discussion, 188 to 98. A proposition passed unanimously claiming that New York had been disobedient.[31]

Although he did not claim to consider all Americans guilty by association with New York, Charles was doing just that. For he juxtaposed the malefactors in New York with suggestions about the want of system. This again demonstrated strategic acumen. When on 13 May he set New York in his sights, he did not formally reveal his plan or his duties, but he did lay out the rationale for them. The problem with New York, and needless to say the rest of America, was, he said, the fact "that the judges and magistrates . . . are now in many colonies dependent every year for their salary or at least a part of it on the Assembly." They ought "to be made independent." He also argued "that a custom house should be established in North America." In this long speech, as one observer argued, Charles "threw out hints" of what he would propose. He suggested that he planned on laying taxes on America, but "that he meant not however to propose these taxes this day." They would, he intimated, not be "internal, because though he did not acknowledge the distinction it was accepted by many Americans and that was sufficient." He reckoned that the duties he would propose would take in £30,000 to £40,000 per year.[32]

To raise the funds to defray the costs of properly construed royal government in America, Charles first floated the idea of offering Americans certain measures of relief from the Navigation Acts, asking that they pay duties on certain goods instead. By law, Americans were not supposed to import goods from places like Spain, Portugal, and France unless they were first shipped to Britain and then reexported to the colonies. Charles first hoped to introduce a bill in Parliament that would allow colonists to import these goods directly, after which a Customs Board in the colonies would collect a duty on what was shipped. As a start, Charles worked on refiguring these duties on wines, oil, and fruit leaving Spain and Portugal. The revenues would stream into the Treasury. The tariff on such goods exported from Britain's chief competitor, traditional rival, and sometime enemy France would be doubled. On the face of it, such a measure—even if it amended the

Navigation Acts—did not amount to anything revolutionary; it merely tinkered with an arrangement, uncontroversial at that, that Grenville had devised in 1763.[33]

Using the "external" tax contrivance, a tactic he presumed would introduce his system "without offence," Charles then sought to put other goods under the umbrella of the duties. These were goods that were exclusively shipped from other imperial posts to the metropole or produced in Britain. Moreover, they were what could be regarded as what one historian calls "articles of little consequence." They included china, all of which was made in Britain, white and red lead paint for ships, certain cuts of paper, and glass. Charles also considered adding tea and salt to the list. Through duties, the Crown could "establish salaries that might be better suited to support the dignity of the respective Officers, and for which to be no longer dependent upon the pleasure of any Assembly." Because, as one of his aides put it, one could not demand "brick without straw," Charles also considered passing a law to allow the colonists to print paper currency "carrying an interest." His aide had drafted such a proposal with Benjamin Franklin only a year earlier. It could be dusted off, and the interest raised could help defray costs as well.[34]

Some saw eye to eye with Charles and the issue of salaries, a fact that certainly made such an innovation palatable. In one of his prescriptions, Thomas Pownall, a prominent official who had spent a great deal of time in the colonies, would advocate such a measure, so long as Parliament did not ride roughshod over colonial consent. Some thought Charles should have gone further, making a point about principle. Grenville did so by pressing for two considerations. First, he proposed that any revenues raised should pay for American defense. He asked "that the Troops to be kept up in America shou'd be Paid by the Colonies respectively for whose defence & benefit they were Employ'd." Charles voted against the measure, and he carried a majority with him. Second, Grenville believed as well that "Ferment and uncertainty" had created a crisis that demanded "some system of measures." No doubt stung over the failure of the Stamp Act, he argued for the imposition of a Test Act to determine which American officials recognized the supreme authority of Parliament and which did not. On 15 May, at around midnight, he tried to force the Test Act through despite evident opposition. He proposed that all elected and appointed officials, from governors to assemblymen, swear an oath "that the colonies and Plantations of America are, and of Right ought to be, subordinate unto, and dependent upon, the

Imperial Crown and Parliament of Great Britain" and that Parliament could make any and all laws binding the colonies in all instances.[35]

Such measures would have made an issue of principle the centerpiece of what Charles was about to embark on. Charles countered that such a measure would prove counterproductive and "ineffectual." Suppose the colonists resisted, he asked, what would then happen to the dignity of Parliament? Far better, he believed, to press for specific measures that made such a point and that also would be followed up with a more systematic approach to government. And though Charles—and George for that matter—would have subscribed to Grenville's sentiment, pursuing the system mattered more. Indeed, Grenville's proposed Test Act unwittingly provided the cover Charles needed to garner support. Charles "opposed it firmly, and even eagerly." It would bring nothing but disgrace to the House, he argued.[36]

It was a brilliant stroke, befitting someone who had displayed over a few days "superior eloquence and influence." By not arguing from principle, he had won points for his principles. "Though he gave his ideas of a tax," it was reported, "yet his motion respected only the disobedience of New York to the Mutiny Act." And so he followed the discussion condemning New York as a renegade colony with his proposal for duties. Ultimately, by 1 June when he laid out his proposed duties to the Committee of Ways and Means, he abandoned the ideas of a new duty on fruit and of changes to the Navigation Acts. He was running into political opposition. The trade in wines, oranges, lemons, oils, capers, and olives would remain as it had been. He also dropped the idea of taxing salt. As one of his advisers put it, "If ever it does take place it will have the same effect as an Act of Parliament to pluck out the eyes or to tear out the hearts of the people of America."[37]

Charles settled on the exported goods—china and glass, some paper, red and white lead and "painter's colours," and tea. The "act for granting certain duties in the British colonies and plantations in America" listed grade after grade of paper (sixty-seven in total), five different sorts of glass, and red and white lead for making paint. True to the rigor of Charles's apprenticeship and expertise, the act distinguished "avoirdupois of green glass" from "avoirdupois of crown, plate, flint, and white glass." It differentiated "Atlas Ordinary" paper from "Bastard" and "Blue Royal." The government would collect a set amount for a certain quantity of goods—say, two shillings for every hundred weight of an item. Together, Charles reckoned, these duties would fetch the Treasury about £45,000, with about £20,000 coming from tea, including that shipped to America and Ireland. This figure represented the requisite amount to at least secure the independence of officials in America.[38]

On the face of it, or so it seemed, Charles had bowed to American concerns by taxing externally produced goods. The state made good on its right to tax, and Parliament asserted its sovereignty in a tangible way. Doing all this did not set Charles apart from others in government and many of those out of government. The Stamp Act, clearly a revenue measure, had passed by a large majority, so most in Parliament believed they should and could tax Americans. Chatham was looking for ways to raise revenues, and taxes undoubtedly were part of any program he would have pursued. Even some of the Rockinghams were considering what taxes they might have to place on Americans if they should come to power again. Taxing and declaring Parliament supreme, therefore, did not distinguish Charles.[39]

Although he was one of a number of competing grandees trying to reform empire in what all regarded as a critical time, the comprehensiveness of the vision he articulated did distinguish Charles. Burke conceded, as a good Rockingham Whig, that the Declaratory Act should hold sway, as it was a "new declaration" of Parliament's "just and unlimited Superiority." He even conceded that he could support some taxes, or the specifics Charles called for, and on balance he considered the taxes proposed "well chosen." Yet, he opposed the measures because of their implications. They asserted the authority of Parliament; but they ignored the consent of colonial assemblies. Moreover, Burke was troubled by the attempt "to secure the dependency of . . . [the] Colonies by Systematic plans of policy." As he observed, "Whole Nations have continued obedient without any principles of Obedience." He intuited that the plan involved much more than "external goods," such as glass, lead, paint, and tea. And it certainly reached much farther than New York. Burke feared that "the moment a principle has been attempted to be forced on them," a new dynamic would grip the colonies. The inevitable "confusion" would lead them to misconstrue "a single measure" as part of a sequence by "taking it with other measures that go along with it." Burke, therefore, opposed the measure, however much he applauded Parliament's supremacy, exclaiming, "If after all our throes and convulsions this Country [he hoped] should be delivered of a System."[40]

The thrust of Charles's plan could not be mistaken. "In the preamble, the assemblies thought they read their own annihilation," Burke noted, however much the act discussed raising revenue. When they would come into force in November, the duties collected would support "the charge of the administration of justice, and the support of civil government," as the act stated. The excess, if there were any, could go toward what the Stamp Act had been designed to do: "Towards defraying the necessary expences of defending, protecting, and securing, the British colonies and plantations in America."[41]

Charles's virtuosity ensured that the measures passed through the Commons easily, so easily, in fact, that one member of Parliament reported on the day of passage—18 June—that "nothing happened material in the House of Commons today." With fifty members present, the bill sailed through, after its third and final reading. It had met no opposition at its first reading on 10 June, its second on 11 June, and in committee on 15 June. The ease with which the proposed legislation passed did not come as a surprise. "Mr. Townshend," an insider noted, "spoke so ably, and with so much effect, as to leave no doubt but that all who had concurr'd in the resolutions, would adhere to them." Or, as one historian argues, "the mood of the moment swept all doubts aside." On 26 June, the king gave his assent to the measures. George III was both surprised by and delighted with what Charles had accomplished. Although he had not "expected that all the great commercial interests should be completely adjusted and regulated in the course of this session," he saw how "a solid foundation is laid for securing the most considerable and essential benefits to this nation."[42]

The principal means of operationalizing the system would be a Board of Revenue for the colonies. The plan for the board recognized the great distance between the colonies and Britain and between the mainland and the Caribbean. The present structure, as Charles argued, with commissioners in London, rendered collection "dilatory and ineffectual." Because of the challenges of "Distance," officers of the revenue, he noted, "are all deterred from executing their Offices with proper Attention and Vigour." Moreover, "litigious persons" in America used the weakness of the commissioners, as well as the courts in America, to skirt many regulations and to intimidate officials. The loose arrangements needed tightening up if the duties were to be collected. Charles proposed that seven commissioners be appointed, of whom three could constitute a board, to be seated, as it was first envisioned, in Philadelphia. Later, it would convene in Boston, and one of the first men named to it was the clerk who had offered Charles such sage advice:

Henry Hulton. He and the other "Plantation Clerks" would coordinate with the provincial collectors and would be answerable for the duties collected to the inspector general of exports and imports in London. The comptroller general in London would supervise management of the board.[43]

The plan Charles was devising also called for a realignment and streamlining of the customs offices already in the colonies. Three new vice-admiralty courts were created and would be systematically tied into the one already established in Nova Scotia. They would be incorporated "into the new Establishment." The creation of the board would cost £5,540, Charles reckoned. The list of those involved included clerks, surveyors, a comptroller general, solicitors, a receiver general, inspectors, and an inspector general; yet, even this simple step of reorganization would save more than £2,000 per year, cutting expenses by half.[44]

There was no doubting what Charles had accomplished. South Carolina's agent in Britain, Charles Garth, who had sat through the debates over Charles's measures, believed that he had witnessed a key turning point for the empire. He knew in the early sessions when Charles had set his sights on New York that he was up to something more. The colonies, Garth guessed, would henceforth have to demonstrate "that dutiful and becoming respect due to the supreme Authority of the Realm." This meant applying the Declaratory Act, to make it more than pious principle. The only question now was "the Mode of Coercion" to "secure the just Dependence of this Colony upon Great Britain, as to maintain and support the Majesty and Authority of Government." Garth understood too the thrust of the duties. "System" would be employed. Charles, Garth said, glided from New York to the whole by way of his duties, ensuring Parliament would "be no longer dependent upon the pleasure of any Assembly." After the duties had passed, Garth explained that the method mattered as much as the particulars. As he put it, "It is said the Colonies will understand the Motive upon which the Measure was founded and to be carried into execution." While some argued Parliament would only interfere where and when it had to, Garth believed that when such a power is used "it must operate to render the Assembly of that Colony rather insignificant."[45]

Fittingly, three days before the king assented to the new law, Charles accepted the freedom of the City of London for "his well tempered zeal in support of the undoubted legislative authority of the king and parliament of Great Britain over all parts of his Majesty's dominions." If he unveiled his system by pillorying New York, without resorting to principle, and by using an "external" tax contrivance he thought absurd, no one could doubt what the measure would mean for empire. What he had done, even a rival conceded in understated fashion, was "imaginative."[46]

Charles's Empire

The basic thrust of Charles's plan for empire dovetailed with his understanding of how the whole could sustain the constituent parts. "If we once lose the superintendence of America," he believed, "this nation is undone." The center depended on the peripheries as much as they relied on the metropole. When Charles imagined empire, he did so in structural terms, seeing how all areas fitted together. Given his apprenticeship with the Board of Trade, such an approach is understandable. Distinctive regions had specific functions or roles to play, and the proper working of empire depended on the relationships between complementary parts. Therefore, Charles conceived of his empire almost like the map on a wall. And, as one historian argues, he was not alone in seeing the world in this way in these years.[47] Animating the map was parliamentary sovereignty, but such sovereignty had meaning only if the pieces worked along the lines he designed. Charles, then, offered a compelling and elegant way to govern space.

Unified sovereignty, of course, could have been achieved by other means. Americans could have traveled to Westminster and sat in Parliament. Adam Smith would later air this proposal as a means of mediating the crisis between Britain and America. Charles certainly read about such proposals. A "scheme for an union between Great Britain and her Colonies" crossed his desk, calling for "Representation in Parliament." Massachusetts, Pennsylvania, and Virginia could send four members to Parliament, and most of the other mainland colonies two or three. Georgia, East Florida, West Florida, and Nova Scotia would be entitled to one each, the same number most of the islands in the Caribbean would send to Westminster. Canada would have three. Dominica, St. Vincent, and Tobago would enjoy representation "when settled." All of the colonies and the islands would then have a direct voice in Parliament. The plan, though, was never pursued, and given the distance between North America and Britain could not have worked.[48]

The plan Charles devised differed from the ones proffered in 1754 as the war was starting and certainly diverged from the one his friend Smith devised. Charles's plan would be driven by London, and the new scheme would create uniform lines of authority between center and periphery. He designed the 1767 plan to address needs and conditions that were systemic in nature. It would make Parliament supreme for taxation and legislation on all sorts of matters, not just for defense and frontier relations with Indians. It was not designed to address one issue. Charles meant it to reform the whole. As Grenville would argue, Charles "stated repeatedly in this House, that this was a beginning only."[49]

Charles, after all, as per his training, thought of the empire systematically, and the plan reflected such a sensibility. He considered the disposition of troops, the expenses of the superintendents of Indian affairs, and the duties collected in American ports as part of a whole tightly connected with Parliament at its head. "In general," he advised at this time, "it did not become Parliament to engage in controversy with its colonies, but by one act to assert its sovereignty." Officials had to be careful because of the interconnectedness of empire. "The provinces" could engage "in common cause."[50] And that is the point. The plan involved more than the duties; its success depended on making the dependencies provinces in ways that Tacitus would have appreciated.

Once authority was established, each constituent part could serve the specific good for which it was best suited. Just consider Charles's nuanced understanding of political economy. Charles ultimately sponsored a broader hybrid plan that mixed what we could call a mercantilist conception of political economy with more free trade ideals. In fact, although "mercantilism" was a concept created by nineteenth-century theorists and historians, almost all officials believed that colonies should benefit the mother country.[51] The means to achieving this end varied. Some called for bullionist approaches, that is, ones focusing on the balance of trade and payments to ensure that more money came into the country than left it. This belief led to calls for a highly regulated economy, one directed by the center. But Charles appreciated that the provinces differed in what they could offer the whole. Perhaps, for some, a different vision of political economy was needed.

And this new vision is just what Charles supplied for the most important parts of the British imperial political economy: the large sugar-producing slave societies of the Caribbean. He believed that there had to be exceptions to his rule. Following up on plans sketched out by the Rockingham administration, the most radical of which would create a free trade empire, Charles adopted the idea of free ports as a "necessity" at times. Under his early watch, a bill was introduced to allow Jamaica and Dominica to import certain goods without having to abide by the Navigation Acts. In fact, he was a chief supporter of the measure. The proposed bill also allowed the exportation of slaves from these ports to "any Foreign Colony or Plantation," as well as many other "goods," stipulated that no foreign rum or spirits could be imported or exported, and that fabrics could be traded duty free to and from Britain. Moreover, the ships of any nation could carry goods to the islands from Britain, Ireland, or North America. In this way, the ports of these islands, which thrived on the most precious commodities of the Atlantic, sugar and slaves, could serve as entrepôts tying the Caribbean islands to the mainland. The Atlantic trading system, after all, required some commerce across imperial boundaries.[52]

Charles's vision of empire drew on what others had been contemplating. Nova Scotia, for instance, with its new capital of Halifax, had been established as a planned colony during Charles's time at the Board of Trade. From its very beginnings, the board had designed it to work in the way Charles wanted all the colonies to function. The ministry paid its royal governor and its officials. Even if a vocal assembly developed as the population grew, the governor would retain his autonomy and by extension ensure that the business of the British Parliament was done. The members of the board envisioned the Floridas, acquired after the war, along the same lines. Few people lived there, but the board hoped settlement would come with time and encouragement. In the meantime, government would take root in a proper way to guarantee that Parliament's wishes were followed. Charles's measures reflected this ideal perfectly.

The plan could also comprehend attempts already under way to integrate former French settlements into the British Empire. Quebec, though under a military government at the time, represented an anomaly, but a telling one. For the moment, the ministry directed affairs through a military governor. Officials respected the distinctive nature of the place, even going so far as tolerating the practice of Catholicism there. Of course, it had little choice. Quebec was more Catholic even than Ireland. Yet, the particulars of local context mattered less than lines of authority. With time, these former French subjects would consider themselves British subjects. When that happened, they would have an assembly and a governor. That governor, of course, would never look to the assembly for his salary. Grenadians found themselves in a similar position. But Grenada would be enmeshed in the system from the very beginning, even if its assembly were composed of French Catholics.[53] Charles's plan could refit the older colonies to work in a similar fashion.

Charles made no real mention of the American West. Like those who ruled before him, he exempted the region from his plan. He and other officials wanted to discourage settlement in the region, already hived off from the East by what was called a Proclamation Line, so that men and women would choose Nova Scotia or the Floridas instead. The board designed the line to keep settlers and speculators away from those regions deep in the interior. Settlements there, if they could be undertaken at all, as Charles learned in office, "[could] have little or no communication with the Mother Country, or be of much utility to it." Therefore, for practical and for ideological reasons, leaving the West out of the system made good sense. It made sense in one other way as well. Troops that would have been policing the West could be shuttled to the East to deal with any disturbances. In practical terms, this approach meant enabling commanders on the ground, who worried over manpower shortages, to dismantle all but the most necessary forts.[54]

All that being said, the system did not include one other place of note: India. In fact, with his views on India, Charles demarked the limits of his system. Although the empire in fact encompassed the globe, the system of sovereignty he was constructing focused on the Atlantic. India received little mention by either Charles or George up to this point because, except as a trading concern or as a site for investment, it did not really concern either of them. Their mother, to be sure, came from a family whose members were key stakeholders in the East India Company. She wrote letters to George discussing the family's investments in the East India Company, as well as a "Townshend sloope" that transported some of the company's funds from Holland. She worried, for instance, that the "India Stock will be worse, for the Parliament never seemes inclined to do them any service."[55] But its affairs, aside from making money, had not concerned Parliament and by extension Charles or George.

That changed when Chatham assumed control of government. He questioned how, or if, the now augmented holdings of the East India Company should be part of any postwar settlement. As usual, the issue came down to money. Through its victories on the subcontinent during the war, the East India Company was transformed from a trading concern to a colonial state. The issues Britons now confronted—or rather that Chatham wanted them to face—were the following: Could a trading company rule this "conquered" territory? How should the relationship of the Crown to the territory be defined? And, most critically, who had the "right" to benefit from the expected revenues? Chatham, by even framing these questions, already knew the answers he sought. To his mind, the state should take over control in some fashion. The Crown had a right to the territories and was sovereign. And the state could expect a share of the revenue in recognition of that right and control. Tapping into the wealth of the Orient, Chatham hoped, could help with the dire fiscal situation he was facing. He then ordered one of his men in the Commons to inquire into the state of the company and its holdings. Eventually, the same M.P. would seek to publish the company's accounts and papers.[56]

Enter Charles Townshend, or rather his detractors. He did not agree with Chatham. He brought himself to support an inquiry, but he wanted it to be limited in scope and certainly not comprehensive. He aimed to avoid a discussion of the rights of the company versus the rights of the state. As Grenville put it, "Mr. Townshend hopes to gain the East India Company by kissing them after the other great Personage has kicked them." Charles did not want the sovereignty of the company compromised in any fashion. "The versatile genius of the Chancellor of the Exchequer was playing tricks and endeavouring to obstruct the measure yet in embryo," Horace Walpole observed. He had, Grafton argued, "marred the business at the outset." And his enemies assumed, understandably, that Charles did so because he had invested in the company. The weathercock was not only fickle and ambitious but venal as well. Although the notion of "conflict of interest" did not have much purchase in the eighteenth century, his critics understood that if Charles stood to gain, he would take a certain course in devising policy. Horace Walpole, once again, seemingly had the last word on his behavior, claiming Townshend wanted to "raise or lower the stock in which he was dealing." As another member of the House argued, because Charles had a vested interest, he proved "very artful, conciliatory, able, and eloquent" in a series of debates over the fate of the company.[57]

He is also remembered in this debate for his famous "Champagne Speech," earning him the sobriquet "Champagne Charlie." It proved an episode that "displayed in a little latitude beyond belief the amazing powers of his capacity, and the no less amazing incongruities of his character." Early on the day in question, Charles dispassionately went over the company's conduct, and he even pointed to the particular care he had demonstrated in doing his homework. He then repaired home, his work apparently done. After the House became entangled in some particulars, however, he was called back. In the meantime he had consumed champagne and hard liquor. Not even knowing what was at issue, as it was reported, he launched into a diatribe about "a descant of the times, a picture of parties, of their leaders, of their hopes, and defects." Only someone with "parts like his own," he thundered, was fit to lead. It was a virtuoso performance that did not speak to the issue of India at all but revealed his inner convictions. "Such was the wit, abundance, and impropriety of this speech, that for some days men could talk or inquire of nothing else," Horace Walpole gushed. All around town, people asked, "Did you hear Charles Townshend's champagne speech?"[58]

Charles had other things to say, things often missing from interpretations of this series of events, that speak to his preoccupation with a system. Some, for instance, wondered, "Could Bengal . . . be stated as a permanent possession?" Had the company conquered or merely plundered the subcontinent, a critical question, especially since the king "was not at war with the Mogul," making it "difficult to know judicially what to do with these acquisitions." Charles supported this motion, asking if Parliament even had any right to claim the sort of sovereignty it did for America. He then joined a commission to look into some sort of arrangement for the company and its vast territories that would reflect these concerns but also address the problems with the Treasury. He encouraged the company to propose its own solution, which would forestall any inquiry.[59]

The record supports this interpretation. Charles noted that if the state tried to milk the company, the whole Indian enterprise could come crashing down. And Chatham overestimated the amount the company could ever pay. It did not have a strong grip on Bengal, and up to this point the state had no stake in the region. India, not America, appeared as a New World for Britain, one yet to be explored and imaginatively amalgamated into the consciousness of the nation. With the issues before him, Charles wrote, he had "held this language from the very beginning, wishing to avoid the necessity of a parliamentary decision upon so very new, mixed, and judicial a question, affecting so large a body of men." Debating the issue given "the circumstances attending the rights claimed, from the nature of the acquisitions themselves, from the impractability of substituting the public in the place of the Company," only compounded confusion. With these uncertainties, the company had a right to its revenues. The state would expect something for its support of the company, but the acquisitions lay beyond its purview.[60]

Therefore, although Chatham hoped the state could claim some sort of right, and he underestimated the implications and complexity of what he was proposing, Charles thought otherwise, pointing out the difficulties that lay ahead if the House took Chatham's course. And Charles did all he could to thwart his patron. He spoke of the "impracticality of the Public in the place of the Company in the collecting, investing, conducting, and remitting the revenue." The potential costs of administering the area, which was then unincorporated in any fashion into the British state either culturally or economically, could be enormous. Moreover, as Charles put it, "the Company had a right to their conquests," something he would not "dispute." Any final settlement, he conceded, would have to be "advantageous to the Company" but also "adequate to the Public." An "amicable" settlement would last and would balance "national justice and Public prosperity."[61] What was good for the East India Company was good for Britain.

Charles had studied a great many things of India. He knew its history, its diversity, the treaties that bound parts of it to the company, and the business of its merchants and nabobs. India was not like America or Ireland. Britons had not settled it. The same dense networks that held the Atlantic together did not tie the subcontinent to the center. The state, he argued, could still derive some benefit from the company but not take on all the risks of administration. The company's formal status was to be left undefined, and for good reason. Charles's system, therefore, would not, and could not, include India. The imperial moment had not yet arrived for the region. Townshend counseled a negotiated settlement through which the company would pay a fee to the state. The company agreed to pay £400,000 a year. Its officials were happy to do so.[62]

The elegance of Charles's system reflected the ways the process of consolidation and imperial competition had shaped the Atlantic. It was not only geared to uniting the empire, almost as an imperial union, but also designed to adhere to true Glorious Revolution principles by rooting legitimacy in Parliament. Once corruption was undone, the rot stripped away, the simple foundation could be laid for an empire that would last and that could function. Once reform took place, and Charles reckoned it should not be difficult if artfully managed, then taxation could begin.

Writing in the mid-twentieth century, Sir Lewis Namier quipped that "the Townshend duties are a thing which any clerk in the treasury would have suggested," adding he could not understand why anyone would ever want to explore, say, "the influence of Adam Smith on Charles Townshend and his American policy."[63] This would appear an oversimplification. Charles had envisioned a structure for empire that could comprehend the diversity of that empire, and he believed he was born to do so. This did not make him exceptional. Nor did the fact that he had a plan. But he had the good fortune to hold the stage alone for a moment, enabling him to implement his vision, even if he believed through his upbringing and experience that he was destined to do so. The conjunction of design and contingency had allowed him to begin the construction of something that he hoped would last through the ages. Of course, it was not to be. Most tragically, Charles would never see his empire, for the simple reason that he would be dead.

Charles's Death

Charles had, of course, always struggled with health issues. If his untimely death stemmed from what he called "the enemy," we will never know. In the summer of 1767, he reported yet another illness, a cold and fever that came and went but that he could not shake. His physician called it "a slow fever of the putrid kind." It could well have been cancer. Whatever it was, Charles did not recover. On Sunday, 6 September, he died in the villa he had acquired through his wife at Sudbrook. Fittingly, his brother George was at his side. Before he died, Charles commended his children to George's care. The following Saturday, the body was "opened up," and as a friend reported, "he had died of a Mortification in his Bowels." He was forty-two.[64]

On Saturday, 26 September, his body was interred at Raynham under St. Mary's Church, which stood about a quarter mile from the house. On a plate, affixed to a crimson velvet-lined coffin, the following words were etched: "Charles Townshend, Chancellor of the Exchequer, Aged 42." The pall was supported by a number of leading lights, including the Earl of Oxford, the Earl of Buckinghamshire, and Lord Walpole. "Sixteen of Lord Townshend's tenants," a newspaper reported, "attended as under bearers." At the time of Charles's death, the family, apparently, planned to erect an "elegant Marble Monument," much like Roger's, in the north side of

Westminster Abbey. The memorial never came off. Roger would be the only Townshend memorialized there.[65]

The death shocked London. "Poor Townshend," one acquaintance observed just after the death, "he is a national loss." Horace Walpole wrote of his brilliance. "Our comet Charles Townshend is dead," he said a few weeks after the passing. As he put it, "that eccentric genius, whom no subsystem could contain, is whirled out of existence." True to form, Walpole saw two sides of Charles even in death. "With such a capacity," he believed, "he must have been the greatest man of his age, and perhaps inferior to no man in any age, had his faults been only in a moderate proportion—in short, if he had had but common truth, common sincerity, common honesty, common modesty, common steadiness, common courage, and common sense." Grenville suggested the same. He lamented what he knew to be "a heavy and unexpected Blow to his Family and which upon the Public's Account I am sorry for as I think his Public opinions as well as his Talents greatly preferable to those of any of his Colleagues in office."[66]

Provincials, too, paid their respects. An Irish newspaper, reporting from an English paper, declared "Trade, manufactures, commerce, colonies, and the finances have an irreparable loss in him." Charles O'Conor, a prominent Catholic and friend to Burke, received a letter from one of Charles's friends and political rivals in which Charles was fondly remembered. "So much Life, spirit, imagination, and talent were scarce ever extinguished in a single man," it read. As O'Conor learned, "Death seems to have shewn his power more imperiously in taking him than in sweeping off a Multitude." One of George's friends in Ireland wrote, "I admired with the rest of the world his eminent abilitys. I was delighted with the vivacity . . . of his wit, but I loved him for his infinite good nature and good humour."[67]

Edmund Burke paid perhaps the most touching tribute to Charles. Some years later, in his "Speech on American Taxation," delivered in the House in 1774, Burke recounted the recent past of all that had happened. He understood that Charles had had a critical role to play in this drama, and that the duties especially had transformed the imperial landscape. In the speech, Burke considered their passage *a,* if not *the,* critical moment. Still, he praised Charles both for his abilities and for his vision. At one point in the speech, in which he discussed the role of "great men" in great events, he said of Charles, "In truth, Sir, he was the delight and ornament of this House, and the charm of every private society which he honoured with his presence. Perhaps there never arose in this country, nor in any country, a man of a more pointed and finished wit; and (where his passions were not concerned) of a more refined, exquisite, and penetrating judgment." Burke summed up his abilities in this way: "He hit the House just between wind and water." Burke, a friend of Charles's, felt the loss personally.[68] He lamented the death even more for Britain and its empire at a critical juncture. Charles was brilliant. "Even before this splendid orb [Chatham] was entirely set," Burke declared, "and while the western horizon was in a blaze with his descending glory, on the opposite heavens arose another luminary." For Burke, Charles was that light.[69]

Charles's death devastated the family. While a friend of the family noted, "The public have a loss," the family, particularly Charles's mother and brother, had suffered a more bitter blow, one "much greater, never to be repaired," which "must be sensibly felt by them to their last moments." The friend was right. Charles's widow kept a steady correspondence with George, in which she continued to refer to Charles as "our dear friend." It was for George and the family a "Distressful Situation."[70]

George struggled profoundly with depression after Charles's death, so much so that some wondered if he would be able to take up his official duties in Ireland. "My brother's Illness," he wrote to a friend, "and his expiring almost in my Arms with the Expressions of our earliest Affections, have left an Impression upon my Frame which has rendered me almost unfit for an easy Correspondence, much more so for so Arduous an Undertaking as Ireland." George wrote of the anguish and "melancholy" he felt at Charles's passing and of the "afflicting stroke which hath befallen our Family," as well as the "irreparable loss" the death represented for him. One of his chief allies could see the effects of the "great Affliction" George was bearing and how "severe" the "Stroke" of the death was for him.[71]

The pain was real, "an Affliction which has not only surpass'd any Thing I ever conceiv'd, but what will certainly sit heavy on my Heart to the latest Hour of my Life." George had lost, he wrote, "my Councellor, my Friend, and my Defence." But he was resolved to work "to do Justice to his Memory." George asked his mother to change the will so that money intended for him would go to Charles's children instead. He suggested, against a great deal of evidence to the contrary, that "his brother did not die in such good circumstances as the World may imagine."[72]

The simple upshot of his untimely death for the empire is this: Charles would not be able to ensure his plan was implemented fully. That task would be left to what remained of the ministry, or rather, its successor. For the instability continued. But before turning to this, let us linger over Charles Townshend's moment. It did not end with his death. In fact, it only began there. How provincials struggled to comprehend a changing world and to disentangle themselves from Charles's system represented the other chapter of what Charles's accomplishments meant.

An American Wake

After his death, the plan Charles bequeathed took on a life of its own once colonists learned of the duties and the suspension of New York's assembly in the summer of 1767. This story is well known and part of the American revolutionary narrative. If American colonists took issue with the Stamp Act, they would bring fevered protests to new heights once they learned of what came to be known as "the Townshend Duties." Writing from Boston to the secretary of state for the Southern Department in late July 1767, a month after the king gave his royal assent to the duties, Governor Francis Bernard noted the stirrings of disorder returning. What he now called "the Faction" had received word of the proceedings in Parliament and, he reported, "hinted that they will occasion fresh trouble in this Town." On 14 August, the anniversary when the effigy of a Stamp Act collector was hanged and burned and a house pulled down, the Sons of Liberty assembled "where those Violences began" to "make another Effort at inflaming the Province and also the Continent against the late resolutions of parliament." He feared they were "in Concert" with their colleagues from New York.[73]

In some respects, Bernard was right. The passage of the duties reignited the sorts of protests that had inflamed American towns and cities in 1765. Only this time the protests had an avowedly more political edge. In this instance, they moved beyond mobbing to more concerted and efficacious resistance. Most conspicuously, Sons of Liberty argued that Americans should refuse to allow the importation of British goods so long as the duties remained on the books. Up and down the coast, local groups published promises to "encourage the Use and Consumption of all Articles manufactured in any of the British American Colonies, and more especially in this Province; and that we will not, from and after the 31st of *December* next, purchase any of the following Articles, imported from Abroad." The lists included goods ranging from gloves to anchors and glue to silks. They even turned back ships. In October 1769, for instance, New Yorkers read how "a vessel arrived there from Scotland, with a considerable quantity of British manufactures, whereupon the sons of liberty assembled and came to a resolution to send her back with her cargo." A newspaper recounted how "they carefully watched her one night to prevent the landing her cargo, with an intention to give any person who might attempt to smuggle, a proper discipline at Liberty-post." The next day "the 'true-born' sons generously subscribed a sum of money, equal to the value of the freight of the ship Home, which they presented to the Captain, and gave him directions to return to the place from whence he came, which he accordingly obeyed on Thursday last, by setting sail for Scotland."[74]

Radical groups from cities along the coast established committees of correspondence to coordinate efforts, to keep each other apprised of what was happening in their communities, and most critically to ensure that the merchants of each town were not circumventing the others. Committees also policed their own neighborhoods. In coordinating their efforts, Americans were acting as true Britons. "Let us," the *Pennsylvania Gazette* implored, "as a Patriot said, when the liberties of England were in like danger from James the first, *petition and petition the King again, as we usually do to God, and without ceasing, till he hear us.*"[75]

Although riots were not surprising, the creation of networks was. Emulating forms of association prevalent throughout the British Isles, these "patriots"—meaning those willing to sacrifice individual interest for the common good—made use of symbols and rites through expert organization to make clear how Parliament had erred.[76] In this instance, they rallied whole communities to wear homespun clothing to demonstrate their contempt for Parliament's presumption to tax them directly or indirectly, internally or externally. They led campaigns to refuse to drink tea exported from India via England, instead brewing their own homemade concoction called Labrador tea, by all accounts a bitter and wretched substitute for the real thing, even if one newspaper claimed it to be "much esteemed and by great numbers vastly preferred to the poisonous Bohea." Vigilance, to use a watchword of the day, was required by all. Some, such as John Adams, read and admired Swift. Others did not. But they certainly were emulating the things that he had proposed when Ireland found itself in similar straits.[77]

From the first rumors of the passage of the duties in 1767 until Americans learned that most of them were to be repealed in 1770, America was stirring with intrigue, intense debate, and heightened political activity. Indeed, it is almost axiomatic to say that the American response to the Townshend Duties represented the start of a significant shift in American political sensibilities, as more and more colonists began to call themselves citizens, as well as subjects, and began to clamor for their rights as men as well as Britons. If we gauge election sermons in Boston in these years, as one historian has, what we find is that what occurred in these years represented the beginning of some sort of turning point in American thinking, that the move toward independence was becoming imaginable. The Stamp Act may have been a mistake, but the duties seemed to signal something more sinister. America's British identity began to erode year by year.[78]

Americans experienced an emotional transformation as well. With the Stamp Act Americans mourned what was happening to them, and with its repeal they rejoiced. Up and down the colonies, they made elaborate speeches of loyalty, lit bonfires, and cracked open barrels of beer, demonstrating a patriotic euphoria as if the whole affair were an anomaly. As a draft of a newspaper advertisement Charles had collected recounted, Americans had indulged in "all Rejoicings and Exhibitions of Joy throughout the Continent on Occasion of the repeal of Stamp Act," including "Illuminations, Ringing of Bells, Bonfires, Firing of Cannon, and other Fireworks" to signal their "Duty and Loyalty to Our Most Gracious Sovereign." The passage of the Townshend Duties elicited a quite different response. "When the enslaving act was repealed," a Connecticut writer argued, "how did every heart swell with joy." It was short-lived. "But Alas!" he exclaimed, "how soon is our joy turned into mourning?" From this point on, Americans resisted consistently with "vigour" and anger. The emotional register of colonists shifted "subtly and substantially" with the duties, as one scholar argues.[79] The actions of colonists, then, suggested unanimity of purpose that was not there before and clarity where confusion had reigned.

This narrative, however, takes on an almost inexorable logic. So accustomed are we to the almost inevitable nature of the American response to the Townshend Duties—that we are marching toward revolution—that we can forget what the moment really meant. If we slow the narrative down, it becomes apparent that concerted opposition did not initially rise out of the ether. It did not emerge unopposed. It did not betoken some sense that history was on the side of the colonists or that revolution was inevitable from this point. The initial reaction to the duties and the meanings people ascribed to them varied, too, and were contingent on events. This story is, therefore, more complex than we may have reckoned with. Moreover, the narrative we have obscures a more profound transformation that was gripping American communities. As they struggled with the duties and what they meant, Americans were also coming to terms with the relationship between Britain and America. This, too, is not a straightforward tale.

The years 1767 and 1768 represented a critical moment for American conceptions of empire and their place in it. The process of imperial debate and redefinition that the brothers participated in, and in which they came to have prominent voices, occurred in America as well. It did so most visibly in the chief organ of eighteenth-century communication and thought, the newspaper. Newspapers played, perhaps, a disproportionately significant role in the American public sphere. In fact, when the unrest began in Boston, Francis Bernard sent clipping after clipping to the Earl of Shelburne in London. "I find myself obliged," he wrote to Shelburne in October, "to continue transmitting the Newspapers to your Lordship upon account of the great flagitiousness of some of the pieces contained in them." These, he reckoned, would give officials an accurate assessment of the situation. Newspaper debate was boisterous and nearly unrestrained. Divergent voices parried in print in what was effectively a provincial culture with a distinctively participatory ethos, one now networked through the expansion and reach of print.[80] Here Americans reckoned with Charles's vision and system but hardly in any foreordained way that would suggest a watershed of fundamental change.

Newspapers kept Americans quite up to date with goings-on in London in 1767. And, though an ocean away, they enjoyed an accurate view of what was happening. To be sure, what colonists saw appeared as snapshots, episodic snippets sometimes taken out of context. Yet reports usually got things right. Over and over, newspapers ran extracts from letters they received from London. Often a paper would publish one of these extracts, and others would follow suit. They borrowed heavily from London correspondents, newspapers, and each other. Bit by bit, taking information from a number of sources and sifting through rumors, men and women up and down the coast were able to assemble a fairly accurate assessment of how those in the center understood them and the developing notions of empire.

In periods of uncertainty, just like all Britons, they followed the rumors closely, trying to get a hold of any bit of useful news. At one point, as all were wondering what sort of ministry would emerge in the tumult of 1766, the *Virginia Gazette* reported that "it is said that Lord Viscount Townshend is to go on an important commission to North America." What he would do was not said. In early 1767, reports flew of how Charles was sponsoring a lottery for raising money. Colonists in Virginia and Massachusetts read, "The state of our finances was the grand object of deliberations . . . at which, we are told, the Right Hon. Charles Townshend communicated a plan for materially lessening the annual expense of the kingdom." All knew he was the master of such affairs. What role he would play in any administration remained unclear. But he was certainly rumored to be at the center of any new plan.[81]

Even though they mixed up which brother would do what and what part Charles would take in any administration, Americans kept themselves abreast of news, and the fact that Charles sponsored the duties was well known. Americans also knew how he was operating through pretext. By April 1767, the *Pennsylvania Gazette* was carrying reports of what was happening in Parliament. New York's "conduct" had transfixed the House, its readers learned. "Most people," they read, "are of Opinion they will certainly enforce the Execution of the Act of Parliament" for quartering troops. The paper reported that troops might be dispatched to that end. The ministry was waiting for Chatham to return from Bath, where, they knew, he was suffering from gout. At this point, they even understood that Charles was taking the reins. He was saying things that offended some of the great and mighty, and he was raising the specter of "Taxing the colonies, in some Shape or other." New Yorkers had alarmed officials, and Charles was using their intransigence to press for change. "The late disputes in New York," an extracted letter read, "have again roused the revengeful spirit of your enemies, and have lost the colonies some, until now, very staunch friends." One name was listed: "Mr. Charles Townshend." Even as early as this date— April 1767—Americans recognized that commissioners for collecting customs in North America might become a central aspect of any plan. The same reports were carried in Virginia newspapers. Americans knew how delicate the times were, that everything reported now "may all be turned Topsyturvey before next Packet." In other words, they had an extraordinarily clear appreciation of metropolitan plans and, of course, the volatility and signal importance of the period.[82]

Through all the rumors and the uncertainty, they recognized what Charles was doing. He hoped to subordinate. "Mr. Charles Townshend, the

Chancellor of the Exchequer," Virginians learned, "urged the propriety of more troops being sent to America, and of their being quartered in the large towns." He also had "a plan preparing, which he would lay before the House, for the raising supplies in America, that the Legislative authority here extended to every colony, in every particular; that the distinction of *internal* and *external taxes* was *nonsense*." He had voted for the repeal of the Stamp Act "not because it was not a good act" but because of expedience. He knew the *"galleries might hear him,"* and thus reports would reach the colonies. *"He did not expect to have statues erected in America."* This report was repeated in paper after paper.[83]

The May parliamentary debates were carried in great detail as well. In extracts Virginians read how "the Ministry still stand their Ground; and Lord Chatham still continues to be incapable of giving the least Attention to Business of any Kind." Illness, along with the medicine prescribed, "had thrown the Disease into his Brain." Virginians still admired him. Now they feared his absence. The issue of what would come of America in the House was an open question. Pennsylvanians knew the voices that cried for lenient treatment. They also knew Grenville remained implacable, "supporting his first Opinion regarding the Stamp Act." Charles, though, stood out. "C-----s T-------d," the *Pennsylvania Gazette* reported, "is for violent Measures." Charles was pressing for "severe compulsory Measures" in America. New Yorkers read the same extracts, with the exception they also read another which argued all that was transpiring was meant "to secure the dependence of the said colonies on Great-Britain." They also knew that "said Duties to be raised in the said Colonies and Plantations," as the *Boston Gazette* explained, "are applied, in the first Place, in making a more certain and adequate Provision for the Charge of the Administration of Justice, and the Support of Civil Government."[84]

Although they had a remarkably well-informed and accurate notion of what was happening in Parliament and what Charles's vision amounted to, the response of American colonists to his plan was, in fact, complex. For a start, some recognized Charles's vision for what it was and cried foul from the beginning, one even going so far as to press for "independence" from a Parliament that had no right to "subordinate" the colonies. The *Boston Evening-Post* carried a series of letters entitled "The Nature and Extent of Parliamentary Power" that declared the moment would create "slavish dependence." Americans had considered themselves free subjects. Now they had become "dependent vassals." Britons "gave birth to my ancestors," the writer conceded. Yet, as he put it, "I consider them as exerting their superior power to reduce their fellow subjects to a state of subordination inconsistent with their natural rights, and not to be reconciled to their spirit of their own constitution." Being born in America "did not divest" him of his rights. Americans had to stand against "the vesting this power in the parliament of Great-Britain."[85]

The reason was simple. The writer believed that the empire was sustained by various arrangements. "In a system so complicated as ours, where one power is continually encroaching upon the other, and where the general balance is so fluctuating and precarious," he tried his best to explain, "a spirit of compliance and moderation in the present age, may lay a foundation for the slavery and dependence of future generations." In this vein, some wondered if the British constitution, which had been refashioned at the time of the Glorious Revolution, even pertained to the colonies. As these writers groped toward an understanding, they relied on older arguments that laid out the distinctive rights of American colonists because of their ancestors' sacrifices at the time of settlement. These writers knew that something was afoot and that it had to be opposed, even if they could never quite say what specifically was happening to Americans and what it would entail.[86]

Surprisingly, and at the other extreme, some even suggested that the Townshend Duties were just. A number of writers in newspapers—and these could be found in papers up and down the coast—did not object to the duties. America was subordinate to the Crown. This went without saying. But the colonies also were subordinate to Parliament. The *New Hampshire Gazette*, for instance, ran a letter to the editor on the front page that urged obedience even if judges and governors would now be rendered "independent of the People." "We have a pleasant Prospect before us," the writer maintained, "which under the influence of Union and harmony, in the several branches of the Legislature, may make us a happy People." Parliament had demonstrated both lenity and wisdom.[87]

British subjects had borne the lion's share of expense for the war; Americans were subjects too and, as some Americans argued, should shoulder their fair share of the burden. Such was one line of reasoning. The *New York Gazette* made this point. After the war, Americans owed a debt to "other subjects," and what Parliament was doing was "reasonable." The paper lampooned those who opposed Charles's plan in this way: "We petition to be freed from every jurisdiction derived from the mother country, such only excepted, as we can controul when we will, and modify how we please." Parliament could regulate trade affairs. Parliament could also tax. So some in the colonies had no truck with the Townshend vision. The *Boston Evening-Post* summed this sentiment up by saying, "*A jealous American at this day must be a very stupid animal.*" "Amicus," writing in the paper, declared Parliament had the right to legislate and enjoyed the "supream legislative authority." Regulating trade and exercising control of the empire was Parliament's "because no such power was or is inherent in the crown." The right was "uncontroverted," rooted in reason and history. The Glorious Revolution now belonged to Americans as well: "The privilege of Britons is just where it ever has been since the revolution, and where it ever ought to be, in the King, Lords and Commons."[88]

Other voices ranged between the two extremes. A writer calling himself "A Friend to this Colony" wrote to the *Providence Gazette* voicing ambivalence. He hated the duties and all they meant. Ultimately, "we must either make our own cloaths, go naked, or augment our debt with Great-Britain to a sum which will in the end enslave the country." What could one do? A writer appearing in the *Connecticut Courant* known as "A Friend" scoffed at those claiming they would face "cannon and redcoats" so that Americans could go on drinking their tea and consuming other "soppish empty notions of grandeur." Still, the duties rankled. Send American rags to mills to make paper, he argued. Scour the beaches for sand to produce glass. Even if this strategy did not work, and the writer had his doubts, at least America was "waking out of her trance." Perhaps good could come of the crisis. After all, he found, "there are too many idle people in this country, who live on the labours of others." Government in America was "so feeble" that it could not guide, direct, or use the powers already lodged in it. One writer in the *New Hampshire Gazette* who supported the measure even suggested that, though Parliament could tax, the duties would force the colonists to learn to live within their means. "I strongly recommend the use and wear of own Manufactures of Cloathing, etc.," he argued, "and to import no unnecessary Articles till we can better afford them."[89]

Some writers proved willing to go along, even if they conceded they did not particularly like the plan. A writer styling himself "Americanus" greeted the duties with a shrug. When the duties were being discussed in Parliament, the paper from New Hampshire asked, "Where lies the

Difference, whether this Duty is stop'd in England or paid in America?" Better it stays in America, he argued: "We shall have the sole use of this Revenue to be appropriated to support the Civil Government of all the Colonies, consequently less burthensome on the People." The *Newport Mercury* also published his views. Another from Connecticut was a bit confused. "Americans," he wondered, "it seems are not only to acknowledge their dependence on the crown as they always have, and hope forever will, but must (if some gentlemen have their will) swear allegiance to the British Parliament." Who was sovereign for the colonies?[90]

What strikes the reader today as most surprising, given the nature of the emotional responses to Charles's plan, is the lack of emotion when it came to Charles and his role. When Americans learned of his death more than two months after the fact, for instance, they reported it without editorial or snide comment. Americans read the report reproduced in a Cambridge newspaper clipped out by Charles's old friend at university, one that hailed him as the empire's expert on trade and America. They read how his remains were interred at Raynham, of the great and good who carried the pall, and how all of London was shocked by his untimely death. The *Virginia Gazette*, hardly likely to support the duties or the system they supported, wrote this of Charles's death: "A great personage, we hear, exclaimed, when he was told of the Right Hon. Mr. Townshend's death, 'Then we have lost the ablest Minister in England.'" The paper carried the news of the death just below a piece that, coincidentally, discussed how "wagers of a hundred guineas to five are offered that a septennial Parliament will not be granted to the people of Ireland," pointing to an issue George would confront on his arrival in Ireland. A while later, after the news of Charles's death had been digested, the paper reported from London: "His great force was in the Senate, where no one ever excelled him in eloquence or ability, to this may be added that there could not be a more affectionate husband, tender parent, a better master."[91]

Others seemed to understand that the man possessed extraordinary talents but also that he did not fit into the standard political mold of the day. He was distinctive. He was, an extract of the letter in London in the *Pennsylvania Gazette* read, "certainly extremely clever." No one could speak like him. "Yet," the report continued in the vein of a Horace Walpole, "he was, at the Bottom, timid." He vacillated, and no one could gain a fix on him. Pennsylvanians read about his work in the debates leading up to the duties he sponsored. Here his work "was superior to any thing I have ever heard in that

House," the extract read. He was "snatched away in the very Prime of Life at the very Moment when he was about to reap the Fruit of his Application, and within Sight of that Station, to which all his Hopes had been directed." In the wake of his death, things in London had reverted to "Confusion and irresolution."[92]

This report, carried in a number of newspapers, demonstrated an interesting American trait.[93] Even those newspaper accounts that named Charles as the person responsible for the duties did so dispassionately. It is as if Americans separated the man from the act, reflecting the fact that from the beginning, despite the riots and the tumult, many did not know quite what to make of the duties. Reading through the newspapers addressing the duties, initially what we find is a very serious, even earnest, discussion about how America should fit into the whole. Americans could not quite situate Charles in the larger story because they had not come to terms with its parameters. They were only beginning to do so.

John Dickinson's Empire

The explanation for the changes in thinking with the Townshend Duties rests with how Americans eventually responded to clarity with clarity, even if their initial reactions to Charles and his plan were muddled. Charles had hoped to use the moment to clarify the relationship between center and periphery, metropole and province. Americans, he suggested, had taken advantage of the ambiguities that governed imperial arrangements to get the best of both worlds: virtual political autonomy along with the benefits of a consolidated Atlantic. Now from the grave he presented Americans with a very different vision of system. And they eventually responded in kind with a vision of their own. The momentous shift in thinking, creating a response that played on history's seeming inevitabilities in ways eerily similar to Charles's vision, that rang unambiguous notes in much the same way he had, and that also relied on a conceit that they were addressing a distinctive moment, occurred because of one person, a lawyer named John Dickinson.

Dickinson, in fact, became the catalyst that created an "American" response and began to create a narrative, that what Americans were facing was a pattern of behavior, not an exceptional or singular vision as Charles believed, and they had to devise distinctive strategies to contest it. Ironically, only Dickinson was able to accomplish what Charles hoped to do. He made America uniform, but he did so in ways Charles, of course, had never intended. He did not do so through the use of novel arguments. Some had made these points before during earlier disputes over the relationship between center and periphery, most conspicuously Franklin. But at this moment, what Dickinson had to say resonated as never before and moved people to concerted action.[94]

The passage of the duties compelled him to act. Born to a slave-owning and merchant father on the eastern shore of Maryland in 1732, Dickinson received a classical education before traveling to London to train for the law, arriving in 1753 to study at Middle Temple. He then returned to America to practice. He served in the Delaware Assembly, and subsequently ran for the larger and more influential Pennsylvania Assembly. Dickinson, then, devoted himself to American legislative politics. He served as a Pennsylvania delegate to the Stamp Act Congress in 1765, at which he drafted a declaration of rights. Although known for his moderate views, he had established himself as a thoughtful and influential British American, with all that this hybrid term conveys.[95]

When the Townshend Acts were passed in 1767, Dickinson was living and working in Philadelphia, the largest city in the colonies. It was a new city, founded only in the 1680s by Quakers, who had designed it for trade and toleration. From its very origins, it was tied to Quaker commercial networks that spanned the globe. It had grown into America's leading city with sustained migration from all over the British Isles and Europe. Peoples and goods came and went at a dizzying pace throughout the century. Pluralistic and contentious, the city abounded in taverns that buzzed with different languages. These taverns created a distinctive culture in the city, in which politics went hand in hand with rum punch.[96]

British in some sense, though ethnically diverse, the city appeared provincial, more rough-hewn even than places like Dublin and Edinburgh. Commerce sustained it. And the ships that came and went to and from the Delaware River brought in migrants and sent out the grain that grew in its hinterlands. Greater Philadelphia reached across the Susquehanna River, down the Great Wagon Road, into the backcountry of Virginia and the Carolinas. It had developed as the Atlantic was integrated; indeed, it epitomized the world that Charles had helped create on the Board of Trade. The city, therefore, thrived on the networks that had emerged in the eighteenth century tying the Atlantic together. Any sort of "system" redefining this

10. John Dickinson, portrait by Charles Willson Peale, circa 1770
(Courtesy of the Philadelphia History Museum at the Atwater Kent,
Historical Society of Pennsylvania Collection)

space and Philadelphia's place in it was sure to stir passions and to capture the imagination of a provincial patriot like Dickinson.

Dickinson put pen to paper and produced a series of letters that addressed the crisis of the day. The first appeared at the end of November in 1767, dated—fittingly—on the fifth of November, Guy Fawkes Day and the anniversary of William III's landing at Torbay during the Glorious Revolution. On this anniversary of events that represented defining moments of British patriotism, Dickinson suggested that Americans needed to open their eyes to a new, grave threat to their liberties. They had not up to this point grasped what was happening to them. Writing as a middling farmer, an everyman, but one with a "liberal education," he made it his task to characterize the real threat America faced. Released in a series of twelve installments and first published in the *Pennsylvania Chronicle and Universal Advertiser*, Dickinson's handiwork would come to be known as *Letters from a Farmer in Pennsylvania*.[97]

Dickinson seemed to understand what Charles had in mind for the colonies and certainly his tactical approach to passing the duties. First to meet Dickinson's scorn was the pretense through which Parliament had targeted New York in passing the "act for suspending the legislation of New-York." Dickinson understood that New York, perhaps, had erred in not complying as readily as some of the other colonies with the Quartering Act. Parliament's remedy, though, struck him as "pernicious to American freedom, and justly alarming to all the colonies." He, therefore, made exactly the same move Charles had in using New York as a wedge, only in this case to discuss the threat to all the colonies.[98] And right from his first letter, he asked if Parliament had the right to do what it did to New York.

Dickinson acknowledged the complex nature of the case he was making. He agreed with some principles of those who saw nothing particularly odious in the duties, as well as with what some of the more radical fringe had to say. He was unambiguous about the status of the colonies under the Crown. The Crown, he thought, could have "restrained the governor of New-York, even from calling the assembly together, by its prerogative in the royal government." Americans regarded Britain as the parent. And no less than a year before, Dickinson had acknowledged his patrimony in 1766: "Every drop of blood in my heart is British; and that heart is animated with as warm wishes for her prosperity, as her truest sons can wish." But what sort of parent-child relationship was it? Dickinson used history to explore the question, ultimately suggesting that the colonies had never been conquered, and that because of this past, colonists enjoyed all the rights of English subjects. Parliament, however estimable an institution, had no place in that historical drama, and the colonies could not be conceived as mere provinces of an expanding empire. History could not be erased in this way. Their sense of autonomy and English heritage suggested that unitary sovereignty could not be foisted upon them. Their assemblies, then, to which they consented, acted as their parliaments, and they could tax.[99]

Dickinson did not reject parliamentary sovereignty. And this is where his stance became quite nuanced. Parliament could regulate certain affairs. In some ways, he advocated views articulated by many Britons, including Chatham, in making his case. Parliament's regulatory powers centered not on trade but on the idea of commonwealth. "We are but parts of a whole," Dickinson argued, "and therefore there must exist a power somewhere, to preside, and preserve the connection in due order." He continued: "This power is lodged in the parliament; and we are as much dependent on Great-Britain, as a perfectly free people can be on another." Parliament's special function was to guarantee the virtue of the whole—"to preserve or promote a mutually beneficial intercourse between the several constituent parts of the empire"—and part of that policing or regulating function involved ensuring that the rights of Englishmen in unconquered colonies were upheld.[100]

What Parliament could not do was to pass laws "for the regulation of trade; not for the preservation or promotion of a mutually beneficial intercourse between the several constituent parts of the empire." Here Dickinson differed a bit from Burke, who argued that Parliament could tax but should not. To Dickinson, laws passed by Parliament to tax the colonies were "unconstitutional." He answered the question about Parliament's ability to levy a tax on the colonists with "a total denial." Ironically, he agreed with Charles on the absurdity of the distinction between internal and external taxation. As he put it, "Here is no distinction made, between internal and external taxes." Of course, he blurred the difference to insist that Parliament had no right to tax, whereas Charles did so to assert that Parliament could do as it saw fit.[101]

In other words, like Charles, Dickinson saw the empire in structural terms. Moreover, he agreed with the Townshend vision of the role of Parliament—Parliament as the guardian of imperial virtue—but it would be at the head of an empire structured along federated lines. Independence did not even cross his mind. "I hope, my dear countrymen," he wrote in *Letter III,* "that you will in every colony be on your guard against those who may at any time endeavour to stir you up, under the pretences of patriotism, to any measures disrespectful to our sovereign and our mother country." As he phrased it, "The prosperity of these provinces is founded on their dependence on Great-Britain," and he urged his fellow colonists to "behave like dutiful children." Yet, he did not counsel the colonists to sit still. He conceded that this was a critical juncture, and that Americans now had to stand up for their rights so "the mistake may be corrected."[102]

Dickinson's vision, as well as his reasoning, are quite compelling even today. The *Letters* read beautifully. The tone is earnest and even, and

Dickinson does not threaten. This is a measured response, one made with "calmness, dignity, and sagacity," one historian writing a century ago argued. Dickinson also relied on the same three strands of thought that so enthralled the Townshends. He gestured toward Scottish moral or commonsense philosophy when he argued, "Benevolence towards mankind excites wishes for their welfare, and such wishes endear the means of fulfilling them." Adam Smith argued along these lines in his *Theory of Moral Sentiments*, as did another thinker the brothers read, Francis Hutcheson. Dickinson wrote of classical antecedents, of the Romans and Carthaginians, to discuss oppression. He also made use of Plutarch, Cicero, and especially Tacitus, Charles's favorite, whom Dickinson called "the judicious historian." Dickinson, therefore, dotted his piece with references to the classical thinkers that Charles and George read, but in this case, he interpreted things very differently.[103]

He also made use of Hume's *History of England*. Fittingly, Dickinson referred to Hume to make the case that the English past was America's past, and that America owed obedience to the Crown as sovereign. Citing Hume as an authority on history over and over again, Dickinson regarded him as "this great man, whose political reflections are so much admired."[104] He also employed Hume to demonstrate that consent went to the very heart of English identity and history. Parliament had not played a part in the colonial story. Dickinson and other Americans, he argued, were planters—not just the planted—and as colonists they had the same rights as any other English subjects.

He cited Chatham a number of times, reciting part of the speech in which he intoned that Americans are "the sons, not the bastards of England."[105] Parliament, even if it safeguarded the virtue of the whole, could not raise revenue from America, because to do so was to tend toward tyranny. And, echoing Hume's logic and adding a twist to Charles's interpretation, Dickinson sensed a singular moment when history could move forward or regress. And individuals could play critical roles in the drama. Only now those in government in London were acting like James II had acted.

One idea that especially featured in Dickinson's letters was the notion that Americans, under the Townshend system, toiled as "slaves." As Dickinson explained, if Parliament could "order us to pay what taxes she pleases . . . we are as abject slaves, as France and Poland can shew in wooden shoes, and with uncombed hair." The idea that those who did not enjoy political liberty could be considered slaves represented a commonplace of the Whig tradition. People bandied about these terms in the wake of the passage of the Stamp Act. But Dickinson gave these ideas a political edge. Parliament was treating Americans worse than "strangers," those outside the political nation and in the realm of rebels, by attempting "to tear a privilege from her own children, which, if executed, must . . . sink them into slaves." Dickinson went a step further, declaring that because they were being treated like "bastards," unable to enjoy the basic rights of Englishmen, they had become "slaves." Their lives, under the new understanding of sovereignty, would engender ones of drudgery and shame. For Charles, provincial status meant Americans had to accept specific roles for the whole to function properly; for Dickinson, such a categorization entailed servile status.[106]

Dickinson clearly saw what was afoot. "Some persons," he lamented, "may think this act of no consequence, because the duties are so *small.*" Such a belief was "a fatal error." He went on, "I am convinced that the authors of this law, would never have obtained an act to raise so trifling a sum, as it must do, had they not intended by it to establish precedent for future use." Here was system. "Unless I am greatly mistaken," Dickinson wrote, "if these purposes are accomplished, according to the express intention of the act, they will be found effectually to supersede that authority in our respective assemblies, which is most essential to liberty." This act, he believed, because of what it was intended to do, was "more dreadful than the *Stamp-Act.*"[107]

Dickinson struck a chord. The same issue of the *Pennsylvania Gazette,* which honored the dead Charles and tried to make sense of his estimable abilities, sang the praises of the second *Farmer's Letter.* One letter writer from the College of Philadelphia explained how his town went so far as to draw up, in his words, "instructions for our Representatives, in which . . . you will perceive that we pursue the Principles laid down by your worthy Farmer, concerning the late Act of Parliament imposing Duties on Paper, Glass, etc., being unconstitutional." The writer wished Dickinson "the greatest Success in his laudable Attempts to convince his Countrymen of their just and most important Rights, and to rouse them in their Defence."[108]

Nineteen of twenty-three English-language newspapers serialized the *Letters,* and community after community in the colonies—following the lead of Boston—published resolutions thanking Dickinson, who was now hailed as "the AMERICAN PITT. Communities met and voted to give the thanks of the town to Dickinson for the *Letters,* "wherein the rights of the American subjects are clearly stated and fully vindicated." New Yorkers toasted "the Farmer of America." On St. Patrick's Day, Philadelphians did the same, as they also raised glasses to Parliament and to the Irish, whom they characterized as likewise struggling for their rights in the empire. The *Virginia Gazette* noted, "Mr Dickinson's Farmer's Letters have carried his name and reputation all over the British dominions." Pennsylvanians argued that his points were "excellent and unanswerable."[109]

When bound together, the *Letters* would become the most-read American pamphlet until *Common Sense,* going through seven editions.[110] Even one of his chief detractors, Francis Bernard, conceded that Dickinson possessed admirable abilities. Before he knew Dickinson was responsible and after reading just a few, Bernard noted that Boston's "Faction" did not have "a Writer of Abilities equal to this Work." The *Letters* would, he feared, find a readership in Boston and New York's newspapers "and I suppose in all others upon this Continent." It seems Dickinson had crystallized what the imperial relationship should be. Ezra Stiles, who later became president of Yale, summed it up best: the *Letters* "alarmed and opend my Eyes."[111]

Throughout the colonies, men and women adopted his phrases and embraced his reasoning, offering the surest example of how what Dickinson said framed how the imperial relationship was being redefined. His understanding, for instance, that the duties were passed for "the sole and express purposes of raising a revenue" became a mantra in America, carried in nearly every newspaper between Portsmouth and Savannah and quoted by Bostonians in a petition to the king. Dickinson used these words eleven times. He emphasized the phrase to try to delimit in specific terms Parliament's powers and to lay out exactly Parliament's relationship to the assemblies. Those who employed the phrase followed it with a clear indication that they knew the duties on glass, tea, paper, and paints were proposed "for the payment of necessary charges of the administration of justice, and the support of civil government." Dickinson's words focused American minds on what Parliament could and could not do and what assemblies were designed to do. Americans knew the duties compromised their assemblies. The words Dickinson repeated, therefore, suggested that although the stumbling block over the duties may have been taxation, it was incidental. The real issue centered on sovereignty, how it would be exercised, where it was located, and why it should now be defined to structure the empire.[112]

Although he would be dubbed the "Penman of the Revolution" and "an American Burke," at this point Dickinson proved to be America's Abbé Sieyès.[113] In much the same way that famous figure from the French Revolution would invoke the idea of the "nation," as if an epiphany, to announce a new form of community that had taken shape but that had to be formally recognized in France, Dickinson offered his vision of empire, one at once simple and by no means novel but compelling, at a time people deemed critical. In the same vein that Sieyès's vision became a clarion call for all, articulating what others knew but could not quite put into words, Dickinson mobilized the thoughts of whole communities. What is the empire, he asked. It was not what Charles had envisioned. Many Americans were at that moment ready to appreciate and act upon these sentiments.

Ireland in this case represented the sum of all fears, "that poor kingdom," as Dickinson called it. "Ireland has," he argued, "with a regular consistence of injustice, been cruelly treated by ministers."[114] America's past, Dickinson reckoned, was not like Ireland's; but Ireland's past could become America's prologue if Townshend's plan worked. Again, he cited Hume in making the parallels. Colonists certainly did not believe that their past mirrored the difficult history of Ireland. Americans were not a subject, conquered people, and if they considered their past, they identified with the English narrative, not the marchland story. But if they did not act swiftly, they would suffer the fate the Irish had a century earlier. Ireland now was ruled by corruption, and the vexed relationship with Britain caused that corruption.[115] Dickinson's breakthrough was not so much to convince Americans to embrace seventeenth-century English discourse as to let them see that under the new system the seventeenth century that subordinated the Irish was now looming over them. All would be Ireland unless something were done quickly. This view, too, had great appeal. A writer in the *Providence Gazette,* for instance, warned: "The American estates are now very valuable, and if joined with the Kingdom of Ireland, would inevitably produce an immense sum to the mother country."[116]

Dickinson selectively remembered and selectively forgot. He accomplished all he did by relying on history every bit as much as Charles had, and reconceiving it as well. He lamented what he called "British prejudice" in trying to shackle the colonists and undermine their rights and assemblies.[117] He considered himself "English" and tried to make England's history that of the colonies. He refused to consider where he lived a province. He still inhabited a colony, but an English one untouched by the tumults that went into creating Britain and making Parliament supreme there. Parliament, a creation of and creator of Britain, could oversee the virtues of the whole, but it could not legislate for English America.

Dickinson, therefore, did much as Charles had done. Charles had tried to manipulate Britain's past to come up with a vision of unitary sovereignty. And in doing so he had forgotten America's seventeenth century, when the colonies had been planted with the blessing of the Crown. Dickinson, too, suffered from amnesia, but in his case he had forgotten the British American eighteenth century, when the colonies were becoming cultural and economic provinces of Britain with the integration of the Atlantic. He harkened back instead to the certainties of the seventeenth century and in doing so created a myth of America. It was never marchland and was only British up to a point. Born English, it remained English. It paid deference to Britain and its Parliament insofar as they sustained an Atlantic community. But community was not constitution. History, in other words, stopped at conception, ensuring that Parliament could only play a symbolically, not a substantively, sovereign role.

In this vein, Dickinson did not especially see a conspiracy afoot, and he was most assuredly not paranoid. He quite calmly argued that a system was being imposed, seeing reality for what it was and arguing that Americans had to act with a sense of urgency. He explained why by recasting the recent past—the Stamp Act—and the more distant past of the archipelago. The Townshend Acts, he argued, represented an "innovation," the sort historically applied in Ireland, but one that first had been tried in America in 1765, a year noted for "the violence of reformation." Dickinson, then, sketched "design," encouraging Americans to connect chronological and geographic dots.[118] Ireland and America had differed; now they might share the same fate because of an unfolding plan to subordinate America unless the measures that Dickinson called for could bring the ministry to its senses.

Dickinson did not only provide definition and focus; he also produced a rallying point. The *Letters* proposed a strategy, attuned to the ideal of sovereignty he developed, to contest the Townshend system. Community after community hailed him and used his ideas as justification for any concerted political action. Assemblies working together would do the job that Parliament was supposed to do: to safeguard the integrity of the whole by inculcating virtue. Presumably, Parliament would learn its lesson by watching

Americans act. He was at pains to say that voluntarily refusing to consume British goods, and this was an old Irish trick, was asking Americans to do nothing illegal or nothing that would challenge the idea of Parliamentary sovereignty. But it would expose how Parliament had erred.[119]

This theme animated many Americans in 1768. The House of Representatives in Massachusetts Bay followed Dickinson's logic to the letter when it sent a circular to the other assemblies in North America. Written by Samuel Adams, the circular resulted from eighteen days of preparation and fulmination. Francis Bernard prophesied what the letter portended. "This present undertaking," he told Shelburne, "is calculated to inflame the whole Continent, and engage them to join together in another Dispute with Parliament, about the Authority of the latter."[120] On this, he was mainly right. Asking the colonies to "harmonize with each other" to contest the duties, the circular also conceded that "His Majesty's high court of parliament is the supreme legislative power over the whole empire." The constitution, however, was "fixed," and local assemblies had the right to tax. "Consent" lay at the very heart of Britishness. The representatives used Dickinson's terms when they said, "Imposing duties on the people of this province with the sole and express purpose of raising a revenue are infringements of their natural and constitutional rights," because they were not represented in Parliament. Their assembly was "a subordinate legislature," but their rights were vested there, and they could not "be reduced in effect to a tributary state." Connecticut followed suit. New Jersey then did much the same, citing Dickinson's language to justify its position. In fact, the assembly there was fixated with the Massachusetts circular, discussing it, as an official alleged, "Day to Day for a course of more than Three Weeks." Pennsylvania took this path in July, as did New Hampshire, again invoking Dickinson's words "sole purpose of raising a revenue" as justification for banding together with other colonies to protect the integrity of local assemblies in the face of the duties. Virginia also sent around its own circular condemning the duties. Even Georgia's assembly issued a resolution.[121]

In London the government responded vigorously. The first Earl of Hillsborough, secretary of state for the newly established American Department, advised all governors to prorogue their assemblies if they heeded the advice of the people from Massachusetts. He then asked Francis Bernard as governor to force the Massachusetts Assembly to rescind the circular. He also ordered military commanders in North America to prepare their troops to move to Boston if needed. Ultimately, Bernard would prorogue the assembly after Samuel Adams had issued a series of "Resolves" condemning the governor, and by implication the government in Britain, for treating the colony as a conquered territory. The assembly, for its part, rejected what Hillsborough demanded by a vote of ninety-two to seventeen. From then on, in these years, ninety-two became a number of great symbolic significance for patriotic opinion.[122]

Even South Carolina issued a petition. Southerners, afraid of the potential of slave risings in their midst, did not contest British measures with the same vigor as northerners. Nonetheless, the duties affected them and the autonomy of their general assemblies. In January 1769, South Carolina took up the matter. The royal governor asked the members of the assembly to "treat with the Contempt it deserves, any Letter or paper that may appear to have the least Tendency to Sedition, or by promoting an unwarrantable Combination, to inflame the Minds of the People, to oppose the Authority of Parliament." The assembly members, however, joined their northern peers. Any letters they received, they accurately asserted, "Are replete with Duty, and Loyalty to his Majesty, Respect for the Parliament of Great Britain, [and] sincere Affection for our Mother Country." That said, they argued that they had to send a "loyal Address" to the king "humbly imploring his Royal Protection and interposition with the Parliament, to relieve his American Subjects from the grievances they labour under in Consequence of the late Acts passed for raising a Revenue in America." The proceedings were aired as far north as Connecticut.[123]

Soon, following Massachusetts's lead and Dickinson's advice, Americans were refusing to import British goods, a practice that struck right at the ways America and Americans had been integrated into the Atlantic. Ironically, they chose this strategy to contest measures Charles had engineered. "Daughters of Liberty" from Charlestown in Massachusetts "offered to spin one day" for a local clergyman and produced enough yarn to make six linen shirts. Harvard students followed suit when they "agreed to take their Degrees the next Commencement in the Manufacture of their own Country." This story was told elsewhere in newspapers, demonstrating how networks were evolving as well. Soon after, Yale students promised to do the same. The well-known tale of nonconsumption, nonimportation, the creation of networks of resistance, and the virtues of homespun goods dates from this moment. Townshend and the Farmer had provided a focus for all to reconsider the relationship of metropole to province and to act accordingly. All in all, by mid-January 1768, just a month after the first of the *Farmer's Letters* was published, twenty-four towns had resolved to abide by boycott agreements. Soon New York and Charleston would follow. As one scholar puts it, "The Townshend Acts . . . changed American resistance from a minority protest to a mass movement."[124]

Critics emerged. Most interestingly, as one scholar argues, J. Hector St. John de Crèvecoeur, the famous author of *Letters from an American Farmer,* may have first drafted his essays to contest Dickinson's understanding of parliamentary power. He was hardly alone. The governor of Georgia argued that Dickinson had "sown the seeds of sedition," which had found fertile ground. The *Boston Evening-Post* ran a series of rejoinders to the *Letters* entitled "Letters in Answer to the Farmer's." The writer summed up his thoughts by saying, "He who denies the authority of Parliament, denies the authority of the King." In one of the pieces, the author alleged that "the Farmer, when he came to distinguish between internal and external taxes, made the analysis with about as much skill as a quack surgeon would attempt to bleed a man with a chizzel or pick-ax." Yet, he went on to suggest that the Farmer had skills. He acknowledged Dickinson's use of subtlety when dealing with parliamentary sovereignty. "There are plenty of those in the colonies who deny this jurisdiction," the writers charged, but not Dickinson: "The Farmer has, indeed, several times in the course of his letters, by a kind of perplexity of expression, acknowledged it in part." He then "took a step too far towards cloathing our assemblies with sovereignty." In the author's mind, Dickinson slipped up here. Once he declared "a subordination to the British Parliament," the Townshend ideal that assemblies had no sovereign power or authority had to hold sway.[125]

His enemies, therefore, conceded that Dickinson had set the terms of debate. He was, according to his critic in the *Boston Evening-Post*, "an industrious spider." Even his harshest opponent, a writer calling himself N.P., who embraced the Townshend vision of empire, conceded that the logic of the Farmer had transfixed America. "The Country," he wrote in a series of letters, "has been deluded and led almost into a state of rebellion by the magic of a tribunitian author, who stiles himself a Farmer." Dickinson, he charged, had crafted a false idol, to which the common people paid homage. In a period marked by confusion, or "hurly burly," only one certainty existed, the one Dickinson tried to have the people refute: "an absolute jurisdiction of the British parliament over the properties and persons of the Colonists, *in every respect.*"[126]

Dickinson had confused the people and blinded them to this essential truth, especially with the mantra of "sole and express purpose of raising a revenue," which had no basis in reality. N.P. likened Dickinson to a delusional Don Quixote, who "contrary to the advice of *Sancho,*" attacked flocks of sheep, claiming them to be an army. Tragically, N.P. suggested, most Americans saw armies and a system of tyranny where he believed none existed.[127]

The Farmer, and many Americans throughout the colonies, thought otherwise. They had met an integrated vision that animated Charles with one of their own. As Benjamin Franklin told his son William, Dickinson had ushered in a new world of understanding, as well as a new appreciation of Parliament's powers and bounds that would not admit compromise, certainly not with the Townshend vision. "I know not," he wrote, "what bounds the Farmer sets to the power he acknowledges in Parliament to 'regulate the trade of the colonies.'" Franklin saw "it difficult to draw lines between duties for regulation and those for revenue." He summed it up this way: "The more I have thought and read on the subject the more I find myself confirmed in opinion, that no middle doctrine can be maintained."[128]

George Townshend's Ireland

A Vision for Ireland

In much the same way as Charles had believed he was engaged in reform during an important window of time, George sensed he was going to Ireland at a critical juncture. "There never was a Time," he was convinced, "when the Service of the Crown stood more in need of its best Subjects." In a series of secret letters, one minister laid out the stakes involved in Ireland in 1767. The ministry feared the sort of crisis that was engulfing the colonies in America, and signs were pointing in such an ominous direction that summer. A Patriot leader named Henry Flood, one of the letters read, "moved a general censure upon the characters and capacity of the judges sent from England, with a view, no doubt, of inflaming the people against all nominations." Such an issue proved challenging for any viceroy sent to firm up the relationship between Ireland and Britain. "The popular party," the letter went on, "are sure to distress the castle to some degree every Session." "The castle" referred to the seat of British control in Dublin. The task of running the Castle without creating discord required poise and perspective. To rule Ireland, the ministry had hitherto used "places, pensions, and honors" among a select few to rule. But the prescription could prove more dangerous than the illness. The lord lieutenant could in theory rule with "ease to himself"; however, doing so "ruined the king's affairs, and enraged the people."[1]

By 1767, when the secret letter was written, the ministry was reevaluating its approach to Ireland. George William Hervey, Lord Bristol, had been appointed to the position of lord lieutenant in the preceding year. This, co-incidentally, is the same George Hervey who had sent George's mother a number of suggestive love letters years earlier. With Bristol's appointment, officials in London were considering whether the lord lieutenant would reside in Ireland. Before 1767, the lord lieutenancy represented a plum job for someone on the way up, a position of responsibility that still allowed the holder to live in England. It was also a job for someone on the way down. But it required little of the holder. In the absence of the lord lieutenant, the real work of executive administration, of standing in as the Crown's representative in the kingdom of Ireland, fell to a group of elites known as the lords justices. These were a mix of homegrown leaders in the church and in the state, as well as a few notable Englishmen dispatched to take up important places in Ireland.

Although the lords justices, in theory, did the real work of government when the lord lieutenant was across the water, even they had little of great consequence to do beyond doling out some spoils. Such was the case because Ireland was run like a twentieth-century Chicago ward. By the mid-eighteenth century, a group called the "undertakers" governed Ireland. For undertaking the tasks of the British administration, they received patronage, place, and positions, which they could then extend to others in exchange for political loyalty. Allowing the undertakers to run the government as what one historian calls "a Namierite paradise" enabled the ministry in Britain to ignore Ireland until, or if, some crisis gripped it. Letting others manage it—however corrupt—ensured that thorny constitutional issues did not have to be confronted. The undertaker system, therefore, guaranteed in some measure an out-of-sight, out-of-mind approach to governance.[2]

In fact, the whole arrangement reflected Ireland's hybrid status. How could one define Ireland's relationship to England and Scotland? Constitutionally, of course, it was a kingdom, one with its own Parliament. Few, however, could deny that it functioned as a colony of Britain, in much the same way Massachusetts or Barbados did. The gray area between the two categories had made it difficult to design both a rationale and a way for ruling Ireland effectively. How did one, after all, "rule" a sister kingdom? How could one do justice to Ireland's status as kingdom yet derive benefits from it as colony? And how did one make this kingdom/colony secure? Moreover, no clear relationship existed between executive and legislature. Accordingly, the Castle had little effective control over what happened in the Irish House of Commons. Mediators were, therefore, necessary, but because patronage became their price, corruption defined how ambiguous relationships functioned. All of these considerations had to be addressed before Ireland could meaningfully contribute to and benefit from the whole. Successive ministries understood the nature of the conundrum. In the 1750s and early 1760s, officials had tried to challenge the prevailing arrangements, airing ideas that George would implement fully during his viceroyalty. What had been missing was the urgency of the moment. Ireland, neglected up to now, would have to be reformed for many of the same reasons Charles had focused his efforts on America.[3]

Lord Bristol, however, never made it to Ireland. He resigned his position as lord lieutenant, ostensibly for health reasons, before he ever set foot in the kingdom. The position opened up, as it appears much else did in the year 1767, by chance. Into the breach stepped George Townshend.

While Charles was laying out his imperial plan in Parliament, Chatham summoned George to offer him the lord lieutenancy. The exact details of why remain murky. One story goes like this: By July 1767, rumors were swirling of George being asked while Charles was voicing dissatisfaction with the way Chatham's governing "arrangement" was evolving. George, then, received the position in Ireland through Charles's influence and efforts, "to please his brother," as Horace Walpole argued. A second interpretation suggests that Charles demanded the post for his brother for agreeing to take the Exchequer position in the first place. Another insider claimed George won the position once Charles "promised his assistance" to Chatham "with every profession of attachment."[4] Given the brothers' previous stances, any other possibility beyond these seems remote.

Historians have debated whether or not George made the decision himself to reside in Dublin during his viceroyalty. They have also asked whether that determination was made before his viceroyalty or during it. We may never know the answers, but it appears that the Chatham administration had decided that residence in the kingdom could secure a better relationship between Ireland and Britain. George would be the first lord lieutenant to live in Ireland on a regular basis, and he would make the point during his viceroyalty that constant residence was critical to maintaining a system that functioned. What is beyond debate is the vision and the perseverance that George brought to the job.[5] As he took the post, he had no intentions of working by half measures. He would, he declared, be motivated by what he called "Duty to the Publick" and an "Ambition to execute my Commission to the King's Approbation."[6]

The lord lieutenant, hoping to reform relationships, faced quite a challenge. He had to appreciate the distinctive cultures of English and Irish political life while devising a workable strategy. Ironically, the more thoughtful brother, Charles, had taken up the more straightforward assignment of reforming the relationship with America, even though he demonstrated an admirable tactical edge to move his reforms through Parliament. The task at hand for George required patience, dexterity, and grace and was given to a man who had not manifested these talents before. As George put it after he had spent some time in the kingdom, the job required "Delicacy."[7] It also demanded a quality George had demonstrated all too often in the past: stubborn tenacity.

The specific task the ministry charged him to accomplish would make his assignment more difficult still and call on all of his skill. At this juncture in time and from this place, Britain needed more troops. Clearly, George took up his post in Ireland to accomplish this end. He knew how pressing the empire's manpower problem had become.[8] Stretched almost to the breaking point as the British had to protect so many exposed and vital frontiers, and in the wake of American urban unrest that had demanded a pronounced military presence, the empire could be undone if more bodies could not be found to fill the ranks. As a military man, who had fought for empire and for a militia, George had spent his professional life, it is fair to say, fixated on the issue of manpower.[9] From his first letters back to the ministry in 1767, just as he was acquainting himself with the people he would have to do business with in the kingdom, he was already discussing the issue. "More troops," he would write a year later, "are wanting in America, in Ireland, and in England." He would, however, have to determine how to secure more bodies for empire and also how political relationships would have to change to make this possible, and the task would not be straightforward. "Lord Townshend will, I think," Grenville predicted, "meet with many Difficulties, and his undertaking the Charge of Ld Lieutenant of Ireland under all the present Circumstances seems to me very hazardous."[10]

On 12 August 1767, the king announced that George was assuming the position of lord lieutenant of Ireland. He officially instructed George to learn all he could about Ireland, including what was "amiss," to see to it that troops were quartered adequately, to survey the castles and forts of the kingdom, to ensure wool was not traded beyond the kingdom, and to advise the king "of every Man's particular Diligence and Care, in our Service there."

These were the usual instructions for any lord lieutenant. Yet, George was not handed a firm set of directions on how to proceed. Indeed, he was leaving for Ireland in what one person called a "sulky" mood, "provoked at their [the ministry] doing nothing, either by way of instruction or support." Although he learned just before he sailed that he would have certain tools at his disposal to win some good will from the Irish, he would have to work out a strategy for securing more troops from Ireland, or an "augmentation" of the existing arrangement, as it was called, when he arrived.[11]

On 9 October, he set off for Dublin. Though a far cry from London in terms of size and significance, Dublin was one of Europe's leading cities and the second city of the empire. George spent much of his time working in Dublin Castle, the site where the English had ruled the Pale for centuries and whence they had attempted to subdue the rest. In the side of the Castle by an old medieval tower, the lord lieutenant presided, slept, and carried out his business. The building had just been renovated. The plasterwork, not so very different from that adorning Raynham's ceilings, was some of Ireland's best, subtle and beautifully crafted. The ballroom and public spaces were appointed for lavish entertainments, and George would outdo any previous lord lieutenant with the use of the state apartments. Balls at the Castle, for instance, became staples of the Dublin season. Outside, the courtyard had also recently been redone to reflect neoclassical tastes. Gates of Fortitude and Justice flanked the old tower and enclosed the cobbled courtyard, making for a new facade on the old Castle structure.[12]

The Castle, as much a symbol as a place and word suggesting central authority, stood as a reminder of a medieval past in a city developing quickly. On the edge of the city, new developments were sprouting up around stylish squares, which would give Dublin its signature Georgian style. Trinity College, punctuating the Castle's environs and newer areas such as Merrion Square, was also undergoing an eighteenth-century refashioning. Across from the main entrance to the college had arisen the splendid Parliament building, a large, well-proportioned structure with classical lines and appointments. By anyone's standards, the building bespoke self-confidence and status.[13] Although a provincial place in the broader British world, Dublin boasted culture and style. The ears of Dubliners, to cite just one telling example, were the first to hear Handel's *Messiah*. And with Swift and Goldsmith, the city had given birth to some of the finest writers in the English language.

For his country estate, George chose the home of some of the leading politicians in Ireland, the Connollys, a place in Kildare called Leixlip Castle. From time to time, the Connollys rented out the place. Ironically, earlier in the century William Connolly, the Speaker of the House, had been Ireland's most famous undertaker. About ten miles from the city, Leixlip lay upon the river Liffey by one of Ireland's great natural wonders, a much-imaged salmon leap. The place was also a strange mix of well-appointed Georgian and medieval, fitting for a ruler who hoped to reform but would have to do so amid the old divisions that had defined the history of the kingdom. Leixlip took on greater importance than serving as a summer residence. There George would spend hours hosting Ireland's great and good, especially those unconnected to the undertakers but with whom he would find ways to cooperate. He also had access to a library as large as the one he had grown up with at Raynham. All in all, it was a place suited to a man of George's temper and aspirations.[14]

In the first months after his arrival, George worked to acquaint himself with the principal men of the kingdom. He received warm wishes from the leading politicians, including John Hely-Hutchinson, one of the leaders in Parliament and a notorious place hunter, and from those who opposed such men. For instance, Charles Lucas, leader of the Patriots, wrote "a very candid and friendly Letter" on George's arrival. Most of the welcomes were self-serving. Connections, as much as in England if not more so, made the kingdom go round, and so currying favor with a new lord lieutenant made good business and political sense. Apprentices, attorneys, politicians, landowners, prelates, and middle-class Catholic businessmen from all over the kingdom sent in their words of congratulations.[15]

George's next order of business involved appointing an able chief secretary. His chief secretary would have to be someone of esteem both in this kingdom and in Britain, as he would have to do business on a daily basis with the grandees of Ireland and to travel to Britain to treat with the ministry. George selected a man who may well have been one of his mother's former lovers, Lord Frederick Campbell, as his first chief secretary. Campbell came from a prominent Scottish family that had served the British cause for generations. He also, most critically, had sat in the Irish Parliament. The other man who served in this capacity from 1769, Sir George Macartney, was as well connected as Campbell, through Butite patronage. His family also had deep roots in Ireland. Macartney had acquired solid legal training and had gained experience with the British world of trade and diplomacy, having served as envoy to Russia. In addition, George would employ Thomas Allan as a lobbyist in London, a man one historian describes as "clever, diligent, tactful and indefatigable."[16]

The first initiatives George sponsored seemed to confirm the good opinion of nearly all. In fact, he cultivated approval by design. In a move calculated to win broad support, he let it be known that he would support a bill to limit the duration of Parliaments. The British ministry also allowed him to push for bills securing the tenure of Irish judges, a militia bill, similar to the one he had sponsored in Britain, and a Habeas Corpus Act. Of these, the so-called septennial bill proved the most vital. Nearly all Irishmen, save the undertakers whose power stemmed from the absence of popular accountability and regular elections, could agree that limiting election to the death of one monarch and the accession of the next seemed to contradict the principles of the Glorious Revolution. The Patriots, who regarded themselves as heirs to the revolution, had long called for a septennial bill. George ultimately sponsored an octennial bill, justifying the subtle difference because the Irish Parliament usually met every second year. This initiative would turn out to be an important aspect of his plan.[17] The ministry in England, hoping that the measure would ensure that Ireland remained quiet in these difficult years, supported the idea. It passed through the Irish Parliament with hardly a whimper. The Irish Privy Council and the British one did not even take heed of the measure, so uncontroversial did it seem on both sides of the water.

George was preparing the ground for his main purpose in Ireland, one that on the surface appeared straightforward but that raised a number of vexing questions. He primarily wanted to tap into Ireland's human wealth, to ensure that it would serve in some capacity as an arsenal of empire. Although we use the term "arsenal" to describe how Highlanders filled the ranks of the British army after the '45, Ireland played a similar role for the British state. It, too, provided manpower for empire. But it could supply more. More precisely, George planned to request a larger Irish military establishment that adhered to British standards. Bringing Irish units up to full British strength, creating uniformity, allowed troops from Ireland to be dispatched to replace other British units. It also increased the number of troops the Irish would have to pay for. Although it was understood that any augmentation would secure more troops from Ireland, these troops might or might not come from the kingdom.

Many Protestants worried about cost, just as they voiced concerns over what augmentation would entail for the security of Ireland. Ireland's Parliament had the responsibility of paying for troops raised for British service. That number had for some time been set and adhered to. Only in times of emergency in Ireland, especially if and when the Ascendancy was imperiled, did the Parliament think it imperative to raise more money to enlist more troops. The crisis now faced, however, was imperial in scope, and troops were sure to be dispatched elsewhere. Even though the Irish Treasury enjoyed budget surpluses in these years, Parliament was not keen to pay to fill such ranks.[18] Its members feared Catholics in their midst, especially if Protestants were siphoned off to secure empire. Catholics could not bear arms or, in theory, enlist. If Protestant soldiers served abroad, the kingdom could be threatened by disaffected Catholics.

Despite the pressing and delicate nature of the task at hand, George would encounter problems Charles did not have to deal with. He had only unsteady support from home, which compounded his worries, so much so that Edmund Burke exclaimed that because George had not received concrete instructions, he had "patched and pieced them together himself." That was putting it charitably. The ministers in Britain fretted over what could happen in Ireland once augmentation was broached. They feared Irish mobs and another, more proximate crisis like that of America. Although they wanted a quiet Ireland, they gave little direction on how to negotiate the many tensions involved in pressing for augmentation. George III fumed, "All the Irish Patriots are daily increasing their demands," yet augmentation had not been implemented. In the king's eyes, Ireland should not operate any differently from the way England or Scotland did.[19]

Officials at home, particularly Shelburne, upbraided him for not making "sufficient" progress, as George complained, even if they failed to give him clear directions. George countered that the ministry in Britain had no idea how different Ireland was. The lord lieutenant had no power because the undertakers controlled all major patronage. George had nothing to work with. He was trying, he explained, to influence the political power brokers of the kingdom, but this would take either patience or a firmness that Britain was not yet willing to subscribe to. In the meantime, he was spending his time trying to win friends and influence the right people. He had, as he put it, "Neither exercise, nor sleep, nor comfort of any sort" and he complained, "My boots [are] on from 7 in the morning . . . till near 5 in the evening."[20]

George seethed over Shelburne's rebukes, but in fairness Shelburne, once confronted, applauded him for the way he had worked with the Irish Parliament and assured him the ministry in Britain appreciated the difficulties he faced.[21] He told George how the British Parliament had proposed a measure that would raise the number of troops on the Irish establishment to more than fifteen thousand men. Shelburne was quick to concede that twelve thousand would be "kept within the Kingdom of Ireland for the Defense thereof," as George had explained that the Irish would never vote for an augmentation that would deprive the kingdom of troops to defend the Protestant interest if necessary. Shelburne left it up to George to decide when and how augmentation would be presented to the Irish Parliament. After all, it would have to pay.[22] And so George had two assignments: to see that the budget passed by the Irish Parliament would support an augmentation of troops supported by the Irish establishment; and to have that augmentation passed through the Irish Parliament. As soon as he sponsored the bill for the limitation of the Irish Parliament, George turned his attention to these difficult issues.

He did not meet with immediate success. In fact, he succeeded in doing something few could hope to pull off: he united Ireland's various political factions, notably undertakers and Patriots, in an alliance, but one destined to defeat his schemes. At the most basic level, George had not built a base of support outside the undertakers and so still needed their votes. Indeed, the octennial bill alienated them, as it struck at the heart of their power, namely, complete autonomy from any electorate.[23] At another level, he had not tried to work with the Patriots in exchanging augmentation for other measures they favored. George, in short, had agreed with the idea that he should reside in Ireland and that he intended to remake the system, but he had not done the things necessary to ingratiate himself to the distinctive customs and culture of Irish politics.

On 19 April, the augmentation measure failed in the Commons by 105 to 101. Even though George had barely lost, it seemed clear, given the hurdles he faced, that any hope for a permanent settlement, one that could meet manpower demands over the long haul without political drama, required a thoroughgoing strategy. He grew incensed with the defeat. His plan had endured "unconstitutional and Insolent attempts in defiance of its authority," which would, he promised, "never prevail over Legal and Parliamentary Jurisdiction." The Irish, he said, had to "decide whether we are to be the subjects of a King or the Slaves to a Mob." And he would not relent. "I observe the least Concession is a mark of great Disunion and severity in Government," he fumed, "and a Removal is a matter of great Triumph to a sett of Men, who have no Plan or System, but can alone derive their Consequence from the Confusion they create." Nor would the other side surrender. "The Speaker [John Ponsonby] and Ld. Shannon," two of the chief undertakers, George complained, "in the interim are indefatigable in Strengthening their Ground."[24]

He resorted to brinksmanship. He began to implement his program in earnest not with the Octennial Bill, nor even with augmentation, but with something called a Money Bill. With this, George was initiating a dispute. In effect, he tried to dictate Ireland's budget and allocations, the money that would be spent, with the direct input of Britain's Parliament. In doing so, he did not pay deference to precedent or the convoluted ways Ireland's Parliament had dealt with its inferior status. The money bill was not, as was the custom, sent to Britain as "heads of a bill," or as an outline of proposed legislation that would be drafted in Dublin and passed on to the Irish and British Privy Councils, before the Irish Parliament voted on it. Such a process suggested that the Irish in some fashion controlled their own purse strings. George now struck at this arrangement.

George's challenge was accepted. George was not only contesting one of the chief prerogatives of the Irish Parliament; he was also resurrecting the terms of a vitriolic debate over a Money Bill that had chilled the relationship between Protestant Ireland and the British ministry in the 1750s. This episode had exercised Lucas and given rise to a vocal, albeit short-lived, Patriot resistance. In what became his first struggle to reform Ireland, George once again tried to win from Ireland's Parliament its nearest and dearest right. As he put it in the wake of the augmentation reversal, "To enlarge the ground of Government, and to recover its vigour and authority . . . depends upon English Government to pursue and confirm this system," because "until this is done, the Lord Lieutenant is a mere pageant of State."[25] When the Money Bill the Castle proposed failed in the House, the one now elected under the Octennial Act, George prorogued the Parliament.

George was now courting crisis, and his masters in London knew it even if they could not offer sound advice because they were of two minds. Townshend was asked to dispatch his chief secretary, Lord Frederick Campbell, to London to answer some questions about his plans for Ireland.

Ministers grew concerned over "Heats and animosities," the "hazardous" implications of pushing too hard for augmentation, as well as what might happen with so many "lower Class People" in Dublin idle because of prorogation. Yet, officials in London were so consumed with augmentation that they did not seem to care what methods George used. Campbell learned as much in 1768 when he met with the king and with the ministry to explain the strategy George was crafting. Augmentation, he counseled, would be "difficult if not dangerous" at this juncture. Campbell discussed how George hoped to use any impasse as a way "to form such a Government as would carry through the Publick Business with Ease to the Crown and Security to Ireland."[26]

Ultimately, the assembled ministers did not quibble too much about strategy but demanded results. "I found the single Point attended to," Campbell reported, "was the augmentation, to which all their Questions led, and upon which I thought their Decision of pushing it on to the utmost was in fact taken." After the meetings, Campbell relayed the message to George that "your Ideas about the Augmentation will be adopted." The "mode" of how this would be done was to be left to George. And ultimately, the ministers went along with George's plan to press for augmentation at this point, even if doing so meant disruption, and with his longer-term goals of redefining the relationship between Ireland and Britain. By 1769, they promised "all that support in the Administration of His Majesty's Affairs in Ireland." The king, they reassured George, would "arm you with the extensive Power of your own Plan."[27]

What followed demonstrated not only the virtues of George's stubbornness but also his political acumen and strategic thinking. With prorogation, the work began in earnest. With Parliament out of session and no political business being accomplished, George used the interlude to prepare to undermine the undertakers and to create a style of government that would have infuriated the patriots. However different the particular circumstances, George was effectively doing what Charles had done in 1767. He was putting first things first by fastening on system, the word they both used over and over again in so many different contexts to suggest institutional order, proper priorities, and fit between broad vision and constituent elements, be they parliamentary or imperial in scope. System was needed before the province could provide for empire. "It is alone by a determined resolution of adhering to system," he wrote as if channeling Charles, "and by constant perseverance on the part of English Government, that its authority and superintendence can be thoroughly maintained and established in Ireland."[28]

After his run-ins with Shelburne, George assiduously kept London up to date with his plans. Wisely, he worked with those he was personally closest to. He plied them with a steady stream of detailed letters that both informed and cajoled. They included his friend Lord Grafton as well as other well-connected political allies. Even though the ministry had trusted George with the reins, he pressed these officials to ensure that they would support his strategies, and they proved more sympathetic than Shelburne, in tone and in substance. George knew that if he were to reform Ireland, some of the most powerful officials there would have their noses bent out of shape, and they would be apt to complain to their friends in England. He worked to forestall such attempts, just as he was suggesting to the ministry that augmentation depended on steady backing of his methods, including providing pensions and peerages for those who had become his friends.[29]

George also did nearly as much preparation as Charles. He traveled far and wide to assess the situation of Ireland for himself and spent time studying the kingdom's capacity to provide manpower. Like Charles, he did his homework by, for instance, reading about the linen trade and Ireland's woolen manufacturing; the former powered the economy, and the latter, some hoped, would do so if Britain would allow Irish woolens to compete on the British market. He prepared budget studies and, most important, read up on the relationship between Ireland's population and the kingdom's economic potential. He drafted reports on the military preparedness, forts, and barracks of the kingdom as well.[30]

Through his studies, he learned of "the oppressed and wretched condition" of Catholics, who would pose a great problem should an invasion occur. Only the British fleet, "the submission of the wealthy Roman Catholicks to His Majesty's Government," and troops served as the guarantors of defense for the kingdom. One had only to explore the westernmost regions of Cork and Kerry and see the true nature of the threat. Here lived "the remnants of the old Popish Clans who kept up a constant Correspondence with France and Spain for smuggling, for Recruits, and for Deserters." Disaffection led the men there to join the armies of France, further compromising Ireland's military potential. These were "a lawless People, mostly armed, frequently forming themselves into Banditti, defying Laws and magistrates, and committing the greatest Outrages." Troops had to march in even for common executions.[31]

One report George commissioned portrayed Ireland as a poor kingdom, no doubt, but one of untapped potential. The report looked into the causes of "the distressed situation of the Poor of this Kingdom and how the same may be remedied." George also studied how "Controverseys and discord" between and among subjects could be eased, as well as methods "on promoting Religion, Agriculture, and manufactures amongst the People." Presumably, most viceroys would have done the same. George, however, did so with an eye to empire and its needs. The report that was presented to him was, for instance, concerned with emigration; at this point migration to America was picking up again. Yet, whereas earlier viceroys and lords justices had voiced similar concerns about the emigration of Protestant subjects, suggesting that if their numbers dipped Catholics would grow in strength, this report concerned itself not with confession but with "the Emigrations of the Poor." Ireland, it argued, could not lose inhabitants, because, echoing theorists of the day, the wealth of a nation depended on population. Tithes, rural insurgency, poverty, lack of industry—all conspired to leave Ireland vulnerable to intrigue. It was, the report continued, "high time something should be done to remedy these great National Evils."[32]

At issue was the good of the empire. Migration, in particular, even to the colonies in America, represented "a loss to the nation of Strength and Publick Stock." Ireland could be "a kind of nursery for sailors when ever their Service Should be wanted," and presumably for soldiers, too. The linen trade had to be protected by Britain. Other industry should be encouraged as well. Development, and by extension manpower for empire, depended on "one Common Interest" between Ireland and Britain. The lord lieutenant would have to avoid "rais[ing] Jealousies and Distrust between two Nations (under the same Sovereign)." Most explosively, the report even toyed with the idea of "relaxing" penal laws, as "the temper [of] the present times [was] much changed from what they were when the Penal Popery Laws were passed." Maybe Catholics, after all, could be persuaded to support the state.[33]

Corruption for a Kingdom

The Irish problem, as far as George was concerned, stemmed from the corrupted nature of the relationship between the two kingdoms, something he realized now had to be remedied. He had two methods at his disposal. On one hand, he could create inducements for the Irish to support what he continually called "English government." One such way, and a means to avoid the Irish finding "common cause" with Americans, involved allowing the Irish to send certain goods to Britain on a duty-free basis. Such a measure would encourage manufacture. So, for instance, George suggested that coarse woolens could be produced in Ireland and sent to Britain, Spain, and Portugal. He also hoped that candles and soap could be exported freely to England. Checked and printed linen should also be encouraged. Throughout his stay in Ireland, George would support such overtures because they could fasten Ireland more securely to England.[34]

On the other hand, he could resort to the sort of "discord" the ministry argued had to be avoided. He could use what one minister called the "mutinous" in Ireland for his broader purposes in much the same way Charles had employed New York's insolence. From 1767, when the crisis began, until his viceroyalty came to an end in 1772, he used corruption to undo what he regarded as corruption. In the short run, the strategy would secure augmentation. In the long run, George would do for Ireland what Charles had aimed to do for America. He would use the period of prorogation, as Campbell counseled, to "Judge with Precision where the Weight of Interest really is, and what can be done to add most to your Weight in Ireland, upon which the Success of your particular Friends must depend."[35]

George had chosen a daunting assignment, so well entrenched had the corrupt system become. Each undertaker had personified the corruption he decried, "straining every Conexion and Obligation to the Crown to his own purposes, and torturing every Man's reserve whom he dares approach, with the most hostile propositions from their private Interests." The implications for the system were pernicious. "You may depend upon it," George declared, "that Faction here is trembling in its very lowest subterfuges and that English Government loses its opportunity to Reestablish itself." Ultimately, George came to appreciate that he had to outdo the undertakers at their own game by securing the support of gentlemen from the country independent of all factions and some "men of business," largely lawyers, some of whom had been attached to the undertakers.[36]

This could only be accomplished by leaving the Castle and even his retreat in Leixlip for the countryside. In 1767 and 1768, he focused his energies in Dublin. In 1769, he took what he called "his intended trip to the Interior parts of this Kingdom, with some friends whose assistance I believe, we shall experience in our future Endeavours here." Up to this point, he had had "no communication with the Powerfull Men whose weight in this Kingdom has enabled them to defeat the measures of the Crown." He needed to win them over in order to circumvent both undertakers and patriots. He had to work, he wrote, with "the considerable Interests of this Kingdom, more ready to adopt and support the King's measures, upon that Idea and Plan, which in my firm opinion can alone place His Majesty's Government upon that basis, by which it may henceforth act with Success and Dignity."[37]

He needed to shift those he met on his journey to a "preference of the measures of the Crown" from "the Cabals" that controlled patronage. This entailed wresting the control of plum positions from the hands of the corrupt. He first, therefore, had to have the ministry's support in making the best prizes his. Alas, the wrong set of men held "the power of creating or increasing salaries" and jobs, "a weight greatly superior to the . . . Patronage of a Chief Governour!" Reluctantly, the ministry supported George's plea to be allowed to make more appointments at his pleasure. George also realized he had to secure oversight of appointments to the Revenue Board, which controlled other moneyed positions in the kingdom. The ministry had suggested he overhaul the board; he hoped to go one step further by assuming control of its patronage instead, prying it away from the undertakers. Control of appointments to the board would, he argued, "give the Essential superiority and strength to the Government here." He could then work for the "Removal" of key undertakers and court some of the very same undertakers, promising the sort of patronage they had come to expect from London, only in this case he would serve as the broker.[38]

This task was not straightforward. The Revenue Board was in theory controlled by the lord lieutenant and the Irish Privy Council. Moreover, it was supposed to comprise two boards: one for customs and another for excise. With the rise of the undertakers, that control was lost, as was the old distinction. Commissioners on the Revenue Board, the chief of whom was John Ponsonby, the Speaker, determined who would serve with them and, therefore, who would win places and raises. George understood he had to win this power back, and he would make it his focus while Parliament was prorogued. Eventually, he came up with the idea of splitting the board back into two, effectively doubling the number of places he would have at his disposal. He also wanted one or two Englishmen appointed, those "regularly bred in the Revenue" and "Men of Sense." The cost of having two boards, he assured the ministry, could be offset with a duty on rum. The British ministry showed lukewarm support for his ideas, but his allies ended up supporting them. Grafton, for instance, counseled George to ensure the move was completely "defensible" so that he could counter the expected objections. True to Grafton's instincts, the undertakers contested the measures. And the Patriots, who decried George's corrupt tactics, tried to use Parliament to stymie his ability to appoint. Nonetheless, through George's dexterity and some strategic dismissals, the lord lieutenant would become the de facto first commissioner of the Revenue Board.[39]

Gaining control of place and position represented only a first step. Next, George had to operate like an undertaker, an especially challenging prospect for someone who had for so long preached the importance of virtue. Playing the undertaker could not be managed in a detached fashion. George had to engage with many actors in Ireland, often meeting them on their own terms, all with the hope of turning their wants, needs, and base instincts to his cause. Moreover, the game of political patronage in Ireland followed a number of scripts depending on status. In most cases, a potential client did not ask for favors. One was asked, or, more precisely, referred. Usually clients only approached to ask a favor if directed to. And one was not picky. So, for instance, Edward Chamberlayne wrote to George by opening with the following: "Mr. de Gray has informed me that your Excellency has thoughts of appointing me to some office in the arrangements which are likely to be made in your Government." He dared not ask for a specific post; instead, the note offered an opportunity to declare his allegiance to George. "It is my wish," he declared, "to be able to serve in any department where you might think proper to place me." Maurice Fitzgerald similarly promised to support George if he would secure a position as a customs officer in Dingle, on the barrack board, or in "any other thing."[40]

For the system to work, George cultivated those far down the status ladder. Here he could pick and choose whom to support to try to further his political agenda. When he let it be known that he would serve as chief dispenser of patronage, people sought to curry favor. Thomas Vereker of Limerick, like others in similar positions in Irish provincial towns, acted as a hinge between regional influence and power in Dublin. George sent him a note declaring, "I have too great a sense of the particular civilities and Attention I have experienc'd from you not to wish to have it in my power to make return in favour of your brother." Finding a position for Vereker's brother would offer "a Mark of my Regard." Vereker could, in other words, win local influence for George, which would prove useful in Dublin. Such men sat in Parliament and had connections to others who could support George. Later, after George had let him know of his regard, Vereker could ask to become barrack master of Limerick with the expectation of success. Loyalty paid. John Lees, who apparently had a change of heart sometime in 1769, shifting from an opponent of George's to a supporter, would still benefit from George's largesse. George spoke of "how far your sentiments are suddenly changed," for which he declared: "I have no doubt of my being able to reward your great services in a manner without hazarding the King's business here which it is my Duty to prefer to any other Consideration."[41]

Potential clients invented connections. Some made mention of their army service for the Crown, a time-tested strategy for securing the support of a lord lieutenant. Others played on George's emotions, using such pleas as a means to skirt protocol. Still others even sent their wives to try to win George's good graces. A petitioner who had helped put down a set of rural insurgents known as the Oakboys in 1763, upon receiving no position for his troubles, sent his wife to request something of George. This was for her an awkward moment, leading her to apologize for the "very uncommon procedure" of applying for help. "I hope you will," she pleaded, "rather pity and pardon a Woman's Weakness than be offended at it." The letter did not make much of an impression. On the back of it, George sketched out the openings and who would likely fill them, including deaneries, bishoprics, and livings. No one of the petitioner's ilk need apply, even if they had put down Oakboys. Audrey Orme similarly sent letter after letter to George, all without an answer. Yet she continued because, she told him, "one Rag of your Protection might make my Family as much beloved and admired in Publick as it is in Private Life." A number also wrote to George's wife, Charlotte, asking her to use her influence with her husband.[42]

Throughout his lord lieutenancy, it was clear that family mattered, and those who realized it tried to leverage George in the most personal way. One, for instance, requested "his Lordship's protection," as, he wrote to him, he had before approached "your Brother with his usual zeal where my interest was concerned." Henry Pelham Davies, an English petitioner for whom George found a position in the Irish establishment, claimed that he had a "connection" to George through Charles. Another, a "Professor Disney," who mentioned his "Connection with my [George's] Brother" in asking for a position, touched on a sensitive subject. George conceded "the memory of my Brother, his Recommendations and his Friends have ever been dear tho afflicting to me." What Disney asked, however, went too far. "You have given me *unnecessary affliction*," George thundered, as Disney's request "treat[ed] that nerve as if it had no Share of Sensibility."[43]

Ultimately, no matter the method used to approach George, a petitioner had to deliver. Someone writing near the end of George's term of office in Ireland even claimed he had given George bread and wine in Germany when George had served in the army. "Eaten Bread," the writer chided, "should not be forgotten, [and] One good turn deserves another." He then made what he called a "moderate" request, to be considered for "halfpay on the [Irish] establishment." George noted to his secretary that this was "a very improper request." George declared, "It would not become me to sign any Commission to which [a] Gentleman would not have his Christian name put to it." Friendship had its limits. Even his chaplain at Raynham Hall, who had asked for a position in Ireland without offering something in return, was disappointed.[44]

Persistence could pay off, even if a potential client did not follow protocol. Consider the case of Robert Clements, a member of the Irish Parliament from Donegal. As soon as George became lord lieutenant, Clements asked to be appointed to the linen board. George counseled him to look for another position, but Clements would not relent. When he learned of someone on the board dying, he tried to visit George in Dublin and Leixlip, apparently missing him each time. Undeterred, he sent letter after letter to George pleading to be appointed. Finally, after being fobbed off one too many times, he told George he had served him loyally in Parliament without asking for any other favor. But he had lost support in Donegal "owing to my having voted for the Augmentation." Finally, two years after his first petition, he wrote to George thanking him for "the Honour to appoint me a Trustee of the Linnen Manufacture." He then swore loyalty to George.[45]

Robert Fitzgerald also refused to take no for an answer. He urged George to consider his friend "Mr. Day," who earned only £200 a year under the Crown, for a post in Meath that would, Fitzgerald suggested, pay more but that would reimburse George handsomely politically. Fitzgerald must have scanned death notices throughout the kingdom, for he put Day up for positions in Meath, Kildare, Kerry, and Cork, all of which opened with a death of a holder. George delivered, but for Fitzgerald himself, whom George singled out for a lucrative post. Fitzgerald thanked him and declared, "[I shall] ever glory in being rank'd among the most zealous and sincere friends of your person and administration, and shall never omit any opportunity of proving with how much truth and respect I am, My Lord, your Excellency's most faithful and most obedient servant." What he called "friendship" bought a semblance of loyalty.[46]

Those on Ireland's highest rungs played by a different set of rules. They expected help without having to bow, scrape, or defer. They simply demanded. One even complained that George had not conferred an honor upon him "sooner," suggesting that he had the "inclination to support His Majesty's Government." The Earl of Altamount, John Browne, simply made a request, with none of the normal niceties, "that I may be promoted, to such a higher Rank of Nobility in this Kingdom." He claimed to have a great deal of money and influence and had demonstrated his loyalty in the past. He promised nothing now. Yet he could deliver. Altamount, who lived in Westport, worked for George's interests in Mayo, looking for openings and having them filled with people loyal to Altamount, each of whom would then support George. Another requested a peerage, and he too could produce. He promised he would name a "friend" that could be counted on for a vacancy in the Irish Commons once he moved to the House of Lords. Each would be a "firm friend to his Majesty's Royal person and government." Their conduct in Parliament would prove helpful. As one nobleman put it, "[I] take the liberty to address your lordship to request a favour," in this case an earldom, "[I am] encouraged from the disposition I see in your Lordship to oblige." George acceded to such demands when doing so would "advance the King's service here, as it will oblige a Nobleman in this Kingdom."[47]

Once George let it be known that the Castle now served as a center of patronage, Ireland's great figures asked him to consider what they wanted. Lord Carrick asked for help placing his second son in the military, which would encourage Carrick "to look upon it as a very high obligation conferred upon me." And George, if he could expect loyalty in the bargain, complied. Lord Donegall, for instance, an owner of large estates in the North whose tenants were engaged in the production of linen and thus a remarkably connected figure, did not even deign to follow the usual rituals when he addressed George. He simply asked "to have a place at the Linen Board" because, he wrote, "I have one of the greatest Estates in the County of

Antrim," as if George had to be told, "where the Linen Manufactures are carried on with great Spirit." He had "a superior right to a favour of this kind." The board oversaw the manufacture and trade of linen. Because linen was not privy to a tariff, as were other goods made in Ireland that competed with British manufacturers, ensuring that the trade thrived was critical for landholders like Donegall, whose tenants depended on sound markets to be able to pay their rents. He ended the letter by stating, "Nor should I wish to meet with a denial when I am sure I am so well Entitled to what I ask." Unsurprisingly, he won what he asked for, in this instance a plum spot on the Irish Linen Board, one of the most important positions in the kingdom.[48]

Soon grandees were inviting George to travel to their estates, as a visit by the lord lieutenant suggested that a landowner enjoyed privileged connections and could provide patronage for his clients as well. Having a great man in one's pocket certainly extended one's influence. Lord Belvedere produced a list of names he hoped George could place for him. Doing so, he suggested, would bolster George, as all he named were "friends of my Interests." As a rule George tried to cultivate these relations as vigorously as he could but only if doing so "strengthen[ed] the Hands of Government."[49]

Once George had embarked on the course he did, the work proved relentless. In 1771, he received a letter from his son, then at Eton and studying Xenophon, professing to be "extremely concerned" for his father. "You are so much confined to the Castle," he wrote, "that you seldom or never have any Exercise, as I know nothing can be more prejudicial to your health than the want of it." The wise petitioner recognized how wearisome George's work was. Charles Ossory of Kilkenny, for instance, did not "presume to present myself to your Excellency amongst Those, who haunt the Castle in the troublesome shape of Petitioners." Yet, of course, he asked for George to make an appointment "in my favour" and said he would "be as grateful as any of Them."[50] The sheer number of requests overwhelmed George. Indeed, it would be fair to say that just keeping up with them and seeing to friends of government took up most of his time from 1767 to 1769, the critical moment for reform in Ireland.

Patronage, of course, brought as well as bought obligations. William Ellis, who had asked for help placing one nephew in a bishopric and another on the Revenue Board, promised George that the newly appointed would retain, as he put it, "a just sense of the high obligation they are under to the King and to your Excellency and that they will shew it in every instance in their Power." One of the nephews indeed helped George with a vacant seat for Thomas-town. "I did no more than justice in declaring to you his zeal to support His Majesty's measures and to render your Government in Ireland, as far as lyes in his power easy and happy," Ellis wrote to George. The nephew, he continued, was "obliged to you for affording him the opportunity of giving you so essential a testimony of his desire of attaching himself personally to you and of his wish for meriting your favour and protection upon proper occasions."[51]

Those who would not be bought by the Castle were exiled to the same sort of wilderness George had endured after his run-ins with Cumberland and with Wolfe's memory. One who failed him would "not find a more sincere Friend than I might have proved," George wrote.[52] Another, Colonel Charles Tottenham, an aide-de-camp to him in Ireland, "was dismissed" for "having followed the speaker's Party during the session, particularly [in] the Great affair of augmentation." George's enemies had given Tottenham an appointment, which infuriated George, but also redoubled his resolve to destroy them. He would, he declared, convince "the Speaker of this Kingdom of the sense of the English Government." He continued, "If they submit, we shall find whether they will hereafter behave as they ought; if the contrary, we shall then have an open enemy to prepare against during the summer." The Castle would do all in its power "to consult and increase our Numbers."[53]

By the end of 1769, George had prepared the ground so well that he could call on the administration in London to rip the patronage away from recalcitrant undertakers and give him the powers. In one fell swoop, on 23 December 1769, he sent letter after letter to his allies in government advising them on which Irish official should lose which plum position, including some of the most powerful, like Ponsonby. He asked that Lord Shannon, for instance, be removed from a position in favor of "a most useful supporter." And that others be replaced on the Irish Privy Council. And that a number on the Revenue Board, such as Ponsonby, be removed or shifted to the Customs Board, a strategy in keeping with George's decision to split these. And that a few of his new supporters be given peerages.[54] The ministry acceded to his demands, and by doing so, enabled George to complete his task.

Ultimately, through his efforts and those of his principal secretary, George turned Dublin Castle into a center of Irish political life. On his side, he believed he had the idea that "nothing retards the King's measures, but the dread of the Country returning under the same people" and their "misdirection of the power of Government." Undoing the undertakers had, he believed, meant "confirm[ing] our friends." The strategy would ensure the "good disposition of the Kingdom in general to the King's service and its contempt for these People."[55] George had undone corruption through corruption, and in the process he had become the greatest man in the kingdom. And within a few years of his arrival, he had transformed Irish politics.

With votes in his pocket and with patronage streaming through his office, the wishes of the British Parliament could be translated effortlessly and seamlessly into action by the Irish Parliament. On 21 November 1768, augmentation had passed, just as George was beginning his work. This represented only a first step, though a necessary one. George had engaged in the sordid business he did to create a permanent system that could ensure Ireland would fulfill its role for empire. The transformation of the corrupt relationship between Ireland and Britain followed as soon as he had secured the votes to make the Castle the chief dispenser of patronage, a task completed by 1770 and helped by the support he received from the ministry and his friends. And this approach would define the rest of his term. Eventually, George would also win on the issue of money bills and, with that triumph, gain effective control of the kingdom. Finally, his allies in Britain could congratulate him on achieving what one described as "success little expected by your friends here, or adversaries in Ireland." What George had accomplished would prove "of infinite use to Government here, and all our ministers do you the Justice to confess it."[56]

What he had accomplished was to redress a political world in which, as he put it, "men have no system." He hoped to create a way of working that would bring order to all for the long term. What he called the "present weakness of government" had to be rectified with a strong Castle party animated by a clear vision. To counteract the "provincial cabal," much like America's assemblies, required "manly and dignified action on the part of English Government." Either "the party" would win or "the system" would. Because of George, the system prevailed, allowing Ireland to contribute its part to the broader Atlantic empire. More critically, he had accomplished all he did without having to touch on constitutional issues. No doubt he still endured struggles in achieving his goals. For instance, when he recalled the Irish Parliament in early 1771, some politicians had planned to make a show of force on College Green. George, however, dispatched troops, with swords drawn, to ensure that Parliament met without a hitch.[57] Usually, though, he did not have to resort to force.

In essence, the lord lieutenant became the chief undertaker, and Britain's agenda would no longer be held hostage to Ireland's Parliament. What the British Parliament wanted to do could be achieved effectively and efficiently, so long as the lord lieutenant retained enough votes by continually cultivating relations. Constant residence now proved critical to the job, as the work of patronage required vigilance and diligence. Political acumen, too, was needed. The lord lieutenant had to work to appreciate the shifting nature of political connections and exploit them. But now the position had real merit. The viceroy from this point on represented more than the Crown or the executive; he also served as the direct agent of the ministry, and by extension Parliament.

What George achieved, therefore, was union between the kingdoms by other means. The two islands would work as one, with a British Parliament at its head. Through his work of "Dispensing happiness to a whole Nation," as one client put it, what George did was effectively melt down the old animating distinction between colony and kingdom.[58] In making Ireland—constitutionally and practically—a province, he undid the ambiguities that had allowed such arrangements as the undertaker system to have taken root. The kingdoms were united, the British Parliament controlled the relationship, and Ireland could, in the minds of the ministry at least, supply its surplus manpower.

On paper, George may have had to concede that more than twelve thousand troops raised in Ireland would stay in Ireland and about twenty-five hundred would be fit for service abroad. In practice, larger numbers sailed in the service of empire from the moment augmentation passed, and this would continue through the Napoleonic Wars.[59]

George's Empire

George harbored even greater ambitions for Ireland. He believed that it could provide even more men for the army, if it could move beyond its past. Irish Protestants did not want to arm Catholics, especially in the service of the Crown. The chief perk of being a churchman in the kingdom was the ability to carry arms and, if called upon, to serve in the military. Catholics could do neither. Cracks, however, were appearing, even if few were willing to admit

that such was the case. During the Seven Years' War, especially as the Jacobite threat had waned throughout the British Isles, more and more Catholics
had been serving. As recruiting sergeants fanned out across Ireland looking
for bodies, they often looked the other way when Catholics enlisted. In most
cases, for common men service did not entail loyalty to the Hanoverians.
Irish-speaking Catholics still embraced Jacobitism, considered themselves
loyal to the exiled king of Ireland, and were not—at this point—republicans.
Increasingly as middle-class Catholics accepted the status quo in the wake in
the suppression of the Jacobite cause in Britain, joining the army did not
carry the same stigma it would have earlier in the century, nor did swearing
loyalty to the Hanoverians. While Catholics still served in the French service,
its popularity was waning, and for many the British service now became a
viable option.[60]

George recognized this changing reality and attempted to make straight
the crooked path Catholics walked into the British military by making what
was happening informally more formal. Doing so would keep them away
from the French army and also tie them more securely to the British cause.
So in 1770 George sent a letter to a secretary of state in Britain making his
case. He had been requested to raise troops by issuing what were called
"beating Orders," that is, by sending recruiting parties beating drums and
beating the bushes to find men for the service. He recognized that "the trade
and manufactures of Ireland are almost totally Carried on by the Protestants," conceding their number was "very Small in proportion to the number
of Papists." Carrying away more and more Protestants for enlistment in the
army could imperil the kingdom. As George put it, "[It] would be of infinite
prejudice to the Kingdom if any considerable number of Protestants should
be taken away."[61]

This was an old argument; however, in the period after the war, when
manpower was stretched, it had new purchase and changed the conventional
calculus. Usually, in times of crisis in Ireland, those Protestants raised agreed
to serve within the kingdom. But what of troops raised to be sent abroad in
an imperial crisis? Here, George pointed to Catholics. Those to be dispatched elsewhere, to serve the cause of empire, might, he reckoned, "be
raised from amongst the Papists." "Mischiefs" would be avoided as well, as a
number of fighting-age men would be sent abroad. Ireland would be secure,
as would the empire, under the arrangement. Moreover, as George suggested, it was a buyer's market. "I think," he wrote, "a considerable Number

of able men might be raised from amongst them in a short space of time, in the Provinces of Leinster, Munster, and Connaught, to which I should wish the recruiting Parties might be restricted, and to the Levying of Papists only." He considered doing so "to be of the Highest National Importance." He promised that he had "at all times a watchfull Eye and a proper attention to the motions and behavior of the Papists in this Kingdom." Yet, like his predecessor in the position of lord lieutenant, Lord Halifax—the same Lord Halifax who had taken Charles under his wing—he took a more liberal view of Catholics.[62]

Catholics could in George's mind be made good subjects, or at least useful ones, so long as they were yoked to the British state. This logic had worked for the Highlanders. They had now embraced empire, even if they had been victimized by British state power in the past.[63] As a Whig with conventional ideas about the relationship between church and state, George did not suggest lifting the disabilities of Catholics. But he did believe, as Halifax too had suggested, that the past could remain in the past, so long as the Catholic issue was not seen narrowly in an Irish context, one in which Catholics ever posed a threat to the Protestant interest. Even if he worried how the most Catholic parts of Ireland could be manipulated to bad ends in the next war with Spain or France, he also saw able bodies in peripheral regions that could be employed gainfully for imperial ends.[64] Unitary sovereignty resolved such a dilemma. It fixed the corrupting nature of the prevailing links between Ireland and Britain, allowing Ireland to serve its proper function for the whole and setting it on a virtuous course. Following this path could also allay the fears of the Ascendancy, as the potentially disaffected could be more securely tied to the interests of the state. With time, George reckoned, Ireland would and could be a critical contributor to the unified state and the united empire. He measured the success of his lord lieutenancy by how he fared in accomplishing this task, and it would be determined by subsuming Ireland within, he wrote, "the Grand Principle of our Constitution, I mean the general superintending and controuling Power of the Mother Country over all its Dependencies."[65]

He also thought a great deal about the economic development of the kingdom, as well as how it would fit into the political economy of the unified state and empire. The older arrangement in which Ireland was hamstrung in competing with British manufacturers could not be sustained if the new union was going to work. With development, George hoped, rural insurgency would end. Maiming cattle by houghing, or hamstringing, them, destroying crops, terrorizing the countryside all occurred before and during his watch. The network of patronage that George was developing, and his visions of economic development in which Ireland became a constituent part of the British state, could address this vexing issue. Just as Charles prophesied how the "oeconomy of North America" would benefit from system, George believed the same would happen for Ireland. Unified British sovereignty promised many blessings.

George, therefore, thought about sovereignty in terms of people and how they related to system. Given the hands-on nature of his apprenticeship, such an approach to empire made sense. For George, sovereignty was not an abstraction. His life had been devoted to inculcating virtue and civility through institutions such as the army and the militia, a sensibility honed in exile. Now in Ireland, George managed the process for the British state in a key imperial province at a time when it had a stake in equipping people for service. Its people, he believed, had to be reformed to serve the whole, and only unified sovereignty could accomplish that feat. In conceiving of empire along these lines, George was providing a means for addressing the postwar imperial conundrum over diversity.

The worlds that Charles had imagined and that George was trying to shape were no longer distinctive places. Through Atlantic consolidation, including the movement of Irish linen and migrants to the colonies, Ireland and America had become as integrated as any two places in the broader British world. Unsurprisingly, George commented on the movement of troops from Ireland to America through the "rotation" of uniformly sized units to support the flow of revenue from the colonies, and how those soldiers returning from America to Ireland, befitting "His Majesty's pleasure," would be placed on the Irish establishment. The bond between the two could help alleviate the empire's debt problems without stretching the capacity of the state's manpower. Ireland and America, therefore, had a symbiotic relationship in the new system, and the transformation of one place along the lines the brothers proposed could help address the problems in the other. Troops raised in Ireland through George's handiwork, to cite just one example, could be used to keep peace in America until its inhabitants returned to their senses and acquiesced to the duties Charles had devised.[66] In many ways, the provinces in their respective schemes complemented one another.

In theory, that is. Writing in 1768, George argued all had entered "Unprincipled and Mad Times," when "too many of the first Men in the Kingdom, seem to be too little aware how deep and far these Evils extend." America and Ireland were part of "the mad vortex of so ungovernable [a] Machine" that needed system.[67] Through the imperial vision of George and Charles's plan, the "machine" could be managed for the benefit of the whole and for the constituent parts. The duties Charles had championed and the scheme George struggled to implement seemed elegant, rooted as each was in history's patterns and in what was developing into a consensual ideal of how British imperial sovereignty had to work. But the problem was this: Americans did not seem to be cooperating with the empire Charles had imagined before he died. And even as George was working to create his empire, the Irish would prove more vexing still.

George's Hand

Even though Charles was dead, his image lived on. The most famous of these hangs in Raynham Hall today, a copy of which can be seen in his college at Cambridge. The story of the painting begins with the moment he became Chancellor of the Exchequer. After his appointment, Charles wasted no time in announcing his new status. Just as he took office, he commissioned the greatest painter of the day and first president of the Royal Academy, Sir Joshua Reynolds, to paint his likeness. He and Reynolds knew each other well. Although Charles had sat for Reynolds when he was working at the Board of Trade during the war, the relationship went well beyond that of painter and client. They counted each other as friends. In fact, they were well enough acquainted that Charles could even offer criticism of Reynolds's work, something the painter did not take kindly to. In his estimation, Charles may have been "a very distinguished person," but he "was little conversant with the art."[68]

In 1765, before he accepted the post in Chatham's government, Charles was planning to sit once again for a straightforward portrait of his head and shoulders. Once he had accepted the position, he asked Reynolds to produce instead a full-length portrait in which he would be wearing his robes of state. By the last of the ten sessions, they were meeting in Charles's new Downing Street office, where he and Adam Smith were working on his plan. He paid the painter twenty-five guineas for the finished product.[69]

11. Charles Townshend, by Robert B. Farren, copy from a portrait made by Joshua Reynolds circa 1765–1767 (By courtesy of the Master, Fellows, and Scholars of Clare College, Cambridge)

The image Reynolds produced plays to his strength in portrait painting, as well as his admiration for classical poses and props.[70] Interestingly, Reynolds set the Exchequer portrait both indoors and out of doors. Draped and bounded by an urn reminiscent of the sort that borders Raynham Hall, Charles gestures to papers on a desk covered with a rug from the Orient. The painting differs from those that have men of trade as their subjects. There is no globe, no ocean and ship in the background, no clue to what Charles has done. Instead, what it shows is what he excelled at. In it, he deals with the correspondence of empire—he is holding a letter with a broken seal in his hand—and with goods, manifest in the rug. Fittingly, he surveys the world from his desk. The classical urn, of course, speaks to the intellectual world that formed him and that also shaped his vision of the world outside his office. Most significantly, the full-length pose testifies to his standing in the world. Charles had assumed his proper station.

George would do the same. He, too, had commissioned Reynolds to paint a portrait, just after he returned from the war. He did so again as soon as he was named lord lieutenant. Wearing armor in it, he holds a baton of command. His hair by this point in his life has turned prematurely white, off-set in the piece by the red sash he is wearing. The painting that remains is of his head and shoulders. Reynolds had originally done a full-length portrait, again on a scale befitting George's new status as viceroy, for which he charged 37 $\frac{1}{2}$ guineas. That painting has gone missing. What we have of it suggests it must have looked like an almost identical full-length portrait Reynolds executed ten years later.

The full-length portrait we have of George mirrors the image of Charles, also painted in two parts with one canvas for the head and another attached for the body.[71] In it, resplendent in armor, George is grasping the edge of a desk, upon which lie the papers of state. He wears the robes of a peer, along with his sword. In the background lies the outer orbit of empire that had made George what he was. Here we see the clouds of war clearing beyond his shoulder. Much like the pose in Reynolds's portrait of Charles, this full-length pose tells a dramatic tale. George would bring clarity where there had been discord through his will and experience. Or so he supposed.

Both images suggest how the brothers believed they were masters of all they surveyed, destined to lead, and exceptional in every regard, able to bend the world to their will. The tangled tale of one other image suggests otherwise. Soon after his appointment, George had thrilled the Irish to such an extent that the Dublin City Assembly commissioned a portrait to be done by the Irish painter Thomas Hickey at "city expence." The assembly chose Hickey because he was "a native of this kingdom." After studying art in Italy, Hickey had returned to Ireland just as George arrived. He now worked from the Society of Arts in Dublin. Later, while George was still serving as viceroy, he would make his way to London and become a member of the Royal Academy. He was, therefore a skilled artist and, just as important, an Irish painter tied into British networks.[72]

12. *George Townshend, 4th Viscount Townshend*, portrait by Joshua
Reynolds, 1778–1789 (Art Gallery of Ontario, Gift of Reuben Wells
Leonard Estate, 1948; © 2016 Art Gallery of Ontario)

Hanging in the drawing room of the Mansion House, the home of
Dublin's lord mayors, the painting shows George resplendent and relaxed in
his attire as lord lieutenant. Hickey's work is straightforward. He painted an
image in which George's pose appears more informal than Charles and
George's sittings for Reynolds. What strikes the viewer is the casual nature
of what George does. He leans into the desk, one leg crossing the other. His

13. George Townshend, portrait by Thomas
Hickey (The Mansion House, Dublin)

face radiates nonchalance. He looks secure. Like Charles in his portrait, though, he stands in his new setting, the state apartments of Dublin Castle. And there is little to take note of, except what he holds in his hand. In it, Hickey was reported to have placed one word on a piece of paper that appears to be a parliamentary bill, the word that won George instant fame in Ireland: "Octennial."[73]

The euphoria was genuine. Even the *Freeman's Journal,* the newspaper of and for patriots in Dublin and Charles Lucas's mouthpiece, hailed George's arrival and first steps. The paper thanked the king for George's appointment in a piece that was reproduced in Belfast. "Date from this," it declared, "a new Aera of Liberty! Engrave it on all your public edifices, *Hibernia Libertata Georgio Tertio Rege.*" As for George, what he did early on in limiting the duration of Parliament "must render him at once the highest object of the envy of his living predecessors, and of the love esteem and admiration of all true friends of Ireland." His administration "will hand down the name of Townshend to posterity, with more honour and renown than that of Poyning's is remembered with hated, infamy and disgrace," a newspaper stated, referring to the law that mandated Irish heads of bills had to be sent to the British Privy Council for approval. The *Freeman's Journal* predicted George would be "as popular and well beloved among the Irish as any Viceroy that ever preceded him."[74]

George was applauded throughout the kingdom, but especially in Dublin, a Protestant-dominated city that held its privileges closely. On Friday, 23 October 1767, just after he had arrived, George demonstrated how well he understood his audience by attending a sermon preached at Christ Church Cathedral on the anniversary of the "Irish Rebellion" in 1641. This date, more than nearly any other, was seared into the minds of the city's Protestants, from lowest to highest, as it represented a moment in Ireland and Britain's past when Catholics had risen up and slaughtered Protestant settlers, setting the scene for much of the tumult throughout the kingdoms in the later seventeenth century. Such sermons represented opportunities for Protestants to remember and to justify their exclusionary rule of the city and the kingdom. At the sermon, George heard of the "corruptions of popery [which] weaken the two main pillars of society, religion and virtue." In Ireland, such sentiments were not mere abstractions, as apparently Protestants had learned in 1641. By attending, George signaled his allegiance to the fundamental status quo in Ireland. On 13 February 1768, George ventured to the Theatre-Royal, where he "was met with the most gracious Reception of any of his Predecessors. Joy was so universally displayed in every Countenance." The crowd shouted and applauded with "overflowing Hearts." Although what George attended would not have struck anyone as unusual, and reports of joy were undoubtedly exaggerated, his arrival promised security for the Protestant interest, or so it seemed.[75]

The Octennial Bill explained such enthusiasm, something felt by "all ranks" in Dublin. At its most basic level, the act imperiled the power of the undertakers. When "Mr. Ponsonby," the Speaker of the House and chief undertaker, heard the news, "His countenance fell. He turned pale." Now, in theory, elections would become meaningful, and because of this, the city of Dublin, a witness recounted, "was one continued bonfire." Members of the House of Commons as well as weavers, journeymen manufacturers, merchants, tailors, tanners, carpenters, joiners and wainscoaters, dyers, and hosiers all cheered George. These Protestant tradesmen had been Lucas's constituency. Now they belonged to George. An editorial in the *Freeman's Journal* summed it up: "It is now universally confessed, that this Kingdom was never blessed with so powerful, so faithful, so loyal, so vigilant, so zealous, a Representative, as at present. . . . The long wished-for Palladium of our Constitution, is at length well nigh established." What George had done vindicated both the aging patriot Charles Lucas and the new leading light, Henry Flood.[76]

Then something changed. In mid-February 1768, the streams of praise began to end, and a new note was sounded. In one issue of the *Freeman's Journal,* two writers calling themselves "Freeman" and "J.F.V." extolled George for passing the Octennial Act. "The Shackles of Hibernian Thraldom," J.F.V. wrote, "have been happily broken in Pieces, and Liberty, constitutional Liberty, once more raises its cheerful Head." He continued in this vein, hailing Ireland's good fortune and its virtue rewarded. "Ha! What pleasing Figure next approaches," he declared. "How revered, yet how sprightly and sportive is his Mien! On the Head of his Crutch, now high exalted, is *Townshend* and *Liberty!* On the Reverse is *the Octennial Bill!*" In the same issue, though, another writer was chastising someone calling himself Philadelphus, who had sounded a warning bell about augmentation. The writer feared augmentation would cause a storm and lead people to forget "Townshend and Liberty." He was right.[77]

And here we come back to Hickey's painting. As the story goes, once George pressed for augmentation and to create his system for Ireland, the Lord Mayor of Dublin sent for a painter to come to the Mansion House on Dawson Street and "ordered him to take out" the word "Octennial" and in its place paint in the word "Augmentation."[78] The story, carried in newspapers, seems almost too good to be true. It probably is. Today, the headline on the paper in George's hand reads, "Act Limiting the Duration of Parliaments." Below those words are mentioned the House of Commons, His Majesty, and Lord Lieutenant. The body of the act follows. The term "octennial" does not appear. It does not look as if the painting was either vandalized or retouched. But given Dublin's vacillations, it should have been.

This apparent indignity paled in comparison to the way George's image was tarnished in the press and in popular culture. George was pilloried as "a blockhead" and "a tool" of Bute. One newspaper reported, "A Lord Lieutenant of Ireland is generally a poor hungry Peer, who is sent to repair his broken fortune." George had tried to steal Wolfe's glory. He caroused and, like a common soldier, drank "till Two in the morning." One story that made the rounds went like this: George stopped at an inn one night, "where he was surprised and charmed to find an extremely good claret, of which he drank copiously." To thank the innkeeper for the fine claret, George made him a knight "under the name of Sir Thomas." The next day, no doubt hung over, he undid the honor. He did much worse. Like Caesar, he oppressed, but even Caesar did not attempt to "enslave the Province he governed." George treated Ireland like "a conquered Country."[79] His plans for undermining the undertakers and making the Castle supreme also stank of corruption. Townshend had "taken from the Dregs of the People, who have been raised from the Dunghill by the unnatural Sunshine of Power." Another intoned, "We pay you the Compliment to esteem you a Criminal." Most galling was how hope turned into despair. With regular elections, it was not to be patriots who ruled in the name of the people. The crafty Townshend had ensured that "the vacant places were filled by the most abject and detested slaves of government."[80]

It seems Horace Walpole's charge that George indulged in "drunkenness and buffoonery," which made him "the scorn even of the populace," was justified. Ireland's confusions stemmed from his "absurd conduct." George's "irregular caprice," as a contemporary wrote, "by which the dignity of government was perpetually degraded, disgusted all men of sense and feeling." That conduct included "shut[ting] himself up with a low woman." George had become the enemy of Ireland. Once it became known that he had "employed such effectual corruption" to remake the Irish system, irate Dubliners smashed the windows of his coach as he passed by Parliament. One newspaper report even accused George of murder to achieve his crooked ends. However much patriots hated undertakers, they disliked him more.[81]

He appeared now like his old mentor, Lord Bute. When George hosted a fancy dress ball at the Castle in March 1770, for instance, he encountered the sort of hostility usually reserved for the likes of Bute. He had made the point that those attending should wear only clothes of Irish manufacture, a patriotic gesture. It would also, he hoped, provide "relief to the poor and Industrious of the City," who had suffered because of the stagnation of trade with prorogation. To critics, he had added insult to injury. This betrayer of Ireland had chosen the date as "the Eve of the great Patron of our Nation," St. Patrick. Writers likened the event to classical times when "Roman slaves were suffered to trifle and gambol in the Presence of their Masters, and wear each the Habit of his own Country." Was it proper, some asked, that Townshend should "treat us like Slaves, and suffer us to dress like wild Irishmen, in the most whimsical Dresses our Fancy can invent?" With such an event, "we are affirmed to be, a conquered People." They were overstating their case. The same sorts of sentiments were aired in the 1750s with the Money Bill dispute. Nonetheless, George's fall from grace was profound. Patriots now clamored to erase him from memory, to paint him out of the picture. One motion in the House declared "an entry in the journals of last session, beginning with the word Townshend, and ending with the words Great Britain, may be expunged from the journals."[82]

George had an active hand in Ireland. He had little choice if he wanted to reform the kingdom along the lines the brothers had laid out. He had to engage in myriad political battles with many þeneath his station, a taxing endeavor for the proud George. He needed agents and emissaries as well. Ultimately, of course, he had artfully worked both the Irish and the British political systems to craft a new relationship between Ireland and Britain, employing as he did what one scholar calls "expert political management." In promulgating his plan, he had won few friends, save those now on the Castle's payroll. The undertakers hated him, and the Patriots even more so.[83]

George's task in Ireland always occasioned more difficulties than had Charles's for America. What George hoped to achieve, of course, required him to live and work in the kingdom and to engage in the dirty business of patronage. While Charles had used pretense and pretext as the means of establishing system for America while far away in London, George had to employ corruption while resident in Dublin. George, therefore, would come face to face with provincials and incur their wrath for what he was trying to achieve. Charles would not endure the same treatment. Of course, the fact that he was dead played a part. But America differed from Ireland. The distinctive past of Ireland, its peculiar status as both kingdom and colony, its rituals of power, its tangled economic and political relations to England all necessitated residency and the plan of action that George designed. More important, distance made reforming America a more straightforward affair. In part, Charles had little choice to see America as part of an integrated structure because he had to imagine and manage it from a desk in London. Distance dictated a time lag in response and counterresponse. Britons prescribed, then Americans acted. Such was not the case for Ireland. Reform did begin as a British initiative, but under George's watch it happened in real time, as plans and the strategies for implementing them were being formulated in light of the moves and countermoves of various groups, each part of a British network. George had to dirty his hands. In part, the implications of this reality ensured that he would face a complex task and that his image would be tarnished, while Charles's would remain inviolate.

Patriot Games

Just as Charles's plan, even after his death, pressed Americans to reconsider what empire meant, George's actions did the same for the Irish. Through what he was doing, they began to see the times in much the way he did: as critical and demanding an urgent response, even if they could not agree on what that response should entail. At first blush, the initial Irish reaction to what a Townshend was doing, albeit more restrained, looks similar to the American one. As in America, responses ranged from mildly supportive to vocally vituperative. More to the point, George's vision occasioned debates and raised all sorts of issues eerily parallel to the American case. George, then, became the focus of either discontent or praise, and even as Patriots pilloried him, others would support him.

Like the American case, the Irish response was mediated by and negotiated in the press. There was a certain irony to this. After all, George had made pioneering use of public opinion during his days in Britain to contest those he opposed; in Ireland, he was on the receiving end. A number of newspapers had prophesied his time in Ireland would "prove highly agreeable to the Irish in general." He had "evinced himself, on several occasions, to be an able Statesman, a good Soldier, a convictive Orator, an excellent writer, a distinguished Patriot, and (of all the most valuable) an honest Man." But, of course, that tune soon changed in the popular press, and now crowds protested his initiative to pass a money bill that had been initiated in Britain, his press for augmentation, his attempts to employ corruption to undermine the undertakers, and his manhandling of the Irish political system.[84] In Dublin, the mobs and those who lambasted him in the press tended to be Protestant.

The Patriot about-face over George represents only one aspect of an initially complex story, one that stemmed from the distinctive nature of Irish political and social life. Fittingly, the "Irish" response to George was mixed at first. Catholics, in fact, initially voiced cautious support for him.

Increasingly, middle-class Catholics cast their lot with the British Parliament as a potential guarantor of their rights, and a lord lieutenant shoring up sovereignty for Parliament could be a critical ally. The head of the Catholic Committee, a group organized to petition for the interests of Catholics in the kingdom, wrote that George Townshend wanted to know everything he could about penal laws and how they worked. Charles O'Conor, who had helped form the committee in the 1750s, saw hope in the viceroyalty, even more so when "the greatest man among us" asked for a copy of the Popery Acts "for his own perusal." So he had grounds to be cautiously optimistic at first. "The clamor about Papists and Popery," he argued, "is drowned in the new political hurricane of a supposed invasion of the constitution." Catholics would be wise to back what the viceroy was doing but keep a low profile as they were doing so. "Under a new political administrator," he prayed, "may our friends escape safe out of the scuffle, for as innocent by-standers they at least merit such a fate."[85]

Catholics had good reason to be hopeful with George's accession. In 1766, the "Old Pretender," the son of James II, died. With the death of this claimant to the throne, the pope absolved Catholics of support for the Jacobite cause. They could now voice allegiance to the Hanoverian regime for the first time. Though avowedly Protestant, the Hanoverians looked a far sight better than their masters in Ireland. Loyalty became the cautious watchword of the Catholic Committee. Catholics could, O'Conor contended, both retain their ancient faith and support temporal powers that rejected the veracity of their faith. Such sentiments, combined with the fact that George introduced modest reforms, such as allowing Catholics to reclaim bogland, ensured that men like O'Conor viewed him during his early days with a sense of guarded respect.[86]

Some greeted what George was trying to do with resignation. A few, who did not find much to like in George's system, thought the Irish had brought this turn of events upon themselves. Employing commonplace ideas about virtue and vice and the cyclical nature of history, the sort of ideas that both Charles and George embraced, some writers argued that the Irish deserved the government they received. "The simplicity of absolute Government," a writer calling himself Thrasea said, "renders it highly favoured in a period of luxury and advanced civilization." Townshend or the British were not to blame. "Our danger, in this country," Thrasea continued, "proceeds not from the ambition of Government, but from the indolence of the

People." Burrhus made the same point, declaring that "the decline of the constitution of government" stems from "a general depravity of the manners of the people."[87]

Not all Protestants protested. Some supported the measures. One writer, signing himself "An Officer," argued that fears of augmentation were overheated, and he took issue with the many "minute Slanders" aimed at George's government. "A Citizen," who also backed George's initiatives, pointed out the irony of how self-styled patriots tried "raising a Mob of Citizens, at one Time, to pay the extravagant Compliment to a Lord Lieutenant, of drawing his Coach, with Scarlet Cords to the Parliament House; and yet in some short Time after, pelting and abusing that same Lord Lieutenant, in all the popular Papers." One writer suggested that with George "a new spirit of activity and disinterestedness appeared in the Castle." Breaking the undertakers had restored virtue to politics. Those who opposed Townshend were the "friend[s] of successful corruption . . . because he does not practise the art of corruption."[88]

A small number of pamphlets appeared defending George's character, arguing that he had played critical roles in British politics and at Quebec, condemning those who would "reproach and defame a Chief Governor of Ireland." One even tried to demonstrate how ridiculous some critics had been. Townshend was, he said tongue in cheek, an "unnatural father." At Quebec, "he contrived to have him [Wolfe] killed." When he left America, "he went in great fear and trembling to Germany, because it was the fashion." He had stayed by Cumberland's side only because there he would be safest in battle. Most egregiously, he had the gall to keep company waiting at dinner for his arrival.[89]

Others supported him for more prosaic reasons. He delivered. One supplicant promised allegiance, observing, "Though you have opened the Road and made a great progress, the Work is not finished but the Power is Certainly in your hands to complete it." Another wrote, a wise client made backing the Castle administration "the sole rule of my actions."[90] Some of these supporters included former undertakers, whom George had tried to woo to the Castle party.

At the other end of the spectrum lay the political agitator par excellence Charles Lucas. George, referring to the great English instigator and champion of rights John Wilkes, even called Lucas "the Wilks of Ireland." Lucas laid into George as soon as augmentation was broached, and however passionately he argued, he claimed to approach the subject from a dispassionate position. "I would not give Sixpence," he thundered, "for a SEAT in the HOUSE." Nor would he cower when critics labeled him "the *shitten* AP-TH-C-RY*," referring to his former profession. He refused, unlike others, to become a "courtier." He stood only for the "constitution of the nation," that is, Ireland's. Such virtue freed him to attack, and attack he did. He welcomed the tumult that George had occasioned. "The Design of all this Violence" leveled at George "was the Nation's Welfare." For this, George tried to have publication of Lucas's work suppressed. Lucas, according to George, had "been playing the devil here and poisoning all . . . with his harangues and writings." Yet, as he put it, "I have treated this nonsensical demagogue as he deserves with his mob at his heels."[91]

Lucas stood by the notion that Ireland was a perfect sister kingdom of England, that the Irish constitution was the same as England's, in that the Ireland he inhabited as a churchman had never been conquered. In an impassioned public letter to George, in which he recounted both legal precedent and history, Lucas noted, "Thus, my Lord, I apprehend, the Political Constitution of England, was in due form of Law, in positive, express terms, made the Political Constitution of Ireland." Ireland was not ruled by a British constitution. Any interference from a British Parliament amounted to "Gallic Slavery."[92] If a Parliament in England would not stand for this sort of insult, a Parliament in Dublin should not either. As a descendant of English Protestant settlers, Lucas argued that his Irish people had not been conquered, and that England's history was theirs as well. He did not, however, believe that the Irish owed anything to a British Parliament. So whereas in Pennsylvania John Dickinson emphasized the colonial condition of Americans, Lucas used the idea of kingdom to characterize Ireland's status. Ireland was not, nor could be, dependent.

Lucas remained a bigot, as did many of the Patriots. He wanted rights for Ireland and for the middling sort, but both of these had to be Protestant. In Dublin, a largely Protestant city, his appeal only grew with George's measures. Lucas remained loyal to the Crown, but he would never allow that Ireland was subordinate. Yet, Catholics would still be subordinated; indeed, Ireland's status depended on Catholic servility. The status quo privileged Lucas but, more important, his many supporters in Dublin, as well as George's most vocal critics in the popular press, and this arrangement hung in the balance at this point.

One thing was certain for Lucas and the other less radical Patriots, and this separates the initial Irish response to George's handiwork from the early American reaction to Charles's system. George solely was to blame. But the Patriots were not the only ones to lay Ireland's woes at his feet. In a remarkable twist, the *Belfast News-Letter* ran reports of debates in Westminster about Ireland that featured a George Grenville who displayed Chatham-like qualities. The government, by 1770 led by Lord North, argued that Ireland had to provide more troops and supported augmentation and Townshend. North would not "press" Townshend to resign and gave him his support. Ironically, Grenville styled himself a patriot, declaring that "the late prorogation was unconstitutional; that the Stuarts had ever been desirous of ruling without Parliament." Townshend had effectively, like Charles II, vested "the power and disposition of all the land and sea forces in the Crown" in pursuing augmentation with prorogation. Even for Grenville, George Townshend bore all the responsibility.[93]

The initial Irish response, then, mimicked the ways Americans had tried to make sense of the Townshend moment. Hard-liners took the extreme. Some supported what George was up to. Just as in the case of what Charles had proposed, George's measures elicited a number of contradictory responses, exposing tensions and revealing cleavages, even if all saw the times as exceptional and requiring action. Amazingly, however, just as in America, a new consensus soon emerged. Someone would develop a coherent vision of empire in exactly the same way Dickinson had. Indeed, Dickinson served as his inspiration.

Henry Flood's Empire

John Dickinson's *Letters* found a ready reception in Ireland, serialized in Dublin in 1768 and 1769.[94] This is not surprising. Publishing houses, and especially newspapers, performed a role similar to the one they played in America. They provided venues for all sorts of debates, just as they represented the very stuff of civil society. Irish debate in pamphlet and newspapers was vigorous, at times unrestrained, and centered on Dublin. And the Patriots had enviable organs to let their voices be heard. They tended to publish in the *Freeman's Journal* and, after 1771, the *Hibernian Journal*.

In the Irish case, through the publication of a series of pieces published in these papers by some talented young upstarts, a consensual redefinition of empire was taking shape. The group included prominent young Patriots in the Irish Parliament such as Sir Lucius O'Brien and, near the end of George's tenure, Henry Grattan. Also playing significant roles were Hercules Langrishe and Gervase Parker Bushe, both Irish M.P.s, as well as James Caulfield, first Earl of Charlemont. Like the others, Charlemont viewed Chatham as a hero and played a prominent role in a number of "patriot clubs" in Dublin, including the Monks of the Order of St. Patrick, known colloquially as "the Monks of the Screw." Whereas the Farmer's *Letters* were written by one man, the Irish pieces were more than likely the work of a number of writers, who employed any number of pseudonyms. The authors called themselves the Native, Rousseau, Philadelphus, Posthumous, and Sindercombe, among others. The veil of anonymity the aliases afforded makes assigning exact authorship of any single piece difficult. Nonetheless, it is clear that Henry Flood became the group's most prolific author and bore responsibility for most of the pieces assailing George Townshend and his vision. Flood shaped patriot opinion more thoroughly than the others, and his name justifiably came to stand for Irish patriotism as it crystallized in the late 1760s. He is with good reason portrayed as an éminence grise of the Patriots. And he, in league with the others, did exactly for Ireland what Dickinson had done for the American colonies in a series of publications.[95]

Flood's life paralleled that of Dickinson in significant ways. Flood, too, was born in 1732 and trained in the law. A student for a while at that bastion of the Protestant Ascendancy, Trinity College, he then made the provincial's trek and entered Christ Church, Oxford. Like Dickinson, he went on to study at the Inns of Court, in his case Inner Temple. No doubt their time there overlapped in 1754. Flood, too, came from a privileged background and had risen to become one of the elite in his province. He did not scruple with the bond to Britain. If Dickinson considered himself a British American, Flood was undoubtedly an Irish Briton. Finally, like Dickinson, he revered Pitt. Indeed, when Pitt came to power at the time of the Townshends, Flood visited him in Bath, offering any service he could to help reform Ireland along Patriot lines.

Flood and Dickinson differed in some important ways as well. Flood was born illegitimate, something that would hound him throughout his life. His true talents lay in debate, and he never worked as a lawyer. Although he, of course, did not come from a slave-owning family, he was a thoroughgoing antipapist. While hailing from provinces with different "others," they

14. Henry Flood, line engraving by an unknown artist (© National Portrait Gallery, London)

remained true both to their station and to the distinctive and fraught histories of the societies that had given birth to them.[96]

Not coincidentally, Flood and the others titled the pieces they wrote early on in George's reign *Letters from a Native of Barataria to His Friend in Pennsylvania*. The *Pennsylvania Chronicle* listed Flood as the "supposed" author of the Barataria pieces that began appearing in the *Freeman's Journal* in early 1768. Later, they were brought together in a collection, much like Dickinson's *Letters*.[97] Although referring to the mythical kingdom Sancho Panza was to rule in *Don Quixote*, the writer of the earliest essays called himself Philadelphus. In a series of letters, just like those of the Farmer from Pennsylvania, this author—and others or the same writer bearing different aliases—lampooned the lord lieutenant but also came up with a precise idea of what was happening to Ireland. It was, he and other patriots feared, being turned into a provincial dependency. This set of writers also devised an exact notion of how the relationship with Britain should work in a post–Seven Years' War Atlantic empire. Flood and his circle, then, served as Ireland's Dickinson in the themes they covered and the service they performed.

Unlike the American response, though, which smacked of earnestness, the Irish variation relied on humor and viciousness. Patriots leveled heavy criticisms at George, using images and popular pressure to discredit him and what he was trying to accomplish. To some extent, the response of Flood and the other Patriots reflected both the nature of George's hands-on, personal approach to system and Ireland and his understanding of empire. George viewed the relationship between center and province through the prism of the civility of a people. These Irish patriot writers would make their approach personal as well, and they would suggest time and time again that it was George who was acting the part of the corrupting barbarian. Like Dickinson, however, Irish writers embraced the idea of the urgency of the moment, justifying the means they employed—fair and foul—to contest George's plan.

Initially, Flood joined the chorus of praise for George, and he worked to secure the limitation of the duration of parliaments. Indeed, Flood knew George personally, and he visited him in the Castle to discuss political matters. George certainly had tried to court him. But soon support turned to scorn, and Flood reached for his pen. The letters began innocently enough. In 1768, the "Native," more than likely Flood, sent a note to his "friend in Pennsylvania," presumably Dickinson. "I have received your anxious letter by the last packet," he said, "and the subject of it has given me occasion of some serious and melancholy reflection." What Dickinson had written, what he had described in America, clearly struck a chord with the Irish. From the very start of what he would write, the Native of Barataria saw system, now incorporating both the Americans and the Irish. "We have both of us read far enough in history," he declared in solidarity with his farmer friend, to understand "like causes must ever produce similar affects; and the same arts, which may be capable of destroying our liberties, must certainly operate strongly against yours."[98]

He framed the issue the Irish faced in ways that demonstrated his mastery of Dickinson and of America. "You are, happily," he told his friend in Pennsylvania, "at too great a distance from ministerial tyranny, to fall an immediate sacrifice to the politics of despotism." Echoing both Chatham and

Dickinson, the Native of Barataria argued: "We have been treated of late, not as the children, but the bastards of our mother country." The circumstances they confronted were "exactly the same." Although the members of Flood's coterie focused on George, they mentioned Charles as well. In one letter, a writer declared to George: "[You] had a brother: a prodigy of parts! In other particulars you may have resembled him." The connection between the brothers had brought George to Ireland. "They would not make him [Charles] the minister in England," the letter charged, "and therefore they made you the viceroy here."[99]

Just as Dickinson had, Flood and the others cited classical authors and Hume. Like the brothers themselves, they made reference to William Robertson, though they did not offer the same reading from shared historical templates. Indeed, using the name Fabricius, one writer likened George to Rome's governors, demonstrating that he knew the Roman antecedents of empire. Irish patriots, too, had read their Tacitus. As Tacitus had argued, and as the Irish now knew, "the true cause of the miseries of the Romans at that period was, that the Senate had lost all its authority, and were become a set of mercenary tools."[100] George and Charles, Flood and Dickinson, were cut from the same cloth.

But whereas the Farmer did not focus on Charles, the Native of Barataria and the others set their sights on George. In Flood's Barataria, George played the part of Sancho. The Native described him as "a plump man, with a merry round, unstudious looking countenance." He was a fool, and according to the Native, "A person who cannot arrive at the heroic virtues, should always affect the social ones." At first, Flood and his group assured their audience that Townshend's bark would be worse than his bite. "It has been whispered, indeed," one piece in the early stages of George's tenure read, "that he is a person of great design." The author knew that George had arrived in Ireland with grand plans, but he did not think George had the talent to achieve what he wanted. What he planned would not, Flood and his allies hoped, last. The Native continued, "I have been told that his execution is rather with the pencil, than the pen," suggesting both the impermanence of what he was aiming to do and his penchant for caricature. Viceroys came, and viceroys went, after all.[101] Early on, Flood and the others believed, the Irish could wait out Sancho.

In the meantime, they artfully used George's past against him. The Irish tended to bring up the Wolfe affair to embarrass and disarm George, and they did so repeatedly. The Irish, one essay argued, had accepted George openly and to his benefit, refusing to dwell on "every former action of his life, from the time he pilfered the fame of his general, before the wounds of the conqueror, or the tears of his soldiers, Had ceased to flow." The Baratarian pieces would focus on these alleged failings. "A fiend," one contended, "only could have envied him [Wolfe] his glory." George aimed "to supplant his monument, and defraud him of his fame." The writers also raised the specter of Cumberland. "You never supported the militia-bill in truth," one author charged, "you only opposed the duke of Cumberland." The duke was "caricatured once; and it was by your lordship." Flood and the rest of the writers reminded their readers how George had "offered to cram the stamp-act down the throats of the Americans." He was, in a word or two, still "the unthinking soldier."[102]

Sancho, of course, did not leave Barataria, and soon, like Dickinson, the young Irish patriots knew what was afoot. "Your government," one piece declared, "had but one object: the augmentation of the army." The Money Bill dispute, it asserted, "was a point-blank shot, let fly directly against the bulwark of our constitution." Subordination would ensure a steady supply of soldiers to police the empire. With the schemes for augmentation and the Money Bill, "we were treated like a ravaged country, where contributions are levied to maintain the very force that oppresses us." Townshend, therefore, was "enslaving" the Irish, and he would "compel us into an union; or at least to induce one, by reducing us to think it more prudent to sell out to a rich, a powerful, and an encroaching neighbor, and so become tenants under his protection." Under Townshend's hand, "we are required to submit to all the inconveniences of an union, without the least prospect of participating in its advantages." Even the Highlanders enjoyed a better deal. All in all, one of the authors declared, invoking Roman history, Townshend planned on "reducing us to become a province only of another kingdom."[103]

Although Flood and the members of his coterie believed that George was to blame, they interpreted George's initiatives as part of some design. "Where he or his advocates have found this idea," they wondered, "I know not. It has not been the system of his predecessors. Nor is it the system of his friends, the Ministry of England." Patriot writers also realized that the tactics George employed may have killed off the older arrangements but did so to perpetuate new evils. "You came to destroy the undertakers in this kingdom," one essay accused him, "and by your late measure you have made their party the party of the nation." It continued: "[You have the power] to remedy the evil of the former system; but . . . you will not have it in your power to remedy the evil of this system, if established."[104]

Ireland was a kingdom with its own integrity, a "sister kingdom," a writer in the Barataria series called Posthumous argued, echoing Lucas. Yet, Posthumous differed from Lucas in one critical way. In line with Dickinson, he conceded that Ireland was dependent. He recognized the fact that Ireland was a younger sister. "Ireland is subordinate, says England, and England is superior. We allow it," said the writer.[105] But Ireland also had constitutional rights, and its Parliament served as the protector of those rights. It did exactly what colonial assemblies were meant to do for America in Dickinson's *Letters*. In the midst of the crisis, Flood and the others were carving out a new ideal attuned to the moment: a Protestant Ireland standing as a sister kingdom, unshackled from the legislating power of the British Parliament but dependent on it for overseeing the whole.

These Irish from the start saw what they regarded as a concerted plan of subordination. They were right in this instance, but their history also suggested as much. Throughout the long eighteenth century, starting with William Molyneux in the 1690s, through Jonathan Swift in the 1710s and 1720s, and Charles Lucas thereafter, the Irish Ascendancy had experience critiquing the relationship, and from time to time events or tensions would bring the vexed nature of the relationship between Britain and Ireland to the fore. In fact, Flood penned the introduction to a 1770 reissue of Molyneux's famous pamphlet *The Case of Ireland's Being Bound by Acts of Parliament, stated*. The pamphlet had addressed one of the tense situations in which England's Parliament had legislated for Ireland, in this case the restriction of an Irish woolen trade that competed with English and Scottish producers.[106] In the 1750s, the Irish also struggled with a constitutional crisis over a money bill dispute, one similar to the one instigated by Townshend. Only with George's ascendency, a new plan was affecting the whole system of which Ireland made up one part, and it did not appear George was leaving. Nor was the ministry relenting, convincing Patriots like Flood that this moment differed in profound ways from earlier periods of constitutional uncertainty. The natives of Barataria writing the essays, therefore, sensed continuities, but also something more pernicious and thoroughgoing.

As Flood and others argued, Townshend's initiatives represented "a despotic government's plan of arbitrary power for Britain and its dependencies." America and Ireland struggled with the same crisis. For the

Irish, ultimately what set this crisis apart and demanded action was its imperial scope. The Irish could look across the ocean and think that perhaps their
fears were not unjustified, and they drew parallels between Ireland and
America. But they did so only up to a point. Dickinson worried that America
would become Ireland. Flood's group feared Ireland would become America, a colonial dependency. American colonies were bit players in the imperial drama, mere provincials. "You were appointed," one of the writers
thundered, "by an administration, the only uniform object of which has been
to injure or insult every part of the British dominions."[107] The ministry was
intent on leveling and subordinating, to treat distinctive regions in the same
way, regardless of constitutional status. In this critical moment, the Irish
were losing their distinctive status as subjects in a kingdom.

As the *Freeman's Journal* put it, "the Liberty and Property of Ireland"
would be sacrificed "to prepare for the Slaughter of Americans." There
was, alas, nothing episodic about this new crisis. It promised to produce
something permanent, to set in stone some sort of subordinated relationship,
in which America and Ireland would become mirror provinces. This was the
chief warning of the writers from Barataria to their farmer friend in Pennsylvania. Patriots agreed with Dickinson. This new arrangement, rooted in
an idea of system, stemmed from "design."[108]

A clear sense of what was happening to the whole tempered this emerging notion of empire, a vision that appeared as uncomplicated as George and
Charles's notion. It drew on and paralleled Dickinson's. It also eschewed
ambiguity. That clarity appears most visibly when Flood was writing in 1770
under the name "Sindercombe." With this alias, he chose a daring and fitting
nom de plume. Miles Sindercombe had dreamed of a pure republic in the
seventeenth century and had participated in a plot to kill the tyrant Oliver
Cromwell to establish it. Ironically, in this drama George played the part of
the very man he had accused Wolfe of resurrecting.

We are on firm ground to believe Flood wrote as Sindercombe. And in
Sindercombe's letters we see understandings of a provincial vision of empire akin to those developed for America by the Farmer. According to
Sindercombe, George had given away offices more corruptly than the undertakers, in one instance giving a bishopric to a man "who is fitter to preside
over a Brothel than an University." George was "the servile Abettor of every
unconstitutional Measure, the Tool of Bute . . . the *Practicer* of Corruption
in every Period of his Life." With his initiatives, Ireland was now clearly

becoming a blighted kingdom, and its status was unambiguous. "The Corruption of a *free State* is over," he charged, "and the Corruption of *Servitude*
is what we are now to experience." Even members of the Ascendancy were
revealed to be mere Irish in the eyes of the ministry. Ireland was a dependency, one that like the provinces of ancient Rome had become a place "into
which all Fugitives and Betrayers are to be received." The upshot was clear:
"A Plan of arbitrary Power has been systematically pursued." And "To
enslave all the Dependencies, it was only necessary to establish the Power of
that Parl-----t over those Dependencies." It was a "system."[109]

Flood playing the part of Sindercombe warned "if the Attack be general, so ought the Defence." His first line involved pointing out the reality all
provincials faced and then defining the federal notion of empire that should
prevail. He argued that a simple arrangement in which Ireland's Parliament
looked after Irish affairs under the Crown "gave all due Pre-eminence and
Authority to England, without stripping this Kingdom of all national
Weight." If such an arrangement prevailed, one that allowed Ireland "national Weight and Dignity" under the Crown, "I am content," he wrote.
"But by the present System, it must be destroyed."[110]

Flood made another point parallel to Dickinson's. Dickinson had spoken of slaves; Flood discussed Catholics. Catholics, or, as Sindercombe
called them, "the natives" of the country, would also be affected. "Were the
present design to prevail," he found, "not an atom of influence would be
suffered to remain in the hands of a native." Granted, Catholics did not have
any substantive political influence under the present Ascendancy, something
Sindercombe was keen to ensure remained intact. This did not stop him
from trying to win Catholics over to his way of thinking. "The natives of a
country may betray it; and the natives, even of greatest consequence, may
sometimes have an interest contrary to that of their country," he argued.
"But not often."[111] The status of Catholics in Flood's Ireland bore a resem-
blance to that of slaves in Dickinson's America. Flood and his circle, too,
sensed how what a Townshend was proposing could have unforeseen implications for those in a servile or subservient position.

The famous Patriot movement in Ireland coalesced around the Townshend lord lieutenancy. The program had first begun to grow earlier in the
1750s, with Lucas leading the way. The year 1767 ushered in a new generation. Not only did a group of young voices emerge in the opposition to Townshend, but more to the point people like Flood created a viable program with

ideological consistency. New certainties took shape. One Patriot argued that "the irresistible opinion of Flood" had "fortified" Irish minds. As Grattan put it after Townshend had succeeded in his plans, the debates that his rule engendered "fix[ed] in the minds of our countrymen some precise principles of constitution."[112] The ideas were not new. It was the arrangement of the ideas, as well as the specific prescriptions that emerged from them, that represented a new departure. Moreover, at this critical moment when the idea of sovereignty was at the forefront of the minds of all Britons, Flood, Grattan, and the rest were able to set the terms of constitutional debate around a crystallized definition of what the relationship between center and periphery should be. This definition, moreover, was gaining more and more appeal among the Ascendancy as the undertaker system was completely compromised, and it would grip the Patriot imagination in the future. With time, one was considered either a Patriot or a member of the Castle party.[113] Unsurprisingly, like Dickinson's *Letters*, the Barataria letters became touchstones for Irish political life, spawning all sorts of praise, denunciation, and imitations.[114]

If it prophesied the future, the work of Flood and the others dwelled in assumptions about the past. The Irish drew connections to what had happened in the past and tied this period into that history. More important, they tied the Irish past and present to what was occurring across the ocean, creating a sense that this time was a watershed. The Americans were beginning to see their provincial crisis as starting with the Stamp Act. The Irish, or better Flood's Irish, also connected dots, but to a different sort of past, a more distant and complex one than Americans had experienced. In the imagined history that this crisis resurrected, Ireland, on the one hand, enjoyed equal status to England as a kingdom but, on the other hand, suffered periods of demeaning subordination. When tensions were heightened between the kingdoms, both pasts reemerged, only this time they did so as subjects across the Atlantic were struggling with the same issues. The renewed and sharpened Patriot program, then, arose not in a vacuum but in a politically charged imperial atmosphere, one that the past, both mythic and imagined, fueled.

The Provincial Moment

The Townshend moment forced provincials into a selective reading of their pasts. This process of misremembering led Americans to erase the eighteenth century, the process of becoming British provincials, and to construe themselves Englishmen much like their forebears, who had arrived from England. They, like their migrating ancestors, were not privy to the process of British state formation that had placed Parliament at the center of sovereignty. Just as the Townshends would use the past to turn American colonies into provinces, writers like Dickinson erased their provincial identity to put in its place a colonial identity—Americans were still dependent colonists but tethered by the Crown and only symbolically by Parliament. That past was also simplified. The coercion that had gone into transforming a wilderness into what they regarded as a settled society went unmentioned. Atlantic commerce, of course, brought civility. So, too, did the work of slaves. These changes were hallmarks of the eighteenth-century Atlantic experience that so shaped the lives of Charles and George. But writers like Dickinson would rather have forgotten such facts. The Irish also forgot, particularly the ways that the ancestors of Grattan and Flood had been complicit in a conquest and process of plantation that made Ireland, de facto if not de jure, subservient to Britain. With a history that paralleled and did not trail that of England's, Ireland, they were at pains to argue, was a dependent kingdom and not a colony. Provincials, therefore, also tried to selectively erase ambiguities, just as the Townshends were trying to do.

However different the provincial responses, they took on a similar valence. Both met certainty with certainty. Both disavowed the arrangements and the uncertainty of the past for exactness and clarity in the future. American creoles and Irish creoles recognized their "dependent" status. But they would not allow dependency to determine their constitutional rights. They were, they believed, partners in the state. Their imagined pasts determined as much. Within a federated empire, their assemblies had critical roles to play and could not be done away with. Americans and the Irish could not be slaves for imperial revenue or proverbial drawers of water and hewers of wood, useful only insofar as they provided bodies for empire. Most important, this crystallization took place as a refined response with great ideological consistency and broad appeal, one crafted in the crucible of debate in both places, to address what people both in the center and on the peripheries were viewing as a watershed.

Whether Dickinson or Flood thought about the seventeenth century and their relationship to it mattered less than what their writing meant. They served as catalysts and offered templates that would allow provincials to make sense of any new contingency in compelling ways.[115] They saw a system confronting them because they found themselves in similar straits at the same moment for the same reasons and because some prominent leaders at the center, like the Townshends, had invested in a system. Moreover, programs to contest the system began to take shape quickly at this time, largely through the work of Dickinson and Flood in the provinces, each of whose interpretations resonated because of their timeliness. Programs of action called for at the right time, not just ideology, mobilized people.

The reimagining of empire in Ireland and in America served as a rallying point for all provincials, who themselves were coming to terms with the effects and implications of Atlantic consolidation. This was, for them as well as for Charles and George, a "moment," forcing all to think about how their societies fit into the dynamically changing whole. How would these provinces figure into the coercive-commercial Atlantic? And at this point they suggested what roles they would not play. Flood lamented how the Irish would pay for augmentation "in order to imbue our hands in the blood of our fellow-sufferers and fellow countrymen, whose sole crime is the love of liberty." Because of this, "the cause of the Provinces is our own cause; the same law that enslaves them enslaves us likewise." Americans would not toil to provide the "revenue" for empire. And for each the time to act was now because each compared their plight to the other's and through this created a provincial connection. The lord lieutenant, Flood argued, was attempting to "poison the fountain of legislature; this end once attained, how easy it is to vote the Irish, Americans, East India Company etc to be horses, asses, and slaves at his pleasure."[116]

This was also, for them as well as Charles and George, "system." Just as the brothers began to believe the empire to be an integrated whole, with each part symbiotically bound to others, so too did provincials. Their understanding of system, however, presented a more jaundiced view. In this context, therefore, it was not unusual for the *Virginia Gazette* to carry reports from Ireland lambasting George and what he was doing to the constitution in Ireland, or for the *Pennsylvania Packet* to pillory him, again culling from a Dublin newspaper, as "the greatest scourge . . . since the days of brass money and wooden shoes." Nor was it strange to read in an American newspaper, say, the *Providence Gazette* in 1768, a letter from a "Gentleman in Ireland" who wrote, "We are not in a less rebellious state here than the people in America. . . . [The ministry] drain us of our Troops to send them to

America, to quell the tumults there." In this newspaper, as in Flood's and Dickinson's writings, the brothers were pursuing complementary plans for the provinces by similar means to achieve an imperial end. The Townshends had effectively subverted "the Liberty and Property of the Inhabitants of Ireland; an Attempt to strengthen the Military against the Civil Power; and so to prepare Slaughter for America, and Slavery for Britain." The Irish would be like "the Scotch," inured to arbitrary government. America would be like Ireland, effectively conquered.[117]

In this regard, Charles had been prophetic, but in ways he could not have foreseen. When he had worried as he introduced his plan to Parliament that the provinces might find "common cause" to contest measures, he did not reckon how his and George's systemic sensibility, worked out hand in hand, would encourage provincials to see the world in similar ways and confront a common crisis arm in arm. They saw the Townshend moment for what it was as they were crafting their own provincial moment.

ACT 5

Making Revolution

Charles's Ghost

In 1777, an anonymous writer published a haunting story. Entitled *Dialogues in the Shades* and printed in London, the pamphlet presented three discourses, "unbiased by party prejudice and free from revengeful passion," on what had become a war between the colonies and Britain.[1] In it, five ghosts, or "shades" as they were called, try to solve the imperial problem. We know four of the ghosts well. Only one makes a new appearance, but his participation in the discourses reveals what happened in the aftermath of Charles's death and John Dickinson's reimagining of empire. In the wake of the Townshend Duties, reconciliation became more and more difficult, and then impossible, after the gulf of misunderstanding grew and as the flow of events pushed Britain and the colonies further and further apart.

In the first discourse, James Wolfe and Richard Montgomery, our new actor, meet by chance in heaven, by all accounts "a delightful place," and begin to debate the issue of who was right: the British or the Americans. In life Montgomery would have known and revered Wolfe, for a time at least. Born in Ireland, Montgomery served as a British officer in the Seven Years' War before settling in New York and rechristening himself a British American, a godson of sorts of the messianic Wolfe. Filial attachment ended with independence, and Montgomery became an ardent patriot. The author chose these two because both had fallen in Quebec. Montgomery met Wolfe's fate in 1775 after he led the Continental Army's failed invasion of Canada, in his case fighting against Britain. As Montgomery's shade notes to Wolfe's, "[I] encountered an honorable death on the same spot where you gloriously fell."[2]

217

In the *Dialogues*, Montgomery and Wolfe share a mutual respect but not the same understanding of the imperial crisis. Wolfe believes Montgomery had "been the leader of seditious men, who revolted against a people to whom they were bound by the most sacred tie of filial duty." Now these men aimed for "Independency." Montgomery, while lavishing praise on the martyr, explains why. What had happened since Wolfe's great victory sundered a transatlantic family.[3]

Wolfe and Montgomery invite David Hume to shed some light on their differences. Hume, "who has analyzed the human mind," had in his life "dared to face Truth in all its splendor." He tries to reconcile the two, explaining how through English history and basic justice each has right on his side. He suggests they need to confront the "first author" of the "wrongs" Montgomery enumerates to see if they can heal the rift. He is not referring to the one figure Americans had fastened on as responsible for their plight in the wake of Stamp Act crisis: Lord Bute. He tells them to invite George Grenville, "the properest opponent to Montgomery."[4]

Discourse II starts with Grenville explaining himself, Wolfe supporting his sentiments, and Montgomery becoming incensed. To Montgomery, the man behind the Stamp Act acted like a rogue. "I think him to be a man initiated in the iniquitous plot intended for our ruin," Montgomery declares. Once the Americans, Grenville's ghost explains, had been "subjects and friends." Now they had become "*rebels* and *enemies*," and the people there had been seduced by "seditious harangues" of some self-styled leaders in the colonies, including presumably Dickinson. Montgomery rejects his arguments out of hand. "Was it justice to tax the Americans without their consent," he thunders, "to deprive them of the benefits arising from a constitution by which they were bound to England? on account of which they were proud of their subjection." Americans like him "dreaded the humiliation of being obliged to envy the condition of those people who are deemed slaves."[5]

When Grenville declares that he had crafted "an useful system," Montgomery shoots back: "O Grenville! if you had viewed the Americans with impartial eyes, you would not have considered them as the descendants of miserable outcasts, who had become by the bounties of England a flourishing, and ungrateful people." Americans had "intrepidly penetrated into a dreadful wilderness to fight savage monsters, and to struggle against a barren soil." Montgomery is at pains to say the issue hinges on what Parliament has done to their "provincial assemblies which constituted our representation," something he regarded as "this innovation."[6] They cannot see eye to eye.

Enter Charles Townshend. Charles, or rather his ghost, ends the second discourse and begins the third. He appears in the dialogue as the "indifferent conciliator," as Grenville puts it, "the very man for your purpose." The Charles Townshend of the *Dialogues* is both brilliant and honorable. When he learns that the Americans are suffering defeats he says, "I shall never rejoice in their misfortune, but on the contrary sincerely pity them." When he is asked to join Wolfe and Montgomery in devising "a lasting peace between the two contending branches of one family," he responds: "With all my heart."[7]

In our ghost story, we see a strange, unrecognizable Townshend. Montgomery says, "I am sensible that I have neither asperity, nor moroseness, to fear from Townshend in this case; for, as he was not an enemy of the Americans from conviction that they were in the wrong, but from a desire of being thought to be himself always in the right, he cannot have brought hither any sort of prejudice against them." Vanity or trying to please all, it seems, remained his weakness.[8]

In the *Dialogues*, Charles tries to find agreeable terms for Montgomery three times and "to settle matters amicably," as Wolfe hopes. He first offers an apology for what he did. As to pushing for the Townshend Acts, Charles argues he did so from the best of intentions. "You may reflect, but too justly, upon my conduct in regard to the American taxes," he tells the specter of Montgomery, adding, "I am very far from justifying it, although I still hold its principle good." Altruism, a concern for the whole, however misplaced, drove Charles. "For, I think the duty of a social being is to strengthen the tie of society," he believes, "by endeavoring to please every one, and I look upon the satisfaction he feels at being admired, as the just reward of his trouble. It is true, the most laudable sentiments may be carried too far, and this was my case when I proposed the renewal of these fatal taxes." He claims he made so many amendments to the bill favorable to the Americans "that I could not foresee they would be exasperated by it."[9]

Montgomery concedes his point. Townshend had, he says, "gilded indeed the bitter pill, but could not render it palatable . . . because our too well-awakened watchfulness took the alarm at the least appearance of danger." Townshend, though, acknowledges his error and hopes to atone for it. "This concession," Montgomery argues, "is worthy of your noble mind."

Charles then turns his mind to a peace settlement. Montgomery, however, rejects his plea.[10]

The ghostly Charles tries a second time, this time urging Montgomery to accept what looks to be a confederated imperial relationship, one along the lines Dickinson has proffered. As Wolfe, Montgomery, and Townshend discuss a new plan for empire that could include Americans and redress past wrongs, Townshend warns Montgomery not to ask for too much and to drop all rancor. "You should not raise so many difficulties," he gently chides. In fact, classical antiquity offers a good reason to embrace the Dickinson model. The British government could, Townshend argues, "think proper to imitate the Romans, who, after their famous social war, granted the requested privilege of being called citizen of Rome, only to some confederate States, and refused it to those who had been very forward in their revolt, in order that the spur of emulation might prompt them to atone for past offences." The Romans employed such an approach "with the inhabitants of the remotest countries, and thus extended their empire to the furthest verge of the then known world." In this way, even rebellious places on the periphery could enter the fold and enjoy rights equal to all others. The ghost had apparently forgotten what the man had done in life. Or rather, he asks for forgiveness. "I acknowledge my error, and should be very willing to atone for it," he pleads, if Montgomery would now accept his new proposal.[11] Montgomery says no. Too much water, or rather blood, has gone under the bridge.

Undeterred, Charles throws out a third idea. Perceptions and ideas, as he now realizes, matter more than social reality. "I should have reflected that men are ruled by words, moved by words, devoted to words, and very little taken with the real substance of things," he concedes.[12] The scales falling from his eyes, he offers Montgomery the most magnanimous terms. Americans could enjoy their treasured independence but do so under the umbrella of commerce and military protection offered by the British. The newly independent, then, could honor older connections, enjoy their natural rights, and not be devoured by other European powers, something in everyone's best interest. All the Americans have to do is pay a yearly subsidy. Astonishingly, Charles seems to hit on a winning formula. Montgomery accepts the proposal, and they are ready to draw up the specifics of the plan.

Meanwhile, however, Charles hears someone snickering behind a tree. David Hume cannot help laughing at the folly of the ghosts. Did not Cicero try to do the same? Did he not hope to leave heaven, return to the world of mortals, and teach the Romans the true path of peace? If Cicero was unable to do so, certainly Montgomery and Townshend could not. Hume reminds them that as ghosts they have no sway in the other world. "Nothing but empty notions, puerile prejudices," he believes, "govern the generality of mankind, and decide the fate of empires." The best-laid plans mean nothing. As Hume knows, complexity and contingency confound.[13] Charles sees the error of his ways. He agrees with Hume and makes a speech about how those in the world of the living, those not yet in the "shade," must suffer the biases of fools and the haughty plans of those who think they know better. Charles has now clothed himself in humility. Ultimately, the debaters leave resigned to the idea that they cannot come up with a solution that will work.

As we turn now from the *Dialogues* themselves, we see that they offer, at first, a comforting story for people in the eighteenth century, suggesting that misunderstanding or miscommunication can be rectified. Yet, the characters in the drama learn otherwise, largely through the different interpretations of Grenville and Charles, as well as the remonstrations of Hume. Complexity, after all, makes for no easy fix and lays bare the fact that broader dynamics cannot be managed, even from heaven, however much the ghosts are fain to admit as much. History, even for the dead, is made of patterns, or so the ghosts believe, but history is tragedy, by and large because people either comply with those patterns as if they are inexorable or believe they can master or shape them, a conceit that never prevails.

For Charles's ghost, what happened after the demise of the man destroyed all he had devoted himself to and demonstrated the futility of his belief in how the world worked. Most significantly, on 5 March 1770, Parliament repealed most of his duties after it had dispatched troops from Ireland and elsewhere to police American cities. The new ministry, led by Lord North, did so to appease English merchants. In the short run, less than £21,000 was collected through the duties to support civil administration in the colonies. Meanwhile British businesses lost £700,000 in one year. Only the tax on tea remained, a constitutional fig leaf for what was characterized as a luxury item. The duty on tea, North argued, would "give additional support to our government and judicatures in America." In a modest way, the remaining tea tax ensured that a modicum of Charles's plan remained. In Massachusetts, a number of royal officials, including the governor, would have their salaries paid by revenue from tea. And for a time, and as nonimportation agreements began to falter with repeal, it looked as though normalcy was returning. In the long run, however, Americans caught up in the transatlantic drama would say opinion pivoted at this time. Later, for instance, Samuel Adams would remember that he imagined independence for America in 1768.[14]

Charles's brother witnessed the unfolding drama with dismay, as everything he and Charles had imagined collapsed before his eyes. As setback followed setback, George grew more and more embittered with the world he and Charles had hoped to master. By the mid-1770s, as the empire was reeling from a systemic crisis, he still saw the problem as system. In Ireland, it was working. But in America it was failing. "May the King's Government," George declared, "when they have adopted system, pursue it, and be intelligible." He warned, "If they shall warp it to particular Interests or Political Coteries, it will all fall back again." The same problem he had complained about in the early 1760s now haunted Britain again, but the stakes had become higher still. And no one, he still believed, had the same sense of vision he and Charles had developed and embraced. The "insolent menaces" of the colonists had been "countenanced and fatally for them cherished by the most audacious faction at home."[15]

In 1775, George rose in the Lords to give a speech on what he saw as a world, and a way of understanding it, falling to pieces. "I shall not hesitate at so awfull a period which I am persuaded will decide upon the Existence of the British Empire," he declared. "Colonial Independence," he prophesied, would challenge all imperial relations. It would affect France and Spain. And what would transpire there would further destabilize the British Empire because France and Spain would abet the rebels in America. As a peer, he had to be concerned with order. "The Saints of Boston, and the Great Constitutional new Erected Legislatures have no such Scruples," he believed. They created the chaos that was engulfing the whole. They subsisted on it. And disorder would only grow. "A German Catholic or a Moravian, an Irish Papist or a Pennsylvania Quaker, nay even the obnoxious Canadians are all invited or compelled to support that new Government which they intend shortly to exhibit," George lamented.[16] Much like the provincial imagination, which drew connections to a recent or distant past to see patterns, George's imagination feared a future of Atlantic revolution, one he and Charles could not have imagined when they initiated the reforms they did.

George believed he understood what had gone wrong. The vision he and Charles had developed had been abandoned. Complaining of what was happening in Boston in 1775 as well as noting what his old nemesis Flood was up to in Ireland, he concluded: "Our reasonings seem to be as tempestuous, our Measures as Uncertain, and our Course as Eventual as the Very Season and Its Effects." America would be lost because of aimlessness and the fickle ways of successive ministries. "At the Moment I write," he continued, "we are debating upon points we ought to have settled many years ago, examining defects we should have cured there two years past, and refining upon Expedients."[17]

Something was also happening that escaped George. By the time Charles's ghost was devising plans for reconciliation, events subsumed what Charles had done and occluded memory. Indeed, history, which Charles had thought he could master, mocked the conceit that he was distinctive. By 1777 when the ghosts debated, the Townshend Duties represented just one point in a long train of abuses, a provincial litany of metropolitan missteps that drove Americans to declare independence and to wage a war against the parent. What at one point had been considered mistakes, even aberrations soon remedied, with hindsight looked like a concerted plan. Lost was any sense of contingency.

As Burke surmised as early as 1769, a tragedy of patterning and misunderstanding was unfolding. "The Americans," he claimed, "have made a discovery, or think they have made one, that we mean to oppress them." Whatever Parliament did from now on would be "poison, gall, and bitterness to the Americans." He went on to say that they were not the only ones seeing things in new ways: "We have made a discovery, or think we have made one, that they intend to rise in rebellion," leading him to conclude, "We know not how to advance, they know not how to retreat."[18] The upshot was that Charles Townshend did not stand out as exceptional at all. He defined the rule for Americans. What he tried to do, as well as its novelty, faded from view. Given the flow of events, it had no time in which to set itself.

The man who during one brief window of time crafted the very system they decried became a ghost to Americans. The signs were there from the very start. The architect of the duties did not feature in Dickinson's *Letters*. Dickinson mentioned Townshend, not by name, but only as "the author" of the "system" in a footnote. The disappearance of Charles would become more conspicuous as the crisis grew. The *Newport Mercury*, for instance, ran one of the *Letters* that pointed to Grenville as the minister responsible for the subordination of the colonies alongside an extract from another paper, which mentioned how Charles after his death was "almost completely forgot."

Charles was not responsible. Grenville, one writer from Boston claimed, is "our greatest enemy," and it was he, the author argued mistakenly, who intoned "*internal and external taxes* are the same in *effect*, and differ but in name." The *Newport Mercury* picked up an anti-Grenville line. It was now he who was trying to "inflame the House against North America." A writer from Connecticut agreed. "The first act passed imploring any such sovereignty was no earlier date than under Mr. Grenville's administration," he argued. What followed seemed to take on the form of logic, as he yoked the Stamp Act to the Declaratory Act to the duties.[19]

Ironically, Grenville, who was overlooked earlier on as the author of the Stamp Act, now stood out as the figure behind the Townshend Duties. In a piece called "The Englishman Deceived," a writer argued that "the late Chancellor of the Exchequer confessed to some of his friends, that he had promised the Gentle Shepard, before he was Chancellor, that he would endeavour to lay an act upon America, which would so far resemble the Stamp Act, as to answer for the same purpose." Charles was "the father of the second child, who though born with smoother features, and weaker limbs, yet may in time become as justly formidable." Grenville was the villain, the father of the first child. "This man, Grenville" the writer charged, "though justly banished from His Majesty's immediate employment, finds means yet to divide and distract and almost destroy, the power and reputation of these great kingdoms."[20]

The reason for the emphasis on Grenville is simple. Americans began to see the duties as part of a broader story that followed a set sequence, what we could call the Stamp Act/Declaratory Act/Townshend Duties saga. "The bait," one newspaper reported, "is now more artfully laid than it was by the bungler who was the author of the Stamp Act." That Charles was cleverer mattered less than who bore initial responsibility. The *Virginia Gazette*, for instance, in a seemingly strange twist, carried praise for the Farmer in the same issue in which it ran the full extract from London lionizing Charles's great abilities and how he had died on the verge of accomplishing all he wanted to do.[21] The same went for the *Pennsylvania Gazette* and the *Providence Gazette*. In November 1768, they reported, based on an extract from a letter from London, that "the passing of this very Law was occasioned solely by a Promise extorted from the late Charles Townshend, by the Opposition, with Grenville at their Head, that some effectual Revenue should be obtained that Session from North America." That such a report was false mattered less than how it meshed with the ways Americans were beginning to misread British motivations.[22] Benjamin Franklin summed it up this way just after the duties were to be repealed: "The Grenvillenians . . . have done all this mischief."[23]

His death certainly shielded Charles from some responsibility. A British witness to the times recalled how Charles "brought forward measures tending to revive the question of the right of the British Parliament to tax the American Colonies; but his premature death protects him from being considered as the author of the American war." Americans, however, did not make that point. The shifts in blame among the colonists suggest something else at work, something beyond Charles's passing. Grenville stood at the very heart of the British parliamentary establishment, and he was the first in a line of ministers pressing for Parliament's supremacy. Charles stood next.[24]

The American interpretation, which forgot Charles, bound the colonies together. In August 1768, the *Boston Evening-Post* ran a "Letter from a Gentleman in Virginia to a Merchant in Philadelphia" that made the same essential points Dickinson had made. They were reading the recent past with new lenses. The Stamp Act now suggested something that was coming to fruition. Grenville had been the designer. Charles Townshend, the writer maintained, "with an artful and penetrating eye, saw clearly to the bottom of your hearts." He designed a system that could put Grenville's principles in operation, using American objections to the Stamp Act against the colonists. It was "your misfortune, and the misfortune of all *America*, that you did not know *him*, as well as he knew *you*." Some merchants were not bothered by the duties, and because of this they did not join with others in protecting American rights. Charles, the writer argued, sewed American divisions into his plans. He served as a clever implementer, but one acting for a disembodied "lurking principle."[25]

The reaction of Americans after the ministry repealed the Townshend Duties, save the tax on tea, in 1770 speaks to the interpretation premised on systematic imperative that Americans had adopted. Colonists had earlier greeted the repeal of the Stamp Act with nothing short of "joy," as one newspaper put it. Jubilation would not be too strong a word to use to describe the collective response, suggesting that Parliament after a lapse had come to its senses and once more was working as a guarantor of liberty. Such did not happen in 1770. No one celebrated. Some condemned Bute and Grenville for maintaining the duty on tea, almost as if they had become symbols and watchwords of tyranny. No one mentioned Charles. If joy at liberty regained captures the mood in 1766, resolve and vigilance over liberty needing to be defended expresses how Americans saw the world in 1770. By this time, they reacted to events with a pattern of thought that disregarded Charles and instead saw a train of abuses likely to continue. Grenville, now the target of colonial scorn, prophesied as much. "If you expect, by that repeal," he declared, "to accomplish the end of satisfying America and reserving to yourselves the power of taxing her, you will be deceived. It cannot be: it will not be."[26]

Losing Charles in the flow of narrative pattern did not make Americans paranoid. It made them revolutionary. For generations scholars have tried to explain what made Americans so prone to seeing things in the ways they did just before the revolution. Was it some sort of sense of provincial inferiority? Or a broader British understanding of human agency within an Enlightenment universe increasingly seen as mechanistic? Or the mind-set of the tumultuous seventeenth century resurrected in the eighteenth?[27] Perhaps the answer is simpler. In contexts fraught with fear and uncertainty, Americans struggled—like George and Charles—to make a narrative of their lives that conformed to social reality. They tried to order the past to manage the future, and in so doing, they took what was singular and made it part of the inexorable. Events, in this way, became moments. There was nothing exceptional about doing so. What one scholar refers to as "carving 'events' out of the chaos of experience" makes history "legible" and compelling. Such thinking turns plausible narratives into "certainties," and in the process becomes "a mechanism by which historical change happens." Patterning the past compels the future.[28]

At this time, the patterning did not only stem from the sorts of ideas Americans espoused, leading them to see the world in almost paranoid ways, or sensing a conspiracy where none existed. The general enthusiasm for Dickinson's ideal of empire emerged at a particular period of time, not just in a hodgepodge of undifferentiated parliamentary initiatives. At this confluence Americans were crafting a new past and a new future in a new historical continuum. The "logic of rebellion," as one prominent historian argues, stemmed from the creation of such patterns, but they were rooted in time— not just in discourse.[29]

Yet, as the ghost story in *Dialogues in the Shades* reveals, the creation of one pattern depends on the end of another. An Irish poet working during a very different age of revolution understood the nature of this dynamic better than nearly any other. William Butler Yeats saw the story of the twentieth century as one of people trying, sometimes against great odds, to make meaning of events within a train of other events, just as certain older ways of making meaning were falling apart. For Yeats, revolution turned on the ways the everyday became mythologized through attempts to come to terms with the "terrible beauty" of reality. In "Easter, 1916" the Easter Rising becomes for him the moment it did once people made it the centerpiece of a new pattern ordering reality.

A new event could be disruptive, especially if it seemed to challenge the prevailing pattern. In such instances, a novelty could, according to the philosopher Alisdair MacIntyre, create an "epistemological crisis," when the relationship between *seems* and *is* breaks down. In tumultuous contexts, the crisis could become the seedbed of a new pattern. Old patterns then become almost unintelligible, and those responsible drift from memory. The new shapes all, accentuating some aspects of experience and muting others.[30] So it is in revolutionary moments.[31] In the years after 1916, the dead and the vanished became ghosts that lived in resurrected forms in the new present, transforming what could be seen in the past as they did so. As Charles was playing the part of a shade, the meaning of what he did was not reborn but vanished at the moment of its greatest import. The pattern that Americans crafted dictated as much. And as the pattern the brothers envisioned died, a new one was being born with each new event.[32]

Events, then, overtook the man. Independence became a watchword. Americans now construed a cultural sensibility of being a people beholden to none as a political principle.[33] Although the critical shift began with Charles and American responses to him, his role was forgotten, however much what he had done would haunt Americans. In other words, making revolution entailed new patterns of how history had to work, remembering and forgetting, as well as turning Charles, who had proudly thought himself an exceptional talent and man of virtue who had discovered his destiny, into a ghost.

Slavery

It could be argued that the Townshend Duties led to American Independence. Although all the talk of Charles starting the "War," as one of those who later recalled his death suggested, may have been overblown, the duties represented a watershed moment in the move to independence, a critical component in a series of moves and countermoves, understandings and misunderstandings, realized plans and abortive plans that convinced many Americans they had to pull away from empire. At this point, some colonists also began to interpret what was happening around the world and in Britain in darker ways. Certainly some historians see it this way. What Charles tried to do laid bare the gulf over constitutional issues that could no longer be avoided, and colonists began to move from patriotic resistance toward independence.[34]

Yet, this is the least of what this episode meant for America. The ghost of Charles hints at something deeper and more fundamental that was stirring in America in these years, something the man bore some responsibility for. At one point during the *Dialogues*, the shade Charles tells Montgomery to be careful what he wishes for in supporting independence. "Your famous Congress," he warns, "is less intended as a bulwark against tyranny, than as a support to an Aristocracy." The admonition points to the use of a term that would fittingly come to define the specter of counterrevolution during the French Revolution; more important, it suggests how this rebellion could have less to do with home rule than with who was to rule at home. In essence, Charles thinks a bid for independence could raise other ghosts of America's past. Revolution or unleashing the furies within a society, in other words, could unwittingly spring from what men like Montgomery and Dickinson had wrought.[35]

Montgomery acknowledges Charles's point. He and others had acted in hope of "preventing future slavery." He concedes, "The wise few have, undoubtedly, influenced the giddy multitude in this resolution, from which they cannot recede without falling into the jaws of destruction." As he puts it, "Prudent leaders . . . [have then] to contain in due bounds those they command, when, from a wavering and inconsistent temper they excite trouble, and threaten division." To gain independence and protect his freedoms, Montgomery is willing to run such a risk. He and others like him, he reckons, could contain any contagion coming from the "fickle vulgar."[36]

He was right and he was wrong. And this gets us to the most significant outcome of the Townshend moment. What the brothers accomplished did not only create a crisis of sovereignty for the empire and precipitate a series of clarifying responses on the part of provincials. It also challenged ruling assumptions that had sustained order in both Ireland and America, because the debates it engendered unleashed older frustrations in each society. The provincial conceit of autonomy within a federated empire could be challenged by British leaders, but as American patriotic leaders struggled against centralization, they revealed how their status could be contested from below. Once the brothers mounted their system, they destabilized even this imperfect system of control that provincial elites used to prop up their status. The question of home rule, then, could not be disentangled from who was to rule at home.

This confluence came to the fore on the very day the duties took effect, 21 November, when a large group of Bostonians, led by Sons of Liberty, marched through the streets with effigies of the commissioners and distributed what one person called "inflammatory" papers.[37] And one of Charles's former aides found himself at the eye of this storm. Henry Hulton traveled to Boston as one of the commissioners on the newly created Board of Customs. Hulton dated the origins of what would be the American Revolution from his entry into Boston. No sooner had he landed than he and the other commissioners, he wrote, "were exhibited in Effigy round the town, along with the Effigies of the Pope, Pretender and Devil, all which were cast into the bonfire at night."[38]

With the duties, Hulton suggested, the lid came off Boston society. The history he wrote of events after the fact was peopled with such "mobs" inflamed by what he called "the sons of violence." He revealed a true Loyalist sensibility: demagogues whipped up an easily duped rabble; the leveling spirit undid all that made a society a society; and only a proper respect for order, and efficacious government, could restore people to their senses. Force was necessary because of the dynamic that now gripped Boston. What Charles had done, Hulton argued, "was now looked on as a means to rivet the Chains of oppression and the resentment of the People." If we look beyond the biases, what we see is a society reeling from both civil strife and an imperial crisis that common people perceived as linked together and forged by Parliament. For this, it should be noted, Hulton held "the Farmer," who had "great influence in riveting the new Doctrines in the minds of the people," responsible.[39]

The royal governor of Massachusetts, Francis Bernard, saw growing radicalization among both the middling and the lower sort—what he called "Men of a lower Rank of Life"—as a response to the duties. "The Minds of the common People," he charged, "are poisoned to a great Degree; so that (to use an Expression of one their partisans) their Bloods are set on boiling." No doubt, he appreciated what Charles had aimed to do, especially in placing system before revenue, and he applauded the fact that, in theory, his salary would not be beholden to an inimical legislature. Townshend earned his praise for "striking at the Root of the American Disorder" by allowing governors to do what they were charged to do. He just questioned the timing. Coming on the heels of the repeal of the Stamp Act, the duties were sure to heighten tensions. The duties also gave an excuse for those Bostonians intent on ruling but cut out by a stratum of better-connected elites—Samuel Adams, James Otis, and John Hancock, to name just three of what Bernard called "Gentlemen Actors"—to mobilize the common sort for their ends. Their twisted ambitions, he argued, "make their destruction of their Country a matter of indifference to 'em."[40]

As a report breathlessly argued, uncertainty reigned because new voices were emerging in the tumult Charles had unwittingly generated. The *Pennsylvania Gazette* noted that by 1769 the colonies were "in an Uproar about their Liberties." With the older bases of order discredited, people who had not been actors before began to assume new roles. This occurred both in Ireland and in the colonies. The Townshend initiatives, of course, created a constitutional crisis, destabilizing both places and leading to an attenuation of authority. This occasioned new opportunities for many in British America. The crisis encouraged the planters, lawyers, and merchants who published pamphlets and wrote for newspapers to find their voices, to articulate a vision of who they were within the empire, and to stake a claim for their right to rule a provincial society.[41]

Yet, all Americans were awakening in these years, and as they did so, tensions emerged. One of the most dynamic things to occur in the late 1760s was the mass politicization of American society, a process Burke summed up in 1769 with this pithy phrase: "America is more wild and absurd than ever." Everyday life was growing more and more political, especially as protests often concerned the very things that defined everyday life: tea and other goods. Perhaps more significantly, more people were stepping into unaccustomed roles as local authority was weakened by protest. With sovereignty questioned and local authority foundering, more and more people acted in self-sovereign ways just as they began to define how they saw their worlds through the political. The impulse to do so, as one historian argues, became "urgent."[42]

Common men had good reason to be resentful. In the wake of the Seven Years' War, local trade in the colonies had been constricted, and even large merchant houses collapsed. In northern cities, the years 1767 to 1769 proved especially difficult. The early 1770s did not see much improvement, driving small shopkeepers into bankruptcy and the poorer sort to the poorhouse. In Boston, British troops were competing with locals for scarce jobs, heightening animosity between these groups, and in this context so fraught with tension, roving bands of young men and British soldiers walked the streets looking for fights.[43]

Such passions led to incidents like the Boston Massacre, in which younger men from the margins of society, just the sort upset with their lot in life after the war, confronted soldiers. Just as significant as the violence were the people involved. John Adams, who defended the soldiers, said at the trial that those who died were "most probably a motley rabble of saucy boys, negroes, and mulattoes, Irish teagues and outlandish jack tars." Indeed, a rope maker, a black sailor named Crispus Attucks, and an Irish immigrant were among the dead. Ironically, the rioters were killed by Irishmen named Hartegan, White, and Killroy under the command of an Irish officer named Thomas Preston serving in the British army.[44] With this incident, George's success in Ireland met Charles's failure for America.

These Bostonians were giving vent to a changing economic system and a shifting understanding of deference and responsibility in a tense political context. What they did had deep political meaning, in terms not only of what they aimed at ideologically—British troops—but also of what their actions meant structurally.[45] The men still believed that the economy and society, as well as the relationship that animated both, had to be constrained by moral laws, that an economy amounted to more than the sum total of supply and demand. When they rioted, as they did throughout Boston in the years between 1767 and 1770, they were articulating a deep sense of frustration with the fortunes of their lives in a quickly changing world. And they took aim at the relationship to Britain, which came to symbolize the idea of subordination. In farming villages as well, the same politicizing dynamic was taking hold. It did so also among new immigrant groups living in rural areas, including even German speakers.[46]

Politicization, however, knew no bounds, and as Americans made rhetorical choices, they opened new avenues of political action. Take the role of women, for instance. As protest increasingly hinged on consumption and nonconsumption, as well as the production of homespun goods to demonstrate political commitment, women began to play critically important roles in protesting Parliament's measures. They were becoming actors. What is critical to understand is that they did so while all America was becoming energized politically. Boston's initial response to the Townshend Duties offers a perfect example. In October 1767, printed subscription sheets appeared on the streets, encouraging townspeople to consume goods made in British America and to refuse to "purchase" any articles "imported from Abroad." The subscription sheets complained less of constitutional issues than of economic realities in Boston. The city was still suffering through a postwar recession. Those 650 signing the list to boycott British goods included not only notables such as Paul Revere and James Otis but also sixty-five women, including one Catherine Thompson, who made her mark on the document. These sixty-five had become key players in a political drama, one transatlantic in scope but deeply local in inflection.[47]

The politicization in the wake of the Townshend Duties occurred in often unpredictable and contradictory ways, challenging elites and moving Americans along unforeseen paths to independence. To understand this dynamic means appreciating the power of one word used over and over again in these years: slave. The use of the terms "slave" and "slavery" to describe the plight of Americans exploded in 1768. In 1765, as rumors flew about the imposition of the Stamp Act, whites had used the terms unapologetically. They did so even more insistently as they began to perceive a pattern: fetters, they believed, were being forged link by link. After the passage of the Townshend Acts, Chatham's words in Parliament and the work of the Farmer, both of which alluded to slavery, galvanized this way of thinking. One scholar has gone so far to suggest that "Dickinson and his ubiquitous *Letters* prepared colonial readers to think of oppressive parliamentary governments as a form of slavery, paving the path to revolution." No North American, he argues, "did more to propagate this tie between slavery and taxation without representation." Of course, such tropes represented commonplaces in the British Atlantic world in the eighteenth century. But for Americans contesting Charles's measures, the term "slave" possessed special meaning. Taxation without consent amounted to slavery. Such a condition made men servile.[48]

These ideas animated American discourse in the North and in the South. South Carolinians protested, "We are as real SLAVES as those we are permitted to command." As a writer styling himself a "Loyal Patriot" put it, "How might the British Patriots ease that Nation, even to the utmost Extent of our narrow Circumstances, by loading her American Children with arbitrary Taxations, under plausible false Pretensions of Justice, Expediency, Necessity, and the great Danger of our growing Opulence and Independency? Slavery might thrive very fast through such Nourishment, and invidious Charges of Rebellion for extorted Invectives." For this writer, the Stamp Act and what Townshend did proved the point of a slavish plot. "That British Commons thus assume the Guardianship of the Subject," he argued, "is even incontestably notorious; and yet now our famous nominal Guardians, through the Plentitude of their Money-raising Power, would freely damn the constitutional Liberty of their American Fellow Subjects, and ignobly intail perpetual Slavery upon us!"[49]

At the most basic level, the slavery trope had some troubling consequences for American elites. George Washington understood the irony even if he would not admit its implications. Washington feared that the British, like Townshend, planned to "make us as tame, & abject Slaves, as the Blacks we rule over with such arbitrary Sway." Others called hypocrisy for what it was. "SINCE you are pleased to enquire what my Sentiments respecting the right of the British Parliament to lay Taxes on the Colonies," a writer calling himself a "Gentleman" argued in 1768, "to raise a revenue, etc.? I think, the best answer to your question, that can be given, in a few words, is by way of reference to the very excellent and adapted letters, signed A FARMER." He went on to say, "The ingenious and discerning Author, has, I conceive, made it sufficiently evident that such a Taxation is Unconstitutional, destructive to England and her Colonies, enslaving to his Majesty's most dutiful Subjects." He did, however, note a troubling problem. "But how can You, Sir," he asked "in *New-England*, join the other Colonies in complaining of Slavery on account of such a Taxation, when, at the same time, you are enslaving and persecuting one another, in matters of much greater Importance, than *merely* a temporary interest can possibly be?"[50]

The discourse that characterized men like Dickinson and presumably "Loyal Patriot" as slaves came at a cost, and hypocrisy was the least of it. The famous quip made by Samuel Johnson, "How is it that we hear the loudest yelps for liberty among the drivers of negroes?" pointed to the uncomfortable truth that American patriots were focusing on a contradiction that underscored the relationship between American slavery and American freedom. One depended on the other, so not surprisingly the charges that the British were acting as slave masters grew in intensity after the passage of the duties when Americans considered their freedoms under assault by a pattern of action. The patterns Americans constructed in their mind gave plausibility to the old Whiggish trope, and as it did so the commonplace took on a political edge. To be a slave meant that one's assembly had no significant power. It meant one did not enjoy the same rights as a Briton in England. It revealed the deepest fears of Americans, that they were not quite equal, that they were, in fact, mere provincials, that they appeared little better than those who toiled in their fields. This anxiety, then, turned most Americans into active political agents and certainly ended any sense of complacency. The fears of slavery did not amount to overblown abstractions, hypocritical rantings, or a basic inconsistency. They had real valence.[51]

Denying they were slaves drew white Americans to their pasts in ways that would encourage them to cast their futures in a new light. Americans like Washington and Dickinson had to reimagine the role of their ancestors to make a plausible case that they could be made slaves because of what Charles Townshend had drawn up. In fact, Americans became entranced with their origins in the late 1760s. They harkened back again and again to the time when the ancestors of Dickinson toiled to carve out a niche in what their descendants called a "wilderness."[52] As Americans confronted Charles's system, they had little choice but to look to their past to contest the measures. Charles rooted his system in Parliament and made arguments about the right of that body to rule the provinces by appealing to the past. Americans used history as much as George and Charles did, but they did so in a way to suggest that their ancestors, as freemen, had tamed a cruel continent without the aid of those in the metropole or the help of those working in the fields. They had integrated the colonies in an increasingly civilized Atlantic world on their own. They were given nothing. They had sacrificed their all to win England its colonies. Such sacrifice counted for a great deal by absolving all sorts of sins, even America's original sins. How could they ever be considered slaves?

Status as a free people who could not be enslaved depended on history. In pamphlets and newspapers, colonists revisited what a colony was and who they were. They hastened to argue that America was not a province, a place animated by the center and ruled by it, and that they were not mere provincials. They constituted part of the empire, but they did so on their own terms.

History had won them that right. In 1768, for instance, a group from New Jersey petitioned the king by endorsing what the Farmer had written. They noted the Townshend Duties were raised "for the sole and express purposes of raising a revenue." They clamored for their rights as "Freemen," continuing with the Dickinsonian tropes, and declared: "Very far is it from our intention, to deny our subordination to that august body or our dependence on the kingdom of Great Britain." They did, though, situate their pleas and their rights in what their ancestors had done, much like the spectral Montgomery. "Our ancestors," they argued, "with the consent of the crown, removed from their native land, then abounding in all blessings . . . to the inhospitable and unknown wilderness of this new world; the horrors of which no consideration could render intolerable; but the prospect of enjoying here that compleat freedom, which Britons thought could be purchased at too great a price." They brought their rights over from England and should have been able to enjoy these unmolested. They were sons, not bastards, as Chatham had said, though they added that their sacrifice had secured their inheritance and their status as free men.[53]

This sentiment enjoyed as widespread an appeal as the Farmer's formulations. Rhode Islanders dedicated a Liberty Tree in 1768 using the same formulation, citing "the extremest toil, difficulty, and danger, [with which] our noble ancestors founded in *America* a number of colonies." Freemen from Pennsylvania followed suit, arguing that their ancestors, too, had "settled in this distant Land then a Wilderness." They had, of course, ascended from such a state of nature and created through work and sacrifice a society, one in which in their minds also made them heirs to the same sorts of Roman thinkers like Tacitus that George and Charles had lionized. As "A Son of Liberty" from Connecticut put it, "We in these American Colonies have been long used to glory in the Thought of our being Englishmen. . . . We knew that we were descended from Britons;—that we had subdued and cultivated, in some Measure, a hideous Wilderness and rendered it a most useful Part of the British Empire." Now, alas, they were prey to "Some evil Genius, some baleful, envious Spirit," which "Whether from France, or Rome, or Hell, I leave the Conjurer to tell."[54] The conjurer was a ghost by now, of course.

Throughout the colonies in these years, Americans reprised an older argument, an invented past, one of wilderness, of merit and sacrifice, of freedom, which determined they would resist being made slaves. They had wrested a living from a stubborn land with the Crown's blessing. Parliament, however important an institution, played no part in the drama, and they enjoyed distinctive rights as settlers, explaining in part why what they regarded as one in a line of tyrannical ministers like Charles had disappeared from the narrative.[55] Actual slaves did not feature in this telling of the past. Neither did Indians. The emerging American origin myth colonists used to counter the conceit of the Townshend plan created a past without dispossessing land from Indians or exploiting slaves, a sanitized and bloodless Atlantic world in which English men and women who migrated played the sacrificial victims. This reimagined past gave the trope of slavery broad and deep appeal.

Slaves, however, were not tropes for those Americans contesting the Townshend Duties. Of course, as we know, enslaved persons found their voices, too, and they began to point out the uncomfortable asymmetry of white elites bellowing about their future as slaves. Quite understandably, blacks began in these years to petition for their rights, most notably in Boston, the epicenter of politicization. "We have in common with all other men," one petition read, "a naturel right to our freedoms without Being depriv'd of them by our fellow men as we are a freeborn Pepel."[56] John Adams argued, "There have been many such cases," as, for instance, a black whaler who sued for his freedom and an enslaved woman from Salem who took her master to court.[57] In the late 1760s and early 1770s, black political life, widely conceived, picked up dramatically.[58]

No doubt, slaves had often risen up to contest their status. Now these instances had a political edge, both in terms of their aims and in terms of how actions and words were interpreted in this period of political anxiety. As white Americans grappled with the meanings of "freedom" and "slavery" because of the attempt to centralize authority, black Americans seized on the glaring distinction between the two categories in their lives. In so doing, as one historian suggests, those in the North "raised the specter of a rebellion within a rebellion."[59]

Blacks acted out of doors in the South as well, where the institution of slavery was most deeply entrenched and where it defined social and economic relations. Slaves in the South also petitioned for their rights, and even some chanted "Liberty" in the streets. This was no "thoughtless imitation," as a planter put it. As one historian argues, with the imperial crisis "slave unrest was more intensive and widespread than in any other previous period."

Slaves, too, were caught up in the political pulses of the times. There is, to substantiate this claim, some evidence that the number of slave runaways was growing in the years after 1767. In South Carolina the number of runaway advertisements in newspapers leaped from sixty-seven to ninety-four. Georgia witnessed a similar pattern beginning in the mid-1760s. Maryland saw more modest but discernible increases beginning in 1768. We can draw no causal connection between the imperial crisis and runaways, and the numbers can be suspect. After all, newspapers came and went, some issues have not survived, and advertisements depended on reporting. So the best we have is a partial and fuzzy snapshot. Nonetheless, such reports suggest that in the eyes of whites, the same eyes that read the newspapers, slaves were voting on the labor regimes of the South with their feet. More critical for our purposes, we know that running away did not always represent an act of desperation; it could be and often was political in intent, a means for voiceless persons to declare their independence.[60]

More troublingly for whites, a series of incidents in the South in these years, in which slaves beat overseers, pointed to the possibility of "conspiracies" in white minds. In South Carolina, fears grew and rumors swirled of intended "insurrections" of slaves. With the specter of such possibilities in the minds of whites as they pushed for their freedom, local officials suppressed any slave action and responded even to rumors with vigor. In one instance, in a fight between whites and blacks known as "bloody Christmas," whites killed a number of slaves in Virginia as fears swept the Tidewater of slave rebellions. In another spot in Virginia, officials hanged seven slaves and had the heads of some of those killed cut off and hung from the courthouse. Indeed, in the years after 1767 the specter of slave insurrection became more persistent throughout the colonies and in the Caribbean. This dynamic stemmed, in part, from the growing radicalization of slaves in the Caribbean, some of whom were being imported into the mainland colonies, what one historian characterizes as a "surge of revolutionary activity by slaves." This sort of "great Ferment," so argues another scholar, gripped the imaginations of many Americans beginning with this moment.[61]

Nothing motivated local elites like the fear of slave uprisings. As James Madison put it in 1774, "It is prudent such things should be concealed as well as suppressed." Were these conspiracies taking place? It is hard to tell, and in point of fact it does not much matter. This much is true: whites were worried about slave risings in their midst. And some saw black politicization as a British-inspired plot, or "instigated insurrections." In 1775, Dickinson argued such was the case, citing "the Danger of Insurrection in Southern Colonies" as part of a series of ministerial "designs." Indeed, studies of the patterns associated with "panics" attributable to fears of slave insurrection demonstrate that they stemmed from deep vulnerabilities on the part of whites. They also suggest how the patterns white provincials in America had created to make sense of their plight in the late 1760s were finding fertile ground for making meaning in the mid-1770s with black politicization.[62]

In the politicized context of the late 1760s and early 1770s, settlers and planters understandably saw such instances through the lens of growing tensions with Parliament. To cite just one telling example, in 1768 an official from South Carolina informed the ministry, "The Circular Boston Letter has been published in every Gazette on the Continent," including the *South Carolina and American General Gazette*. He was referring to the concerted response to the duties in the wake of the Farmer's *Letters*. He also related how disputes over rights in the western part of the colony, in which politicized settlers were contesting local authorities, could not be quelled by troops. "The only resource where a Military Force for such service can be raised," he believed, "must be among our Maritime Settlements, where White Inhabitants are few and a numerous domestic Enemy is thick sown in our Plantations." By "domestic enemies" he meant slaves. These unruly enemies, he argued, "require our utmost attention to keep them in order." The fear of slave insurrection could not be detached in his mind from what he regarded as the disorders gripping all the colonies and the particular form that mass politicization was taking in South Carolina.[63] Heightened anxiety played on politicization, creating an environment in which panic and rumor flew.[64]

The Townshend moment, then, revived provincial ghosts. It revealed quite clearly the basis of order within American colonies. And the response of people like Dickinson revealed the nature of inclusions and exclusions to political life in all of the colonies, leading to what one historian studying a very different revolutionary moment refers to as the "dynamic destabilization" of American society.[65] To sustain the idea that Americans had rights, that they could not be considered second-class subjects, meant that Dickinson and others had to go back to the seventeenth century to demonstrate how they had a justification to make the claims they did. They remembered settlement. They recounted their mastery of the land as well as its native people.

They also had to grapple, of course, with the meanings of slavery. This was far from a rhetorical point. With the creation in their minds of the pattern of abuses that had transformed Charles into a ghost, colonists believed that they were excluded from the rights of citizenship, that they were suffering a political death. They were gesturing to a powerful but perverse inversion: the masters were becoming slaves themselves. Their status as leaders at home, which was born through their ancestors driving "savages" off their land and capturing "drudges" to work their fields, was imperiled once Parliament was asserting its right to control their land and their persons. The issue not only pointed squarely to a sordid past, it also went to the heart of what made colonists, even in their subservient position in the empire, estimable men.

The predicament white Americans found themselves in was this: if they wanted to assert their rights and stand up to what Charles had done, they had to clarify relationships. Doing so necessitated a review of their history, something they would rather have left untouched. It also required an explanation of the basis of their current authority as masters in their colonies. This, too, they would have preferred not to explore. The unspoken, the hidden, the assumed, all became fair game once they decided to contest Charles's plan.

The divisions emerging over the duties also revealed all sorts of rifts in American society. Those swearing to oppose Charles's plan—those rioting and those behind the riots—saw their status in society imperiled. The war had created a new class of wealthy merchants that had thrived with the consolidation of the Atlantic. While these men had risen, others had fallen. Women saw with protest new possibilities of asserting themselves. Others, wealthier but still a rung below the truly elite, worried that they would never rule in America so long as the status quo reigned. The looming divisions created opportunities for them not so much to climb the ladder as to pull it down. The riots gripping cities sprang from these tangled dynamics. Charles's plans, then, fractured American cities. It also forced many to take stock of their lots in life and to ask if, under the current circumstances, they could hope to fare as well as their parents had.

The upshot, as far as Charles and his ghost were concerned, is that the plans had misfired in ways the mortal Charles, and his specter for that matter, would never have believed. The patriot Paul Revere provided a fitting example of how they had gone awry. Revere, who had signed on to nonimportation agreements, produced an image of British troops arriving in

15. *A View of Part of the Town of Boston in New-England and British Ships of War Landing Their Troops, 1768,* engraving by Paul Revere

Boston in 1768, many of them from Cork, which was where they had been stationed. They marched, Revere reported, from Long Wharf up King Street "with Insolent Parade" and "Drums beating, Fife playing, and Colours flying." Each soldier carried "16 rounds of Powder and Ball."[66] Revere's interpretation pointed out the perversity of what was happening. Politicization in the wake of what Charles had done had created an urgent need to bring the troops from the kingdom George was reforming. This symbiotic relationship was not what the brothers had imagined, or what Revere could have prophesied even a few years earlier. But in Revere's mind, as well as the minds of more and more members of the American elite, this was all in keeping with a new pattern that was becoming deeply ingrained. Such patterning determined that slavery was design.

After 1770, America would calm down, especially as the ministry backed off and revoked nearly all of the duties. Nonetheless, from 1767 until 1770, new ways of appreciating the past had emerged. New voices were heard. None of these would remain quiet when, or if, Parliament acted again. The world, through the provincial moment, had changed utterly.

Vanishing Acts

For Americans, Charles had to vanish, given the ways they were beginning to see the empire and their plight. Ironically, the vanishings took place because what Charles had done became a catalyzing event that encouraged Americans to invent the patterns that erased him. The same happened in Ireland. George, too, disappeared, but for different reasons and with different implications. Most prosaically, he disappeared in 1772 by being replaced as lord lieutenant.

In 1772, George left Ireland, recalled by Lord North. He did so with some bitter memories and with lingering anger. Most painful of all, in September 1770 his wife had died in Leixlip Castle. Friends tried to console his "unspeakable loss." In writing to North, George had portrayed her death as a "heavy Calamity," one that had pulled him into the sort of darkness he had experienced on Charles's passing. Nonetheless, when he returned to England, his feistiness remained. In fact, in 1773 he accepted and fought a duel in England against an Irish client for whom he had done a favor. In London at Mary-le-bone fields, armed with small swords and pistols, George doffed his hat to his opponent, was given the first shot, and fired. His ball wounded his adversary in the groin. The man was carried off the field in a chair in great pain, but survived.[67]

George's best years were behind him. In 1773, he was married again, to Anne Montgomery, the daughter of an Irish M.P., with whom he would have six more children, and continued a life dedicated to public service. He served on the Ordnance as soon as he left Ireland and did so again later. He retained an interest in the militia and assumed the role of lord lieutenant of the County of Norfolk, a powerful local position, but nothing akin to the post he had held in Ireland. He also held a number of honorific titles, including governor of Chelsea, governor of Hull, and field marshal and governor of Jersey. Most conspicuously, he was elevated to the rank of marquess in 1787 in recognition of all that he had done for Britain over the course of his life. He had also lobbied for the elevation ever since Charles had been Chancellor of the Exchequer. He then devoted himself to the concerns of the country. As the famous political economist Arthur Young wrote, he came up with a "discovery in feeding cattle and sheep with the trimmings of plantations." In his retirement, he lamented how men such as him, who had served and then led, had "been treated as the meer Machinery of Government." Though put out to pasture, he would continue, he said, "[to] express my attachment to the Constitution and its Scepter," even if he did so from the margins.[68]

Most forgot George once he left Ireland. Still, he followed events in Ireland closely, even speaking in the House of Lords a number of times on Irish trade issues, and he sent long notes to his successor, Lord Harcourt, telling him of his challenges, what to watch out for, and how Ireland now functioned. "No one can be more aware," he wrote, "of the arduous task you undertake than I am, and I hope that the many vicissitudes and hard struggles which I have experienced, tho' supported by a gracious master and a firm administration, will be found to have rendered your Lordship's Government less difficult and painfull." George took pride in what he had done, what he called "the favourable circumstances of Government." He was especially pleased with how he had mastered the undertakers. As he put it, Lord Shannon arrived in Parliament "robed and carried a sword of State" but "afterwards appeared at the Castle with his principal friends." George also claimed to have triumphed over "vain and fruitless opposition." He was referring to the Patriots, of course.[69] A betting man would have put his money on Charles achieving his vision rather than George. The younger brother had been the visionary and the extraordinary talent. Yet George, the more stubborn of the two, had triumphed in his immediate task.

However different the fortunes of the brothers, George also vanished in both the Irish and the broader imperial story. Let us start with the imperial story. George vanished most conspicuously in one of the most famous and enduring images of the period, one that focused on his and Charles's old patron, and hero to Flood and Dickinson, the Earl of Chatham. The story starts in Parliament. On 7 April 1778, the peers in the House of Lords argued over whether or not to let the colonies go their own way. With the British embroiled in a war against France, their troops and navies stretched beyond capacity, and with no end in sight in putting down what they called a colonial rebellion, common sense suggested that they should cut their losses and come to some sort of accommodation with an independent America. Chatham, who had made America the centerpiece of his maritime empire, would have none of it. If America went, so would all he had struggled for. The Duke of Richmond made an impassioned argument for the British to let the colonies be and to make peace with America. Helped to his feet with his crutches, the gouty Chatham delivered an extraordinary performance, explaining why America mattered so much to the whole. If America left,

Britain would decline. "I will as soon *subscribe* to *Transubstantiation* as to *Sovereignty, by Right,* in the Colonies," he had declared to the Earl of Shelburne just before the session. When he stood to speak a second time, he fell backward and fainted, suffering a stroke. He died a month later.[70]

In a letter written soon after the event, George reported on the episode. On the day of the collapse, George sent a letter to one of his old friends, sharing how he had "this moment returned home from the House of Peers." He wrote how "Lord Chatham has been on the point of Death, just as he was preparing to rise, as it seemed to me who was opposite, to reply a second time to the Duke of Richmond." He recounted the whole scene that took place before his eyes. "Lord Chatham," he reported, "came into the House very feeble, seemingly to me who met him as he came in, and spoke to him." George said, "His first Speech was very short and spoke in great pain, and appeared to me to sink under the oppression of his Disorder." He saw, however, "much animation and decision." In George's telling, Chatham played his role as guardian of the empire. "He lamented," George continued, "the critical and wretched situation of the British Empire, but he reprobated and disdained the Indecision of the Ministers and the degrading and degenerate Language of the Houses of Parliament of the Nation." George, it seems, put some of his own words into Chatham's mouth, but he did appreciate the gist of the speech. Chatham "particularized by a Dismemberment of one 3rd of their Dominions—viz. America—and reprobated the idea of offering Independence. His voice sank afterwards."[71]

George's breathless letter serves as a witness to the event. When the moment came, we read, "he appeared to me preparing to rise, when a deadly convulsion struck him." Many crowded round Chatham. "I ran for water, which I procured immediately." When Chatham collapsed, George moved to support his patron, leaving only when other members did so "to give him air." George waited for the physician to arrive and have him carried out, and long enough to learn that by 8 P.M. Chatham was feeling a bit better. "It was," George concluded, "a Melancholly Scene." Not only was George present, he was one of the few to act.[72]

The vanishings then began. Benjamin West produced a small piece, really a study, of the scene filled with peers in the chamber at the precise moment Chatham collapsed, which he hoped later to turn into something on a larger scale. He never finished it. A Sotheby's auction catalogue, which includes the key, reveals that George is not in the painting.[73] Exclusion, since

George had been in the Lords when Chatham fell, almost certainly would have been deliberate, so crowded is the scene West populated, only more so because Chatham, after all, was one of George's heroes and had brought him into government in 1767.

Later, John Singleton Copley completed his masterpiece of the scene, now in the National Portrait Gallery in London. This is a study of empire, of rise and most especially of fall. Chatham, the architect of empire at the time of Seven Years' War, collapses in a room as the British cause is collapsing in America. Behind him on the wall of the chamber is a tapestry commemorating the defeat of the Spanish Armada. For the American Copley, Chatham was the last great hope for empire. The painting of Chatham and his fall represented his lament over the fall of the empire, one that he thought as a loyal American belonged to him as well. It had arisen in the late sixteenth century with the Armada, paving the way for the settlement of the colonies; it had fallen when the great hero, Chatham, had collapsed while he made a final futile gesture to try to reconcile metropole and province.

16. John Singleton Copley (1738–1815), *The Collapse of the Earl of Chatham in the House of Lords, 7 July 1778*, 1779–1780 (Photograph © Tate, London, 2016)

Copley's painting serves as a companion piece to West's *Death of General Wolfe*. Copley clearly mimicked West's composition. Chatham, the new Wolfe, dies not with a bang but with a whimper, in a room of deliberation. There, Copley suggests, empire was lost. It had been won by the likes of Wolfe through war and sacrifice. Politicians now sacrificed it with words and self-interest. And this is the other intriguing aspect of the painting. To finish it Copley had to travel far and wide over two years to complete more than fifty portraits of those in the Lords when Chatham collapsed. He combined the virtues of both portraiture and history painting to make something he hoped would be accurate but would also tell a tale. As he put it, he aimed for "uniting the value of living characters to the dignity of an historical fact . . . which no other picture extant has to boast of in any degree equal to this."[74]

The people in the painting matter to the theme. When looking at the key, however, we see that George Townshend is nowhere to be found. The exhibition drew thousands to see the painting at the Great Room in Spring Gardens, for which Copley charged a fee. Throngs queued to see it—on some days as many as eight hundred. Within six weeks, twenty thousand had viewed it. Published for the exhibition was a "description of Mr. Copley's Picture," along with "a list of portraits." The description was meant to entice viewers to purchase an engraving of the image, all the more impressive because "this is the most arduous work of the kind hitherto undertaken in any Country." The Italian artist Francesco Bartolozzi produced a key to the engraving, which shows the faces of each of those in this history painting of portraits. Twenty-five hundred large engravings were sold. George does not appear. Copley even placed George's eldest, estranged son in the painting: Lord Ferrers, with whom George had had a falling out after his first wife's death. He appears in a key position in the piece, with his hand on the Armada tapestry, thereby playing a critical role in the composition, even if, as one critic charged, he "was once so genteel and thin a gentleman" but in the painting looked like "a fat Dutch mastiff."[75] He is there. But not George.

Copley, like West, would have many of his subjects in such paintings sit for portraits before composing something on a grand scale. And perhaps this is the reason for the exclusion.[76] Maybe George Townshend did not pay for a portrait, and Copley was consumed with making money from his paintings. Moreover, George had sat for his friend Reynolds a number of times, and chances are he may not have wanted to do so for West or Copley. And Copley had a difficult relationship with Reynolds. Maybe George was still shunned by the painters because of the Wolfe affair. Whatever the reason, and we may never know, he once again vanished. He had disappeared in West's vision of the origins of empire; he disappeared in Copley's requiem for empire.

The vanishing act is fitting. And this gets us to the Irish disappearance. On the face of it, just as Charles's ghost was wringing his hands over America, all that George had done for Ireland seemed to disappear. Events soon swallowed his vision as well. On the surface of things, it looked as though George would lose to the Patriots once he destroyed the undertakers. Indeed, the story of the Patriots appears as one success after another leading also to independence. Just as event after event seemed to form an American pattern, the flow of what happened in Ireland after George's departure made for an Irish litany. Once he left, the Patriot movement coalesced, especially as its leaders followed events in America closely.[77] Emulating the Americans, they began to press for the rights of the Irish nation. They set their sights on the end of trade restrictions and the undoing of Poynings' Law and the Declaratory Act, hoping to make Ireland a kingdom with its own integrity.

The Patriots, in their focus on what George had done, reknitted a narrative extending from Molyneux and Swift to Lucas and Flood. The reprinting of Molyneux's work is a case in point. The story would, another author calling himself "The Farmer" wrote, link their present to a patriotic past. The years of Townshend joined a long imagined line of resistance, beginning in the previous century and reaching a new high-water mark with Lucas's defense of Dublin's liberties, the Money Bill dispute of the 1750s, then the entrance of Flood on the stage. Just as Charles went missing, therefore, so too did George. The construction of memory and its patterns were responsible. And this essential narrative would animate all of Ireland as the knitting of the new narrative grew even more deeply entrenched. The persuasiveness of that story would only grow as event after event was added to the patriotic pattern.[78]

The pattern reached its culmination ten years after George left. With the war in America, Irish Protestants formed themselves into "Volunteer" units, ostensibly to defend Ireland from French invasion, but in fact to demonstrate their resolve to stand for what they characterized as Ireland's freedom within the British state. Indeed, George worried that they would not be able to defend Ireland, that fleets and troops would have to be mobilized or else, he wrote, "Ireland, I fear, will soon have Spain as well as France to look to." He needn't have worried. In fact, he could not have foreseen what the Volunteers would eventually do for Ireland. In 1782, they would win their ultimate prize, legislative independence, largely through the efforts of Volunteers out of doors and the skills of Patriot orators such as Henry Grattan indoors. In what would be known as "the revolution of 1782," the Ireland of Flood and Grattan would finally gain control of a destiny imagined by Swift and Lucas. These years witnessed Ireland gaining its economic autonomy and its constitutional rights, two victories—perhaps revolutionary in themselves—that by any measure finally fulfilled the promise of the Glorious Revolution. As Grattan declared in 1782, "Spirit of Swift, spirit of Molyneux, your genius has prevailed, Ireland is now a nation."[79] All that George had struggled to accomplish seemed to vanish. It seemed fitting that he disappeared from the Irish and imperial narrative.

Popery

Appearances can deceive. "Grattan's Parliament," as it was later called, did not initiate true reform of the institution of Parliament. Moreover, it certainly did not transform the kingdom or its relationship to Britain in any fundamental way. The Castle still ruled, appearances to the contrary. Parliamentary independence, most visibly, did little for the status of Catholics, and even if some Protestants believed Catholics should be free to worship as they saw fit, few would make the case that they deserved full political rights. In fact, the measure, in part, sought to strengthen the hold of the Ascendancy over the kingdom. It arose as much from anxiety as it did from confidence. And men like Flood and Grattan had ample reason to be anxious. They owed this fear—in its immediate manifestation—to George as well.[80] The "independence" of the Irish Parliament, or better the attenuated nature of that independence, emerged as Ireland, like America, became politicized because of a Townshend initiative.

To explain the nature of independence means uncovering other sides of the Irish story. The implications of George's actions paralleled those that his brother's ghost wrestled with, though they differed in subtle ways. No doubt, Flood and Grattan, too, worried about "slavery." They, too, used the term to describe what they regarded as political oppression. This potentiality, however, amounted to little more than an abstraction for them and was not freighted with the same meaning that it held for Americans.[81] Anxieties for them stemmed from Ireland's history and its marginalized people: Catholics. "Popery" was not an abstraction in Ireland, and the exalted status of churchmen depended on the denigration of Catholics. The position of Patriots also relied on tacit agreements not to disturb the political arrangements that ensured Catholics did not contest their position. Catholics were not "socially dead," as slaves in America were. Nor were they politically debilitated to the same degree. Nonetheless, political power in Ireland hinged on their disempowerment.

In George's wake, all were drawn into political affairs. It could not be otherwise. In a kingdom in which power was laid out and defended along confessional and socioeconomic lines, the justifications underscoring elite rule would be aired at the moment George implemented his system, especially as patriots in Ireland, like those in America, refined their understandings of sovereignty. Once patriots crystallized what the nature of the relationship between center and periphery should be, they had to expose exclusions and revisit their bases, many now obsolete. They too would have to grapple with the past and their own ghosts, however reluctant they were to do so.

In the Irish case, politicization created an almost kaleidoscopic sort of response to George's overtures. At the most basic level, with the Octennial Bill passed, Ireland now had regular elections. Voters had to be courted. It also meant places like Dublin pulsed with political energy. "Many of the counties and boroughs," George observed, "are strongly contested, and considerable sums of money have already been lavished, to the great encouragement of idleness and riot amongst common people." Of course, much of the country was "discontented and irritated" with George, and through the offices of men such as Lucas "was in a flame, and riotous mobs assembled about the avenues of the house, swearing and otherwise insulting the more obnoxious members." Lucas especially seemed to grow in stature on the energized political stage. He was playing the part, George wrote in 1768, of the "vile incendiary," trying to whip up "the citizens of Dublin against us."[82]

Elections represented troubling times for any administration in Ireland. Voices cried out for reform, and the Patriots were emboldened even if George had outmaneuvered them. He faced now "plausible objections from the Patriots" for his plans, and he was discovering, while the Castle was gaining ascendancy in the kingdom, that he was stirring resentments. "I own I am sick of these silly unprincipled indecorous politics," he fumed in 1769, "this low imitation of French Stratagem, where System and Decency are to be the sacrifice of a social hour, and a proper measure must at least have the appearance of ripened by some Petticoat Patronage." Dublin now seethed with political intrigue, especially since the Patriots had found a voice and focus. As one writer put it, with George's reforms, "Every Thing is in the utmost Confusion, and from Cork to Derry, the whole Country is in a Flame."[83]

Just as in America, the process of politicization began to change the roles of women in Ireland. Simply put, as the Castle became more and more prominent in the political life of the country, women now had outsized roles to play in protecting family interests, working with their husbands to secure place and position during a period of flux. Women also became more politically visible. As George reported to his successor, the new measures he put in place created difficulties he had not imagined. He had learned to "divide and subdivide their connexions" to control patronage. This had an unintended consequence. "Their ladies," he reported, "will solicit when their husbands threaten, and what is more indecent, the Ladies menace when the Men profess friendship." The politicization of Castle patronage now made all who worked with the Castle, including women, political actors. Those women who rejected the patronage offered by the Castle for patriotic reasons found critical roles to play as well, particularly as early attempts to undue parliamentary subordination focused on economic and, necessarily, household affairs. Paralleling what American patriots were doing to contest Parliament's presumption to tax, Irish Protestant women in Dublin also made homespun goods and policed consumption.[84]

Just as in America, common men found their voices. In Dublin, Protestant mobs could and did make their presence felt in response to what George was working to accomplish. Tied to the civic patriotism of Lucas, they let their displeasure be known most visibly on that infamous St. Patrick's Day in 1770, when the well-to-do made their way up Dame Street to the Castle in their domestic manufactures to attend the ball George was hosting. George, of course, thought he was doing the lower sort a favor by offering work while Parliament was prorogued. Most thought otherwise, and their actions went far beyond the war of words Patriots waged in the press. Some vandalized carriages with the words "Wilkes and Liberty," while others pressed the merrymakers to discover whether they were Patriots or not. This sort of behavior was not unprecedented, but it did become almost exclusively focused on the issues Flood and Lucas championed, particularly if Dubliners feared that George's initiatives betokened union. In 1771, to cite just one instance, "a great multitude of people from the liberty," an area dominated by Protestant weavers, "assembled in College Green," accosting members of Parliament "and compelling them to take oaths to be true to the interests of the country." Various guilds in these years also issued resolutions supporting shorter parliaments and voicing their displeasure over augmentation. Working men formed themselves into "Pitt clubs," supporting what they thought to be the Chathamite vision of what empire should be. They did so the very moment George began his work. As George put it, "The spirit of debate seems now to be transferred from the Parliament to some newborn oratorical societies in Dublin."[85]

Catholics, on the other hand, saw something to support in George's plan, and they took a more deliberate political stance as George's vision touched off constitutional debates. As O'Conor observed, Townshend was "huzzaed" by the Catholics. In many respects, the acclaim that some middle-class Catholics showed George was puzzling. One observer asked, "What particular service has Lord Townshend rendered the Papists?" O'Conor believed that Protestant Ireland's troubles under Townshend could be Catholic Ireland's opportunity. Throwing their weight behind him offered Catholics protection from the Ascendancy. It also provided them with an opening they had not had for nearly twenty years, when a Money Bill dispute challenged the political status quo. And so, unsurprisingly, agents for the Catholic Committee that Charles O'Conor headed up publicly thanked George for his "lenity" during his administration. Moreover, they used the occasion as an opportunity to emphasize "[our] loyal disposition, and that every act of ours shall always tend to the tranquility of this kingdom, and the support of his Majesty's person and government." Recognizing George in such a way left few doubts about the fully evolved political stance of middle-class Catholics. They had embraced loyalty.[86]

Catholics, especially those who were well-to-do, entered the political fray once more, but they did so more insistently than in the past. In doing so, they demonstrated that they did not fit into the conventional categories of Ascendancy politics. The *Dublin Mercury*, a Dublin newspaper catering to the Catholic merchant community and run by a Catholic, praised the lord lieutenant without qualification for challenging the many enemies of Catholics in the city. Indeed, as the Patriots were coalescing behind opposition to George, the paper ran a series written by John Courtenay, an Irish supporter and then client of the lord lieutenant. Courtenay aimed to counter the

Patriot press, and he found a willing audience in the readership of the *Mercury*. Calling himself Jeofrey Wagstaffe in a column he entitled "The Batchelor," Courtenay crystallized the middle-class Catholic response to what was happening in Ireland after 1767. He decried Lucas and the other Patriots as children. They, not George, were the "internal enemies" to the constitution. Courtenay lambasted undertakers and Patriots alike, suggesting that Ireland's problems stemmed not from the nature of the relationship to Britain but from venal landlords and rack renters. He derided those who protested the augmentation scheme. As he put it, just as Patriot protest was growing in vehemence, "we shall always consider the Octennial . . . and the Augmentation Bills, as the strongest instances of your M-----y's paternal care and affection." The bills "will always make the aera of L--- T------d's administration dear to us."[87]

More significantly, the Catholic Committee came to life again after a period of dormancy. In fact, it had been, as one historian argues, "moribund" before 1767. It revived itself because of two issues. The first had to do with the status of Catholic tradesmen, who were required to pay a tax called a "quarterage" in order to work. Emboldened by the charged political atmosphere in Ireland in the wake of the Octennial Act, Catholic tradesmen began pressing for their rights, and soon their cause was adopted by the Catholic Committee. The second issue was O'Conor's drafting of a statement of Catholic political principles, including what sort of oath of loyalty Catholics could countenance and what they could not, all of which encouraged groups of well-to-do Catholics to petition the administration in both Ireland and England to address their grievances. They did so, as one historian argues, "with a vigour in sharp contrast to the timidity of only a decade earlier." George, then, found himself an unwitting dupe in the politicization of the Catholic artisanal and middle classes. The imbroglio over quarterage and the support George had from the Catholic Committee only further inflamed Patriot opinion. George could be seen, as a later chronicler would put it, as showing "Popish partiality."[88]

Catholic loyalties presented vexing problems for Patriots, problems revealed by a telling episode involving Cork. As early as September 1769, Cork Catholics sent their congratulations to George for all he had been doing, much like their Protestant counterparts in Dublin; however, they also did so after he pressed for augmentation. The weavers and manufacturers of the city and the county wrote "with all Humiliation and with the most unfeigned Loyalty to our most gracious Sovereign" to thank George for visiting Cork and the western parts of Ireland. They promised their support: "[We] pray, that the Almighty may influence the Hearts of all Honest men to support your Excellency's good intentions of making the Military of this Country more useful, by a seasonable and proper Augmentation of its Numbers."[89]

This step, really a modest and careful show of support, infuriated Patriots. Just days after the report of the Cork address in the *Freeman's Journal,* writers sent letters to the paper condemning the weavers and manufacturers. These were a people, one wrote, "who had a Property to lose, and wished for an Augmentation of the Army to secure it." A writer using the poorly chosen sobriquet "Impartial" argued, "[They] are almost entirely Papists. These are the People pinched upon by the Agents of Government to address the L--d L--------t in behalf of a Measure held in Execration by the whole of the Kingdom." The Corkmen were, he believed, influenced by British "Tools of Power." He declared, "We ought however to despise these infamous Tools who were busy enough to supply the L--d L--------t with such political Counselors as a Banditti purchased at the Expence of *five Guineas.*"[90]

The Patriot press lampooned the Cork Catholics, in one instance calling them a "Race of Prostitutes." Opponents condemned the "Popish printer" who published the address in Cork. Those supporting George and augmentation were written off as "Jacobites, Papists, and other avowed Enemies of our Establishment." Undermining what Patriots hoped Ireland would become, the "Mob at Cork," little more than "hired Popish Vagabonds," would plunge all of Ireland into a "Thralldom," a political and ecclesiastical form of slavery, one that dovetailed with the vision coming from the Castle.[91]

It was not only Anglicized Catholics who entered the political arena. Irish speakers, too, voiced support for George. In an unexpected gesture, one of the most visible Irish-language poets of the eighteenth-century, Maurice O'Gorman, wrote a poem praising Townshend as soon as he took up his post. O'Gorman lived up the standard image of the Irish poet. Hard-drinking and womanizing, he sought out patrons from Ireland's Catholic elite to support him. But he was not above seeking patronage from the lord lieutenant. He had written a praise poem for an earlier viceroy and would also draft one for George's successor. Nonetheless, the poem to George speaks to the ways that Irish speakers like O'Gorman were accommodating themselves, on the surface at least, to a Hanoverian order and how they, too, were not so much becoming political actors—they had always been—as reorienting that political activity toward the status quo, whether that meant contesting it, or in O'Gorman's case, supporting it. The poem said:

> Happy it is for you, O Ireland,
> To have found your spouse at last,
> Who will not neglect your grievances
> In private council or assembly. . . .
>
> Lord Townsend is the man
> Most noble in charity ever conceived;
> . . . .
> A merciful heart without blemish.

Heaping praise upon praise, the poem extolled George's complexion, his deeds, and the joy he had brought to the kingdom. It ended on a similar note:

> You have received praise and fame abroad,
> Honor and triumph for your country,
> May your name by many people
> Be remembered on account of your great deeds.
>
> May your line be long-lived,
> As loyal heirs to the Lordship,
> For as long as water flows in streams
> And grass grows on smooth hillocks.[92]

O'Gorman wrote the poem to Ireland's "spouse," as he put it, in order to procure patronage, and it strains credulity to think he meant much of what he wrote. However overblown the rhetoric, it followed conventions for an Irish praise poem. O'Gorman worked for a long time under O'Conor, and he had no doubt learned a great deal about picking one's way nimbly through competing loyalties. He may have earned O'Conor's support, but in praising George and expecting a return for his investment, he was disappointed. There was little George needed that O'Gorman could offer.[93]

O'Gorman was not the only Irish speaker to begin this subtle reorientation to the status quo. Many now began to have a more conscious sense of themselves as a people with a coherent sense of community and with a common identity. They also now imagined some sort of "practical coexistence," as one scholar puts it, with the Hanoverian state. This shift started during the period of George's viceroyalty.[94] With the Townshend program of sovereignty, more and more Catholics began to think of their status anew.

The Catholic response to George and the Patriots' invigoration, therefore, was anything but simple or predictable. In general, men such as O'Conor supported the regime in an effort to win rights for Catholics. They cultivated loyalty cunningly. The same goes for those lower down the socioeconomic ladder, though they did so in different ways reflecting their status in the confessional state. They did not so much come to peace with the status quo as appreciate that they had to recognize its terms of debate. Certainly, at least a veneer of Jacobitism remained—if not a continued hope in the Stuart cause—but it was added to a newfound engagement with the political debates of the day as these were being framed by George, the patriots, and men like O'Conor. Actors on a political stage, they now aimed their resentment at the sort of arrangements both George was building and the Catholic Committee was supporting, on the one hand, and the alternative proposed by the Patriots, on the other hand. Poets spoke of "the rightful king," but such a role was to deliver the kingdom from the clutches of all who were refining their understandings of political arrangements in these years.[95]

This much is certain: whether arrayed for or against the status quo, Catholic political action challenged the assumptions on which the Ascendancy assumed power. Irish popery sustained Irish freedom in much the way American slavery underscored American freedom. And all understood the equation. Some were willing to confront it; others were now willing to contest it; still others acknowledged it as they tried to finesse it. None could ignore it; for the period's politicization had ensured the historic bases of inclusion and exclusion had to be recognized anew.

Dissenters, especially those in the North, also voiced their discontent with the status quo. In large part, they had already cultivated a vigorous political profile. Earlier in the century, through a series of theological debates, church leaders had developed sophisticated ideas of consent and liberty, which they employed to champion the rights of dissent in a confessional kingdom. With the 1760s, however, Presbyterians began stepping out of doors to assert their rights as Protestants and as Britons. Recession and the drop in the linen trade accentuated the urgency of their appeals for rights and for the "Protestant interest." This sensibility found its clearest expression in volunteering. Bearing arms, a Protestant's right, in defense of the Crown and Protestantism in Ireland as troops headed to America tied volunteers into older ideas of protecting their interests. Volunteering, of course, quickly became a way of focusing discontent and anxiety on the relationship with Britain that Patriots like Flood had clarified. Embracing patriotism, while they pressed for their rights, became yet another instance of how economic and social grievances were channeled into political demands that hinged on Ireland's sovereign status within the state.[96]

Politicization, however, much as in America, did not only depend on words. It stemmed from deeds as well. And Ireland also experienced a shocking increase in what many perceived as politically oriented violence in these years. It had long struggled with rural insurgency, and the eighteenth century witnessed spasms in both the North and the South at different moments. Before the 1760s, most insurgents engaged in protest or ritualistic violence to contest those who were imperiling traditional arrangements, especially in economic matters. In the late 1760s, as new instances gripped various regions of Ireland, such episodes seemed to have taken on a political edge. Catholics in Munster and in south Leinster now revived groups that were in abeyance, such as the Whiteboys, so called because of the white clothing they wore. And fresh waves of rural violence broke out in these years in Tipperary and Cork, terrifying the members of the Ascendancy who lived there.[97]

Not only Catholics engaged in this sort of behavior, however. Dissenters did as well, especially in Ulster. Some acted with Catholics, some against, but they always did so in opposition to the state even if they claimed loyalty. Most of these called themselves Oak-Boys or Hearts of Oak. Numbers were now rising in Presbyterian strongholds under the name "Hearts of Steel" or "Steel-boys." "There are some disturbances in the County of Antrim," a correspondent from Coleraine wrote to George in 1770, "by a set of People who call themselves Hearts of Flint, who are treading in the steps of the Oak Boys." He went on to say, "I really believe they have been driven by Despair by the severity of the Land Lords, as several Gentlemen have lately raised their Lands in that County to an unanswerable Price." Dissenter insurgents also complained of "places given to Papists," suggesting fear over Catholic politicization, as well as tithes, illustrating unease with the Ascendancy and with their political and religious disabilities.[98]

The year 1770 marked a troubling watershed for the state. "There is a wild and ungovernable disposition in the people in many parts of the kingdom," George wrote in March 1770, "which neither the common law nor the civil magistrates are able to restrain, as appears from the constant applications for the assistance of troops, and for military stations." He added, ominously, "There are quantities of arms in the Catholic parts." From 1767 through 1769, the government issued proclamations asking for the capture of rural insurgents. The following year, the number of such instances grew larger. The lord lieutenant's office called for the apprehension of rural insurgents in Cork, Kerry, and Antrim, as well as Whiteboys in Kilkenny and Tipperary. In that year, men calling themselves "Captain Fearnought, Lieutenant Calfskin, and Ensign Leather Coat" were attacking tithe collectors. Another group killed the man who had executed a priest accused of colluding with insurgents. And insurgents from "Antrim, Down, Armagh, [the] city and country of Londonderry, and county of Tyrone" had assembled and bore responsibility for killing a Presbyterian minister. Sometimes Protestants killed Catholics; at other times, those responsible were "tories, robbers, and rapparees . . . of the Popish religion." In 1771 and 1772, the government was searching for Steelboys in the North, too, as well as less organized men in the south of Ulster.[99]

Perhaps most troubling of all, in these years the normal ritualistic forms of violence that defined Irish rural life began to shift in significant ways. While poets cautiously praised the lord lieutenant, the discontented targeted people who were cooperating with the regime. Reports began to arrive in the Castle of a grisly practice in some of the provinces of Ireland. In Munster and South Ulster, officials were learning, some men were houghing soldiers, cutting their hamstrings. A number of houghings even took place in Dublin. In August 1770, for instance, a soldier was dragged from Thomas Street, cut across the back, and then "hamstrung." Some of these incidents no doubt had to do with the employment of soldiers by master butchers to crack a skinner's labor organization. In other words, the immediate precipitants of violence were the same sorts of issues that animated insurgents in America at the time of the Boston Massacre.[100]

Houghers, or "chalkers," as they were called, maimed soldiers with troubling regularity in the early 1770s, especially as troops were being raised for America. And by 1774 the government issued a proclamation after confronting a spate of such incidents. Eight soldiers, it announced, had been maimed in Dublin. Seven suffered horrific wounds to their hamstrings or Achilles' tendons. One lost the use of his hand. Later in the year, one soldier

had half of his tongue "feloniously and inhumanly cut off." All were attacked by a number of men, one of whom intoned that "they would soon
have more of them." It was clear that urban Catholics, men of no property,
bore responsibility. Indeed, in the later 1760s and early 1770s, scores of soldiers were houghed in Ireland, their numbers growing into the hundreds
over the next decades.[101]

Did these represent political acts? It is difficult to say with certainty,
and historians have debated the issue.[102] Nonetheless, this sort of ritualized
violence played upon worries about Ireland's constitutional relationship
with Britain, especially since soldiers—some of them Irishmen of many
confessional stripes employed by the British state—were the targets. In politicized Ireland, insurgents targeted cattle and men, all of which suggested
intent. They appeared to be demonstrating not only their allegiance to
a Jacobite cause but also their growing disaffection with the Hanoverian
regime, even if their wealthier coreligionists were declaring their loyalty.
More to the point, such actions in this context were ipso facto political, as
what could be called "the political" was becoming the chief means by which
men and women made sense of the world. The patterns they created, in the
midst of a vigorous and acrimonious debate over the constitution, which
drew all in, now focused on the state.[103]

Just as significantly, these sorts of insurgents laid bare the contradictions rooted in history that sustained provincial patriotism. Augmentation,
which now depended on Catholics to fill the ranks, occasioned not only a
constitutional or imperial crisis but a domestic one also, putting Ireland's
elites in an awkward spot. The Catholic *Dublin Mercury* happily pointed
out their fix. "We hear that the committee of the Free-Press," it reported in
1770 referring to Lucas's group, "have hit on an excellent expedient to counteract the pernicious effects of augmentation." It went on to say, pointing
out the ironies the Ascendancy found itself caught up in, that Lucas and his
followers would "pay a reward of 40s. to every person who hamstrings, or
otherwise maims and disables a soldier. This scheme is thought will furnish
sufficient employment to our chalkers and street robbers, and render them of
some service to the community."[104]

The Castle responded vigorously to insurgency because of the very
real political threat it represented in the official mind. In late 1771, George informed the government in London of barracks going up in Limerick and
Cork to, as he put it, "quell the mobs which rise to plunder Dublin goods in

a supposition that they are English manufacture." He also laid out plans for barracks construction for Waterford, to protect the customs house there, and Kenmare in Kerry and parts of Dublin where armed Catholics supported smugglers. Troops also quieted Steelboy disturbances in the North. They did so in part because they believed insurgents acted with political intent. The Steelboys, for instance, though they claimed to be loyal Protestants, also intimidated the troops sent to quell their disturbances, in one instance firing "their guns on every side in the air to provoke." The same was happening in Cork, with the "Papists" also armed.[105]

Yet, just as in America, fear and panic mattered more than reality because, as in the case of slave insurrection, insurgency was interpreted as a political act in these years. In this case, even if a *grande peur* was without foundation, appearances did matter.[106] As in America, these sorts of insurrections threatened governing arrangements and assumptions as well as the very fabric of the social order, thereby tapping into deep anxieties of those who styled themselves a ruling class. A traveler named Thomas Campbell called such activity, aptly, "the many-headed monster now being roused." There was no mistaking how such instances were seen in a new light after 1767. In an address to the House of Commons, Sir James Caldwell saw these old forms in a new way. "In Ireland," he declared, "a Popish mob is the most dreadful instrument that could possibly fall into the hands of either a foreign or domestick enemy, and will always endanger for a time, the subversion of the state."[107]

Members of the Ascendancy saw such acts as deeply political for a number of reasons. First, the world they now inhabited had become energized by what George had done. All Irish life had political valence in this context. Second, because of the exclusions that animated Irish political life, actions of the excluded that hinted at disaffection with the state and the status quo threatened the established order. The politicized kingdom reeled from what one historian calls the evident "mismatch between the institutional life and demographic reality" that had become apparent by what George had set in motion.[108] The clarifying debates about sovereignty, and the concomitant constitutional crisis, determined that such considerations could no longer be dodged. Finally, those who were houghing soldiers were now focusing their discontent on the very symbol of the relationship between Ireland and Britain: the soldier. By attacking soldiers, they were, just as eloquently as Flood, trying to bring purifying refinement to understandings of sovereignty.

Catholic political involvement still entailed loyalty to the Jacobite cause, at least for Irish speakers, but now they were freed up to voice their allegiance to or rejection of the Hanoverians. The nature of the British connection now became a point of focus for the Irish, whereas it had not necessarily been so during the years of undiluted Jacobitism.

The period, though distinctive because of its tensions, was not unique. Politicization ebbed and flowed, but each episode betrayed the particular context in which it took place. Middle-class Catholics had first found their voice in the 1750s with the creation of the Catholic Committee and with the Money Bill dispute, when the Ascendancy had been divided in much the same way it would under Townshend. It was during this earlier time that O'Conor published a number of pamphlets arguing for the repeal of the penal laws. At this stage they came to naught, and the political crisis of the 1750s passed and with it the impetus for reform. Yet, that moment was followed by others when, as one historian argues, "public opinion bared its teeth" once again. And as it did so, it would have dramatic implications for the tumultuous period that followed not too long after George's stay in Ireland. As another scholar finds, political awareness during George's viceroyalty grew as never before, with the result that the "political world had been substantially enlarged."[109] With the increasing pressure for money and manpower in the empire, the destruction of the undertaker system, the rise of a more determined Patriot movement, renewed and assertively political insurgency, and the concomitant crisis in the American colonies, politicization for Catholics had new troubling implications. In such a context, some members of the Ascendancy could be easily panicked.

The time that immediately followed George's years in office would be relatively quiet. Like America, Ireland, too, would calm down after these years of tumult. The tenure of George's successor, Lord Harcourt, would prove rather uneventful; he would even be able to pass a Stamp Act for Ireland. But what had made George's stay in Ireland so critical mirrored what happened in America in the same years. Ways of seeing the world had changed profoundly, especially because Ireland's process of politicization at the time occurred in a context that bridged the Atlantic. If America reignited, or if the ministry made missteps in Ireland, or if the Ascendancy did not attend to Catholic concerns, a politicized people would not long remain quiescent.

Nonetheless, despite or because of this sense of panic, reform would eventually come, but the sort designed to recognize the limitations imposed on provincial rulers by Catholic politicization. In 1778 a Catholic Relief Act passed in both the British and the Irish Parliaments. With the war in America, and France allying itself with the Patriot cause there, concerns about disaffected Catholics were becoming widespread, and the ministry in Britain asked the lord lieutenant to see to it that something passed in Ireland. It was a modest reform that did not undo political disabilities.[110] The Ascendancy had little choice in supporting the measure. Some preached practicality as the reason for doing so. Others declared that toleration was in keeping with the spirit of the times and that middle-class Catholics had demonstrated their loyalty by condemning rural insurgents and by offering to raise troops for the war effort in America. Most did as they were bidden by the Castle. The Relief Act alleviated stresses that the whole kingdom was experiencing in a highly volatile political atmosphere, one in Ireland and one in the whole Atlantic system. Ironically, the Patriots had brought this on themselves by matching George's clarifying vision with one of their own, by creating a new and potentially revolutionary patterning of events.

Provincial Dilemmas

America and Ireland differed in some fundamental ways. Proximity to or distance from London and the differing nature of interests tying each place to the center made for distinctive sorts of relationships to Britain. This, of course, explains why Charles and George had developed their particular approaches to reform. But whether treating empire as a map on a wall or engaging it in a more hands-on fashion, the parallels between America and Ireland—because of what the brothers had tried to do—became striking. In a new political environment old fears came to the fore in both places. In Ireland, with elections now occurring on a regular basis, and with the new opportunities for grievance, lobbying, and jockeying open to all, many worried that Catholics would be reenergized. This led, as much as it did in America, to unfounded fears and rumor. Slaves in America and papists in Ireland represented the sum of all fears for their respective societies, so bound up was the status of each group with power and with history. They did so as symbol and, because of heightened political uncertainty, specter. George offered an instructive example in 1768. "Certain Irish Priests," he alleged, "are set out for this Kingdom to be present during the ensuing Elections and to feel the Pulse of the Commonality." With each election season, the question of who ruled and why they ruled could come to the surface. Such moments, George feared, beckoned Catholics. "There are," he fretted, "many Roman Catholicks, Irish Persons both of Cloth and the Sword, Coming over at this time as well." Whether they did or not is beside the point. He added that they did so "for bad purposes."[111] Officials were saying the same things about slaves in the colonies. And if such concerns were overblown, they pointed to the anxieties felt by many in both provincial societies. These years were defined by threat.

No doubt, popery and slavery, as categories, loomed in the imagination of patriots on both sides of the ocean as the most troubling manifestation of broad and deep politicization. Yet, the most tangibly pressing concerns George and British officials in America faced were common people: lower-class whites in America and their Protestant peers in Ireland. If they followed their patriotic leaders, stability would be lost. So by 1772, a new official narrative was emerging in both places that went something like this: rabble-rousers recognized the fundamental tensions in each society and exploited them in a naked bid for provincial power. In doing so, or so the story went, they were playing with fire. As one official from the North of Ireland argued, "That a Spirit of Licentiousness, opposition to lawfull authority, and violence, has possess'd the Minds of the lower ranks of People, throughout the whole Country is to me, but too apparent."[112] Officials like Francis Bernard and Thomas Hutchinson in Massachusetts echoed these sentiments on an almost daily basis from 1767 onward.

This is not to say that "elites" in each society, with all that the word conveys, mendaciously manipulated all with an eye to maintaining power in the face of threats to their provincial autonomy from those in Britain and challenges to their mastery from those below. It was not that simple. Rather, they surveyed the possibilities and constraints, imposed by a charged Atlantic context and politicized provincial worlds, to determine what course they could take. They acted, in other words, exactly as the Townshend brothers had. At this moment, members of the Ascendancy in Ireland and the well-to-do in the colonies had to consider a great many pressures and tensions as they filtered all through the Whiggish principles of the day, the political lingua franca of both groups and of the Townshends. And they fully appreciated the difficulties of doing so, that they were indeed playing with fire.

As they engaged in this imaginative process, in both places, patriots convinced themselves they knew the proximate, if not the exact, culprits for this state of affairs. In both places, they argued that British officials acting in their respective societies bore responsibility. In 1768, Lucas had laid out a dystopic vision of what could happen to Ireland unless Patriots practiced vigilant virtue to contest what George was up to. "It is Cruelty not to be parallel'd," he warned, "when the private Lust of Power hurries Men to embarrass and fight against Government, to embroil a nation, dissolve the social intercourse and destroy the tender Charities of Father, Brother, Husband, Son and Friend." These connections, he argued, "make Life worth enduring." As he put it, "Ambitious Men" threatened "the sweet Peace of this Kingdom, and by well contriv'd Alarm frighted it into Commotions, into all the Poverty and almost the Rage of War!"[113] Samuel Adams used the same imagery to contest Charles's measures, characterizing the governor and lieutenant governor of Massachusetts as tyrants who had created the crisis of politicization.

And he used similar tactics. Adams preached resistance and watchfulness to the people, believing it his job to keep an "unthinking herd," as he put it, "awake to their grievances." As long as the common sort stayed within the bounds of pressing for their legitimate rights as they were traditionally defined and as long as violence remained at acceptable levels—and thereby could be channeled—Adams supported popular action. Lucas did much the same. Fittingly, Adams drew on Lucas directly when he and others publicized the Boston Massacre and interpreted it as yet another event in a long pattern of abuses. And he, too, as his critics alleged, was willing to inflame tensions to awaken common people to the reality of this pattern.[114]

Charles and George Townshend, then, placed white American colonists and the Irish Ascendancy in the same bind. They were peoples who sat between two worlds. They struggled with what we could call a provincial dilemma. The conventional definition of the term posits that provincials wanted both autonomy and to be accepted as equals in the metropole and that, because of this, they had a simultaneous attraction to and repulsion from the center. This predicament, of course, lay at the heart of the case Dickinson and Flood were making; in fact, they offered the crystallizing logic that made this dilemma so salient to so many.[115] The dilemma worked in other ways. Provincial patriots also found themselves caught between Britons in Britain, on the one hand, and those further down the socioeconomic ladder in their own societies, on the other, as well as groups that had been defined out of the British equation through history. Slaves and papists, neither free nor Protestant, respectively, were negative images of everything Brit-ishness stood for, vivid reminders for whites in America and Protestants in Ireland of what could happen to them if they could not maintain control over the cacophony of voices in their volatile societies.

Both Americans and Irish Protestants used the terms "popery" and "slavery" promiscuously and emotionally. Doing so spoke to their deep belief in Whiggish ideas, and to the fact that through the narratives they were crafting, they were living in places in time that imperiled their status within the empire. They signaled two other things by holding fast to each. First, the use of such terms demonstrated a belief in their mastery of their respective societies. Each group had, after the tumult of civil war in Ireland and the struggles of settlement in America, come of age in the eighteenth century, in their minds anyway. Invoking cherished British ideas, they announced their status as true-born Britons, "fully encased," as a sociologist observes, in their identities as masters of their societies.[116] Second, and perhaps more critically, the terms suggest existential fear. Ever watchful, ever worried, Americans and Irish Protestants vigilantly looked to see if the seventeenth century would revisit them, especially with the disorder occasioned by imperial crisis. And in this case, the twin fears of popery and slavery resonated differently in each society. Popery, an abstraction in America, especially after the French had gone, was very real in Ireland. Slavery, which had only Whiggish political connotations in Ireland, represented something quite tangible in America.

These histories, much like Charles's ghost, came back to haunt both Americans and the Irish, especially as both had to reckon with unseemly pasts they would rather have suppressed. The eighteenth-century imperial crisis resurrected the coercion, bloodshed, and oppression of the seventeenth century that had given rise to the stability of the eighteenth. The presump-tion of men like Flood and Dickinson to rule each of their provinces was based on the sacrifices their ancestors had made in the past during the era of settlement, a rationale that served as the most persuasive argument for au-tonomy and provincial rights within the empire. Nonetheless, their status also stood on the bloody ground of past conflicts and past exploitation, often couched as "improvement," which, if revisited, threatened their security at home. Each would be vexed, fittingly, in a distinctive way by calculating how to balance these two predicaments. Each group of elites, in other words, would have to make a wager as to how far they were willing to go to claim independence in risking resurrecting the furies of the earlier age.[117]

Patriots proved more daring in encouraging politicization in America than in Ireland, even if on paper it threatened them. The decision to declare independence, of course, stemmed from many motives, from high-sounding principles to base economic concerns, all of which appeared clearer and clearer as each new event was tethered to the revolutionary pattern. What made the decision compelling, even perhaps "self-evident," was the belief that American patriots possessed the ability to channel, manage, or control the swelling forces beneath them, as they stood up for their rights as Britons. The reason has to do with confidence. Boston's leaders understood that those involved in mob action had foisted many of their frustrations onto the British. In parallel fashion, even when it came to confronting the most deep-seated of fears, white Americans in a place like South Carolina could act with some assurance of security, certainly more so than planters in places like Jamaica. One historian argues, "Slave revolts were everywhere feared and they were also expected, but few slaveholders doubted that they could be suppressed."[118] Independence, then, was a calculated gamble that those Americans who had prospered with Atlantic integration believed they could win. They could contest the unjust actions of Parliament without imperiling their place at home.[119]

Ireland, even if the "moment" presented the same process of politicization for almost the exact same reasons, differed from America. To be sure, clarifying relationships led to an unwanted but necessary exploration of the past, revealing presumptions to power and the galling contradictions that sustained them. Irish provincial dilemmas, however, presented churchmen with an answer different from the one fastened on by Americans. One of the impulses animating parliamentary independence was to allow members of the Ascendancy to resume control after a moment of destabilization, while securing as much autonomy as they dared within the British state system. However much it appeared like a revolutionary course, it was not, nor could it be. Ireland's Patriots had little means, besides British troops, to retain their hold on the reins of power in a country in which Protestants were a minority. In Ireland the most marginalized made up the majority of the population; in America, they did not. These blunt proportions determined the tipping point, or moment, for independence. Therefore, where white Americans were willing to gamble on independence, Irish churchmen were not. Appearances to the contrary, Grattan's Parliament and the Relief Act of 1778 changed little substantively in Irish political life. Revolutionary change would have entailed contesting the hold the executive now had on Irish political life. This the Ascendancy would not do. George's reforms had been thoroughgoing, and the Ascendancy had to keep such an arrangement in place.[120]

Irish and American elites, when push came to shove, were not brothers in arms. As they weighed the merits of their dilemmas, they had to decide on relative or absolute autonomy from the center; the narratives they had created, and British responses to them, gave them little choice. That Americans were willing to chance their places in society for independence demonstrated the lengths they would go to in order to defend their status as Whiggish-minded freemen. Ultimately, they had a belief, despite substantive anxieties, that could manage disorder. Breaking away, then, presented the only sure way out of both sorts of provincial dilemmas: the one that Dickinson brought into focus over home rule, and the other that emerged from a politicized world of fear that centered on rule at home. To hold onto their status, to come to peace with their past, and to maintain their dignity in the face of what many Americans had come to see as a pattern of tyranny meant independence.

The Irish dealt with their dilemmas differently. To be sure, when Americans were engaged in war against their British brethren, some Irish patriots raised their glasses to this thought: "May the gates of Temple Bar be speedily decorated with the heads of those who advised the employing military force to enslave our fellow subjects in America." More significantly, and this was George's legacy in part, Irish troops were streaming into American ports. By 1776, more than one-fourth of all British battalions serving in America came from the augmented Irish establishment, voted for and passed by the Irish Parliament. Many were Catholics, even if recruiting them troubled the Ascendancy. Ultimately, more Irish supported the Crown than supported the American rebels.[121] Most conspicuously, the Irish Parliament, while it was baying for its rights, voted to condemn the Americans as "rebels" once war broke out, taking its cues from the Castle. The M.P.s did so reluctantly, but they did so nonetheless.

The Castle controlled the kingdom. The Irish Parliament did not. The lord lieutenant held firm to the purse strings. And as long as he did, he would have the votes and the allegiance of powerful people in the kingdom. The year 1782 proved an anomaly. In the 1770s and 1780s, members of the Ascendancy asked themselves whether, as Grattan put it, "we shall be a

Protestant settlement or an Irish nation." They chose the former and would not challenge the executive.[122] Appearances can deceive. Beneath the surface, even if he had vanished, even if he had slipped into irrelevance, and even if he no longer featured in the stories of empire, George had prevailed.

But politicization is an unpredictable dynamic that defies control. Ireland, George sensed even after he had left the kingdom, lay on the brink. As events moved Ireland toward volunteering and parliamentary independence, he saw "a most critical and difficult period" officials would have to face. "When if one spark of that horrid Flame," he feared, "which rages on the other side of the Atlantic and glows on this [side], had caught your part of the King's Dominion, the consequences [would have been] immeasurable." He was right about potential consequences. He was wrong about predicting Atlantic dynamics. The spark had already lit a flame. History, contingency, and the tortured calculus over the provincial dilemmas, though, had fashioned a longer fuse for Ireland.[123]

What If?

Writing from England years after he had left Ireland, George wondered what he would see if he could return as a ghost to Ireland's Parliament. "O my late friends," he declared, "couldst then look out of thy graves and meet the departed Vice Roy and steal onto the Gallery during the sessions." What would a ghost learn, or, as he put it, "How much should we wonder . . .?" What could he have done differently? Such musings gave him perspective but little solace. George finished the exercise certain of one thing: "What poor Tenants we are of a very short time here, and that we do a great deal in making it habitable for our own Time." His visit from the world beyond raised more questions about possibilities lost and opportunities missed than he could answer.[124]

Both Charles's and George's ghost stories and George's disappearance in Copley's painting pose these questions about what might have been. In the *Dialogues in the Shades*, ghosts meet to discuss paths not taken, as well as the cruel twists that brought them to where they were. The spectral George and his friends attend sessions in Parliament and wonder if what they did mattered. Copley's lament on empire does the same thing, asking us to consider a different outcome had his protagonist's vision, never mind the man himself, carried the day.

The idea of a "Townshend moment" also raises similar issues. Suppose George had not crossed swords with Cumberland or sullied the memory of Wolfe? Imagine if Charles had not been able to assume control of the House. What if Chatham's gout or his emotional issues had not incapacitated him? The counterfactual question—the "What if?"—poses the sternest challenge to any argument emphasizing contingency. If not Charles and George, then surely someone else would have done what they planned to do. Certainly, the Americans would have rebelled at one point or another. Irish society would have, without a doubt, become politicized in the way that it did. All of this was, after all, inevitable, especially since empires come into being and revolutions occur on a scale far beyond human control. Or is this the case?[125]

The question is worth considering. What would have happened had the Townshends not come to power when they did? Others in and out of government harbored similar visions for the whole, and some of their plans were nearly as well formulated as the brothers'. Moreover, most subscribed to the idea that Parliament had to be supreme and that the critical times called for more centralized approaches to empire. The limits of what could be imagined were, in fact, quite narrow.[126] This much we can say. Although George and Charles considered themselves uniquely equipped to rule, they were not exceptional. They were part of a chorus of like-minded men convinced they could devise the answer to the most thrilling, urgent, and universally acknowledged problem of the day, and others would have taken up the roles had they not. Probably, that is. Put another way, George and Charles were not alone in what they read, in how they approached the problem of empire, or even in their belief in their destiny. Surely someone would have done what they did and initiated the same crises in the provinces. Or maybe not . . .[127]

If "making empire" more than likely would not have set the brothers apart, the same cannot necessarily be said of provincials and "making revolution." And here we get to the more problematic aspect of contingency and counterfactual. What of the chain of events? Had the brothers not done what they did when they did it, would the provinces have responded as they did when they did? The question itself suggests the complexity of the problem. If George had not been given five years to enact his vision, would Ireland have been changed? Would some other lord lieutenant, with different strengths and different foibles, have encouraged others to craft a crystallized provincial response? Would members of the Ascendancy have interpreted insurgency differently if this had been the case? On the American side, had

Charles not come to power with a well-developed plan or had the Townshend Duties not been passed when they were, would provincials have been
able to connect the dots as they had from the Stamp Act? Would tensions
have simmered down? Would fears of slave risings and "mob" action have
been perceived as apolitical?

The possibilities and questions are endless. And that is just the point.
When we venture to ask "What if?" especially as we try to imagine how one
eventuality leads to the next, ultimately the best we can come up with is
"Who knows?" A much better question, one that the ghost stories conjure
for us, is why men and women at this moment were asking "What if?" People
both at the center, most notably the Townshends, and at the peripheries became actors and created empire or revolution when they created patterns.
They took the contingencies of their lives and transformed them into what
they regarded as patterns of inevitability, allowing them to make sense of the
new contingencies the world threw at them. And this created the need for
ghosts. Because all crafted a "moment," in other words, all had to confront
"what if."

Ghosts transfixed men and women in these years for these reasons. In
1770, for instance, an Irish writer calling himself "Lucius" wrote of how an
"honest shade," as he styled it, "would conceive me to be a strayer from the
infernal regions, not an observer of the ways of men" if he were to witness
"the political machine . . . at a stand" with "the suspension of one of its most
active and essential powers." Lucius was referring to the prorogued Parliament, of course. He hoped he could convince the ghost that "there are men
in this country, whose penetration is not easily imposed upon by appearances
and pretences." He implied that only the greatest diligence could move history from the tack it had taken. This shade, though, was an exception. Irish
ghosts would not make regular appearances until the late 1780s, when the
bonds of society seemed to be breaking with the tumult of the age of revolution and as more and more Irishmen and women saw the reforms of the early
part of the decade as illusory. As they now understood how George had triumphed despite parliamentary independence, they began asking a number of
"what if's" by conjuring ghosts.[128]

Americans knew such uncertainty earlier, by and large because the
effects of what Charles had set in motion could not be wished away as phantoms. And unsurprisingly ghosts appeared with greater regularity in the
early 1770s. They came as the undead spirits of those killed in the Boston

Massacre to issue warnings. They appeared in the form of Wolfe to ask what had happened to British notions of liberty. A dead Britannia arose to "gnaw" the hearts of the living. The specter of Oliver Cromwell, adorned in armor, even visited London, as it seemed Parliament had become like the Stuart monarchs of old. As Mercy Otis Warren, one of the first to publish a history of the American Revolution, wrote in 1774, "The wonderful appearance of an angel, devil, and ghost" in Boston could "be attributed to the distresses that have of late fallen upon that unhappy metropolis." Another writer in 1771 observed how "fleeting Spectres" arrived to "mourne the present [to] Contrast with a sigh." Paul Revere appreciated the power of such images. In the wake of the Boston Massacre, he assembled an "Exhibition" at his house replete with images of the fallen and wounded, the figure of America, and the ghost of Christopher Seider, an eleven-year-old killed in a disturbance just days before the Massacre. In Revere's hands, Seider comes back from the dead and "fresh bleeding stands, And Vengeance for his Death demands." The most inspiring shade to appear in these years emerged from the pen of a writer named Elizabeth Graeme Fergusson. As one scholar who came across her work discovered, Fergusson in 1768 wrote a poem entitled "The Dream" that conjures a number of ghosts. Fergusson appears in her own poem and encounters the ghost of William Penn, who appears as "haughty" Britain seeks to dominate the colonists. He recounts the nature of the colony he had founded, one noted for freedom and virtue. He wonders what has happened to his vision. Amazingly, at this point Penn offers a scroll to Fergusson, who then passes it on to none other than John Dickinson. By reminding Dickinson what should have been the proper path of history, the ghost of Penn, then, serves as the inspiration for his *Letters*. Penn's ideas, the poet suggests, animated the *Letters*. Such a poem, the scholar who unearthed the poem argues, "alleges precisely such counterfactuals" to make a political point in a fraught context. And only a ghost could deliver them and make sense of such a jarring moment.[129]

Ghosts appeared because of the way people believed a "course of events" had been set in motion. What was happening to them struck them as unworldly. The ghosts reminded them of other possibilities, especially as they wondered how courses of events had taken the turns they had, just as the conjurings absolved the living of forging such chains themselves. The brothers' experiences and ghost stories teach us that these dynamics are heightened during periods of profound flux and uncertainty, when people are struggling to find interpretive handholds to manage events and heightened stakes, such as when a broad system is changing before their eyes. Contingency matters even more in these contexts, and what powerful people do can have far-reaching and unforeseen implications. But so too does the narrative of inevitability. When sovereignty comes under scrutiny, men and women craft their patterns with an eye to supporting or contesting the state. This is what happened at this time for people on both sides of the Atlantic. At such moments when people begin to see pattern where there had been contingency before, the results can be revolutionary. And in 1767 it began with the brothers.

The Americans and the Irish were right. The moment presented them with inexorable patterns. But their experiences and those of the brothers point to one conclusion: all conspired to create such destinies.[130] And this is the gist of the dilemma all were struggling with in this moment. All the players involved created narratives of their own design, especially those who found themselves standing between the marginalized in their own communities and Britons on the other side of the water. They made the case for inevitability out of events to imagine what they had to do to fight the brothers at their own game and to secure their own societies. To accomplish both, provincials had to make Charles and George vanish, even as they had to conjure their troubled pasts and consider their futures almost foreordained.

George's Passing

On 14 September 1807 George Townshend passed away at Raynham. He was eighty-three. About an hour before he died, the story goes, he called for a glass of wine and drank to "the Health of the Best King that ever Graced the British Throne." He reclined and went back to sleep. He never awoke.[131]

His family laid his body to rest next to Charles's in the family vault in St. Mary's. "The mournful procession was awfully grand," a report noted. The coffin was topped in red crimson, beautifully embroidered. One hundred "principal" tenants and George's immediate family and his many grandchildren followed it. Poorer tenants and servants, almost "innumerable," came at the end of the cortege. George left his family "in a state of great opulence." He bequeathed thousands to each of his children from his two marriages. His widow would live on £3,000 per year and have access to ready cash in excess of £30,000.[132]

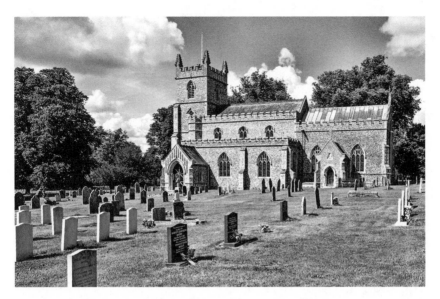

17. St. Mary's Church, East Raynham (Photograph by James P. Miller)

A great deal of water had passed under many bridges between 1767 and the day George died. The American colonies were now the United States. They had survived both the War of Independence and a revolution, though not one as radical and violent as France's. America's leaders had enacted a new constitution and put the ghosts of the past, of the colonial and provincial periods as well as of the tumult of politicization, behind them. Ireland had done much the same. After the blood-stained Rebellion of 1798 and the brutal crackdown, the Irish Parliament voted itself out of existence. Ireland became a constituent part of the United Kingdom. Patriot politics were a distant memory for Protestants. With a few notable exceptions, only Catholics thought of home rule. India, which Charles had argued could not constitute part of his system, had become the very center of British imperial ambitions. Renewed war with France, during what had now clearly appeared to be an "age of revolution" and combating radicalism at home, preoccupied the political class.

Memorials of George's death reflected these changes. Americans did not even note his passing. A few months before George died, one American newspaper had written about him in a snide piece concerning the appointment of a new lord lieutenant for Ireland, an act "thinned a little by the Union." The paper explained how during George's reign he had bought off the

Irish with whiskey to accomplish all he wanted to do. "[He] used to boast it cost him 60,000l. when Lord Lieutenant of Ireland to *drink down* the aristocracy of the country."[133] But nothing else appeared. The story of George and the whiskey said much less about Townshend and Ireland than it did about internal changes in the United States. On the face of it, lampooning an "aristocracy," a new favored word for tyrants of any ancien régime, reassured Americans of their proper republican credentials.

Something else was at work in America beyond giving voice to radical aspirations, something very much the opposite, in fact. As a fitting epilogue to a bygone age in which Ireland and America were tied together, and in the wake of a period of revolutionary ferment that bound patriots in America to their confreres in Ireland as brothers in arms, the story spoke of how Americans saw Ireland as an alien place, the perverse mirror image of all Americans held dear. Rural and largely Catholic, under an authoritarian regime politically and a thralldom religiously, the Irish appeared to postrevolutionary Americans as the anti-Americans. And after the tumult of the French Revolution and the violence of revolutionary Ireland, which tossed many radicals onto American shores, most Americans were happy to forget about Ireland. Why should Americans have remembered George? He was no longer part of their sovereign or intellectual universe, nor was the chaos and disorder afflicting Europe that gave rise to fears of radicalism and aristocracy.[134]

The Irish—Protestants, that is—remembered him fondly. George would be elected to what had been the Patriot-controlled Monks of the Screw, the first Englishman so honored.[135] Ironically, even the *Freeman's Journal* praised all he had done, forgetting how in the heady days after 1767 its writers had held him up as an enemy to Irish freedom. The paper near the time of his death recounted how for more than three decades men in Ireland had met to toast George on his birthday, harkening back to earlier days of stability that gave them faith in the present moment and allowed them to forget the intervening period of bloodshed and difficulty. He represented all that yoked the kingdoms together in a period of uncertainty. By the time of his passing, Patriots had become Unionists. On one occasion when they remembered George, sixty-seven grandees toasted "The Marquis Townshend, the friend of Ireland." On 10 March 1807, the paper ran a notice about the celebration of his birthday for the following day. This marked the thirty-ninth time his supporters had done so. They were to meet at a bar on Dawson Street for dinner and drinking at precisely 6 P.M.[136]

The *Freeman's Journal* noted his death on 25 September 1807 with a hint of sadness. "The death of the late Most Noble Marquis Townshend is universally regretted throughout Ireland," it wrote, "and particularly in the City of Dublin." In a stroke of revisionist history, the paper declared: "This country, grateful for the many services derived under his Lordship's administration of His Majesty's Government among us for five successive years (among which was the passing of the Octennial Bill in the Irish Parliament)." His memory, the paper solemnly noted, was celebrated by the great and the good. The Octennial Bill should indeed have been noted parenthetically. For that is all that legislative autonomy for Ireland had become, a parenthetical moment that punctuated a longer period of subordination and by 1807 disappearance. A month after his death, the paper even published verse that George had drafted during his stay in Ireland, in which he had written of "Intrepid Lucas, lame and old, Bereft of eye-sight, Health, and Gold." The paper noted, as if the readers had to appreciate, that Lucas was "the celebrated demagogue." The readership of the *Freeman's Journal*, therefore, had come to see eye-to-eye with George only as he passed away.[137]

The British universally praised him, in almost a nostalgic manner. "An Admirer" even penned a poem entitled "The Late Marquis Townshend," trying to put into some perspective for the reading public the life of "the Hero, Statesman, Father, Friend." The Admirer declared,

> To each emotion of his heart so true,
> You saw his manly soul in every view!
> So pure his heart, no fault had he to hide,
> For e'en his failings leant to Virtue's side

There was, of course, some truth in that line. He did turn his shortcomings into the stuff of proclaimed virtues. The Admirer asked:

> Wilt thou not weep? With me a while deplore?
> Thy fav'rite Son, thy Townshend is no more!
> Great in his day, he shone with brightest glory,
> And shar'd with Wolfe in his immortal story!
> Inspir'd by thee, no realms wou'd he enslave,
> Led by thine hand, he conquer'd but to save![138]

Much of the North America George had "conquer'd but to save" had, of course, by now been lost. And the poem served as a call harkening back to an age that preceded the unrest that had gripped the world he and Charles had helped fashion.

Forgotten in the British papers that covered his death were his clashes with Cumberland and his sullying of the memory of Wolfe. Notices of his death lauded George without qualification, paying particular attention to his role in the "revival of that Constitutional Force, the British Militia." What such reports failed to note was the fact that, in part, George's beloved Norfolk militia scheme helped the American patriot cause, as a drill book for the Norfolk unit served as a template for the Continental Army and local America militias. The papers invariably mentioned his service at Quebec, the fact that he had fought side by side with the hero Wolfe and had assumed command after what one paper called "the deplored death of the immortal Wolfe." The only critical note, if we could even call it that, was mention of the "unfortunate event" of one of his duels.[139]

The *Times* noted George's many experiences and participation in the epic events of the eighteenth century without comment, except when it came to Ireland. "His Viceroyalty," it noted, "was distinguished by a total change in the Parliamentary Constitution of the sister kingdom." It ended with an appreciation of his personality: "In his private character he was lively, unaffected, and convivial. He possessed an acute mind, and enlivened his conversation with that original pleasantry, which is so very visible in the works of his pencil when he chose to display it." *The Times* suggested how an age was passing with his death. "No one," its obituary read, "enjoyed life more than the Marquis Townshend. He suffered, indeed, some heavy afflictions, but he bore them with resignation; and closed a life, protracted beyond the common date of man, with the general respect and estimation of his country."[140]

One obituary, however, suggested that George had outlived his era. "There are few men of the present day," it argued, "who have seen a greater variety of service." He had been a giant. Noting the litany of his accomplishments and experiences, the paper argued how not many of his contemporaries could have measured up. "Few noblemen of that day were better adapted for this eminent station" of serving as viceroy in troubled Ireland. "His Lordship," it continued, "was gallant, gay and shewy in his person and address." The Irish needed an aristocrat. George "possessed a popular eloquence, and was calculated to win the confidence of the people over whom he was delegated to rule." His status, something decried in a democratic age, helped him then. But times had changed. A friend who wrote an appreciation of his life for a London newspaper compared George to Charles, who was "more eloquent." But George's steeliness "succeeded in overturning, after a sharp struggle, the old vicious system of governing that kingdom by a set of leading men, then called Undertakers." Reform he could manage. Revolution was another matter. "To his [the king's] wisdom and firmness," the friend wrote, "Lord Townshend was persuaded his subjects owe their having been preserved from the alternate contagion of anarchy and despotism, which threatened us from a neighbouring nation": the contagion of liberty that had transformed France.[141]

It is trite to say it, but his world had changed profoundly since his apprenticeship.[142] In fact, George had helped bring into being, often unwittingly, the world he saw fall apart. While the movement of peoples, goods, and ideas from Ireland had, in part, bound the Atlantic together and tied Ireland to America, the chaos that followed the brief ascendancy of Charles and George undid those ties.[143] In other words, the changes the brothers had served as midwives to sundered the relationship between Ireland and America. The process of consolidation had tied the two, and to a great extent what each brother tried to do in each place, respectively, reflected the entanglement. Money from America and troops from Ireland in a centralized empire in which provinces played subordinate but critical roles promised stability, peace, and virtue for the whole. One province could not function well without the other in an empire that was greater than the sum of its parts. Tragically for the brothers, the two places fell apart in ways that dovetailed with how they had been integrated. The coercive model epitomized by George bound Ireland to the center and made it a functioning part of the Atlantic system. To make it a part of the whole meant that Catholics would be politically marginalized. They paid the price for consolidation. Integration for Americans followed Charles's commercial model. And, of course, the abasement of Africans and the institution of slavery served as the hidden driver to this commercial Atlantic system. Without such labor, Americans could not have had any role to play in the Atlantic system.

When the brothers forced all to confront their past, they ensured that these ghosts in each provincial society would haunt Ireland and America. Flood and Dickinson had descended from the same England that had peopled places like Leinster and Pennsylvania in the seventeenth century. Their ancestors were part of a broader world of motion that through trade and exploitation had established settler societies in each. The "moment" revealed the simmering realties of the seventeenth-century Atlantic that were still under the surface in each society, tensions that had not been effaced by the changes of the eighteenth century. Distant pasts now presented themselves once more.

Politicization in both Ireland and America did, of course, create a sense of common purpose for a great many. The process focused discontents and energies on the relations between center and periphery in a way that could not be denied or wished away, leading ultimately to independence for America and quasi-independence for Ireland. The process, however, also revealed and then exacerbated deep and defining fault lines in each society. These lines cohered to history, just what George and Charles believed could rescue the empire. Now history was bringing it down. Lord Fitzgibbon summed up the genies Charles and George had unleashed from the bottle by believing they could manage complex societies with simple plans. "If the People of England," he chided, "would but see the danger and folly of making Experiments upon this giddy country, we might still do well, notwithstanding the many Blunders which have been committed in the Government of Ireland." He could easily have said the same for America.[144]

The lives of the brothers reveal a few ironies that defined their time. Some are simple enough to appreciate. Through a series of unforeseen twists and turns, the brothers, blind to the contingencies of their own lives and instead sure of their mastery of the world's patterns, created an empire based on the idea that history's processes could be managed. The moment of hubris touched off the furies in each society and brought the whole Atlantic system—and nearly the British state—crashing down. Through their reading, the brothers would have known the story of the furies. They would have also appreciated how the Greeks believed peripeteia, or a dramatic reversal of fortune, inevitably followed hubris, and that the nature of a rise prefigures the nature of any fall. The experience of all in the British Atlantic during this moment confirmed this age-old bit of wisdom.[145]

Another set of ironies is more difficult to reckon with. The people on the margins of the world they tried to recast also had their "moment." It, too, centered on their devising their own narratives out of the stuff of events, a process that created all sorts of dilemmas. And each society would be cursed by the distinctiveness of its history, haunted really, until order could be restored again. The brothers played formative roles in bringing these eventualities into being in ways they could not have conceived, and in order for them to have been as formative as they had been, they would have to be forgotten. This explains why Charles disappeared, or became a ghost, and why George vanished.

Charles's specter seemed to appreciate this story. In his last murmurings in the *Dialogues,* the dead Charles suggests that history hinges on patterns, what is discerned and what is created. As people tried to grasp history's essential course, they transformed events but could not manage them. "Who can foresee the consequences of the simplest, the justest, the best action?" Charles wonders. "We are all doomed to the task of making such or such a link in the chain of events," he laments.[146] The real Charles had made many links of the fortunes and misfortunes of his life, as had George. But he had never realized that what he had forged would have unforeseen implications. The ghost, it seems, understood the nature of history better than the man.

What do these hauntings and vanishings teach us? In light of what we know, or should know, from other ages of revolution, the Townshend moment offers a vivid reminder of difficult truths we would rather forget. Even if the stage the brothers strode was Atlantic in scope and the imperatives of Atlantic empire defined their lives, the lessons they offer also speak to global dynamics, those encountered since and even those we confront today. Maybe, when all is said and done, the recurring pattern across time and space of men such as George and Charles believing they can control contingency to master systems suggests that little in the past is contingent after all.[147]

Such a quixotic belief in mastery of the world and its patterns, as the Townshend moment illustrates, rests on the conceit of control. It denies the agency of others. It has been and remains the aphrodisiac of the powerful. But the world rarely cooperates with attempts to bend reality to one's will. As the brothers should have learned from Charles's fellow ghost David Hume, "all plans of government, which suppose great reformation in the manners of mankind, are plainly imaginary."[148] Those in power can, of course, effect change, especially during times of volatility and uncertainty; but it does not follow that the change is what they envision. The powerless in faraway places, they often learn, have voices of their own, and that same volatility and instability that amplify the influence of the powerful offer a space for those marginalized to press for their own vision of how society should work. Sometimes the patterns or inevitabilities they construct can be liberating. Sometimes they can be terrifying.[149] Revolutions, after all, are as unpredictable as they are unexceptional, and when we glibly declare one over, events—or contingencies—confound us. So it was during the Townshend moment, and so it is today.

Above all, the brothers, their world, and their experiences seem to demonstrate certain immutabilities, even as they remind us that nothing is inevitable: appearances deceive, the ghosts of the past haunt all of us, and pride cometh before the fall.

Notes

Prologue

1. For a similar visit to Raynham, some of the details about its extent today, as well as a discussion of how Lord Townshend now works to make the estate profitable, see James Meek, "How to Grow a Weetabix," *London Review of Books* 38 (2016), 7–16. My thanks to D. G. Rogers for this reference.

2. For "moment" used this way, in reference to a "Cromwellian Moment," see Nicholas Canny, "Atlantic Empire and the Peoples of the British Monarchy, 1603–1815," in *Oxford Comparative History of Empires*, edited by C. A. Bayly (forthcoming).

3. On this idea of moment, see J. G. A. Pocock, *The Machiavellian Moment: Florentine Political Thought and the Atlantic Republican Tradition* (Princeton, 2003), viii–ix. For Pocock, however, a moment could last centuries.

4. For a similar sense of capturing an image as a "moment," I was intrigued by Geoff Dyer's description of "the Lightning Field moment," when lightning struck a piece of public art he had seen and rendered its meaning anew. See *White Sands: Experiences from the Outside World* (New York, 2016), 79. On the embeddedness of historical thinking, the need to craft narratives from events, and hanging meaning on such structures, see Mark Lilla, *The Shipwrecked Mind: On Political Reaction* (New York, 2016), 134.

5. The phrase is an adaptation from the classic two-volume study, since republished and reintroduced by David Armitage, on the subject by R. R. Palmer entitled *The Age of Democratic Revolution: A Political History of Europe and America, 1760–1800* (Princeton, 2014).

6. On how versus why and the role of agency or contingency, see Christopher Clark, *The Sleepwalkers: How Europe Went to War in 1914* (New York, 2014).

Act 1. Making Empire

1. Manuscript Genealogy of the Townshend Family, Charles Townshend Papers, Buccleuch Manuscripts, Clements Library, Ann Arbor, Mich., 296/6/7.

2. Horace Walpole, *Memoirs of the Reign of King George the Second*, vol. 1 (London, 1847), 163–64. For an excellent discussion of the ideas of the second and third viscounts, see Linda Frey and Marsha Frey, "Townshend, Charles, Second Viscount Townshend (1674–1738)," *Oxford Dictionary of National Biography* (Oxford, 2004) (hereafter *ODNB*).

3. For both the second and third viscounts, see Frey and Frey, "Townshend, Charles, Second Viscount Townshend (1674–1738)," *ODNB*.

4. CT (Charles Townshend) to Lord Lynn (his father), 8 September 1735, CT to Lord Townshend, 17 July 1748, GT (George Townshend) to Lord Townshend, 15 July 1748; Historical Manuscripts Commission, *The Manuscripts of the Marquess Townshend* (London, 1887), 354, 363 (hereafter HMC).

5. George Hervey, afterward the Earl of Bristol, to Lady Townshend, 22 May 1742, George Hervey to Lady Townshend, 19 August 1742, HMC, 357–58.

6. John Martin, "Townshend, Etheldreda, Viscountess Townshend (c. 1708–1788)," *ODNB* (Oxford, 2004).

7. Verses on Lady Etheldreda Townshend in *Cambridge Chronicle* of 1 Nov. 1766; Character of the two Right Honorable Brothers, collected by Rev. Mr. Cole, Add. Mss. 5834, British Library, 434; John Campbell to Lady Townshend, 30 September 1746, HMC, 360–62; Martin, "Townshend, Etheldreda, Viscountess Townshend," *ODNB*.

8. Cornelius P. Forster, *The Uncontrolled Chancellor: Charles Townshend and His American Policy* (Providence, 1978), 2.

9. The Townshends subscribed to three volumes of this standard eighteenth-century work. See Colen Campbell, *Vitruvius Britannicus: The Classic of Eighteenth-Century British Architecture* (Mineola, N.Y., 2007).

10. Charles Hind and Irena Murray, eds., *Palladio and His Legacy: A Transatlantic Journey* (Venice, 2011).

11. David Cholmondeley and Andrew Moore, *Houghton Hall: Portrait of an English Country House* (New York, 2014), 83.

12. That is, unlike his former friend and now political enemy, Sir Robert Walpole, whose home Houghton Hall pulled out all the stops. The Townshends thought the grandiose corrupt and aimed for restrained grandeur. See Susan Weber, ed., *William Kent: Designing Georgian Britain* (New Haven, 2014),

202–5, 497–99. On Kent's Italian leanings, and criticisms thereof, see John Brewer, *Pleasures of the Imagination: English Culture in the Eighteenth Century* (New York, 2007), 213.

13. Truth be told, they envied Walpole's exquisite Houghton Hall, designed by the same team that had renovated Raynham; indeed, he had built it on such a scale to outshine its only Norfolk rival, Raynham. Lord Townshend, it was reported, "considered every stone that augmented the splendor of Houghton as a diminution of the grandeur of Raynham." Cholmondeley and Moore, *Houghton Hall*, 42–43, 64.

14. Forster, *The Uncontrolled Chancellor*, 4; D. A. Winstanley, *The University of Cambridge in the Eighteenth Century* (Cambridge, 1922); John Gascoigne, *Cambridge in the Age of the Enlightenment* (Cambridge, 1989).

15. Walpole, *Memoirs of the Reign of King George the Second*, vol. 1, 340–41.

16. Walpole, *Memoirs of the Reign of King George the Third*, vol. 1 (London, 1845), 39, 21, 23.

17. Observations on the Townshends by Rev. Mr. Cole, Add. Mss. 5834, British Library, 434; *The Life and Letters of Lady Sarah Lennox, 1745–1826* (London, 1901), I:40; CT to -----, 6 March 1763, PRO 30/8/64, National Archives, Kew; L. B. Namier and John Brooke, *Charles Townshend* (New York, 1964); CT to Lord Townshend, 1 September 1745, HMC, 359; *The Correspondence of King George the Third with Lord North from 1768 to 1783*, ed. William Donne (London, 1867), 78.

18. Walpole, *Memoirs of the Reign of King George the Third*, vol. 1, 23.

19. Namier and Brooke, *Charles Townshend*, 2, 5–6, 130; and Namier and Brooke, *The House of Commons, 1754–1790* (New York, 1964), 549. This is quoted in Martyn J. Powell, "Townshend, George, First Marquess Townshend (1724–1807)," *ODNB* (Oxford, 2004).

20. See, for instance Forster, *The Uncontrolled Chancellor*, xiii; Thomas Bartlett, "The Townshend Viceroyalty, 1767–1772," Ph.D. dissertation, Queen's University, Belfast (1976), 46–51; and "The Townshend Viceroyalty," in *Penal Era and Golden Age: Essays in Irish History, 1690–1800* (Belfast, 1979), edited by Thomas Bartlett and D. W. Hayton, 94. See also the excellent and indispensable entries for the brothers by Martyn Powell for George and by P. D. G Thomas for Charles in the *ODNB* (Oxford, 2004). On the pull of Namier, see Geoffrey Holmes, *British Politics in the Age of Anne* (New York, 1967), 3. My thanks to Alex Barber for guidance and perspective on this point.

21. On this limitation of the "Namierist" vision as far as Americanists are concerned, see Edmund Morgan, "The American Revolution: Revisions in Need of Revising," *William and Mary Quarterly*, 3rd ser., 14 (1957), 8; and T. H. Breen, "Ideology and Nationalism on the Eve of the American Revolution: Revisions *Once More* in Need of Revising," *Journal of American History* 84 (1997), 13. A thoughtful response to Namier is found in John Shy, "The Spectrum of Imperial Possibilities: Henry Ellis and Thomas Pownall, 1763–1775," in *A People Numerous and Armed: Reflections on the Military Struggle for American Independence* (Ann Arbor, Mich., 1990).

22. For persuasive salvos against Namierite approaches from the British and Irish perspectives, see Richard Bourke, *Empire and Revolution: The Political Life of Edmund Burke* (Princeton, 2015), 223. For what he calls "Namierland," see Jim Smyth, *Cold War Culture: Intellectuals, the Media, and the Practice of History* (London, 2016).

23. Geoffrey Holmes writes, "Biographical evidence has to become the historian's servant and not his master; it has, after all, no inherent superiority over other types of evidence, and it carries the dangerous liability that by focusing attention exclusively on the trees it can easily persuade us that it is they and not the wood which really matter." See *British Politics in the Age of Anne*, 6–7.

24. For a similar approach, one that offers a sympathetic interpretation of often misunderstood leaders, albeit for figures on the losing end of the struggle for empire, see Andrew O'Shaughnessy, *The Men Who Lost America: British Leadership, the American Revolution, and the Fate of Empire* (New Haven, 2013), 1–14.

25. CT to Lord Townshend, 8 December 1748, HMC, 366–67. On Charles's progression, see Peter D. G. Thomas, "Townshend, Charles (1725–1767)," *ODNB*; Walpole, *Memoirs of the Reign of King George the Second*, vol. 1, 421.

26. Andrew Beaumont, *Colonial America and the Earl of Halifax, 1748–1761* (Oxford, 2015); James Henretta, *"Salutary Neglect": Colonial Administration Under the Duke of Newcastle* (Princeton, 1972), 342–45. On the board and the centralizing vision, see S. Max Edelson, *The New Map of Empire: How Britain Imagined America Before Independence* (Cambridge, Mass., 2017). My thanks to Max Edelson for sending me a copy of his book manuscript. See also David Flaherty, "The Board of Trade and American Policy," Ph.D. dissertation, University of Virginia (2017).

27. Notes on the State of the Newfoundland Fisheries; Minutes of the Committee on the Petition of the Makers of and Dealers in Hats, January 1752,

Microfilm of Charles Townshend Papers at Dalkeith in the Possession of the Duke of Buccleuch at Dalkeith House, Midlothian, compiled by T. C. Smout (hereafter called "Buccleuch Mss. at Dalkeith"), Reel 1, Reel 2; List of Officers of the North Department of Indian Affairs, 9 December 1766, CT Papers, Clements, 8/2/1/d; Difference between the Trader and Smuggler in Cambricks, Buccleuch Mss. at Dalkeith, Reel 2; Accounts of Sundry Merchandize Ship'd from New York to Ireland, December 1766–March 1767, Charles Townshend Papers, Clements, 8/31/10.

28. Notes on America, the Minutes of America, and Study of Encroachments in America, Buccleuch Mss. at Dalkeith, Reel 1; CT's Notes on Cases to Show the Effect of Alterations Made in the Standard of Money, CT Papers, Buccleuch Mss., Clements, 296/7/8; Notes on American Revenue, n.d., Buccleuch Mss. at Dalkeith, Reel 2.

29. CT to Buccleuch, 10 April 1764, CT Papers, Buccleuch Mss., Clements, 296/1/3. See also the reports, all signed by Charles, held in CO5/402, National Archives, which is included in the "Colonial America" database (www.colonialamerica.amdigital.co.uk).

30. April Lee Hatfield, *Atlantic Virginia: Intercolonial Relations in the Seventeenth Century* (Philadelphia, 2007); Alison Games, *Migration and the Origins of the English Atlantic World* (Cambridge, Mass., 2001).

31. On this, I am indebted to Richard Drayton, who elaborated on the idea of "mimetic rivalry" among European imperial powers in a talk entitled "Northwestern European Macro-Regions and the Connected Histories of French and British Imperialism," University of Notre Dame, London Centre, 12 July 2016.

32. Bernard Bailyn, *The Peopling of British North America: An Introduction* (New York, 1986). On the construction of such an empire, as well as the contingencies that shaped it, see Nicholas Canny, "Atlantic Empire and the Peoples of the British Monarchy, 1603–1815," in *Oxford Comparative History of Empires*, edited by C. A. Bayly (forthcoming). For the merchants, their ideology, and the theme of integration, see David Hancock, *Citizens of the World: London Merchants and the Integration of the British Atlantic Community, 1735–1785* (New York, 1995).

33. On these themes, see the introduction to Nicholas Canny and Philip Morgan, *Oxford Handbook of the Atlantic World* (New York, 2013); as well as the essay in that volume by Joyce Chaplin, entitled "The British Atlantic." David Hancock also explores how capital flows, as well as the movement of peoples and material, were transforming the Atlantic into a community. See

Citizens of the World. For the many ways of casting the transformation, see Jack Greene and Philip Morgan, "Introduction: The Present State of Atlantic History," and Trevor Burnard, "The British Atlantic," in *Atlantic History: A Critical Appraisal* (New York, 2009), 18–20, 118–19.

34. See, for instance, CT Papers, Clements, 8/22/16; and *Proceedings and Debates of the British Parliaments Respecting North America, 1754–1783,* vol. 1, edited by R. C. Simmons and P. D. G. Thomas (Millwood, N.Y., 1982), 141. A strikingly similar narrative of trade in the Atlantic system and commercial empire (in a model biography) is offered by Perry Gauci in *William Beckford: First Prime Minister of the London Empire* (New Haven, 2013).

35. Estimates of the Amount of Quit Rents in each Colony; and Regulations with respect to Quit Rents and Grants of Lands in North America, Buccleuch Mss. at Dalkeith, Reel 2. Also see Marianne Wokeck, *Trade in Strangers: The Beginnings of Mass Migration to North America* (University Park, Pa., 1999).

36. He read, for instance, a Memorandum on the charter of New England, dating from 1691 (CT Papers, Clements, 8/22/30); and Abstracts from several acts of Parliament to the Plantations, Buccleuch Mss. at Dalkeith, Reel 2, vol. 2. Also see Bernard Bailyn, *The Origins of American Politics* (New York, 1968).

37. Peter Coclanis, "Atlantic World or Atlantic/World?" *William and Mary Quarterly,* 3rd ser., 63 (2006), 725–42; Philip Stern, *The Company State: Corporate Sovereignty and the Early Modern Foundations of the British Empire in India* (New York, 2011).

38. Abigail Swingen, *Competing Visions of Empire: Labor, Slavery, and the Origins of the British Atlantic Empire* (New Haven, 2015); Vincent Brown, "The Eighteenth Century: Growth, Crisis, and Revolution," in *The Princeton Companion to Atlantic History,* edited by Joseph Miller (Princeton, 2015), 36–40.

39. William Pettigrew, *Freedom's Debt: The Royal African Company and the Politics of the Atlantic Slave Trade* (Chapel Hill, 2013); Simon Newman, *A New World of Labor: The Development of Plantation Slavery in the British Atlantic* (Philadelphia, 2014). On rum and sugar, see CT Papers, Clements, 8/34/1–6.

40. Memorandum dated 27 January 1747, Buccleuch Mss. at Dalkeith, Reel 2; Bill for Board, Lodging and Clothing of Two Black Princes, August 1748, and Receipt for Necessaries to the Black Boys, Buccleuch Mss. at Dalkeith, Reel 2; Account of the Disbursements for the African Gentlemen by David

Crichton, Buccleuch Mss. at Dalkeith, Reel 2; Principal Articles in Demand [along African coast], n.d., Buccleuch Mss. at Dalkeith, Reel 2. On how slavery transformed Africa, see Walter Hawthorne, *Planting Rice and Harvesting Slaves: Transformations Along the Guinea-Bissau Coast, 1400–1900* (Portsmouth, N.H., 2003).

41. Notes on Whether the Exportation of European Goods to North America ought to be prohibited, n.d., Buccleuch Mss. at Dalkeith, Reel 2.

42. Observations on the Vouchers procured by the Committee for the Delivery of the Cargoes at Cape Coast Castle, n.d., Buccleuch Mss. at Dalkeith, Reel 3; Receipt for Cupid, a Black Boy, to John Maguire Debtor, 1747, Buccleuch Mss. at Dalkeith, Reel 2.

43. See Philip Morgan, *Slave Counterpoint: Black Culture in the Eighteenth-Century Chesapeake and Lowcountry* (Chapel Hill, 1998); Ira Berlin, *Many Thousands Gone: The First Two Centuries of Slavery in North America* (Cambridge, Mass., 1998); and Peter Wood, *Black Majority: Negroes in Colonial South Carolina from 1670 Through the Stono Rebellion* (New York, 1974).

44. Report to the Lords of the Privy Council from Halifax, Pitt, Grenville, and CT, 6 August 1751, CO 5/402/286–291.

45. Memorandum of Andrew Symmes, n.d., Buccleuch Mss. at Dalkeith, Reel 2; Notes in CT's hand on rum, sugar, and slaves, n.d., Buccleuch Mss. at Dalkeith, Reel 2.

46. Notes on Forts in America, and An Estimate of Expenses of Transporting Provisions, CT Papers, Clements, 8/31/1 and 16; and List of "Encroachments" in America, Buccleuch Mss. at Dalkeith, Reel 1; Distances of Several Parts of America, Buccleuch Mss. at Dalkeith, Reel 2. For more on these frontier places see Lawrence Hatter, *Citizens of Convenience: The Imperial Origins of American Nationhood on the U.S.-Canadian Border* (Charlottesville, 2017); and Catherine Cangany, *Frontier Seaport: Detroit's Transformation into an American Entrepôt* (Chicago, 2014).

47. Daniel Richter, *The Ordeal of the Longhouse: The Peoples of the Iroquois League in the Era of European Colonization* (Chapel Hill, 1992); Francis Jennings, *The Ambiguous Iroquois Empire: The Covenant Chain Confederation of Indian Tribes with English Colonies from Its Beginnings to the Lancaster Treaty of 1744* (New York, 1984).

48. Notes on Duties from America, n.d., Buccleuch Mss. at Dalkeith, Reel 2.

49. See Account of Charges Incumbent in Supporting and Maintaining the Settlement of His Majesty's Colony in Nova Scotia, 1749–1752, Buccleuch Mss. at Dalkeith, Reel 2.

50. "Journal, January 1750: Volume 58," in *Journals of the Board of Trade and Plantations*, vol. 9, edited by K. H. Ledward (London, 1932), 1–39; Mary Patterson Clarke, "The Board of Trade at Work," *American Historical Review* 17 (1911), 19. My thanks to Dylan Leblanc for his help on these matters.

51. Paul Langford made this formulation in his *A Polite and Commercial People: England, 1727–1783* (Oxford, 1989).

52. See Richard Drayton, *Nature's Government: Science, Imperial Britain, and the "Improvement" of the World* (New Haven, 2000), 57.

53. Linda Colley, *Britons: Forging the Nation, 1707–1837* (New Haven, 1992); David Armitage, *Ideological Origins of the British Empire* (Cambridge, 2000).

54. Notes on a Bill to Introduce Security, Industry, and Moveable Property, Buccleuch Mss. at Dalkeith, Reel 2.

55. Rosalind K. Marshall, "Townshend, Caroline, *suo jure* Baroness Greenwich (1717–1794)," *ODNB* (Oxford, 2004); Lord Townshend to CT, 20 January 1753, HMC, 381; Forster, *The Uncontrolled Chancellor*, 10.

56. Namier and Brooke, *Charles Townshend*, 57.

57. Brian Bonnyman, *The Third Duke of Buccleuch and Adam Smith: Estate Management and Improvement in Enlightenment Scotland* (Edinburgh, 2014), 2–4, 8, 26–30; Andrew Mackillop, *"More Fruitful Than the Soil": Army, Empire, and the Scottish Highlands, 1715–1815* (East Linton, 2000).

58. Walpole, *Memoirs of the Reign of King George the Second*, vol. 1, 421–22; Walpole, *Memoirs of the Reign of King George the Second*, vol. 2, 5.

59. Walpole, *Memoirs of the Reign of King George the Second*, vol. 2, 132; John Nicholls, *Recollections and Reflections, Personal and Political, as Connected with Public Affairs, During the Reign of George III* (London, 1822); *Proceedings and Debates of the British Parliaments Respecting North America, 1754–1783*, vol. 1, ed. Simmons and Thomas, 135. Another contemporary called him a "young florid speaker." See William Reed, ed., *The Life of Esther De Berdt, Afterwards Esther Reed, of Pennsylvania* (Philadelphia, 1853), 91–92.

60. Walpole, *Memoirs of the Reign of King George the Second*, vol. 2, 147–48; Grafton Diary, in *Autobiography and Political Correspondence of Augustus Henry, Third Duke of Grafton*, edited by W. R. Anson (London, 1898), 126, 128.

61. Notes for the Private Book of GT's Memoirs, 6806–41–1–1, George Townshend Papers, National Army Museum, Chelsea, 1.

62. Walpole, *Memoirs of the Reign of King George the Third*, vol. 1, 23.

63. Brendan Simms, *Three Victories and a Defeat: The Rise and Fall of the First British Empire, 1714–1783* (New York, 2008); Vincent Brown, "The Eighteenth Century," in *The Princeton Companion to Atlantic History,* ed. Miller, 36–40.

64. Journal of George Townshend's Life and Service, 6806–41–1–2, GT Papers, National Army Museum, Chelsea; Notes for the Private Book of GT's Memoirs, 6806–41–1–1, GT Papers, National Army Museum, Chelsea, 1–2.

65. Notes for the Private Book of GT's Memoirs, 6806–41–1–1, GT Papers, National Army Museum, Chelsea, 3; Walpole, *Memoirs of the Reign of King George the Second,* vol. 1, 56–58, 95; John Carswell and L. A. Dralle, eds., *The Political Journal of George Bubb Dodington* (Oxford, 1965), 103.

66. Michael Hechter, *Internal Colonialism: The Celtic Fringe in British National Development, 1536–1966* (Berkeley, 1975); John Morrill, "The British Problem," in *The British Problem, c. 1534–1707: State Formation in the Atlantic Archipelago,* edited by Brendan Bradshaw and John Morrill (New York, 1996); GT's Dedication to a pamphlet entitled *A Plan of Discipline Composed for the Use of the Militia of the County of Norfolk* (London, 1759), iv.

67. Charles Vere Ferrers Townshend, *The Military Life of Field-Marshal George* (London, 1901), 100.

68. Notes for the Private Book of GT's Memoirs, 6806–41–1–1, GT Papers, National Army Museum, Chelsea, 2.

69. See Geoffrey Plank, *Rebellion and Savagery: The Jacobite Rising of 1745 and the British Empire* (Philadelphia, 2006).

70. GT to George Selwyn, 1 October 1746, in John Heneage Jesse, *George Selwyn and His Contemporaries: With Memoirs and Notes* (London, 1843), vol. 1, 112–16.

71. GT to George Selwyn, 1 October 1746, in Jesse, *George Selwyn and His Contemporaries: With Memoirs and Notes,* vol. 1, 112–16.

72. On this theme, see Matthew Dziennik, *The Fatal Land: War, Empire, and the Highland Soldier in British America* (New Haven, 2015).

73. GT Diary, 6806–41–1–2, GT Papers, National Army Museum, Chelsea.

74. GT to Lord Townshend, 27 December 1748, dated from Craven Street, GT to Lord Townshend, 15 October 1748, HMC, 368, 365; Walpole, *Memoirs of the Reign of King George the Third,* vol. 1, 23.

75. Bartlett, "The Townshend Viceroyalty, 1767–1772," 49–50. Also see his excellent treatment of George in the *Dictionary of Irish Biography* (Cambridge, 2009).

76. See Powell, "Townshend, George, First Marquess Townshend (1724–1807)," *ODNB.* For Cumberland, refer to W. A. Speck, "William Augustus, Prince, Duke of Cumberland (1721–1765)," *ODNB* (Oxford, 2004).

77. Erroll Sherson, *The Lively Lady Townshend and Her Friends* (New York, 1927), 160–61; Walpole, *Memoirs of the Reign of King George the Second,* vol. 1, 40.

78. Diana Donald, "'Calumny and Caricatura': Eighteenth-Century Political Prints and the Case of George Townshend," *Art History* 6 (1983), 44–66; Herbert Atherton, "George Townshend Revisited: The Politician as Caricaturist," *Oxford Art Journal* (1985), 14; Eileen Harris, ed., *The Townshend Album* (London, 1974), nos. 37–39. My thanks to Tom Bartlett for this last source.

79. Powell, "Townshend, George, First Marquess Townshend (1724–1807)," *ODNB;* George Townshend, *A Brief Narrative of the Late Campaigns in Germany and Flanders in a Letter to a Member of Parliament* (London, 1751), 4, 10, 41, 43, 50. On changing fortunes on the Continent, as well as this shifting focus, see Eliga Gould, *The Persistence of Empire: British Political Culture in the Age of the American Revolution* (Chapel Hill, 2000), 33–71.

80. GT to Lord Townshend, 16 December 1750, Add. Mss. 63079, British Library, 52.

81. Notes for the Separate Book of GT's Memoirs, 6806–41–1–6, GT Papers, National Army Museum, Chelsea; Herbert Atherton, "George Townshend, Caricaturist," *Eighteenth-Century Studies* 4 (1971), 437–46; Donald, "'Calumny and Caricatura.'"

82. Hambleton Custance to GT, 6 December 1753, HMC, 382; "Survey of London, Vol. 40, The Grosvenor Estate in Mayfair, Part 2," http://www.british-history.ac.uk/report.aspx?compid=42152; Walpole, *Memoirs of the Reign of King George the Second,* vol. 2, 19. At one point, in 1751, George even made the case that parliaments could also become oppressive if they served for too long. See Walpole, *Memoirs of the Last Ten Years of the Reign of George II,* vol. 1, 144. On the development of the brothers' neighborhood, see Jerry White, *London in the Eighteenth Century: A Great and Monstrous Thing* (London, 2013), 30.

83. CT to his mother, 29 December 1755 and 23 June 1757, Add. Mss. 63079, British Library, 83, 87.

84. CT to his mother, 15 July 1757, Add. Mss. 63079, British Library, 42.

85. Fred Anderson, *Crucible of War: The Seven Years' War and the Fate of Empire in British North America, 1754–1766* (New York, 2000).

86. Stephen Brumwell, *Redcoats: The British Soldier and War in the Americas, 1755–1763* (Cambridge, 2002); Vincent Brown, "The Eighteenth Century," in *The Princeton Companion to Atlantic History*, ed. Miller, 36.

87. Forster, *The Uncontrolled Chancellor*, 5.

88. Carla Mulford, *Benjamin Franklin and the Ends of Empire* (New York, 2015); Timothy Shannon, *Indians and Colonists at the Crossroads of Empire: The Albany Congress of 1754* (Ithaca, N.Y., 2000).

89. Beaumont, *Colonial America and the Earl of Halifax*.

90. Charles's objection was lodged in a long report to Newcastle. See CT to Newcastle, 13 September 1754, Add. Mss. 32736, British Library, 508–9; and the attached "Remarks upon the Plan for a General Concert," 510–14. The following paragraphs draw from these.

91. This is covered in two reports in Charles's hand. See Notes on Inactivity of the Colonies; and Minutes of America, 18 February 1756, CT Papers, Clements, 8/4/1, 8/4/3.

92. Stanley Katz, *Newcastle's New York: Anglo-American Politics, 1732–1753* (Cambridge, Mass., 1968); Charles quoted in Bartlett, "The Townshend Viceroyalty, 1767–1772," 49; Forster, *The Uncontrolled Chancellor*, 5–7.

93. In another memo to Newcastle, he discussed the urgency of the moment. He argued that what we could call rapid-deployment forces had to be established in America. These, he thought, should be dispatched to Canada and deliver a coup de main. Regarding money and distance, he argued that raising troops in Britain would prove too costly and take too much time. He counseled Newcastle to press for "an offensive instead of carrying on a defensive War in America," which could break Britain and only encourage further French aggression. See Enclosure of CT to Newcastle entitled "A Scheme for the Improvement and Employment of His Majesties Forces in America," Add. Mss. 32736, British Library, 515–18.

94. *Proceedings and Debates of the British Parliaments Respecting North America, 1754–1783*, vol. 1, ed. Simmons and Thomas, 94–95; Walpole, *Memoirs of the Reign of King George the Second*, vol. 2, 80.

95. *Proceedings and Debates of the British Parliaments Respecting North America, 1754–1783*, vol. 1, ed. Simmons and Thomas, 110; Walpole, *Memoirs of the Reign of King George the Second*, vol. 2, 96.

96. CT to his mother, 18 October 1757, Add. Mss. 63079, British Library, 108.

97. CT to GT, Ms. Eng. Hist., d. 211, Bodleian Library, 3; Walpole, *Memoirs of the Reign of King George the Second*, vol. 2, 62–63.

98. Chesterfield to Solomon Dayrolles, 19 December 1755, 4:179; and Chesterfield to his Son, 30 September 1763, 4:371, in *The Letters of Philip Dormer Stanhope, Earl of Chesterfield* (London, 1847); Richard Lyttelton to Pitt, 2 November 1756, *The Correspondence of William Pitt, Earl of Chatham*, edited by W. S. Taylor and J. H. Pringle (London, 1838–1840), vol. 1, 181–82; Earl Temple to Pitt, 9 November 1756, *Correspondence of William Pitt*, vol. 1, 186–87.

99. CT to GT, n.d., but 1756, Add. Mss. 41198, British Library, 97.

100. CT to GT, 13 May 1759, MS Eng. Hist. d., 211, Bodleian Library, 5; Walpole, *Memoirs of the Reign of King George the Second*, vol. 2, 304; CT quoted in Beaumont, *Colonial America and the Earl of Halifax*, 179.

101. Walpole, *Memoirs of the Reign of King George the Second*, vol. 2, 64, 154, 302–3.

102. For this issue, see J. R. Western, *The English Militia in the Eighteenth Century: The Story of a Political Issue, 1660–1802* (Toronto, 1965). On George's reasoning and the manpower issue, see *The Caledonian Mercury*, 19 November 1759. My thanks to Bry Martin for bringing this to my attention. GT's Dedication to a pamphlet entitled *A Plan of Discipline Composed for the Use of the Militia of the County of Norfolk*, iii. The best discussion of the militia bill is in Gould, *The Persistence of Empire*, 75–79.

103. Draft of a Speech before the House of Commons, on Army v. Militia, 1757, OSB MSS 161/4, Beinecke Library, Yale University; Gould, *Persistence of Empire*, 42, 87–88.

104. Walpole, *Memoirs of the Reign of King George the Second*, vol. 2, 303; Walpole, *Memoirs of the Reign of King George the Second*, vol. 3, 7, 34.

105. Memorandum in the hand of GT, 18 June 1757, HMC, 393.

106. Mr. Rigby to Duke of Bedford, 18 June 1757, in Lord John Russell, ed., *Correspondence of John, Fourth Duke of Bedford*, vol. 2 (London, 1843), 251–52.

107. Walpole, *Memoirs of the Reign of King George II*, vol. 2, 97–99; GT to Pitt, 14 February 1757, and GT to Pitt, 15 January 1757, *Correspondence of William Pitt*, vol. 1, 223, 216; Notes for the Private Book of GT's Memoirs, 6806–41–1–1, GT Papers, National Army Museum, Chelsea, 4; Walpole, *Memoirs of the Reign of King George the Third*, vol. 1, 87–88. On George and the anti-Cumberland angle for a militia, as well as Charles's enthusiasm for the measure, see Western, *The English Militia in the Eighteenth Century*, 122–23, 136.

108. GT to CT, 4 July 1757, Ms. Eng. Lett., c. 386, Bodleian Library, 116.

109. GT to CT, Ms. Eng. Lett., c. 386, Bodleian Library, 118.

110. Walpole, *Memoirs of the Reign of King George the Second*, vol. 2, 228; Powell, "Townshend, George, First Marquess Townshend (1724–1807)"; Namier and Brooke, *The House of Commons, 1754–1790*. For an idealist reading of George and his work as caricaturist, one at odds with the Namierite reading, see Herbert Atherton, "George Townshend Revisited: The Politician as Caricaturist," *Oxford Art Journal* 8 (1985), 3–19. Quotation from p. 3. On Hogarth and George, see Donald, "'Calumny and Caricatura,'" 44.

111. Atherton, "George Townshend Revisited"; Walpole, *Memoirs of the Reign of King George the Second*, vol. 2, 245–46.

112. GT to Lord Leicester, 24 January 1759, Add. Mss. 57823, British Library, 198.

113. GT to CT, n.d. (but presumably 1757), Ms. Eng. Lett., c. 386, Bodleian Library, 120; GT to CT, 4 July 1757, Ms. Eng. Lett., c. 386, Bodleian Library, 116; CT to GT, n.d. 1760, Ms. Eng. Hist., d. 211, Bodleian Library, 11.

114. CT to Earl of Grenville, 19 March 1760, Ms. Eng. Lett., c. 386, Bodleian Library, 111–12; Charles quoted in Namier and Brooke, *Charles Townshend*, 77–78.

115. Namier and Brooke, *Charles Townshend*, 56.

116. This is Namier's interpretation in his and John Brooke's *Charles Townshend*.

117. W. A. Speck, "William Augustus, Prince, Duke of Cumberland (1721–1765)," *ODNB* (Oxford, 2004); CT to Lady Townshend, 26 September 1758, HMC, 394–95.

118. CT to Lady Townshend, 26 September 1758, HMC, 394–95; Roger Townshend Commissions, 24 August 1758, 1 February 1758, CT Papers, Buccleuch Mss., Clements, 297/6/14–15; Fragment of Letter by Roger Townshend, 20 July 1759, 297/6/11.

119. GT to Pitt, 27 August 1758, *Correspondence of William Pitt*, vol. 1, 345–47; GT to Pitt, 2 May 1758, National Archives, 30/8/64.

120. Notes for the Private Book of GT's Memoirs, 6806–41–1–1, GT Papers, National Army Museum, Chelsea, 5; and 6806–41–1–1; Walpole, *Memoirs of the Reign of King George the Third*, vol. 1, 21.

121. Richard Littleton to GT, 28 December 1758, Jeffrey Amherst to GT, 14 March 1759, Roger Townshend to Lady Ferrers, 7 June 1759, HMC, 306–8; Walpole, *Memoirs of the Reign of King George the Second*, vol. 3, 172.

122. GT to Charlotte Townshend, 18 February 1759, GT Papers, Clements, vol. 1; Journal of the Voyage to America and the Campaign against Quebec, 1759, 6806–41–4–2–1, GT Papers, National Army Museum, Chelsea; Note and Sketchbook accompanying Journal of the Voyage to America and the

Campaign against Quebec, 1759, 6806–41–4–2–3, GT Papers, National Army Museum Chelsea.

123. GT to Lady Ferrers, 6 September 1759, HMC, 309; Continuation of Journal of the Voyage to America and the Campaign against Quebec, 1759, 6806–41–4–2–2, GT Papers, National Army Museum, Chelsea; Murray to George Townshend, 5 October 1759, in Townshend, *The Military Life of Field-Marshal George,* 247. On Wolfe and his brigadiers, and the hatred they had for him, see D. Peter MacLeod, *Northern Armageddon: The Battle of the Plains of Abraham and the Making of the American Revolution* (New York, 2016), 126.

124. Copies of Papers That Were Wrote by General Wolfe and the Brigadiers before the Operations above the Town of Quebec in 1759, Buccleuch Mss. at Dalkeith, Reel 3.

125. Samuel Morris Diary, 25 July 1759, Misc. Bound Manuscripts, Clements. My thanks to Brian Dunnigan for this information. On Roger, I have also drawn from "The Townshends: A Short History from the 12th to the 19th Century"; my thanks to Lord Townshend for this unpublished pamphlet.

126. GT to Audrey Townshend, 6 September 1759, Add. Mss. 50006, British Library, 10. My thanks to Tim Shannon for bringing this memorial to my attention.

127. GT to Lady Ferrers, 6 September 1759, HMC, 308–9.

128. GT to Lady Ferrers, 20 September 1759, HMC, 313; E. J. Chapman and R. P. Goodman, "Quebec, 1759: Reconstructing Wolfe's Main Battle Line from Contemporary Evidence," *Journal of the Society for Army Historical Research* 92 (2014), 5; MacLeod, *Northern Armageddon,* 177; GT to Audrey Townshend, 20 September 1759, Add. Mss. 50006, British Library, 12.

129. Copies of Papers That Were Wrote by General Wolfe and the Brigadiers before the Operations above the Town of Quebec in 1759, Buccleuch Mss. at Dalkeith, Reel 3; Townshend, *The Military Life of Field-Marshal George,* 243. On Wolfe's death, see Simon Schama, *Dead Certainties: Unwarranted Speculations* (New York, 1992).

130. George's description in letter to Pitt dated 20 September 1759, in Townshend, *The Military Life of Field-Marshal George,* 234–39; Anderson, *Crucible of War,* 362–63; MacLeod, *Northern Armageddon,* 231, 265; General Townshend's Book of General Orders, 1759, 6806–41–4–1, GT Papers, National Army Museum, Chelsea; Articles of Capitulation, in Townshend, *The Military Life of Field-Marshal George,* 239–41.

131. Townshend, *The Military Life of Field-Marshal George,* 242.

132. James Jones to Lady Townshend, 26 October 1759, Add. Mss. 50006A, British Library, 36; Rev. R. Leeke to Lady Ferrers, 30 October 1759, HMC, 317; Richard Lyttelton to Pitt, 18 October 1759, *Correspondence of William Pitt*, vol. 1, 442; CT to Lady Ferrers, 29 September 1759, HMC, 315.

133. General Townshend's Book of General Orders, 1759, 6806–41–4–1, GT Papers, National Army Museum, Chelsea; MacLeod, *Northern Armageddon*, 283.

134. George Townshend's Orders issued from June to October 1762, Loudon Papers, LO 10250, Huntington Library, San Merino, Calif.; GT to John Campbell, Earl of Loudon, 30 August 1762, Loudon Papers, LO 10249, Huntington Library.

135. Patrick Lindesay to CT, 7 February 1761, YO 540, Huntington Library; Edward Williams to CT, 23 June 1761, YO 831, Huntington Library; William Windham, 25 June 1761, YO 834; and Armine Woldenhouse to CT, 21 August 1761, YO 835, Huntington Library.

136. See a number of letters to CT (YO 666, 475, 552, 485, 636, 642) in the Huntington Library.

137. Walpole, *Memoirs of the Reign of King George the Second*, vol. 2, 154.

138. Walpole, *Memoirs of the Reign of King George the Second*, vol. 2, 157–58, 172–74; Viscount Barrington to Earl of Buckinghamshire, 17 December 1762, in Historical Manuscripts Commission, *Report on the Manuscripts of the Marquess of Lothian* (London, 1905), 245; Thomas Nuthall to Lady Chatham, 14 October 1762, in *The Correspondence of William Pitt, Earl of Chatham*, edited by W. S. Taylor and J. H. Pringle (London, 1838–1840), vol. 2, 182–83.

139. Horace Walpole, *Memoirs of the Reign of King George the Third*, vol. 1 (London, 1845), 102.

140. Forster, *The Uncontrolled Chancellor*, 20–21.

141. Townshend, *The Military Life of Field-Marshal George*, 245; CT to Lady Ferrers, 15 September 1759, Lord Townshend to Rev. Robert Leeke, 15 September 1759, HMC, 311.

142. Lord Townshend to CT, n.d., Ms. Eng. Lett., c. 386, Bodleian Library, 109–10; Namier and Brooke, *Charles Townshend*, 33.

143. John Dalrymple to CT, 12 February 1761, Ms. Eng. Lett., c. 386, Bodleian Library, 50–53. For more on Adam, see Henry Hope Reed, ed., *The Works in Architecture of Robert and James Adam* (London, 1975).

144. For an excellent study of the Wolfe–Roger Townshend issue, as well as an excellent reading of both of their monuments in Westminster, see Alan McNairn, *Behold the Hero: General Wolfe and the Arts in the Eighteenth Century* (Montreal, 1997).

145. He was memorialized, for instance, in Stowe.

146. On the monument and its design, see John Fleming, "Robert Adam, Luc-François Breton and the Townshend Monument in Westminster Abbey," *Connoisseur,* July 1962. And especially McNairn, *Behold the Hero.*

147. Adam Drawings, Sir John Soane Museum, London, vol. 19, nos. 9, 10, 66, 67, 68, 71, 72; vol. 54, set 2, no. 8, 9, 27; set 7, no. 17.

148. By war's end, seven hundred Iroquois were serving with the British. On this, see Anderson, *Crucible of War,* 410. The drawings of the Indians, however, show powder horns embellished with fleurs-de-lis. Only if the Mohawks had captured such powder horns from their enemies would they be carrying anything with the French symbol of royalty. My thanks to Stephen Astley, Curator of Prints at Sir John Soane's Museum, for the knowledge he shared about Adam. On the image of the Indian in eighteenth-century Britain, see Troy Bickham, *Savages Within the Empire: Representations of American Indians in Eighteenth-Century Britain* (Oxford, 2005); and Eric Hinderaker, *The Two Hendricks: Unraveling a Mohawk Mystery* (Cambridge, Mass., 2011).

149. On this monument, see McNairn, *Behold the Hero.*

150. Fleming, "Robert Adam, Luc-François Breton and the Townshend Monument in Westminster Abbey," 169, 171; Funeral Fee Book, Westminster Abbey Archives, London.

151. Adam quoted in Loyd Grossman, *Benjamin West and the Struggle to Be Modern* (London, 2016), 133.

152. On the theme of the nation-state-capital nexus, see Kojin Karatani, *The Structure of World History: From Modes of Production to Modes of Exchange* (Durham, N.C., 2014). My thanks to Richard Drayton for bringing this to my attention.

153. On the challenges of bringing the two together, see Steven Pincus, "Addison's Empire: Whig Conceptions of Empire in the Early Eighteenth Century," *Parliamentary History* (2012), 115–16. For a very different interpretation of these visions of empire, one that would lead to fundamental tensions that could not be resolved and that would result in an inevitable crisis, see Nick Bunker, *An Empire on the Edge: How Britain Came to Fight America* (New York, 2014).

154. Will of Viscount Charles Townshend, PROB 11/898/28, National Archives; Lord Townshend to CT, 12 January 1760, 14 January 1760, Ms. Eng. Lett., c. 386, Bodleian Library, 105–8; Lord Townshend to CT, 5 August 1758, Ms. Eng. Lett., c. 386, Bodleian Library, 101–4.

155. CT to his mother, Add. Mss. 63079, British Library, 129.

Act 2. Britain's Imperial Reckonings

1. Horace Walpole, *Memoirs of the Reign of King George the Second,* vol. 3 (London, 1847), 222.

2. Walpole, *Memoirs of the Reign of King George the Second,* vol. 3, 227; Walpole, *Memoirs of the Reign of King George the Second,* vol. 3, 230; "Letter" reprinted in Charles Vere Ferrers Townshend, *The Military Life of Field-Marshal George* (London, 1901), 253–61. In a satire written in 1762 lampooning Bute, the writer imagines a grand procession in Westminster "as soon as the definitive Treaty is signed," after which Bute becomes "minister for life." George should have marched seventh in the procession, leading "the most formidable Troop of duelists, their Standard a Deaths Head." George, however, fittingly, arrived too late to lead his band. See "A Satire on Bute's Ministerial Power, Late 1762," in *The Memoirs and Speeches of James, 2nd Earl Waldegrave,* edited by J. C. D. Clark (Cambridge, 1988), 238–40.

3. Elizabeth Montagu to Lord Lyttelton, 23 October 1759, in *The Letters of Mrs. Elizabeth Montagu,* edited by Matthew Montagu, vol. 4 (London, 1813), 251–54; CT to his mother, 24 June 1760, Add. Mss. 63100, Townshend Papers, British Library, 145; CT to his mother, 6 October 1760, Add. Mss. 63100, Townshend Papers, British Library, 147.

4. "A Refutation of the Letter to an Honble. Brigadier General, Commander of His Majesty's Forces in Canada," in Townshend, *The Military Life of Field-Marshal George,* 261–84.

5. Carole McNamara, *Benjamin West: General Wolfe and the Art of Empire* (Ann Arbor, Mich., 2012), 49–51. On the reading of the image that follows, see Patrick Griffin, *America's Revolution* (New York, 2012), 1–5.

6. On the influence of Adam on West, and in particular the use of Indians in the Roger Townshend monument, see Loyd Grossman, *Benjamin West and the Struggle to Be Modern* (London, 2016), 132–33.

7. Earl of Buckinghamshire to Lady Suffolk, 10 July 1764, in Historical Manuscripts Commission, *Report of the Manuscripts of the Marquess of Lothian* (London, 1905), 186.

8. Philip Stern, *The Company State: Corporate Sovereignty and the Early Modern Foundations of the British Empire in India* (New York, 2011). For a sense of the immensity of the challenges Britons faced, as well as the struggle to devise plans, see H. V. Bowen, "British Conceptions of Global Empire, 1756–83," *Journal of Imperial and Commonwealth History* 26 (1998), 1–27.

9. He seemed to see some wisdom in what his contemporary Voltaire quipped, that ultimately Britain had won "a few acres of snow in Canada" and that the British were "spending more on this lovely war than all Canada is worth." See Voltaire, *Candide*, edited by Daniel Gordon (Boston, 1999), 98.

10. Walpole, *Memoirs of the Reign of King George the Third* (London, 1845), vol. 1, 232.

11. *Proceedings and Debates of the British Parliaments Respecting North America*, vol. 1, edited by Simmons and Thomas (Millwood, N.Y., 1982), 419; Walpole, *Memoirs of the Reign of King George the Third*, vol. 1, 105.

12. On the interest and Crown income, see Robert Chaffin, "The Townshend Acts of 1767," *William and Mary Quarterly*, 3rd ser., 27 (1970), 91.

13. Nancy Koehn, *The Power of Commerce: Economy and Governance in the First British Empire* (Ithaca, N.Y., 1994), 3, 9, 64.

14. David Armitage, *Ideological Origins of the British Empire* (Cambridge, 2000).

15. On 1676 and the Caribbean, respectively, see Edmund Morgan, *American Slavery, American Freedom: The Ordeal of Colonial Virginia* (New York, 1975), and Andrew O'Shaughnessy, *An Empire Divided: The American Revolution and the British Caribbean* (Philadelphia, 2000). For garrison government see S. S. Webb, *The Governors-General: The English Army and the Definition of Empire, 1569–1681* (Chapel Hill, 1979). On the lack of connections, see John Murrin, "A Roof Without Walls: The Dilemma of American National Identity," in *Beyond Confederation: Origins of the Constitution and American Identity,* edited by Richard Beemen, Stephen Botein, and Edward C. Carter II (Chapel Hill, 1987).

16. On this, see Lauren Benton, *A Search for Sovereignty: Law and Geography in European Empires, 1400–1900* (New York, 2009). James Sheehan described the eighteenth-century European dilemma thus in a talk entitled "The Making of the Modern Political Order: States," 28 April 2015, University of Notre Dame. My thanks to Jim for his guidance on these points.

17. Walpole, *Memoirs of the Reign of King George the Third*, vol. 1, 135; *Proceedings and Debates of the British Parliament Respecting North America, 1754–1783*, vol. 1, ed. Simmons and Thomas, 386; CT to GT, n.d. 1763, Ms. Eng. Hist., d. 211, Bodleian Library, 16; Richard Bourke, *Empire and Revolution: The Political Life of Edmund Burke* (Princeton, 2015), 8.

18. Linda Colley, *Britons: Forging the Nation* (New Haven, 1992); Armitage, *Ideological Origins of the British Empire;* Brendan Simms, *Three Victories and a Defeat: The Rise and Fall of the First British Empire, 1714–1783* (New York, 2007), 501–32.

19. On this, see John Shy, "The Spectrum of Imperial Possibilities: Henry Ellis and Thomas Pownall, 1763–1775," in *A People Numerous and Armed: Reflections on the Military Struggle for American Independence* (Ann Arbor, Mich., 1990), 54.

20. Bute to GT, 2 November 1762, GT Papers, Clements, vol. 1; John Brewer, *Party Ideology and Popular Politics at the Accession of George III* (New York, 1976), 106. On the empire and Bute, I am indebted to Rachel Banke, who is completing a dissertation on Bute's American policy entitled "Bute's Empire: Reform, Reaction, and the Roots of Imperial Crisis," University of Notre Dame (2017).

21. For Bute, see Karl Wolfgang Schweizer's entry in the *ODNB* (Oxford, 2004); see the entry for Grenville by J. V. Beckett and P. D. G. Thomas as well. For the period, and the volatility, see Brewer, *Party Ideology and Popular Politics*, 3–11, 126–27, 132.

22. Bute to GT, 6 April 1763, GT Papers, Clements, vol. 1; CT to Earl Temple, 11 September 1763; CT to Earl Temple, 3 October 1763, *The Grenville Papers: Being the Correspondence of Richard Grenville Earl Temple, and George Grenville, Their Friends and Contemporaries,* edited by William James Smith (London, 1852), vol. 2, 121, 133; GT to CT, n.d. (but presumably 1764), Ms. Eng. Lett., c. 386, 134.

23. CT to Halifax, 8 December 1762; Halifax to CT, 10 December 1762, SP 44/139 f. 193, *State Papers Online;* Halifax to Lord Sandys, 22 February 1763, in *Calendar of Home Office Papers of the Reign of George III,* edited by Joseph Redington, vol. 2 (London, 1879), 266; Halifax to Lord Sandys, 22 February 1763, *Calendar of Home Office Papers,* vol. 2, 266; CT to GT, 7 October 1763, Ms. Eng. Hist., d. 211, Bodleian Library, 20; Walpole, *Memoirs of the Reign of King George the Third,* vol. 1, 209–10. Others quote Charles as calling it "a lutestring ministry." It would, or so he argued, "last the summer." On this, see David Bromwich, *The Intellectual Life of Edmund Burke: From the Sublime and Beautiful to American Independence* (Cambridge, Mass., 2014), 196.

24. Earl of Bristol to William Pitt, 6 April 1763, and CT to Pitt, 31 October 1763, *Correspondence of William Pitt Earl of Chatham,* edited by W. S. Taylor and J. H. Pringle (London, 1838), vol. 2, 218, 266; Walpole, *Memoirs of the Reign of King George the Third,* vol. 1, 295, 264; Brewer, *Party Ideology and Popular Politics,* 84; Duke of Newcastle to Pitt, 9 April 1763, *Correspondence of William Pitt,* vol. 2, 221; CT to ----------, 10 November 1762, CT Papers, Buccleuch Mss., Clements, 296/7/7.

25. CT to GT, n.d. 1763, Ms. Eng. Hist., d. 211, Bodleian Library, 16; GT to CT, 12 July 1764, Ms. Eng. Lett., c. 386, Bodleian Library, 124.

26. CT to GT, n.d. 1762; same to same, n.d. 1762, Ms. Eng. Hist., d. 211, Bodleian Library, 12, 14; CT to Buccleuch, 10 April 1764, CT Papers, Buccleuch Mss., Clements, 296/1/3; CT to GT, 16 October 1763, Ms. Eng. Hist., d. 211, Bodleian Library, 22.

27. CT to Duke of Newcastle, 30 April 1764, HMC, 398–400.

28. CT to Duke of Newcastle, 30 April 1764, HMC, 398–400.

29. CT to Newcastle, 30 April 1764, Osb. Mss., 161/2, Beinecke Library, Yale University.

30. GT to Mr. Whiston, 8 January 1766, HMC, 402.

31. Hunt Walsh to GT, 5 June 1766, HMC, 402.

32. Notes on Forts in America, CT Papers, Clements, 8/31/2; Expence of North America, Reel 2, vol. 2, Buccleuch Mss. at Dalkeith; also in CT Papers, Clements, 8/31/1.

33. Edmund and Helen Morgan, *The Stamp Act Crisis: Prologue to Revolution* (Chapel Hill, 1953), 21–35. See also James Henretta, *"Salutary Neglect": Colonial Administration Under the Duke of Newcastle* (Princeton, 1972), 342.

34. John Brooke, *The Chatham Administration, 1766–1768* (London, 1956), 28. As one scholar argues, "No theory, no vision of empire, dictated that policy's shape." See Fred Anderson, *Crucible of War: The Seven Years' War and the Fate of Empire in British North America* (New York, 2000), 570. The other view is found in Steve Pincus, *The Heart of the Declaration: The Founders' Case for an Activist Government* (New Haven, 2016), 51–88.

35. Jack Greene, *Evaluating Empire and Confronting Colonialism in Eighteenth-Century Britain* (New York, 2013), 84–91; Pincus, *The Heart of the Declaration*.

36. Walpole, *Memoirs of the Reign of King George the Third*, vol. 2, 46–47.

37. See Eliga H. Gould, *The Persistence of Empire: British Political Culture in the Age of the American Revolution* (Chapel Hill, 2000), 108–19; Grenville quoted on p. 110. Zachary McLeod Hutchins, "Introduction: The Stamp Act, from Beginning to End," in *Community Without Consent: New Perspectives on the Stamp Act,* edited by Zachary McLeod Hutchins (Hanover, N.H., 2016), xiii.

38. Francis Bernard to the Board of Trade, 15 August 1765 and 22 August 1765, in *The Papers of Francis Bernard, Governor of Colonial Massachusetts, 1760–1769,* edited by Colin Nicolson, vol. 2 (Boston, 2012), 302, 316. All of these American responses are covered in Patrick Griffin, *America's Revolution* (New York, 2012).

39. Anderson, *Crucible of War*, 562. On rioting in early modern Britain and Ireland, see Jim Smyth, *The Making of the United Kingdom, 1660–1800: State, Religion and Identity in Britain and Ireland* (Harlow, U.K., 2001). Pauline Maier makes the case that there was nothing unusual about rioting in the colonial city of Boston or in the Atlantic world generally, in *From Resistance to Revolution: Colonial Radicals and the Development of American Opposition to Britain, 1765–1776* (New York, 1972). For Boston rioting, see also Brendan McConville, *The King's Three Faces: The Rise and Fall of Royal America, 1688–1776* (Chapel Hill, 2006), 1–2, 58–59; Peter Messer, "Stamps and Popes: Rethinking the Role of Violence in the Coming of the American Revolution," in *Between Sovereignty and Anarchy: The Politics of Violence in the American Revolutionary Era*, edited by Patrick Griffin et al. (Charlottesville, 2015), 114–38. On the Stamp Act not serving as the first chapter of the American Revolution, see Hutchins, "Introduction: The Stamp Act, from Beginning to End," in *Community Without Consent*.

40. This insight comes from Rachel Banke, "Bute's Empire: Reform, Reaction, and the Roots of Imperial Crisis," Ph.D. dissertation, University of Notre Dame (2017).

41. Forster, *The Uncontrolled Chancellor: Charles Townshend and His American Policy* (Providence, R.I., 1978), 91–92; Thomas Bartlett, "The Townshend Viceroyalty, 1767–1772," Ph.D. dissertation, Queen's University, Belfast (1976), 49; GT to Grenville, 2 May 1765, Add. Mss. 57825, British Library, 1; GT to CT, 2 September 1765, CT Papers, Buccleuch Mss., Clements, 296/3/31.

42. George Cooke to Pitt, 17 December 1765, *Correspondence of William Pitt*, vol. 2, 351; Walpole, *Memoirs of the Reign of King George the Third*, vol. 2, 236; George Onslow to Pitt, 15 February 1766, *Correspondence of William Pitt*, vol. 2, 384–86; Earl of Chesterfield to his son, 17 August 1765, in *The Letters of Philip Dorner Stanhope, Earl of Chesterfield*, edited by Lord Mahon (London, 1847), vol. 4, 402.

43. *Proceedings and Debates of the British Parliaments Respecting North America, 1754–1783*, vol. 2, ed. Simmons and Thomas, 13.

44. Walpole, *Memoirs of the Reign of King George the Third*, vol. 2, 77–78; Townshend quoted in Forster, *The Uncontrolled Chancellor*, 91–93. On the struggle between the two, and for a fascinating interpretation of the intractability of the problem officials were confronting at this time, see Neil York, "When Words Fail: William Pitt, Benjamin Franklin and the Imperial Crisis of 1766," *Parliamentary History* 28 (2009), 354–55.

45. *Proceedings and Debates of the British Parliaments Respecting North America, 1754–1783*, vol. 2, ed. Simmons and Thomas, 13. For their history of clashes, see Lord John Cavendish to Duke of Grafton, 15 December 1761, in *Autobiography and Political Correspondence of Augustus Henry, Third Duke of Grafton*, edited by W. R. Anson (London, 1898), 36.

46. Charles quoted in Forster, *The Uncontrolled Chancellor*, 52.

47. Conway to the King, 17 December 1765, in *The Correspondence of King George the Third from 1760 to December 1783, Printed from the Original Papers in the Royal Archives at Windsor Castle*, edited by John Fortescue (London, 1927), vol. 1, 201–2. On the so-called Black Boys, see Patrick Griffin, *American Leviathan: Empire, Nation, and Revolutionary Frontier* (New York, 2007); and Gregory Dowd, *War Under Heaven: Pontiac, the Indian Nations, and the British Empire* (Baltimore, 2002).

48. Greene, *Evaluating Empire and Confronting Colonialism in Eighteenth-Century Britain*, 97–105. One such leader who supported "coercive" measures, and who would later encourage Charles to tax Americans to support the army, was Lord George Germain. On him, see Andrew O'Shaughnessy, *The Men Who Lost America: British Leadership, the American Revolution, and the Fate of Empire* (New Haven, 2013), 174.

49. Francis Bernard to Richard Jackson, 9 July 1764; same to John Pownall, 11 July 1764; same to same, 18 August 1765, Bernard to Lord Barrington, 23 November 1765, in *The Papers of Francis Bernard*, vol. 2, ed. Nicolson, 98, 100, 308, 414–15.

50. On Pownall, see Eliga Gould's entry in the *ODNB* (Oxford, 2004); and especially John Shy, "The Spectrum of Imperial Possibilities: Henry Ellis and Thomas Pownall, 1763–1775," in *A People Numerous and Armed: Reflections on the Military Struggle for American Independence* (Ann Arbor, Mich., 1990), 43–80.

51. See Peter Miller, *Defining the Common Good: Empire, Religion, and Philosophy in Eighteenth-Century Britain* (New York, 1994), 214.

52. *Sir Henry Cavendish's Debates of the House of Commons*, vol. 2 (London, 1841), 10, in Robert Chaffin Papers, Jefferson Library, Monticello, Folder 68.

53. Pincus, *The Heart of the Declaration*.

54. For Pitt's uncertainties, see Marie Peters, "The Myth of William Pitt, Earl of Chatham, Great Imperialist: Part 2, Chatham and Imperial Reorganization, 1763–1778," *Journal of Imperial and Commonwealth History* 22 (1994), 393–431. For a similar position of someone who stood for the rights of Americans and for the rights of Parliament, see Perry Gauci, *William Beckford: First Prime Minister of the London Empire* (New Haven, 2013).

55. On this theme, see Gould, *The Persistence of Empire.*

56. *Freeman's Journal*, 5 October 1765. On neglect and the relationship, see Patrick McNally, *Parties, Patriots, and Undertakers: Parliamentary Politics in Early Hanoverian Ireland* (Dublin, 1997), 197. For the how and why of the system, and why it lasted as long as it did, see Eoin Magennis, *The Irish Political System, 1740–1765* (Dublin, 2000).

57. On Lucas and the Stamp Act, see Patrick Griffin, "America's Changing Image in Ireland's Looking-Glass: Provincial Construction of an Eighteenth-Century British Atlantic World," *Journal of Imperial and Commonwealth History* 26 (1998), 37.

58. *Proceedings and Debates of the British Parliaments Respecting North America, 1754–1783*, vol. 2, ed. Simmons and Thomas, 59, 98, 167, 173, 185.

59. *Proceedings and Debates of the British Parliaments Respecting North America, 1754–1783*, vol. 2, ed. Simmons and Thomas, 59, 98, 167, 173, 185.

60. Earl of Sandwich to Grenville, 23 November 1764, *The Grenville Papers*, vol. 2, 466; George Grenville's Diary in *The Grenville Papers*, vol. 2, 482; L. B. Namier and John Brooke, *Charles Townshend* (New York, 1964), 99; Mr. Morton to Grenville, 15 October 1764; Mr. Jenkinson to Grenville, 20 November 1764, and entries from Grenville's Diary for 1764, *The Grenville Papers*, vol. 2, 465, 448, 482; Grenville's Diary for March 1765 in *The Grenville Papers*, vol. 3, 120.

61. CT to GT, 26 September 1765, Ms. Eng. Hist., d. 211, Bodleian Library, 37; Namier and Brooke, *Charles Townshend;* Bourke, *Empire and Revolution*, 230.

62. Grenville to Lord Sandwich, 7 July 1765; same to same, 9 July 1765; Grenville to Earl Temple, 6 July 1765; Grenville to Duke of Bedford, 7 July 1765, George Grenville Letterbook, st. 7, vol. 2, Huntington Library; Burke to CT, 25 June 1765, CT Papers, Buccleuch Mss., Clements, 296/1/46.

63. The king to Lord Egmont, 9 July 1765 (two letters), in *The Correspondence of King George the Third*, ed. Fortescue, 148, 152; Earl of Sandwich to the Duke of Bedford, 10 July 1765, in *Correspondence of John, Fourth Duke of Bedford*, ed. Lord John Russell, vol. 2 (London, 1843), 307.

64. Grenville's Diary, July 1765, in *The Grenville Papers*, vol. 3, 209, 210.

65. Thomas Gray to James Brown, in *Correspondence of Thomas Gray: 1766–1771*, ed. Paget Toynbee (Oxford, 1935), vol. 3, 924–26; Thomas Pelham-Holles, *A Narrative of the Changes in the Ministry, Told by the Duke of Newcastle in a Series of Letters to John White*, edited by Mary Bateson (New York, 1898), 25.

66. CT to Dowdeswell, 25 May 1765, CT Papers, Buccleuch Mss., Clements, 296/1/15; GT to Grenville, 24 May 1765, Add. Mss. 57825, British Library, 38. Some understood this stance. See Egmont to GT, 25 June 1765, Add. Mss. 47014 B, British Library.

67. Walpole, *Memoirs of the Reign of King George the Third*, vol. 2, 149; CT to Buccleuch, 30 December 1765, CT Papers, Buccleuch Mss., Clements, 296/1/9; CT to GT, 24 November 1765, Ms. Eng. Hist., d. 211, Bodleian Library, 40.

68. CT to GT, 4 July 1765, Add. Mss. 57285, BL, 121. Also in CT Papers, Buccleuch Mss., Clements, 296/1/18.

69. GT to CT, 22 July 1765, CT Papers, Buccleuch Mss., Clements, 296/1/23.

70. Grenville's Diary, May 1766, *The Grenville Papers*, vol. 3, 235; Francis Bernard to Thomas Gage, 13 September 1765, in *The Papers of Francis Bernard*, vol. 2, ed. Nicolson, 359.

71. On Burke and the Rockinghams and this point, see Bourke, *Empire and Revolution*, 233, 235. Also see Bromwich, *The Intellectual Life of Edmund Burke*, 196. For those who shared these views, see Neil York, "William Dowdeswell and the American Crisis, 1763–1775," *History* 90 (2005), 509. For Ireland and the Rockinghams, see Martyn Powell, "British Party Politics and Imperial Control: The Rockingham Whigs and Ireland 1765–1782," *Parliamentary History* 21 (2002), 325–50.

72. CT to Buccleuch, 30 December 1765, CT Papers, Buccleuch Mss., Clements, 296/1/9; CT to GT, 3 July 1765, Add. Mss. 57825, British Library, 119; CT to GT, 16 June 1766, Ms. Eng. Hist., d. 211, Bodleian Library, 45; CT to GT, 21 July 1766, Ms. Eng. Hist., d. 211, Bodleian Library, 45.

73. Walpole, *Memoirs of the Reign of King George the Third*, vol. 1, 381.

74. Namier and Brooke, *Charles Townshend*, 28–29; GT to his son, 13 November 1768, GT Papers, Letterbook, Clements, vol. 1.

75. The contents of the library are contained in two sources: "A Catalogue of Books in the Library of Raynham Hall, 1764," Grolier Club, New York; and *A Catalogue of the Magnificent Library, Books of Prints, and Manuscripts of the Late Most Noble George, Marquis of Townshend* (auction book by Leigh and Sotheby, 1812), from the Huntington Library. What follows is based on these.

76. Charles was quite fluent, for instance, in French history. See CT to Buccleuch, 22 April [no year], CT Papers, Buccleuch Mss., Clements, 296/1/6.

77. See James Livesay, *Civil Society and Empire: Ireland and Scotland in the Eighteenth Century Atlantic World* (New Haven, 2009).

78. GT to George Macartney, 8 February 1769, D 572/1/5, Public Record Office Northern Ireland (hereafter PRONI), 15–18; *A Catalogue of the Magnificent Library, Books of Prints, and Manuscripts of the Late Most Noble George, Marquis of Townshend*, 138; Books left at Norton Lodge (found among the papers of Lord Charles Townshend, 1700–1764), Osb. Mss. 161/4, Beinecke Library, Yale University.

79. Peter Thomas, *The Townshend Duties Crisis: The Second Phase of the American Revolution, 1767–1773* (Oxford, 1987), 11; Gregory Dowd, *War Under Heaven;* Patrick Griffin, "Destroying and Reforming Canaan: Making America British," in *Between Sovereignty and Anarchy*, ed. Griffin et al., 40–59.

80. Britons shared this understanding with other Europeans, and it has been expertly dissected by John Pocock in his *Barbarism and Religion*, 5 volumes, but especially volume 3, entitled *The First Decline and Fall* (New York, 2003). See also Karen O'Brien, *Narratives of Enlightenment: Cosmopolitan History from Voltaire to Gibbon* (London, 1997); and David Worlesly's excellent introduction to Edward Gibbon, *The History of the Decline and Fall of the Roman Empire, Volume I* (London, 1994). This section draws from what these three have written.

81. Namier and Brooke, *Charles Townshend*, 7; GT to his son, 13 November 1768, GT Papers, Letterbook, Clements, vol. 1.

82. H. V. Bowen, "British Conceptions of Global Empire, 1756–1783," *Journal of Imperial and Commonwealth History* 26 (1998), 8–10.

83. Books left at Norton Lodge (found among the papers of Lord Charles Townshend, 1700–1764), Osb. Mss. 161/4, Beinecke Library.

84. On West and the painting, see John Dillenberger, *Benjamin West: The Context of His Life's Work* (San Antonio, 1977), 24–29; C. P. Stacey, "Benjamin West and 'The Death of Wolfe,'" *National Gallery of Canada Bulletin* 7 (1966), 1–5; Simon Schama, *Dead Certainties: (Unwarranted Speculations)* (New York, 1991); and the entry by Dorinda Evans in the *Dictionary of National Biography*. Also see Hugh Howard, *The Painter's Chair: George Washington and the Making of American Art* (New York, 2009); and Ann Uhry Abrams, *The Valiant Hero: Grand-Style History Painting* (Washington, D.C., 1985).

85. "The Present," Jeremy Black writes, "with reference to the classical past was commonplace in eighteenth-century Britain." See Jeremy Black, "Gibbon and International Relations," in *Edward Gibbon and Empire,* edited by Rosamond McKitterick and Roland Quinault (London, 1997). Also see Peter Miller, *Defining the Common Good*, 186, 193–94.

86. O'Brien, *Narratives of Enlightenment*.

87. As Pocock concludes, "The Enlightened history of antiquity [was] more concerned to confront this tension [between libertas and imperium] than to overcome it." Pocock, *Barbarism and Religion*, vol. 3, 375.

88. More to the point, as we know, so did British officials responsible for New World policy. The designers of the Proclamation Line, for instance, were informed by these ideas as they imagined a West in which Indians would with time and influence become subjects. And they reread the archipelagic history of the seventeenth century, in which Ireland and Scotland were subjected, through these stadial lenses. See Griffin, *American Leviathan*.

89. Copies of Hume's *History of England* and Smith's *Theory of Moral Sentiments* could be found at Raynham and also at a place called Norton Lodge: Books left at Norton Lodge (found among the papers of Lord Charles Townshend, 1700–1764), Osb Mss 161/4, Beinecke Library.

90. Andrew Millar to Adam Smith, 26 April 1759, in *The Correspondence of Adam Smith*, edited by E. C. Mossner (Oxford, 1987), 39–40. Twelve volumes of Robertson's works were listed at Norton Lodge. See Books left at Norton Lodge (found among the papers of Lord Charles Townshend, 1700–1764), Osb. Mss. 161/4, Beinecke Library.

91. Drew R. McCoy, *The Elusive Republic: Political Economy in Jeffersonian America* (Chapel Hill, 1980); Pocock, *Barbarism and Religion*, vol. 3.

92. Extracts from Hume's *History of England* in the Hand of the Hon. Charles Townshend, Add. Mss. 63100, Townshend Papers, British Library, 155. On the Norman Conquest in Hume's thought see James Harris, *Hume: An Intellectual Biography* (New York, 2015), 309.

93. J. Shelbean to CT, 3 September 1760, CT Papers, Buccleuch Mss., Clements, 296/4/16; Forster, *The Uncontrolled Chancellor*, 15–16; Hume to Mme. Marie Charlotte Hippolyte Boufflers-Rouverel, 16 May 1766, in *The Letters of David Hume*, edited by J. Y. T. Greig, vol. 2 (Oxford, 1932), 44–48.

94. John Dalrymple to CT, 12 February 1761, Ms. Eng. Lett., c. 386, Bodleian Library, 50–53.

95. CT to Buccleuch, 10 April 1764, CT Papers, Buccleuch Mss., Clements, 296/1/3; CT to Smith, 25 October 1763, in *The Correspondence of Adam Smith*, ed. Mossner, 95–96; Account for Books Supplied for Henry Scott, c. October 1759, in *The Correspondence of Adam Smith*, ed. Mossner, 57; CT to Buccleuch, 10 September 1760, CT Papers, Buccleuch Mss., Clements, 296/1/1; Adam Smith to CT, Ms. Eng. Lett., c. 386, Bodleian Library, 99–100.

96. For this relationship, see Brian Bonnyman, *The Third Duke of Buccleuch and Adam Smith: Estate Management and Improvement in Enlightenment Scotland* (Edinburgh, 2014), 34–52. Charles is quoted on p. 49.

97. Robertson to CT, 25 October 1759, 23 July 1760, CT Papers, Clements, 295/3/21, 22; John Dalrymple to CT, 12 February 1761, Ms. Eng. Lett., c. 366, Bodleian Library, 50–53.

98. For an interpretation of Hume that focuses on such dramatic shifts and the critical role of leadership in creating stability, see Andrew Sabl, *Hume's Politics: Coordination and Crisis in the History of England* (Princeton, 2012).

99. On this, see Reinhart Koselleck, *Futures Past: On the Semantics of Historical Time* (Cambridge, Mass., 1985), 117. My thanks to Asher Kaufman for the reference.

100. CT to Buccleuch, 10 June 1764, CT Papers, Buccleuch Mss., Clements, 296/1/4–5.

101. Harris, *Hume: An Intellectual Biography*, 337, 320; Colin Kidd, "The Ideological Significance of Robertson's *History of Scotland*," in *William Robertson and the Expansion of Empire*, edited by Stewart Brown (Cambridge, 2008), 132–35.

102. In such circumstances, a leader, like a new Augustus, could reform or retard, in much the same way the emperor had done ages ago. As David Womersley notes, an Augustus "was both savior and destroyer, oppressor and preserver." Womersley, "Introduction," in Gibbon, *The History of the Decline and Fall of the Roman Empire* (London, 2000), xxvii. See also Pocock, *Barbarism and Religion*.

103. Bourke, *Empire and Revolution*, 3–4. For a fascinating study of reading habits and Hume and Robertson, see John Brewer, *Pleasures of the Imagination: English Culture in the Eighteenth Century* (New York, 2007), 180–82.

104. Brendan Simms, *Three Victories and a Defeat: The Rise and Fall of the First British Empire, 1714–1783* (New York, 2007), 537; Gabriel Paquette, *Enlightenment, Government, and Reform in Spain and Its Empire, 1759–1808* (London, 2011). For the French and reform, see Michael Kwass, *Privilege and the Politics of Taxation in Eighteenth-Century France: Liberté, Egalité, Fiscalité* (New York, 2006). The best statement on this conundrum may be Jeremy Adelman, "An Age of Imperial Revolutions," *American Historical Review* 113 (2008), 319–40.

105. This is something akin to what historians would call Gibbon's "empire of republican forms." See O'Brien, *Narratives of Enlightenment*.

106. Bartlett, "The Townshend Viceroyalty, 1767–1772," 50. GT to Bute, 9 July 1768, 29 March 1768, GT Papers, Letterbook, Clements, vol. 1, 85–88.

107. Burke quoted in Forster, *The Uncontrolled Chancellor*, 82.

108. Holland quoted in Forster, *The Uncontrolled Chancellor*, 71–72.

109. *The Letters of Thomas Gray*, edited by Duncan Tovey (London, 1900), vol. 1, 285.

110. CT to GT, n.d. 1766, Ms. Eng. Hist., d. 211, Bodleian Library, 43; *Autobiography and Political Correspondence of August Henry, Third Duke of Grafton*, edited by W. R. Anson (London, 1898), 65.

111. CT to GT, n.d. 1766, Ms. Eng. Hist., d. 211, Bodleian Library, 43.

112. GT to Egremont, 3 July 1765, Add. Mss. 47014 B, British Library; GT to Edward Jerningham, 15 April 1765, JE 950, Huntington Library; CT to GT, 3 July 1765, Add. Mss. 57825, British Library, 119.

113. Grenville to GT, 19 November 1765, George Grenville Letterbook, st. 7, vol. 2, Huntington Library; CT to GT, 29 September 1765, Ms. Eng. Hist., d. 211, Bodleian Library, 38.

114. GT to Pitt, 21 April 1766, *Correspondence of William Pitt*, vol. 2, 413–14; GT to CT, 2 July 1764, Ms. Eng. Lett., c. 386, Bodleian Library, 122.

Act 3. Charles Townshend's America

1. Perhaps because of Pitt's uncertain association with Charles, and the king's opinion of that relationship. See the King to the Marquis of Rockingham, 9 January 1766; Rockingham to George III, 15 January 1766, in *Memoirs of the Marquis of Rockingham and His Contemporaries*, edited by George Thomas, vol. 1 (London, 1852), 266, 270, 311. For a sense of the tangled politics of the period, see John Brewer, *Party Ideology and Popular Politics at the Accession of George III* (New York, 1976).

2. On this, as well as the hoped-for stability, see John Brooke, *The Chatham Administration, 1766–1768* (London, 1956).

3. CT to --------, 13 June 1766, Ms. Eng. Lett., c. 144, 272, Bodleian Library; CT to Charles Dingley, June 1765, cited in *The Correspondence of William Pitt, Earl of Chatham*, edited by W. S. Taylor and J. H. Pringle (London, 1838–1840), vol. 2, 462.

4. John Brooke, *The Chatham Administration, 1766–1768* (London, 1956), 9–10; Horace Walpole, *Memoirs of the Reign of King George the Third*, vol. 2 (London, 1845), 346; CT to Pitt, 22 July 1766, *Correspondence of William Pitt*, vol. 2, 456; L. B. Namier and John Brooke, *Charles Townshend* (New York, 1964), 149; the King to Pitt, Pitt to the King, 26 July 1766, in *The*

Correspondence of King George the Third, vol. 1, edited by John Fortescue (London, 1927), 382; CT to Duke of Grafton, 25 July 1766, in *Autobiography and Political Correspondence of Augustus Henry, Third Duke of Grafton*, edited by W. R. Anson (London, 1898), 96.

5. CT to Grafton, 25 November 1766, in *Autobiography and Political Correspondence of Augustus Henry, Third Duke of Grafton*, ed. Anson, 104; Lord Holland to CT, 24 July 1766, Ms. Eng. Lett., c. 386, Bodleian Library, 76–77; Brooke, *The Chatham Administration*, 33.

6. GT to the King, January 1767, in *The Correspondence of King George the Third*, vol. 1, ed. Fortescue, 442.

7. Burke quoted in David Bromwich, *The Intellectual Life of Edmund Burke: From the Sublime and Beautiful to American Independence* (Cambridge, Mass., 2014), 215.

8. "R.B." to CT, 15 July 1766, Ms. Eng. Lett., c. 386, Bodleian Library, 3–4; Brooke, *The Chatham Administration*.

9. Grenville to Earl of Burks, 27 January 1767, Grenville Letterbook, st. 7, vol. 2, Huntington Library; Grenville to Gen. Fraser, 17 February 1767, Grenville Letterbook, st. 7, vol. 2, Huntington Library.

10. Robert Chaffin to Thad Tate, 20 November 1968; and Chaffin's Notes on Reader's Report, in Chaffin Papers, Jefferson Library, Monticello, Folder 71; Earl of Chesterfield to his son, 1 August 1766, 13 February 1767, 3 March 1767, in *The Letters of the Earl of Chesterfield to His Son*, edited by Charles Strachey, vol. 2 (London, 1901), 458, 465; CT to Buccleuch, 16 September 1766, CT Papers, Buccleuch Mss., Clements, 296/1/12.

11. Merchants of New York to CT, 16 December 1766, CT Papers, Clements, 8/31/13. For the longer, formal petition to Parliament, see 8/31/14; Petition of New York Merchants, 20 February 1767, Buccleuch Mss. at Dalkeith, Reel 2. On the free ports see Frances Armytage, *The Free Port System in the British West Indies: A Study in Commercial Policy, 1766–1822* (London, 1953).

12. CT to C. Yorke, n.d., Add. Mss. 35639, 333, British Library. For two very different interpretations of Charles's planning (whether he had thorough plans or not) and his single-mindedness, see Robert Chaffin, "The Townshend Acts of 1767," *William and Mary Quarterly*, 3rd. ser., 27 (1970), 90–121; and P. D. G. Thomas, "Charles Townshend and American Taxation in 1767," *English Historical Review* 83 (1968), 33–51. Both, despite the differing positions, offer excellent narratives of the ins and outs of the passage of the duties.

13. Proposed Duties upon Wine, Oil, and Fruit to America, 1766; Study of Duties on Goods Sent to America, 1767, CT Papers, Clements, 8/31/9, 8/31/12.

14. Walpole, *Memoirs of the Reign of King George the Third*, vol. 2, 447; Notes on Commons Debate, 30 April 1767, in *Proceedings and Debates of the British Parliaments Respecting North America, 1754–1783*, edited by R. C. Simmons and P. D. G. Thomas, vol. 2 (Millwood, N.Y., 1982), 457; Lists of an Extract from several papers laid before the Parliament relative to the Disturbances in America, 8/22/17; Reports from *Maryland Gazette* and Reports from *New-York Gazette or Weekly Post-Boy*, 8/22/18–19; Memorandum on the Charter of New England, 1691, CT Papers, Clements, 8/22/30; Stephen Sayre to Mr. Reed, 19 June 1766, in W. B. Reed, ed., *The Life of Esther De Berndt, Afterwards Esther Reed, of Pennsylvania* (Philadelphia, 1853), 85–86.

15. Report of the Board of Trade of the Establishment of the Salaries of Governors, Judges, and Other Officers, CT Papers, Buccleuch Mss., Clements, 296/5/12; The Gross Produce of the Several Duties, which Constitute Excise, 1760, 1761, 1762; Account of the Nett Sums Arising from the Revenue of Customs and Payed into the Exchequer, 1716–1764; and Balance Sheet Showing National Debt with the Charge for Annuities, 5 January 1764; A List of Certain Officers under the Present American Establishment of Customs, 6 January 1767, CT Papers, Clements, 8/3B/2, 8/3B/3, 8/3B/10, 8/31/18; Cornelius P. Forster, *The Uncontrolled Chancellor: Charles Townshend and His American Policy* (Providence, 1978), 112.

16. Neil Longley York, ed., *Henry Hulton and the American Revolution: An Outsider's Inside View* (Charlottesville, 2010), 44–45, 92.

17. Examination of Brook Watson before the Committee for American Affairs, 27 March 1766, CT Papers, Buccleuch Mss., Clements, 8/34/27; Queries and Answers Relative to North America, CT Papers, Buccleuch Mss., Clements, 8/34/35.

18. "Adam Smith at Downing Street, 1766–1767," *Economic History Review* 6 (1935), 79–89; Abstracts Re: The Sinking Fund, 1688–1697, CT Papers, Clements, 8/3B/1.

19. Charles asked questions 123, 124, 144, 145, and 158–162 in the session. See *The Complete Works of Benjamin Franklin*, ed. John Bigelow (New York, 1887–1888), 407–53.

20. Namier and Brooke, *Charles Townshend*, and Forster, *The Uncontrolled Chancellor*.

21. Notes on Commons Debate, 18 February 1767, in *Proceedings and Debates of the British Parliaments Respecting North America, 1754–1783*, vol. 2, ed. Simmons and Thomas, 428–29; Grenville to Earl of Burks, 27 January 1767, Grenville Letterbook, st. 7, vol. 2, Huntington Library.

22. Notes on Commons Debate, 18 February 1767, in *Proceedings and Debates of the British Parliaments Respecting North America, 1754–1783*, vol. 2, ed. Simmons and Thomas, 428–29.

23. Sarah Byng Osborn to her brother Jack, April 1767, 12 August 1766, in *Letters of Sarah Byng Osborn, 1721–1773*, edited by John McClelland (Palo Alto, 1930), 128–29, 110; Walpole, *Memoirs of the Reign of King George the Third*, vol. 2, 8–9.

24. Response to Petition of New York Merchants, 14 March 1767, CT Papers, Clements, 8/31/18.

25. Copy of the Journal of the General Assembly of New York, November 1766, in Buccleuch Mss. at Dalkeith, Reel 2.

26. At this time Charles also had to overcome his isolation in the cabinet. He enjoyed no substantive support. Chatham, ambiguous with his plans for America at the best of times, was now thoroughly incapacitated and would talk to no one, except the incompetent Grafton. Moreover, Charles was hearing rumors that Chatham was threatening to find a new Chancellor of the Exchequer. Yet Charles still knew Parliament had to stand up against the insolence of New York's assembly. For this episode, as well as a blow-by-blow description of the political twists and turns Charles dealt with, see Chaffin, "The Townshend Acts of 1767," 90–121.

27. Notes on Commons Debate, 30 April 1767, in *Proceedings and Debates of the British Parliaments Respecting North America, 1754–1783*, vol. 2, ed. Simmons and Thomas, 457; Notes on Commons Debate, 13 May 1767, in *Proceedings and Debates of the British Parliaments Respecting North America, 1754–1783*, vol. 2, ed. Simmons and Thomas, 463–64.

28. Notes on Commons Debate, 13 May 1767, in Simmons and Thomas, eds., *Proceedings and Debates of the British Parliaments Respecting North America, 1754–1783*, vol. 2, ed. Simmons and Thomas, 463, 467.

29. Notes on Commons Debate, 13 May 1767, in *Proceedings and Debates of the British Parliaments Respecting North America, 1754–1783*, vol. 2, ed. Simmons and Thomas, 467; Eric Nelson, *The Royalist Revolution: Monarchy and the American Founding* (Cambridge, Mass., 2014). For the centrality of Charles in this drama, see Thomas, "Charles Townshend and American Taxation in 1767," 33–34.

30. CT to Pitt, 26 July 1766, *Correspondence of William Pitt*, vol. 2, 465; Forster, *The Uncontrolled Chancellor*, 100; Notes on Commons Debate, 13 May 1767, in *Proceedings and Debates of the British Parliaments Respecting North America, 1754–1783*, vol. 2, ed. Simmons and Thomas, 466, 464. Some have claimed that Charles did not intend an imperial overhaul at all but proposed the revenue measures he did, if we could even call them that, because the government had lost on a land tax initiative. Money had to come from some place, after all. Charles, though, launched his American plan a month before the land tax setback. See Namier and Brooke, *Charles Townshend*, 175, and Thomas, "Charles Townshend and American Taxation in 1767," 42.

31. Richard Bourke, *Empire and Revolution: The Political Life of Edmund Burke* (Princeton, 2015), 306–7. For a broad outline of the plan, and especially the New York Restraining Act, see Robert J. Chaffin, "The Townshend Acts Crisis, 1767–1770," in *The Blackwell Encyclopedia of the American Revolution*, edited by Jack Greene and J. R. Pole, 126–32.

32. Notes on Commons Debate, 13 May 1767, in *Proceedings and Debates of the British Parliaments Respecting North America, 1754–1783*, vol. 2, ed. Simmons and Thomas, 464.

33. Forster, *The Uncontrolled Chancellor*, 131; Namier and Brooke, *Charles Townshend*.

34. *Autobiography and Political Correspondence of Augustus Henry, Third Duke of Grafton*, ed. Anson, 126; Chaffin, "The Townshend Acts Crisis, 1767–1770," 127; Notes on Commons Debate, 13 May 1767, in *Proceedings and Debates of the British Parliaments Respecting North America, 1754–1783*, vol. 2, ed. Simmons and Thomas, 470–71; Huske to CT in Namier and Brooke, *Charles Townshend*, 187–88.

35. John Shy, "The Spectrum of Imperial Possibilities: Henry Ellis and Thomas Pownall, 1763–1775," in *A People Numerous and Armed: Reflections on the Military Struggle for American Independence* (Ann Arbor, Mich., 1990); Conway to the king, 22 February 1767, in *The Correspondence of King George the Third*, vol. 1, ed. Fortescue, 251; Grenville to Lord Clive, 19 July 1767, Grenville Letterbook, st. 7, vol. 2, Huntington Library; Notes on Commons Debate, 15 May 1767, in *Proceedings and Debates of the British Parliaments Respecting North America, 1754–1783*, vol. 2, ed. Simmons and Thomas, 475.

36. Notes on Commons Debate, 13 May 1767, in *Proceedings and Debates of the British Parliaments Respecting North America, 1754–1783*, vol. 2, ed. Simmons and Thomas, 465; Notes on Commons Debate, 15 May 1767, in

Proceedings and Debates of the British Parliaments Respecting North America, 1754–1783, vol. 2, ed. Simmons and Thomas, 478.

37. Notes on Commons Debate, 15 May 1767, in *Proceedings and Debates of the British Parliaments Respecting North America, 1754–1783*, vol. 2, ed. Simmons and Thomas, 479; Notes on Commons Debate, 13 May 1767, in *Proceedings and Debates of the British Parliaments Respecting North America, 1754–1783*, vol. 2, ed. Simmons and Thomas, 468; Chaffin, "The Townshend Acts Crisis, 1767–1770," 131; "Letter from John Huske to CT, 9 April 1767," in Namier and Brooke, *Charles Townshend*, 188; "Preliminary Draft of the Townshend Duties," in Namier and Brooke, *Charles Townshend*, 189–91; Forster, *The Uncontrolled Chancellor*, 134.

38. "An act for granting certain duties in the British colonies and plantations in America; for allowing a drawback of the duties of customs upon the exportation, from this kingdom, of coffee and cocoa nuts of the produce of the said colonies or plantations; for discontinuing the drawbacks payable on china earthen ware exported to America; and for more effectually preventing the clandestine running of goods in the colonies and plantations," in *The Statutes at Large*, vol. 27, edited by Danby Pickering (London, 1767), 505–12; John Philip Reid, *Constitutional History of the American Revolution: The Authority to Tax* (Madison, Wis., 1987), 30–31; Committee of Ways and Means Notes, *Proceedings and Debates of the British Parliaments Respecting North America, 1754–1783*, vol. 2, ed. Simmons and Thomas, 504.

39. P. J. Marshall makes this point in his *The Making and Unmaking of Empires: Britain, India, and America, c. 1750–1783* (Oxford, 2005), 307–8.

40. "Speech on Townshend Duties, 15 May 1767," *Writings and Speeches of Edmund Burke*, edited by William B. Todd, vol. 2, 61–64; Reid, *Constitutional History of the American Revolution: The Authority to Tax*, 30; Bourke, *Empire and Revolution*, 309.

41. Burke quoted in Reid, *Constitutional History of the American Revolution: The Authority to Tax*, 220; "An Act for Granting Certain Duties," *Statutes at Large*.

42. "Charles Townshend and American Taxation in 1767," 50; Forster, *The Uncontrolled Chancellor*, 139; *Autobiography and Political Correspondence of August Henry, Third Duke of Grafton*, edited by Anson, 179; King George III quoted in Chaffin, "The Townshend Acts Crisis, 1767–1770," 131–32. On the mood, see P. D. G. Thomas, *The Townshend Duties Crisis* (Oxford, 1987), 31, as cited in Bromwich, *The Intellectual Life of Edmund Burke*, 470.

43. A Plan for the Establishment of a Board of Revenue for managing the Duties imposed by Parliament in the American Colonies, Clements, 8/31/17. On Hulton, see York, ed., *Henry Hulton and the American Revolution*.

44. Gordon Wood, *The American Revolution: A History* (New York, 2002), 31; A Plan for the Establishment of a Board of Revenue for Managing the Duties imposed by parliament in the American Colonies, Clements, 8/31/17; A List of certain Offices under the present American Establishment of the Customs proposed to be incorporated into the new Establishment, 6 January 1767, Buccleuch Mss. at Dalkeith, Reel 2. The new board would be designed to work efficiently and would be required to keep exacting records. See A List of Books Proposed as Requisite to be Kept under the Care of the Secretary to the American Board of Customs, CT Papers, Buccleuch Mss., Clements, 296/5/17.

45. Joseph Barnwell and Charles Garth, "Garth Correspondence (Continued)," *South Carolina Historical and Genealogical Magazine* 29 (1928), 223, 225, 227, 299, 300.

46. Marshall, *The Making and Unmaking of Empires*, 310; *Autobiography and Political Correspondence of Augustus Henry, Third Duke of Grafton*, ed. Anson, 123.

47. Charles quoted in Marshall, *The Making and Unmaking of Empires*, 274. For this view of the Board of Trade and imperial political economy, as well as the reliance on mapmaking to animate it, see S. Max Edelson, *The New Map of Empire: How Britain Imagined America Before Independence* (Cambridge, Mass., 2017).

48. Scheme for an Union between Great Britain and her Colonies, Buccleuch Mss. at Dalkeith, Reel 2.

49. *Sir Henry Cavendish's Debates of the House of Commons*, vol. 2, 495, in Chaffin Papers, Jefferson Library, Monticello, Folder 68.

50. Namier and Brooke, *Charles Townshend*, 176–79.

51. See Philip Stern and Carl Wennerland, "Introduction," in *Mercantilism Reimagined: Political Economy in Early Modern Britain and Its Empire*, edited by Stern and Wennerland (New York, 2015).

52. Notes on Free Ports, CT Papers, Buccleuch Mss., Clements, 8/34/67; Edited draft of a Bill for Opening and Establishing certain Ports in the Islands of Jamaica and Dominica, Buccleuch Mss. at Dalkeith, Reel 2; Regulations for Opening the Island of Dominica as a Free-Port, Buccleuch Mss. at Dalkeith, Reel 2. Burke was responsible for the most radical approach, though it never saw the light of day with the collapse of the Rockingham

ministry: see Bourke, *Empire and Revolution*, 235–36. On the significance of the free ports to imperial political economy and Atlantic trade, see Gregory O'Malley, *Final Passages: The Intercolonial Slave Trade of British America, 1619–1807* (Chapel Hill, 2014); Armytage, *The Free Port System in the British West Indies*, 40.

53. Notes Concerning the Trade, Economy, and Dependence of Granada, 1764; Papers Concerning Lands in North America, Buccleuch Mss. at Dalkeith, Reel 2.

54. Paper concerning Land in North America, Buccleuch Mss. at Dalkeith, Reel 2; Craig Yirush, *Settlers, Liberty, and Empire: The Roots of Early American Political Theory, 1675–1775* (New York, 2011), 234–35; Report on Forts, 1766, CT Papers, Clements, 8/31/1. For more on policy and ideology in the West see Patrick Griffin, *American Leviathan: Empire, Nation, and Revolutionary Frontier* (New York, 2007).

55. H. Harrison to Lord Lynne, 13 December [1769?]; H. Harrison to GT, 12 June [1770?]; Harrison to GT, 5 July [1770?], George Townshend Papers, Dublin Castle Archival Material, Oireachtas Library, Dublin (hereafter Oireachtas Library).

56. Forster, *The Uncontrolled Chancellor*, 107–8. For the dynamic between Charles and Chatham, and especially Charles's role in stymying his plans, see Brooke, *The Chatham Administration*, 73–74.

57. Forster, *The Uncontrolled Chancellor*, 108–10; Grenville to Earl of Burks, 27 January 1767, Grenville Letterbook, st. 7, vol. 2, Huntington Library; Walpole, *Memoirs of the Reign of King George the Third*, vol. 3, 393; *Autobiography and Political Correspondence of Augustus Henry, Third Duke of Grafton*, ed. Anson, 122; Walpole, *Memoirs of the Reign of King George the Third*, vol. 2, 394–95. On the pecuniary interest, see Namier and Brooke, *Charles Townshend*, 160.

58. Walpole, *Memoirs of the Reign of King George the Third*, vol. 3, 23–25.

59. Walpole, *Memoirs of the Reign of King George the Third*, vol. 2, 408; vol. 3, 2; Brooke, *The Chatham Administration*, 74.

60. Namier and Brooke, *Charles Townshend*, 161–62, 164; Brooke, *The Chatham Administration*, 73.

61. Marie Peters, "The Myth of William Pitt," *Journal of Imperial and Commonwealth History* 22 (1994), 404; H. V. Bowen, *Revenue and Reform: The Indian Problem in British Politics, 1757–1773* (Cambridge, 2002), 57–59, 87; CT to Chatham, 4 January 1767, CT Papers, Buccleuch Mss., Clements, 296/3/23. My thanks to Rachel Banke for bringing the Bowen reference to my attention.

62. CT Papers, Clements, 8/33 and 8/38; Bowen, *Revenue and Reform*, 57–59, 87; Namier and Brooke, *Charles Townshend*, 159–61; Walpole, *Memoirs of the Reign of King George the Third*, vol. 2, 427. Burke took a similar stand also for principled reasons, though his motives have been questioned in much the same ways Charles's were. Richard Bourke uncovers Burke's "humanitarian" concerns in *Empire and Revolution*, 361.

63. Lewis Namier to J. H. Plumb, 20 March 1957, Plumb Papers, Cambridge University Library (uncatalogued). My thanks to Jim Smyth for the reference.

64. CT to Earl Temple, 21 October 1763, in *The Grenville Papers: Being the Correspondence of Richard Grenville Earl Temple and the Right Hon. George Grenville*, edited by W. J. Smith, vol. 2 (London, 1852), 143; Forster, *The Uncontrolled Chancellor*, 141; Report on Charles Townshend's Death by Rev. Mr. Cole, Add. Mss. 5808, 226, British Library.

65. Epitaph of Charles Townshend from *Cambridge Chronicle*, Add. Mss. 5850, 226, British Library.

66. Charles Frederick to Marquess of Granby, 11 September 1767, in Historical Manuscripts Commission, *The Manuscripts of His Grace the Duke of Rutland Preserved at Belvoir Castle*, vol. 2 (London, 1889), 292; Walpole to Mann, 27 September 1767, in *The Letters of Thomas Gray*, edited by Duncan C. Tovey, vol. 3 (London, 1912), 159; Walpole, *Memoirs of the Reign of King George the Third*, vol. 3, 100; George Grenville to Earl of Thomond, 7 September 1767, George Grenville Letterbook, st. 7, vol. 2, Huntington Library. A friend, who had studied at Cambridge with him, clipped out a piece from the *Cambridge Chronicle*, in which it was said, "His great Fort was in the Senate, where no one ever excelled, if any ever equaled him, in Eloquence or Ability." See Report on Charles Townshend's Death by Rev. Mr. Cole, Add. Mss. 5808, 226, British Library.

67. *Belfast News-Letter*, 15 September 1767; Henry Seymour Conway to Charles O'Conor, 5 September 1767, T2812/12/7, PRONI; W. Ellis to GT, 13 September 1767, T2930/4, PRONI.

68. *Speech of Edmund Burke on American Taxation, April 19, 1774* (London, 1775), 79–82. On this, see Bourke, *Empire and Revolution*.

69. Burke's speech cited in Forster, *The Uncontrolled Chancellor*, 141. For Burke's read on Charles after the death, see Bromwich, *The Intellectual Life of Edmund Burke*, 216–17. Burke even forgave him for formulating the duties that he thought had created a grave imperial crisis. On this, see Edmund Burke, Speech on American Taxation, 19 April 1774, in *Writings and Speeches of*

Edmund Burke, edited by Paul Langford, vol. 2, 453ff. My thanks to Richard Bourke for this reference.

70. *Letters of Sarah Bing Osborn, 1721–1773: From the Collection of the Hon. Mrs. McDonnel,* edited by John McClelland (Palo Alto, 1930), Letter LXXXI, 8 September 1767, 132; Namier and Brooke, *Charles Townshend,* 183; GT to Duke of Leinster, 9 September 1767, GT Papers, Letterbook, Clements, vol. 1, 14.

71. GT to Lord Lyttleton, 26 September 1767, GT Papers, Letterbook, Clements, vol. 1; GT to Lord Shannon, 6 September 1767; GT to Lord Granby, 19 September 1767, GT to Lord Hillsborough, 10 September 1767, GT Papers, Letterbook, vol. 1, Clements Library, 12–13, 28–29, 21; Richard Jackson to GT, 12 September 1767, GT Papers, Clements, vol. 1.

72. GT to Dr. Barnard, 4 October 1767, GT Papers, Letterbook, Clements, vol. 1, 53–56; Epitaph of Charles Townshend from *Cambridge Chronicle,* Add. Mss. 5850, 226, British Library.

73. Carl Kaestle, "The Public Reaction to John Dickinson's Farmer's Letters," *Proceedings of the American Antiquarian Society* 78 (1969), 323; Francis Bernard to the Earl of Shelburne, 27 July 1767, 24 August 1767, 14 September 1767, in *The Papers of Francis Bernard,* edited by Colin Nicolson, vol. 3 (Boston, 2013), 379, 384–85, 403.

74. T. H. Breen, *The Marketplace of Revolution: How Consumer Politics Shaped American Independence* (Oxford, 2004), 236; *New-York Journal; or, the General Advertiser,* 19 October 1769.

75. Jack Rakove, *Revolutionaries: A New History of the Invention of America* (Boston, 2010), 23; "Divide & Impera. *Divide and Tyrannize,*" *Pennsylvania Gazette,* 14 April 1768.

76. Breen, *Marketplace of Revolution;* Colin Kidd, "North Britishness and the Nature of Eighteenth-Century British Patriotisms," *Historical Journal* 39 (1996), 361–82.

77. Extract from *Connecticut Courant,* 14 December 1767, in Chaffin Papers, Monticello, Folder 65; John E. Ferlin, *John Adams: A Life* (Knoxville, Tenn., 1992), 174.

78. Jeremy Stern, "Anglicization Against the Empire: Revolutionary Ideas and Identity in Townshend Crisis Massachusetts," in *Anglicizing America: Empire, Revolution, Republic,* edited by Ignacio Gallup-Diaz, Andrew Shankman, and David Silverman (Philadelphia, 2015), 153–80.

79. Fred Anderson, *Crucible of War: The Seven Years' War and the Fate of Empire in British North America, 1754–1766* (New York, 2000), 709;

Advertisement in Boston Paper, CT Papers, Buccleuch Mss., Clements, 266/5/24; *Connecticut Courant*, 11 January 1768, Chaffin Papers, Monticello, Folder 65; Nicole Eustace, *Passion Is the Gale: Emotion, Power, and the Coming of the American Revolution* (Chapel Hill, 2008), 418–25.

80. Bernard to Shelburne, 8 October 1767, in *The Papers of Francis Bernard*, ed. Nicolson, vol. 3, 412–13. In this letter, he sent nine clippings. For the best, and most recent, studies of the reach of print and of newspapers in particular before the Revolution, see Robert Parkinson, *The Common Cause: Creating Race and Nation in the American Revolution* (Chapel Hill, 2016), and Breen, *Marketplace of Revolution*.

81. *Virginia Gazette*, 14 March 1766; *Virginia Gazette*, 15 January 1767; *Boston Post-Boy*, 19 January 1767; *Boston Gazette*, 23 March 1767. All citations of the *Virginia Gazette* refer to the Purdie and Dixon edition of the paper.

82. Extracted letters in *Pennsylvania Gazette*, 23 April 1767; *Virginia Gazette*, 7 May 1767, 21 May 1767; *Pennsylvania Gazette*, 21 May 1767.

83. *Virginia Gazette*, 21 May 1767. Also see *Pennsylvania Gazette*, 30 April 1767.

84. *Boston Post-Boy*, 6 July 1767; *Boston Gazette*, 6 July 1767; *Boston Evening-Post*, 6 July 1767. Reports also carried in *Pennsylvania Gazette*, 16 July 1767; *Pennsylvania Gazette*, 27 August 1767; *New York Mercury*, 31 August 1767; *Boston Gazette*, 31 August 1767.

85. *Boston Evening-Post*, 15 February 1768; 22 February 1768.

86. *Boston Evening-Post*, 15 February 1768; 22 February 1768. This vision is laid out most clearly in Yirush, *Settlers, Liberty, and Empire*, 229–33.

87. *New Hampshire Gazette*, 17 July 1767.

88. *New York Gazette*, 13 July–20 July 1767; *Boston Evening-Post*, 2 November 1767.

89. *Providence Gazette*, 14 November 1767; *Connecticut Courant*, 14 November 1767; *New Hampshire Gazette*, 20 November 1767.

90. *New Hampshire Gazette*, 16 October 1767; *Newport Mercury*, 26 October 1767; Extract from the *Connecticut Courant*, 12 October 1767, in Robert Chaffin Papers, Jefferson Library, Monticello, Folder 65.

91. *Providence Gazette*, 5 December 1767; *Boston Chronicle*, 28 December–4 January 1768; *Virginia Gazette*, 10 December 1767; *Virginia Gazette*, 31 December 1767.

92. *Pennsylvania Gazette*, 28 January 1768.

93. For example, see *Massachusetts Gazette*, 11 February 1768; *Boston Post-Boy*, 15 February 1768; and a shorter version in *New York Gazette* and *Weekly Mercury*, 1 February 1768.

94. For the development of similar ideas over the course of the eighteenth century, see Yirush, *Settlers, Liberty, and Empire*. On Franklin and the early provincial appreciation of the need to create a federated empire, see Carla Mulford, *Benjamin Franklin and the Ends of Empire* (New York, 2015).

95. John Dickinson, *Letters from a Farmer in Pennsylvania, to the Inhabitants of the British Colonies (with an Historical Introduction by R. T. H. Halsey)* (New York, 1903), xx. Also see James Truslow Adams, "Dickinson, John," in *The Dictionary of American Biography* (New York, 1928); and Elaine K. Ginsberg, "Dickinson, John," in *American National Biography* (Oxford, 1999).

96. Peter Thompson, *Rum Punch and Revolution: Taverngoing and Public Life in Eighteenth-Century Philadelphia* (Philadelphia, 1999).

97. Dickinson, *Letters from a Farmer in Pennsylvania*, xvii, xix; Letter 1, 5; Chaffin, "The Townshend Acts Crisis, 1767–1770," 132.

98. Dickinson, *Letters from a Farmer in Pennsylvania*, Letter 1, 7.

99. Dickinson, *Letters from a Farmer in Pennsylvania*, Letter 1, 9; William Murchison, *The Cost of Liberty: The Life of John Dickinson* (Wilmington, Del., 2013), 38. For the best studies of the ideas Dickinson espoused, see Bernard Bailyn, *Ideological Origins of the American Revolution* (New York, 1968), and Pauline Maier, *From Resistance to Revolution: Colonial Radicals and the Development of American Opposition to Britain, 1765–1766* (New York, 1972).

100. Dickinson, *Letters from a Farmer in Pennsylvania*, Letter 2, 13–14. On this, see J. C. D. Clark, *The Language of Liberty, 1660–1832: Political Discourse and Social Dynamics in the Anglo-American World* (Cambridge, 1994), 100–101.

101. Dickinson, *Letters from a Farmer in Pennsylvania*, Letter 2, 19, 13; Letter 4, 37, 41.

102. Dickinson, *Letters from a Farmer in Pennsylvania*, Letter 3, 30, 33–34, 31. On Dickinson and moderation see Jack Greene, *The Constitutional Origins of the American Revolution* (Cambridge, 2011), 114.

103. R. L. Brunhouse, "Effects of the Townshend Acts in Pennsylvania," *Pennsylvania Magazine of History and Biography* 14 (1930), 357, in Chaffin Papers, Monticello, Folder 21; Dickinson, *Letters from a Farmer in Pennsylvania*, Letter 1, 6; Letter 2, 25; Letter 6, 62; Letter 7, 72; Letter 12, 140.

104. Dickinson, *Letters from a Farmer in Pennsylvania*, Letter 4, 39; Letter 5, 51; Letter 8, 85; Letter 9, 88; Letter 9, 96.

105. Dickinson, *Letters from a Farmer in Pennsylvania*, Letter 4, 43.

106. Dickinson, *Letters from a Farmer in Pennsylvania*, Letter 2, 25; Letter 5, 56; Letter 7, 77; Letter 9, 98–99; Bailyn, *The Ideological Origins of the American Revolution;* Maier, *From Resistance to Revolution*.

107. Dickinson, *Letters from a Farmer in Pennsylvania*, Letter 7, 75; Letter 9, 87; John Phillip Reid, *Constitutional History of the American Revolution: The Authority to Tax* (Madison, Wis., 1987), 220.

108. *Pennsylvania Gazette*, 28 January 1768. For more details of the reaction, including appendices covering newspaper coverage, see Kaestle, "The Public Reaction to John Dickinson's Farmer's Letters."

109. Kaestle, "The Public Reaction to John Dickinson's Farmer's Letters," 325, 327; *Boston Chronicle*, 21 March 1768; *New York Journal*, 26 March 1768, which reports on Boston; *New London Gazette*, 15 April 1768; *Virginia Gazette*, 13 April 1769; *Pennsylvania Gazette*, 14 April 1768.

110. Kaestle, "The Public Reaction to John Dickinson's Farmer's Letters," 326.

111. Francis Bernard to John Pownall, 9 January 1768, in *The Papers of Francis Bernard*, ed. Colin Nicolson, vol. 4 (Boston, 2015), 63; *Extracts from the Itineraries and Other Miscellanies of Ezra Stiles*, edited by F. B. Dexter (New Haven, 1916), 471, in Chaffin Papers, Monticello, Folder 25.

112. Copy of a Letter written by the Hon. The House of Representatives, in *Boston Chronicle*, 21 March 1768 (Boston); *The True Sentiments of America Contained in a Collection of Letters Sent from the House of Representatives of the Province of Massachusetts Bay* (London, 1768), 8; *Connecticut Courant*, 27 February 1769, in Chaffin Papers, Monticello, Folder 65; and Petition of New Jersey Assembly to the King, 1768, *Documents Relating to the Colonial History of the State of New Jersey*, edited by F. W. Ricord and Wm. Nelson, vol. 10 (Newark, 1886), 18, and *Documents and Records Relating to the Province of New Hampshire*, edited by N. Bouton, vol. 8 (Nashua, N.H., 1873), 190, in Chaffin Papers, Monticello, Folder 20, Folder 16; Kaestle, "The Public Reaction to John Dickinson's Farmer's Letters," 341; *The True Sentiments of America Contained in a Collection of Letters Sent from the House of Representatives of the Province of Massachusetts Bay* (London, 1768), 30.

113. See Murchison, *The Cost of Liberty*, 3, 33.

114. Dickinson, *Letters from a Farmer in Pennsylvania*, Letter 10, 105, 103.

115. Dickinson did see some instance of hope, however; ironically, he cited the "Lord Lieutenant" in October 1767—George, in other words—granting concessions to the patriots for curtailing the duration of Parliaments there. Little did he know what would follow that concession. See Dickinson, *Letters from a Farmer in Pennsylvania*, Letter 10, 108.

116. Dickinson, *Letters from a Farmer in Pennsylvania*, Letter 10, 113; *Providence Gazette*, 1 August 1767, Chaffin Papers, Monticello, Folder 66.

117. Dickinson, *Letters from a Farmer in Pennsylvania*, Letter 9, 91.

118. Dickinson, *Letters from a Farmer in Pennsylvania*, Letter 2, 19; Letter 7, 68; Letter 12, 142. This focus on chronological and geographic connections is also noted in Kaestle, "The Public Reaction to John Dickinson's Farmer's Letters," 333.

119. See Dickinson, *Letters from a Farmer in Pennsylvania*, Letter 3.

120. Chaffin, "The Townshend Acts Crisis, 1767–1770," 132–38; Francis Bernard to Earl of Shelburne, 18 February 1768, in *The Papers of Francis Bernard*, vol. 4, ed. Nicolson, 98. Nicolson sees this as a critical turning point; see *The Papers of Francis Bernard*, 99. For a general sense of how a Dickinson-like understanding of empire worked, though he does not point out Dickinson as the genesis, see Greene, *The Constitutional Origins of the American Revolution*, 105–48.

121. *Massachusetts Gazette*, 23 June 1768; *The True Sentiments of America Contained in a Collection of Letters Sent from the House of Representatives of the Province of Massachusetts Bay* (London, 1768), 39; *Boston Evening-Post*, 27 June 1768; "Petition of the Province of New Jersey to His Majesty," carried in *Boston Chronicle*, 18–25 July 1768, and *New York Gazette*, 25 July 1768; Hillsborough to William Franklin, 16 August 1768, in *Documents Relating to the Colonial History of the State of New Jersey*, ed. Ricord and Nelson, vol. 10 (Newark, 1886), 46, in Chaffin Papers, Monticello, Folder 20; *Boston Chronicle*, 1–8 August 1768; Chaffin, "The Townshend Acts Crisis, 1767–1770," 135; Georgia Assembly's Agreement of Resolution against Townshend Duties, Chaffin Papers, Monticello, Folder 27.

122. Chaffin, "The Townshend Acts Crisis, 1767–1770," 133–34; Maier, *From Resistance to Revolution*, 170.

123. *Connecticut Journal*, 6 January 1769. On South Carolina, see Chaffin, "The Townshend Acts Crisis, 1767–1770," 135–36.

124. *Boston Chronicle*, 15–22 August 1768. See also *Virginia Gazette*, 29 September 1768; *Essex Gazette*, 15–22 November 1768; *Connecticut Gazette*, 25 November 1768; *Connecticut Journal*, 6 July 1769; Chaffin, "The Townshend Acts Crisis, 1767–1770," 137; Bromwich, *The Intellectual Life of Edmund Burke*, 217. For more on American resistance strategies see Breen, *Marketplace of Revolution*, 240.

125. Chaffin, "The Townshend Acts Crisis, 1767–1770," 132; *Boston Evening-Post*, 13 February 1769; 29 May 1769; 6 March 1769. Zachary McLeod Hutchins, "The Slave Narrative and the Stamp Act, or Letters from Two American Farmers in Pennsylvania," in *Community Without Consent: New Perspectives on the Stamp Act* (Hanover, N.H., 2016), 117.

126. *Boston Evening-Post,* 3 April 1769; *Boston Evening-Post,* 6 February 1769.

127. *Boston Evening-Post,* 20 February 1769.

128. Murchison, *The Cost of Liberty,* 61–63.

Act 4. George Townshend's Ireland

1. GT to Grafton, 1 August 1767, GT Papers, Letterbook, Clements, vol. 1, 1–3; Grafton Autobiography and Camden to Grafton, 29 September 1767, in *Autobiography and Political Correspondence of Augustus Henry, Third Duke of Grafton,* edited by William Reynell Anson (London, 1898), 157, 158–59.

2. R. F. Foster quoted in Eoin Magennis, *The Irish Political System, 1740–1765* (Dublin, 2000), 13.

3. For Irish parliamentary dynamics and corruption, see Patrick McNally, *Parties, Patriots, and Undertakers: Parliamentary Politics in Early Hanoverian Ireland* (Dublin, 1997), 202–6. On earlier attempts setting the stage for what was to come after 1767, see Martyn Powell, "The Reform of the Undertaker System: Anglo-Irish Politics, 1750–1767," *Irish Historical Studies* 31 (1998), 19–36. Eoin Magennis argues that the imperial moment made reform of the undertaker system imperative. See *The Irish Political System,* 172–98.

4. William Gerard Hamilton to Earl Temple, 22 July 1767; Augustus Hervey to Grenville, 31 July 1767, in *The Grenville Papers,* edited by W. J. Smith, vol. 4 (London, 1853), 92, 130; Horace Walpole, *Memoirs of the Reign of King George the Third,* vol. 3 (London, 1845), 98; *Autobiography and Political Correspondence of Augustus Henry, Third Duke of Grafton,* ed. Anson, 153.

5. Thomas Bartlett, "The Townshend Viceroyalty, 1767–1772," in *Penal Era and Golden Age: Essays in Irish History, 1690–1800,* edited by Thomas Bartlett and D. W. Hayton (Belfast, 1979), 88–112; and Martyn Powell, *Britain and Ireland in the Eighteenth-Century Crisis of Empire* (New York, 2003). On the debate, see Martyn Powell, "Reassessing Townshend's Irish Viceroyalty, 1767–1772: The Caldwell-Shelburne Correspondence in the John Rylands Library, Manchester," *Bulletin of the John Rylands Library* 89 (2013), 155–76.

6. GT to Mr. Jenkinson, 8 August 1767, Ms. Eng. d. 3837, 86, Bodleian Library.

7. See GT to George Macartney, 11 December 1768, D 572/1/3, 8–10, PRONI. For the role of the lord lieutenant, see James Kelly, "Residential and Nonresidential Lords Lieutenants—the Viceroyalty, 1703–1790," in *The Irish Lord Lieutenancy, c. 1541–1922,* edited by Peter Gray and Olwen Purdue (Dublin, 2012), 66–96.

8. Charles Ivar McGrath, *Ireland and Empire, 1692–1770* (London, 2012), 139–43.

9. See, for instance, a report George received of a mob hanging British soldiers. Thomas Allen to GT, 25 April 1770, GT Papers, Clements, vol. 2. On George and manpower, see GT to Attorney General De Grey, 21 October 1768, GT Papers, Letterbook, vol. 1, 221–29.

10. GT to Earl of Shelburne, 27 October 1767, *Calendar of Home Office Papers of the Reign of George III, 1766–1769* (Nendeln, Liechtenstein, 1967), 196–97; and GT to Lord Granby, 1 August 1768, GT Papers, Letterbook, vol. 1, 137–39; Grenville to Mr. Astle, 9 August 1767, Grenville Letterbook, st. 7, vol. 2, Huntington Library. For more on the connection between manpower issues and George's plans see Bartlett, "The Townshend Viceroyalty."

11. The King's Declaration in Council, 12 August 1767, 6806–41–2–1, GT Papers, National Army Museum, Chelsea; Extracts from the King's Instructions to the Lord Lieutenant, 1767, 6806–41–7–1; Instructions for the Lord Lieutenant of Ireland, 1767, 6806–41–7–2, GT Papers, National Army Museum, Chelsea; Mr. Whately to Grenville, 5 October 1767, in *The Grenville Papers,* ed. Smith, vol. 4, 171.

12. Powell, *Britain and Ireland in the Eighteenth-Century Crisis of Empire*, 97; Edward McParland, *Public Architecture in Ireland, 1680–1760* (London, 2001).

13. On Dublin and these buildings, see David Dickson, *Dublin: The Making of a Capital City* (Cambridge, Mass., 2014).

14. Ultan Gillen, "Ascendancy Ireland, 1660–1800," in *The Princeton History of Modern Ireland,* edited by Richard Bourke and Ian McBride (Princeton, 2016), 61; Desmond Guinness, "Leixlip Castle, Co. Kildare," unpublished pamphlet. My thanks to Mr. Guinness, who has done so much to preserve Ireland's eighteenth century, for kindly opening his home to me during my research.

15. John Hely-Hutchinson to GT, 13 August 1768, Add. Mss. 63100, 135, British Library; GT to Lucas, 16 November 1767, GT Papers, Letterbook, Clements, vol. 1, 63–64. For more welcomes see the February 1768 editions of the *Freeman's Journal.*

16. Thomas Bartlett, "Viscount Townshend and the Irish Revenue Board, 1767–1773," *Proceedings of the Royal Irish Academy* 79 (1979), 163. On Macartney, see the entry by Bartlett in the *Dictionary of Irish Biography* (Cambridge, 2009).

17. GT to Shelburne, 13 November 1767; and same to same, 16 February 1768, *Calendar of Home Office Papers,* vol. 2, 616, 778; Powell, *Britain and Ireland*

in the Eighteenth-Century Crisis of Empire, 98; Shelburne to GT, 2 February 1768, 30/29/3/1/24, National Archives, Kew.

18. On the budget surplus and what it meant for Anglo-Irish relations, see Michael Brown, *The Irish Enlightenment* (Cambridge, Mass., 2016), 344.

19. Powell, *Britain and Ireland in the Eighteenth-Century Crisis of Empire*, 99; "Thoughts on Lord Townshend's Proposals [In the King's handwriting]," in *The Correspondence of King George III from 1760 to December 1783*, edited by John Fortescue, vol. I (London, 1927), 512–13.

20. Shelburne to GT, 14 March 1768, GT Papers, Clements, vol. 1; GT to Marquess of Granby, 10 November 1767, 3 December 1767, in Historical Manuscripts Commission, *Duke of Rutland* (London, 1889), 293–97. On Shelburne and his knowledge of the situation, see Powell, "Reassessing Townshend's Irish Viceroyalty, 1767–1772," 173.

21. See, in particular, an exchange between the two in October and November 1767, in *Calendar of Home Office Papers of the Reign of George III*, vol. 2, 196–201.

22. Shelburne to GT, 2 February 1768, 30/29/3/1/24, National Archives, Kew; GT to Shelburne, 3 May 1768, *Calendar of Home Office Papers*, vol. 2, 862. The numbers ended up as 12,815 troops to be stationed in Ireland and 2,420 for service abroad, though many more would serve in places like America. See McGrath, *Ireland and Empire*, 142.

23. See Powell, *Britain and Ireland in the Eighteenth-Century Crisis of Empire*.

24. Powell, *Britain and Ireland in the Eighteenth-Century Crisis of Empire*, 105; GT to Macartney, 20 February 1768, D 572/1/6, 19–22, PRONI.

25. GT to Shelburne, 17 May 1768, *Calendar of Home Office Papers*, vol. 2, 887.

26. Draft of Directions and Queries from GT to Lord Frederick Campbell, 20 February 1768, GT Papers, Oireachtas Library, Dublin; Campbell to GT, 1 March 1768; same to same, n.d.; same to same, 8 March 1768, GT Papers, Oireachtas Library.

27. Campbell to GT, 1 March 1768; same to same, n.d.; same to same, 8 March 1768, GT Papers, Oireachtas Library; Thomas Weymouth to GT, 9 June 1768, Osb. Mss. 1616/14, Beinecke.

28. GT to Earl of Rochford, 9 January 1772, *Calendar of Home Office Papers*, vol. 3, 1026.

29. Grafton to GT, 18 October 1768, GT Papers, Clements; GT to Grafton, December 1768, GT Papers, Letterbook, Clements, vol. 1, 301–4; Weymouth to GT, 8 July 1769, GT Papers, Clements, vol. 1; GT to Weymouth, 27 December 1769; GT to Grafton, 23 December 1769; GT to Weymouth,

7 March 1770, Letterbook, Clements, vol. 2, 1–19, 25–31, 93–95; GT to Lord Rochford, 22 December 1771, Letterbook, Clements, vol. 3, 165–68.

30. Sketch-book of Irish towns, roads, and fortifications, 6806–41–7–3, GT Papers, National Army Museum, Chelsea; G. Trotter to GT, as well as Extract of a letter from London to G. Trotter, n.d., M 667, National Archives of Ireland, Dublin; William Horton to George Macartney, 19 November 1770, M 661, National Archives of Ireland; GT to Earl of Rochford, 16 October 1770, 6806–41–7–5, GT Papers, National Army Museum, Chelsea, 3, 12, 30.

31. GT to Earl of Rochford, 16 October 1770, 6806–41–7–5, GT Papers, National Army Museum, Chelsea, 3, 12, 30; also held in Copy of a Military Dispatch of Lord Townshends', 16 October 1770, Add. Mss. 33118, British Library, 1–24.

32. Observations on the Commercial Policy of Ireland, n.d., 6806–41–7–3, GT Papers, National Army Museum, Chelsea, 1, 4, 12, 38, 44, 82. On these themes, see R. J. Dickson, *Ulster Emigration to Colonial America* (London, 1966).

33. Observations on the Commercial Policy of Ireland, n.d., 6806–41–7–3, GT Papers, National Army Museum, Chelsea, 1, 4, 12, 38, 44, 82, 102.

34. See GT to Weymouth, 25 September 1770, GT Papers, Letterbook, Clements, vol. 2, 198–207.

35. Camden to Grafton, 29 September 1767, in *Autobiography and Political Correspondence of Augustus Henry, Third Duke of Grafton*, ed. Anson, 162; Campbell to GT, 16 July 1768, GT Papers, Oireachtas Library.

36. Powell, *Britain and Ireland in the Eighteenth-Century Crisis of Empire*, 108–9; GT to Macartney, 20 May 1769, D 572/1/31, 107–10, PRONI.

37. GT to Macartney, 8 February 1769, D 572/1/5, 15–18, PRONI.

38. GT to Macartney, 8 February 1769, D 572/1/5, 15–18, PRONI; Campbell to GT, July 1768, GT Papers, Oireachtas Library; GT to Macartney, 17 July 1769, D 572/1/49, 187–90, PRONI; Campbell to GT, 9 July 1768, GT Papers, Oireachtas Library.

39. On this, see Thomas Bartlett, "Viscount Townshend and the Irish Revenue Board, 1767–1773," 153–75; GT to Weymouth, 27 December 1769, GT Papers, Letterbook, Clements, vol. 2, 1–19. On lukewarm support from Britain, see Grafton to GT, 18 December 1768, GT Papers, Clements, vol. 1. For more fulsome support, see Grafton to GT, 3 January 1771, GT Papers, Clements, vol. 2. For rum, see GT to North, 25 September 1770, GT Papers, Letterbook, Clements, vol. 2, 212.

40. Edward Chamberlayne to GT, 15 September 1770, Osb. Mss., 161/9, Beinecke; Fitzgerald to GT, 23 August 1768, GT Papers, Clements, vol. 1.

41. GT to Thomas Vereker, 9 October 1768; Vereker to GT, 8 March 1770; John Lees to GT, 19 April 1769, Osb. Mss. 1616/12, Beinecke.

42. McNally, *Parties, Patriots, and Undertakers;* Mrs. Blacker to GT, 19 May 1768, Osb. Mss. 1616/8, Beinecke; Audrey Orme to GT, 8 December —, GT Papers, Oireachtas Library; Richard Woodward to Charlotte Townshend, 22 November 1768; M. Maintry to Charlotte Townshend, n.d., Osb. Mss. 161/2, Beinecke. Similar cases were those of Lady Anglesey and Henrietta Macartney, who played on emotions for employment for a son and brother, respectively. See Lady Anglesey to GT, 17 October 1772; and Henrietta Macartney to GT, 11 February 1768, GT Papers, Clements, vol. 1.

43. James Cunningham to GT, 29 September 1767, Osb. Mss. 1616/2, Beinecke; Davies to GT, 19 June 1769, GT Papers, Oireachtas Library; GT to Disney, 20 November 1768, GT Papers, Letterbook, Clements, vol. 1, 293–96.

44. Thomas Milloe to GT, 1 January 1772, with note in George's hand attached, Osb. Mss., 1616/6, Beinecke; Henry Parish to GT, n.d., GT Papers, Oireachtas Library.

45. Clements to GT, 5 October 1768, 20 March 1769, 30 March 1769, 14 August 1769, M 670, 671, 672, 673, National Archives of Ireland, Dublin.

46. Robert Fitzgerald to GT, eight letters, 1767–1768, Osb. Mss., 161/2, Beinecke; Fitzgerald to GT, 30 October 1772, Osb. Mss. 1616/2, Beinecke.

47. Earl of Carrick to GT, 26 October 1767, Osb. Mss. 1616/8, Beinecke; Altamount to GT, 30 October 1767, Osb. Mss., 1616/8, Beinecke; Altamount to GT, 17 August 1768, Osb. Mss. 161/8, Beinecke; William Henry Dawson, 8 May 1768, Osb. Mss. 161/9, Beinecke; Powerscourt to GT, 14 May 1768, Add. Mss. 63100, 98, British Library; GT to ----------, 17 June 1770, Ms. Eng. d. 3837, 88, Bodleian Library.

48. Lord Carrick to GT, 19 May 1771, M 683, National Archives of Ireland; Marquess of Donegall to GT, 2 November 1767, Osb. Mss., 161/9, Beinecke; Donegall to GT, 20 March 1768, GT Papers, Oireachtas Library.

49. Archibald Acheson to GT, 19 July 1772, M651, National Archives of Ireland; Belvedere to GT, 18 August 1768, M 689, National Archives of Ireland; GT to Macartney, 12 June 1769, D 572/1/40, 147–50, PRONI.

50. McNally, *Parties, Patriots, and Undertakers;* George Townshend (son) to GT, 2 January 1771, Osb. Mss. 161/2, Beinecke; Charles Ossory to GT, 16 December 1771, GT Papers, Oireachtas Library.

51. Ellis to GT, 4 August 1767, 9 February 1768, 24 September 1767, T 2930/1, 7, 5, PRONI.

52. GT to Mr. Wollaston, 24 July 1768, GT Papers, Letterbook, Clements, vol. 1, 124–25.

53. GT to Macartney, 26 February 1769, D 572/1/10, 35–37, PRONI.

54. GT to Grafton, 23 December 1769; GT to Lords of the Treasury, 23 December 1769; GT to Weymouth (three letters), 23 December 1769, GT Papers, Letterbook, Clements, vol. 2, 25–31, 33–36, 40–42, 42–43, 44–46. Also see GT to Weymouth, 27 December 1769, 1–19.

55. GT to Macartney, 14 September 1769, D 572/1/19, 64–67, PRONI.

56. GT to Weymouth, 31 December 1769, GT Papers, Letterbook, Clements, vol. 2, 60–64; Powell, *Britain and Ireland in the Eighteenth-Century Crisis of Empire*, 109; Lord Barrington to GT, 25 March 1771, GT Papers, Clements, vol. 2.

57. GT to Macartney, 8 February 1769, D 572/1/5, 15–18, PRONI; GT to Macartney, 7 April 1769, D 572/1/15, 51–54, PRONI; Dickson, *Dublin*, 193.

58. John Crozier to GT, 5 November 1768, Osb. Mss. 161/9, Beinecke.

59. McGrath, *Ireland and Empire*, 165.

60. See Thomas Bartlett's essay on the Irish and the military entitled "Ireland During the Revolutionary and Napoleonic Wars, 1793–1815," in *Cambridge History of Ireland*, vol. 3 (forthcoming).

61. GT to Rochford, 27 December 1770, M 2446, vol. 1, National Archives of Ireland. My thanks to Sam Fisher for bringing this to my attention. Also in GT Papers, Letterbook, Clements, vol. 2, 326–29.

62. GT to Rochford, 27 December 1770, M 2446, vol. 1, National Archives of Ireland; Andrew Beaumont, *Colonial America and the Earl of Halifax, 1748–1761* (Oxford, 2014).

63. On this, see Matthew Dziennik, *The Fatal Land: War, Empire, and the Highland Soldier in British America* (New Haven, 2015).

64. For sketches and for economic development of Ireland, see GT Papers, National Army Museum, Chelsea.

65. GT to Lord Rochford, 22 December 1771, GT Papers, Letterbook, vol. 3, 165–68.

66. GT to Lords of Treasury, 30 November 1768, T 1/474/188–89, National Archives, Kew; Frederick Campbell to GT, 28 July 1768, GT Papers, Oireachtas Library.

67. GT to Lord Egmont, 5 July 1768, GT Papers, Letterbook, Clements, vol. 1, 160–66.

68. Martin Postle, *Sir Joshua Reynolds: The Subject Pictures* (Cambridge, 1995), 210.

69. For Charles and Reynolds, see David Mannings and Martin Postle, *Sir Joshua Reynolds: A Complete Catalogue of His Paintings* (New Haven, 2000), vol. 1, 181, 371; vol. 2, 446.

70. Jules David Prown, *John Singleton Copley in England* (Cambridge, Mass., 1966), 279.

71. For George and Reynolds, see Mannings and Postle, *Sir Joshua Reynolds*, vol. 1, 261, 390, 498; vol. 2, 446–47.

72. Linde Lunney, "Hickey, Thomas," in *Dictionary of Irish Biography* (Cambridge, 2009).

73. See *Belfast News-Letter*, 19 April 1768; *Freeman's Journal*, 1–5 March 1768. On the Townshend portrait in Dublin, I am indebted to the Lord Mayor, who sent an unpublished piece entitled "Portraits in the Mansion House." My thanks, too, to Lisa Caulfield, who arranged a viewing.

74. *Belfast News-Letter*, 19 February 1768; *Freeman's Journal*, 25–29 August 1767.

75. William Lord, Bishop of Drumore, *A Sermon Preached in Christ-Church, Dublin . . . Before His Excellency George, Lord Viscount Townshend* (Dublin, 1767), 8; "Memoirs of His Political Life," in Historical Manuscripts Commission, *The Manuscripts and Correspondence of James, First Earl of Charlemont*, vol. 1, 1745–1783 (London, 1891), 24. See also the February 1768 editions of the *Freeman's Journal*.

76. "Memoirs of His Political Life," 26; *Freeman's Journal*, 9–13 February 1768; 13–16 February 1768; 16–20 February 1768; 20–23 February 1768; 23–27 February 1768; "Memoirs of His Political Life," 24. So great was his early achievement that a New Yorker named William Kelly told George of how he and some others were working to have a township in the colony named Townshend. Kelly also sent George seeds from America for his garden. See William Kelly to GT, 8 January 1769, GT Papers, Clements, vol. 1.

77. *Freeman's Journal*, 16–20 February 1768.

78. *Freeman's Journal*, 9–12 December 1769.

79. "Cantilena to the Printer, with two ballads.—Proceedings of Lord Townshend's second Sessions verified," in *Baratariana: A Select Collection of Fugitive Political Pieces, Published During the Administration of Lord Townshend in Ireland* (Dublin, 1773), 293; Report noted in *Belfast News-Letter*, 20 December 1771; *Freeman's Journal*, 16–18 November 1769, 13–16 January 1770. For the innkeeper story, see the Chevalier de Latoncnaye, *A Frenchman's*

Walk Through Ireland, 1796–1797 (London, 1798), 94–95. My thanks to Tom Bartlett for this.

80. *Freeman's Journal,* 6–9 January 1770; "Memoirs of His Political Life," 30. For more on public opinion and George, see Martyn Powell, "Managing the Dublin Populace: The Importance of Public Opinion in Anglo-Irish Politics, 1750–1772," *Irish Studies Review* 16 (1996), 8–13.

81. Walpole, *Memoirs of the Reign of King George the Third,* vol. 3 (London, 1845), 110, 375; "Memoirs of His Political Life," 24; Walpole, *Memoirs of the Reign of King George the Third,* vol. 4, 348, 283; Powell, *Britain and Ireland in the Eighteenth-Century Crisis of Empire,* 117.

82. *Freeman's Journal,* 1–3 March 1770; GT to Weymouth, 17 January 1770, GT Papers, Letterbook, Clements, vol. 2, 64–66; "Memoirs of His Political Life," 30.

83. A good example of this delicacy is in GT to George Macartney, 16 December 1768; and same to same, 20 February 1769, D572/1/3–5, 8–10, 15–18, PRONI. For more on George's situation at this point see Bartlett, "The Townshend Viceroyalty," 101. On the inept image of George, see Neil Longley York, *Neither Kingdom Nor Nation: The Irish Quest for Constitutional Rights, 1698–1800* (Washington, D.C., 1994), 76–77.

84. *Belfast News-Letter,* 18 August 1767; *Freeman's Journal,* 8–11 August 1767; Martyn Powell, "Ireland: Radicalism, Rebellion and Union," in *A Companion to Eighteenth-Century Britain,* edited by H. T. Dickinson (Oxford, 2002), 415–16.

85. Charles O'Conor to John Curry, 9 December 1767; O'Conor to Curry, 19 July 1770; O'Conor to Curry, 1 January 1773; O'Conor to Curry, 30 October 1767, in *The Letters of Charles O'Conor of Belangare,* edited by Catherine Coogan Ward and Robert E. Ward (Ann Arbor, Mich., 1980), 233, 273, 231.

86. Dickson, *Dublin;* Powell, *Britain and Ireland in the Eighteenth-Century Crisis of Empire;* and Vincent Morley, *Irish Opinion and the American Revolution, 1760–1783* (Cambridge, 2002); Thomas Bartlett, *The Fall and Rise of the Irish Nation: The Catholic Question, 1690–1830* (Dublin, 1992), 67; Powell, *Britain and Ireland in the Eighteenth-Century Crisis of Empire.*

87. *Belfast News-Letter,* 4 June 1771.

88. *Freeman's Journal,* 7–10 October 1769; *Freeman's Journal,* 14–17 October 1769; Broghill to Sindercombe, "Vindication of Lord Townshend," in *Baratariana,* 105, 110.

89. *An Essay on the Character and Conduct of His Excellency Lord Vsc. Townshend* (Dublin, 1771), 4; *An Epistle from Gorges Edmond Howard, Esq. to Alderman G. Faulkner* (Dublin, n.d.), 11.

90. Archibald Acheson to GT, 26 August 1772, Townshend Papers, National Archives of Ireland, M554; Lord Carrick to GT, 8 May 1768, Townshend Papers, National Archives of Ireland, M680.

91. GT to Marquess of Granby, 5 April 1768, Historical Manuscripts Commission, *The Manuscripts of His Grace the Duke of Rutland*, 303; Charles Lucas, *A Second Letter to the Free Citizens and Free Holders and Tradesmen of the City of Dublin* (Dublin, 1768), 3–6, 8.

92. Charles Lucas, *The Rights and Privileges of Parlements Asserted upon Constitutional Principles* (Dublin, 1770), 9, 28.

93. *The Correspondence of King George the Third with Lord North from 1768 to 1783*, edited by W. B. Donne (London, 1867), 15; *Belfast News-Letter*, 22 May 1770.

94. Dickson, *Dublin*; Powell, *Britain and Ireland in the Eighteenth-Century Crisis of Empire*, 121. My thanks to James Kelly for help with these connections.

95. On Charlemont, see James Kelly's entry in the *Oxford Dictionary of National Biography;* and "Lord Charlemont and Learning," *Proceedings of the Royal Irish Academy* 106C (2006), 395–407. For the Flood emphasis, see Bartlett, "The Townshend Viceroyalty," 150. Martyn Powell emphasizes the Flood-Grattan line: Powell, "Reassessing Townshend's Irish Viceroyalty, 1767–72," 176. For a differing interpretation, see York, *Neither Kingdom Nor Nation* (Washington, D.C., 1994), 79.

96. York, *Neither Kingdom Nor Nation*, 80; James Kelly, *Henry Flood: Patriots and Politics in Eighteenth-Century Ireland* (Notre Dame, Ind., 1998), 123ff. My thanks to Jim Kelly for his help on these points.

97. James Kelly, "Flood, Henry," in *Dictionary of Irish Biography* (Cambridge, 2009).

98. GT to George Macartney, 7 April 1769, D572/1/15, 51–54, PRONI; "From a native of Barataria to his friend in Pennsylvania—Condition of Barataria—Character of *Sancho* the Chief Governour—of *Caledon* his Secretary—of *Col. Promise*—of *Serjeant Rufinius*" in *Baratariana*, 1–2.

99. "From a native of Barataria to his friend in Pennsylvania—Condition of Barataria—Character of *Sancho* the Chief Governour—of *Caledon* his Secretary—of *Col. Promise*—of *Serjeant Rufinius*," in *Baratariana*, 1–2; "Sindercombe to Lord Townshend on his publick conduct in Ireland, England, and America," in *Baratariana*, 86.

100. "John Jacques Rousseau to the Writers of the Bachelor—Vindicates the Constitution of Ireland from the misrepresentations of the authors of that paper," in *Baratariana*, 245; "Cantilena to the Printer, with a ballad on the

same subject," in *Baratariana*, 263; "Fabricius to Lord Townshend on his being divested of the government of Ireland," in *Baratariana*, 343–44; *Belfast News-Letter*, 29 October–2 November 1773.

101. "From a native of Barataria to his friend in Pennsylvania—Condition of Barataria—Character of *Sancho* the Chief Governour—of *Caledon* his Secretary—of *Col. Promise*—of *Serjeant Rufinius*," in *Baratariana*, 4–5.

102. "Sindercombe to Lord Townshend on his publick conduct in Ireland, England, and America," in *Baratariana*, 93, 94, 92; "Posthumous to the people of Ireland, on the Chief Governour's Protest, the prorogation and threatened dissolution of Parliament," in *Baratariana*, 77.

103. "Sindercombe to Lord Townshend on his publick conduct in Ireland, England, and America," in *Baratariana*, 87; "From the same to the same—History of *Rufinus* continued . . .," in *Baratariana*, 32, 33, 39, 40, 52; "E. S. to the Printer, with the answer of the inhabitants of Barataria to the speech of Sancho Panca their Governour," in *Baratariana*, 57.

104. "Sindercombe to Broghill—Makes good the charges brought against Lord Townshend in Letter 12—Address to the people of Ireland on the present crisis," in *Baratariana*, 119, 131; *Baratariana*, 67.

105. "Posthumous to the people of Ireland, on the Chief Governour's Protest, the prorogation and threatened dissolution of Parliament," in *Baratariana*, 75; "Sindercombe to Broghill—Makes good the charges brought against Lord Townshend in Letter 12—Address to the people of Ireland on the present crisis," in *Baratariana*, 132.

106. For the centrality of the Molyneux-Swift-Lucas genealogy to Patriot self-conception, see York, *Neither Kingdom Nor Nation*. For Flood's introduction, see Kelly, "Flood, Henry."

107. Kelly, *Henry Flood: Patriots and Politics in Eighteenth-Century Ireland*, 140; "Sindercombe to Lord Townshend on his publick conduct in Ireland, England, and America," in *Baratariana*, 85.

108. "Sindercombe to Broghill—Makes good the charges brought against Lord Townshend in Letter 12—Address to the people of Ireland on the present crisis," in *Baratariana*, 125, 126.

109. *Freeman's Journal*, 3–5 April 1770; 5–7 April 1770. On Flood as Sindercombe, see the entry for Flood in the *Dictionary of National Biography*, edited by Leslie Stephen, vol. 19 (London, 1889), 331.

110. *Freeman's Journal*, 3–5 April 1770; 5–7 April 1770.

111. "Sindercombe to Broghill—Makes good the charges brought against Lord Townshend in Letter 12—Address to the people of Ireland on the present crisis," in *Baratariana*, 127.

112. "Memoirs of His Political Life," 34; Kelly, *Henry Flood: Patriots and Politics in Eighteenth-Century Ireland*, 159.

113. We could say, akin to Neil Longley York's subtitle, that patriots now saw their cause as a "quest for constitutional rights" or, as York put it in chapter 1 of his *Neither Kingdom Nor Nation*, "A Constitutional Tradition."

114. On the importance of these letters, as well as how the Townshend administration proved critical for the development of a coherent set of patriot ideas, see James Kelly, *Sir Edward Newenham, M.P., 1734–1814: Defender of the Protestant Constitution* (Dublin, 2004), 80–81.

115. See introduction to Eric Nelson, *The Royalist Revolution: Monarchy and the American Founding* (Cambridge, Mass., 2014) for methodology.

116. "E. S. to the Printer, with the answer of the inhabitants of Barataria to the speech of Sancho Panca their Governour," in *Baratariana*, 58; Flood's preface to the republication of William Molyneux, *The Case of Ireland Being Bound by Acts of Parliament, Stated* (Dublin, 1770).

117. *Hibernian Journal* report carried in *Virginia Gazette*, 31 October 1771; *Pennsylvania Packet*, 29 June 1772; *Providence Gazette*, 26 November 1768; *Freeman's Journal*, 10–14 October 1769, 19–21 October 1769.

Act 5. Making Revolution

1. *Dialogues in the Shades, Between General Wolfe, General Montgomery, David Hume, George Grenville, and Charles Townshend* (London, 1777). I first learned of this pamphlet through the excellent work of Alan McNairn, whose *Behold the Hero: General Wolfe and the Arts in the Eighteenth Century* (Montreal, 1997) focuses on Wolfe's role in the drama.

2. *Dialogues*, iii, 4. The two had a great deal more in common. Montgomery, not coincidentally, had become a cult hero, much like Wolfe had. In fact, Montgomery was the first American martyr of the war, and his funeral compared in scope to Wolfe's. See Sarah Purcell, *Sealed with Blood: War, Sacrifice, and Memory in Revolutionary America* (Philadelphia, 2002), 103.

3. *Dialogues*, 6, 14, 25.

4. *Dialogues*, 21–22, 33, 34.

5. *Dialogues*, 41, 42, 44, 45.

6. *Dialogues*, 54, 72, 73.

7. *Dialogues*, 80–82.

8. *Dialogues*, 86.

9. *Dialogues*, 89, 93–94.

10. *Dialogues*, 94, 99.

11. *Dialogues*, 104–5, 98.

12. *Dialogues*, 110.

13. *Dialogues*, 115. For this vision of Hume's thought, see James Harris, *Hume: An Intellectual Biography* (New York, 2015), 25, 32.

14. Gordon Wood, *The American Revolution: A History* (New York, 2002), 33, 35; P. J. Marshall, *The Making and Unmaking of Empire: Britain, India, and America, c. 1750–1783* (Oxford, 2005), 317–18; Chaffin, "The Townshend Acts Crisis, 1767–1770," in *A Companion to the American Revolution*, edited by Jack Greene and J. R. Pole (Malden, Mass., 2000), 138–40. North quote in *Sir Henry Cavendish's Debates of the House of Commons*, edited by J. Wright (London, 1841), vol. 2, 486, in Chaffin Papers, Monticello, Folder 68. For the political vision of North, one that started out on the coercive end of the spectrum but ended up on the more conciliatory end, see Andrew O'Shaughnessy, *The Men Who Lost America: British Leadership, the American Revolution, and the Fate of the Empire* (New Haven, 2014).

15. GT to Harcourt, 2 December 1776, GT to Harcourt, 9 February 1775 MS. Eng. d. 3837, Bodleian Library, 138, 116.

16. Notes on a Speech by Lord Townshend in Lords, 26 October 1775, Add. Mss. 50006, Townshend Papers, vol. 1, British Library, f. 49.

17. GT to Edward Sexton Pery, 5 November 1775, PE 323, Huntington Library.

18. "Speech on Townshend Duties," 19 April 1769, in *The Writings and Speeches of Edmund Burke*, edited by Paul Langford, vol. 2 (Oxford, 1981), 231–32.

19. John Dickinson, *Letters from a Farmer in Pennsylvania, to the Inhabitants of the British Colonies (with an Historical Introduction by R. T. H. Halsey)* (New York, 1903), Letter 11, 130–131; *Newport Mercury*, 15 February 1768; *Boston Evening-Post*, 7 March 1768; *Newport Mercury*, 7 March 1768; *Connecticut Courant*, 11 January 1768, in Chaffin Papers, Monticello, Folder 65. On Grenville bearing responsibility, even as he was in Opposition, see Pauline Maier, *From Resistance to Revolution: Colonial Radicals and the Development of American Opposition to Britain, 1765–1776* (New York, 1991), 171.

20. This was carried in the *Providence Gazette*, 15 October 1768, in Chaffin Papers, Monticello, Folder 66.

21. *Virginia Gazette*, 25 February 1768. All citations of the *Virginia Gazette* refer to the Purdie and Dixon edition of the paper.

22. *Providence Gazette*, 31 October 1767, in Chaffin Papers, Monticello, Folder 66; *Pennsylvania Gazette*, 17 November 1768; *Providence Gazette*, 26 November 1768. Report also carried in *Essex Gazette*, 22–29 November 1768. Not so

ironically, the man that Americans now cast as their nemesis did not see Dickinson as the sum of all fears. As he wrote, after he had perused the Letters, "Arguments on both sides are I believe contained in some of the Pamphlets which were publish'd on this Subject in the Years 1764 and 1765." He added, "There is very little new in them." He was right, of course. The ideas Dickinson employed were not novel. But the way of arranging them at a particular moment was. Although unmoved by Dickinson, Grenville went on to try to refute his positions, point by point, citing Locke to do so, but adding nothing to what he had already said on the matter. Grenville to William Knox, 16 August 1768, George Grenville Letterbook, st. 7, vol. 2, Huntington Library.

23. Franklin quoted in Chaffin Papers, Monticello, Folder 4a, 199.

24. John Nicholls, *Recollections and Reflections, Personal and Political, as Connected with Public Affairs, During the Reign of George III* (London, 1822), 27; Jack P. Greene, *Evaluating Empire and Confronting Colonialism in Eighteenth-Century Britain* (New York, 2013), 91–97.

25. *Boston Evening-Post*, 15 August 1768. Steve Pincus offers a similar take in *The Heart of the Declaration: The Founders' Case for an Activist Government* (New Haven, 2016), 89–90.

26. *New Hampshire Gazette*, 4 July 1766; *Pennsylvania Gazette*, 12 June 1766; *Virginia Gazette*, 20 June 1766; *Boston Evening-Post*, 2 June 1766; *New York Gazette*, 21 April 1766; *Boston Gazette*, 7 April 1766; *Essex Gazette*, 26 June–3 July 1770; *New Hampshire Gazette*, 14 September 1770; *New York Gazette*, 23 July 1770, 30 July 1770; *Pennsylvania Journal*, 8 November 1770; *Sir Henry Cavendish's Debates of the House of Commons*, vol. 2, 217 in Chaffin Papers, Monticello, Folder 68. On the emotion of joy at repeal, see Nicole Eustace, *Passion Is the Gale: Emotion, Power, and the Coming of the American Revolution* (Chapel Hill, 2008).

27. See Bernard Bailyn, *The Ideological Origins of the American Revolution* (Cambridge, Mass., 1967); and Gordon Wood, "Conspiracy and the Paranoid Style: Causality and Deceit in the Eighteenth Century," *William and Mary Quarterly*, 3rd ser., 39 (1982), 401–41.

28. Mark Lilla, *The Shipwrecked Mind: On Political Reaction* (New York, 2016), 133–36.

29. On the broader idea of pattern, see Bailyn, *The Ideological Origins of the American Revolution*, 94–95. On the idea of a new continuum, see Reinhart Kosseleck, *Futures Past: On the Semantics of Historical Time* (Cambridge, Mass., 1985), 23, 105.

30. Alisdair MacIntyre, "Epistemological Crises, Dramatic Narrative and the Philosophy of Science," *Monist* 60 (1977), 453–72. My thanks to Evan Ragland for this reference.

31. Beckett has a similar interpretation. For him, memory acted like a clothesline. All hung bits of laundry—the events—along their lines. More often than not, new events increased the tautness of the line, making it more unflappable, but at the same time they strained the line. Memory, then, was "unruly" and could snap at any moment, even as it became more sure of itself. Samuel Beckett, *Proust* (New York, 1957), 7–20. My thanks to Joe Buttigieg for this insight.

32. For these readings of this idea of event and moment, I am indebted to Declan Kiberd, who led a discussion of Yeats's "Easter, 1916" in a seminar in Buenos Aires in 2015.

33. Thomas P. Slaughter, *Independence: The Tangled Roots of the American Revolution* (New York, 2014).

34. John Phillip Reid makes this point emphatically in his *Constitutional History of the American Revolution: The Authority to Tax* (Madison, Wis., 1987), 281–82. On the ways the outside world fueled the transition, see Maier, *From Resistance to Revolution*, 162–83. See also Eliga Gould, *The Persistence of Empire: British Political Culture in the Age of the American Revolution* (Chapel Hill, 2000), 134–35.

35. *Dialogues*, 95. For the pithy "home rule" formulation, see Carl Becker, *The History of Political Parties in the Province of New York, 1760–1776* (Madison, Wis., 1909), 22. On the furies of revolution, see Arno Meyer, *The Furies: Violence and Terror in the French and Russian Revolutions* (Princeton, 2002).

36. *Dialogues*, 97.

37. Colin Nicolson, *The "Infamas Govener": Francis Bernard and the Origins of the American Revolution* (Boston, 2001), 155. This book is the best account of what happened in Boston in the wake of the duties.

38. The writings of Hulton have been edited by Neil Longley York in *Henry Hulton and the American Revolution: An Outsider's Inside View* (Charlottesville, 2010). Quotations are from pp. 193, 236, 117, 123. My thanks to Professor York for bringing this to my attention.

39. York, ed., *Henry Hulton and the American Revolution: An Outsider's Inside View*, 193, 236, 117, 123.

40. Nicolson, *The "Infamas Govener,"* 153, 117, 12. On boiling blood, see Bernard to Shelburne, 21 September 1767, in *The Papers of Francis Bernard*, edited by Colin Nicolson, vol. 3 (Boston, 2013), 410.

41. *Pennsylvania Gazette*, 30 March 1769; Marshall, *The Making and Unmaking of Empires*, 277.

42. Burke quoted in Richard Bourke, *Empire and Revolution: The Political Life of Edmund Burke* (Princeton, 2015), 316; T. H. Breen, *Marketplace of Revolution: How Consumer Politics Shaped American Independence* (New York, 2004), 235; Patrick Griffin, *America's Revolution* (New York, 2012); Robert Parkinson, *The Common Cause: Creating Race and Nation in the American Revolution* (Chapel Hill, 2016).

43. Gary B. Nash, *The Unknown American Revolution: The Unruly Birth of Democracy and the Struggle to Create America* (New York, 2005), 92–93, 97; Robert Middlekauff, *The Glorious Cause: The American Revolution, 1763–1789*, rev. ed. (Oxford, 2005), 200–209; Hiller B. Zobel, *The Boston Massacre* (New York, 1970), 102–3; Richard Archer, *As If an Enemy's Country: The British Occupation of Boston and the Origins of Revolution* (Oxford, 2010), 128–29. The best treatment of these events can be found in Eric Hinderaker, *Boston's Massacre* (Cambridge, 2017).

44. Middlekauff, *The Glorious Cause*, 203–7; John Adams, December 4, 1770, Boston Massacre Trial, in *American State Trials*, edited by John D. Lawson (St. Louis, 1918), 10:486; *History of the Boston Massacre, March 5, 1770*, edited by Frederic Kidder (Albany, 1870).

45. This is Ian McBride's formulation, from his *Eighteenth-Century Ireland: The Isle of Slaves* (Dublin, 2007), 339.

46. E. P. Thompson, *The Making of the English Working Class*, new ed. (Harmondsworth, U.K., 1972); Robert A. Gross, *The Minutemen and Their World* (New York, 1976), 10–29, 76–93; Aaron Fogleman, *Hopeful Journeys: German Immigration, Settlement, and Political Culture in Colonial America, 1717–1775* (Philadelphia, 1996).

47. The subscription lists were discovered by Karen Nipps in 2013. Harvard University's Houghton Library holds the originals (pAB7.B6578.767w). A copy was printed in *The Colonial Society of Massachusetts Newsletter* 18 (2013). For more on women and resistance to the duties see Breen, *The Marketplace of Revolution*, 282–84.

48. A Son of Liberty, *A new song, address'd to the sons of Liberty, on the continent of America; particularly to the illustrious, glorious and never to be forgotten ninety-two of Boston* (Boston, 1768); Nicolson, *The "Infamas Govener,"* 114; Bailyn, *The Ideological Origins of the American Revolution*; Zachary McLeod Hutchins, "The Slave Narrative and the Stamp Act, or Letters from Two American Farmers in Pennsylvania," in *Community Without Consent: New Perspectives on the Stamp Act*, edited by Hutchins (Hanover, N.H., 2016), 115–16.

49. Douglas R. Egerton, *Death or Liberty: African Americans and Revolutionary America* (Oxford, 2009), 49; *Some observations of consequence, in three parts. Occasioned by the stamp-tax, lately imposed on the British colonies* (Philadelphia, 1768), 19, 57.

50. Egerton, *Death or Liberty*, 48; *A letter from a gentleman at a distance to his friend at court* (1768).

51. On the contradictions, and how they worked together, see Edmund Morgan, *American Slavery, American Freedom: The Ordeal of Colonial Virginia* (New York, 1975); and David Brion Davis, *The Problem of Slavery in the Age of Revolution, 1770–1823* (New York, 1999), 277–84.

52. For this idea of wilderness in the seventeenth century, see Samuel Fisher, "Fit Instruments in a Howling Wilderness: Colonists, Indians, and the Origins of the American Revolution," *William and Mary Quarterly*, 3rd ser., 73 (2016), 647–80.

53. *Boston Chronicle*, 18–25 July 1768. Also see *The True Sentiments of America Contained in a Collection of Letters Sent from the House of Representatives of the Province of Massachusetts Bay* (London, 1768), 6.

54. *A Discourse Delivered in Providence, in the Colony of Rhode-Island upon the 25th Day of July, 1768 at the Dedication of a Tree of Liberty* (Providence, 1768), 3–5; *Boston Post-Boy*, 20 February 1769; Carl Kaestle, "The Public Reaction to John Dickinson's Farmer's Letters," in *Proceedings of the American Antiquarian Society* 78 (1969), 336; *Connecticut Journal*, 6 January 1769.

55. For settlers' rights and how they developed, see Craig Yirush, *Settlers, Liberty, and Empire: The Roots of Early American Political Theory, 1675–1775* (New York, 2011).

56. Davis, *The Problem of Slavery in the Age of Revolution*, 276.

57. Egerton, *Death or Liberty*, 46.

58. See Egerton, *Death or Liberty*; Gary Nash, *Red, Black, and White: The Peoples of Early America* (Englewood Cliffs, N.J., 1974); Edward Countryman, *Enjoy the Same Liberty: Black Americans and the Revolutionary Era* (Lanham, Md., 2012); Peter Wood, "Liberty Is Sweet," in *Beyond the American Revolution: Explorations in the History of American Radicalism*, edited by Alfred F. Young (DeKalb, Ill., 1993).

59. Davis, *The Problem of Slavery in the Age of Revolution*, 276.

60. Sylvia Frey, *Water from the Rock: Black Resistance in a Revolutionary Age* (Princeton, 1991), 51, 49; Lathan Windley, *Runaway Slave Advertisements: A Documentary History from the 1730s to 1790* (Westport, Conn., 1983); Nash, *Red, White, and Black*.

61. Egerton, *Death or Liberty,* 50; Nini Rodgers, *Ireland, Slavery, and Anti-Slavery* (New York, 2007), 72–74; Michael Mullin, *Africa in America: Slave Accultura-tion and Resistance in the American South and the British Caribbean, 1736–1831* (Chicago, 1992), 215, 219–21; Parkinson, *The Common Cause,* 20, 85.

62. Madison quoted in Frey, *Water from the Rock,* 53; Parkinson, *The Common Cause,* 87, 94; Jason Sharples, "The Flames of Insurrection: Fearing Slave Conspiracy in Early America, 1670–1780," Ph.D. dissertation, Princeton University (2010). My thanks to Jeff Bain-Conklin for bringing this to my attention.

63. Gerald Horne, *The Counter-Revolution of 1776: Slave Resistance and the Ori-gins of the United States of America* (New York, 2015); Frey, *Water from the Rock,* 52; William Bull to Hillsborough, 10 September 1768, and *The South Carolina and American General Gazette,* 26 August–2 September 1768, 6 Sep-tember 1768, CO 5/391 in "Colonial Office" database: http://www.coloni alamerica.amdigital.co.uk.proxy.library.nd.edu/Documents/SearchDe-tails/CO_5_391_010#Snippits.

64. For this dynamic and how it works, see Gregory Evans Dowd, *Groundless: Rumors, Legends, and Hoaxes on the Early American Frontier* (Baltimore, 2015), 290–91. On these dynamics in France, see Timothy Tackett, *The Com-ing of the Terror in the French Revolution* (Cambridge, Mass., 2015). The rise of Indian confederations and British fears in these years are covered by Rob-ert Owens, *Red Dreams, White Nightmares: Pan-Indian Alliances in the Anglo-American Mind, 1763–1815* (Norman, Okla., 2015). It seems the Brit-ish were more particularly afflicted with these fears; American colonists, ex-cept those on the frontier, less so.

65. See Roy Foster, *Vivid Faces: The Revolutionary Generation in Ireland, 1890–1923* (New York, 2015).

66. Nicolson, *The "Infamas Govener,"* 172, 183; Hinderaker, *Boston's Massacre,* 73, 112, 116.

67. Richard Jackson to GT, and Barrington to GT, 14 September 1770, GT Pa-pers, Clements, vol. 2; GT to North, 25 September 1770, GT Papers, Letter-book, Clements, vol. 2, 212; *Belfast Newsletter,* 12 February 1773.

68. Earl of Buckinghamshire to Lord George Germain, 16 September 1780, His-torical Manuscripts Commission, *Report of the Manuscripts of the Marquess of Lothian* (London, 1905), 373; Arthur Young to GT, 30 January 1786, HMC, 412; GT's Note for a Speech in the Lords, October 1775, Add. Mss. 50006A, British Library, 49.

69. *The Morning Post,* 31 October 1807; Martyn J. Powell, "Townshend, George,

First Marquess Townshend (1724–1807)," *Oxford Dictionary of National Biography,* vol. 55 (Oxford, 2004), 159; GT to Lord Harcourt, 29 June 1772, MS. Eng. d. 3837, Bodleian Library, 90.

70. Jules David Prown, *John Singleton Copley in England* (Cambridge, Mass., 1966), 276–78. Chatham quoted in Marie Peters, "The Myth of William Pitt," *Journal of Imperial and Commonwealth History* 22 (1994), 410.

71. GT to Edward Sexton Pery, 7 April 1778, PE 326, Huntington Library.

72. GT to Edward Sexton Pery, 7 April 1778, PE 326, Huntington Library.

73. Sotheby's catalogue copy for West's *The Death of the Earl of Chatham* from the Yale Center for British Art. My thanks to Abigail Armistead for sending along a copy of the Sotheby's companion piece to the painting.

74. Robert Plate, *John Singleton Copley: America's First Great Artist* (New York, 1969), 124; Prown, *John Singleton Copley in England,* 279.

75. Prown, *John Singleton Copley in England,* 284, 286; *Description of Mr. Copley's Picture of the Death of the Earl of Chatham,* printed by H. Reynell (London, 1780); Plate in Prown, *John Singleton Copley,* 124–26; Key to the Death of the Earl of Chatham, T. 1213, Harvard Art Museum. Thanks to the museum staff for sending a copy of the key. See also Martha Amory, *The Domestic and Artistic Life of John Singleton Copley* (New York, 1969), 83.

76. Prown, *John Singleton Copley,* 298.

77. See, for instance, *The Case of Great-Britain and America, Addressed to the King, and Both Houses of Parliament* (Dublin, 1769), 1, in which they read how in 1769 "the affairs of Great-Britain and her Colonies, are at a crisis." On the well-known links, see Neil Longley York, *Neither Kingdom Nor Nation: The Irish Quest for Constitutional Rights, 1698–1800* (Washington, D.C., 1994); Maurice O'Connell, *Irish Politics and Social Conflict in the Age of the American Revolution* (Philadelphia, 1965); and Owen Dudley Edwards, "The Impact of the American Revolution on Ireland," in *The Impact of the American Revolution Abroad* (Washington, D.C., 1976).

78. On patterns, see Jacqueline Hill, *From Patriots to Unionists: Dublin Civic Politics and Irish Protestant Patriotism, 1660–1840* (Oxford, 1997), 127; for the next period, and its "density," see Padhraig O'Higgins, *A Nation of Politicians: Gender, Patriotism, and Political Culture in Late Eighteenth-Century Ireland* (Madison, Wis., 2010).

79. GT to the Earl of Buckinghamshire, 21 August 1778, HMC, *Lothian,* 337; Grattan quoted in James Kelly, "Patriot Politics, 1750–91," in *The Oxford Handbook of Modern Irish History,* edited by Alvin Jackson (Oxford, 2014).

80. George, of course, also served as some sort of catalyst for constitutional is-
    sues to come to the fore, and some historians have seen George's role for
    what it was. See, for instance, York, *Neither Kingdom Nor Nation,* 75–82. On
    the idea of retreat, and what he calls the concomitant "fracturing of the En-
    lightenment," see Michael Brown, *The Irish Enlightenment* (Cambridge,
    Mass., 2016), 346–47. The best statements on the nature of what this form
    accomplished and did not accomplish are James Kelly, "Patriot Politics,
    1750–91," in *The Oxford Handbook of Modern Irish History,* edited by Alvin
    Jackson (Oxford, 2014); Ian McBride, " 'The Common Name of Irish Man':
    Protestantism and Patriotism in Eighteenth-Century Ireland," in *Protestant-*
    ism and National Identity: Britain in Ireland, c. 1650–c. 1850, edited by Tony
    Claydon and Ian McBride (Cambridge, 1998), 236–60.
81. McBride, *Eighteenth-Century Ireland,* 278–79. On how and why the Irish did
    not take the road of the Americas, see H. T. Dickinson, "Why Did the
    American Revolution Not Spread to Ireland?" *Valahian Journal of Historical*
    Studies 18–19 (2012–2013), 155–80. My thanks to Professor Dickinson for
    sharing this essay.
82. GT to Shelburne, 10 May 1768, in *Calendar of Home Office Papers of the*
    Reign of George III: 1760–1775, edited by Joseph Redington (London, 1879),
    vol. 2, 871. Around elections, "the feelings of a people roused from a long
    state of apathy are usually violent, and never silent," as one Patriot put it.
    "Their wishes," he continued, "were strongly conveyed to their representa-
    tives in peremptory instructions, and to Parliament in spirited petitions." See
    "Memoirs of His Political Life," in *The Manuscripts and Correspondence of*
    James, First Earl of Charlemont (London, 1891), vol. 1, 30, 25; GT to Mar-
    quess of Granby, 7 May 1768, Historical Manuscripts Commission, *Rutland,*
    305.
83. GT to Macartney, 31 August 1769, D 572/1/18, PRONI, 60–63; GT to Ma-
    cartney, 27 May 1769, D 572/1/34, PRONI, 119–22; David Dickson, *Dub-*
    lin: The Making of a Capital City (Cambridge, Mass., 2014), 192–93;
    Freeman's Journal, 22–28 December 1769.
84. GT to Harcourt, 12 March 1773, MS. Eng. d 3837, Bodleian Library, 104; Mc-
    Bride, *Eighteenth-Century Ireland,* 390. On Irish women and homespun in
    the 1770s, following the example of America, see Higgins, *A Nation of Poli-*
    ticians.
85. GT to Earl of Rochford, 28 February 1771, *Calendar of Home Office Papers,*
    vol. 3, 557; Hill, *From Patriots to Unionists,* 128, 130–32; GT to Lord Roch-
    ford, 8 April 1771, *Calendar of Home Office Papers,* vol. 3, 633.

86. Charles O'Conor to John Curry, 1 January 1773, in *The Letters of Charles O'Conor of Belangare*, edited by Catherine Coogan Ward and Robert E. Ward (Ann Arbor, Mich., 1980), 35; my thanks to Macdara Dwyer for this reference. *Belfast Newsletter*, 17 November 1772.

87. Roland Thorne, "Courtenay, John (1738–1816)," in *Oxford Dictionary of National Biography*, vol. 13 (Oxford, 2004), 682; *Dublin Mercury*, 1 September 1770, August 2, 1770; *Dublin Mercury*, 15 August 1770.

88. S. J. Connolly, *Divided Kingdom: Ireland, 1630–1800* (Oxford, 2008), 394; Thomas Bartlett, *The Fall and Rise of the Irish Nation: The Catholic Question, 1690–1830* (Dublin, 1992), 76–81. On quarterage and George, see Sir Thomas Wyse, *Historical Sketch of the Late Catholic Association of Ireland*, vol. 1 (London, 1829), 85. My thanks to Martyn Powell for this reference.

89. *Freeman's Journal*, 16–19 September 1769.

90. *Freeman's Journal*, 19–23 September 1769.

91. *Freeman's Journal*, 10–14 October 1769, 17–19 October 1769.

92. Muiris Ó Gormáin, "Ar George Townshend," in *Muiris Ó Gormáin: Beatha agus Saothar Fileata*, edited by Nioclás Mac Cathmhaoil (An Clóchomhar, 2013), 231–32. My thanks to Sam Fisher for both the citation and the translation from the Irish.

93. Desmond McCabe, "Ó Gormáin (Mac Gormáin, O'Gorman, Gorman), Muiris (Maurice)," in *Dictionary of Irish Biography* (Cambridge, 2009). On coexistence, see Brown, *The Irish Enlightenment*, 362–63.

94. On this, see Nicholas Wolf, *An Irish-Speaking Island: State, Religion, Community, and the Linguistic Landscape in Ireland, 1770–1870* (Madison, Wis., 2014), 18–19, 181–85.

95. Vincent Morley, *Irish Opinion and the American Revolution, 1760–1783* (Cambridge, 2002), 46–47. For an interpretation that questions the centrality of Jacobitism, but that does agree with increasing levels of political engagement throughout the eighteenth century, see Ultan Gillen, "Ascendancy Ireland, 1660–1800," in *The Princeton History of Modern Ireland*, edited by Richard Bourke and Ian McBride (Princeton, 2016), 59.

96. Ian McBride, *Scripture Politics: Ulster Presbyterians and Irish Radicalism in the Late Eighteenth Century* (Oxford 1998).

97. For a political interpretation relying on broad and local context, as well as contemporary fears, I am relying on David Dickson's work, especially "Novel Spectacle? The Birth of the Whiteboys, 1761–1762," in *Ourselves Alone? Religion, Society, and Politics in Eighteenth- and Nineteenth-Century Ireland: Essays Presented to S. J. Connolly*, edited by D. W. Hayton and

Andrew Holmes (Dublin, 2016). See also Morley, *Irish Opinion and the American Revolution*, 48–51.

98. Richard Jackson to GT, 16 November 1770, Add. Mss. 63100, Townshend Papers, British Library, f. 32; GT to Earl of Rochford, 27 March 1772, *Calendar of Home Office Papers*, vol. 3, 1189. On the politicization angle, see Eoin Magennis, "County Armagh Hearts of Oak," *Seanchas Ardmhacha: Journal of the Armagh Diocesan Historical Society* 17 (1998), 19–31; and "A 'Presbyterian Insurrection'? Reconsidering the Hearts of Oaks Disturbances of 1763," *Irish Historical Studies* 122 (1998).

99. GT to Lord Weymouth, 2 March 1770, *Calendar of Home Office Papers*, vol. 3, 59. The priest was Fr. Nicholas Sheehy. See *The Proclamations of Ireland, 1660–1820*, edited by James Kelly and Mary Ann Lyons, vol. 4, part I (Dublin, 2014), 139, 147, 188, 121, 122–23.

100. *Dublin Mercury*, 7 August 1770; Dickson, *Dublin*, 194.

101. *The Proclamations of Ireland, 1660–1820*, ed. Kelly and Lyons, vol. 4, part I, 207–10, 212; Morley, *Irish Opinion and the American Revolution*, 90–94; Diarmuid O Grada, *Georgian Dublin: The Forces That Shaped the City* (Cork, 2015), 248–49. On the men of no property, see Jim Smyth, *The Men of No Property: Irish Radicals and Popular Politics in the Late Eighteenth Century* (New York, 1992).

102. On rural insurgency caused by "economic xenophobia," see James Donnelly, "Irish Agrarian Rebellion: The Whiteboys of 1769–1776," *Proceedings of the Royal Irish Academy* 83 (1983), 293–331. For the counterargument, one that stresses the "insecurities of the decade," most especially political issues, see Maurice Bric, "The Whiteboy Movement in Tipperary, 1760–1780," *Tipperary: History and Society*, edited by William Nolan and Thomas McGrath (Dublin, 1985), 148–68.

103. Martyn Powell, "Money for the Maimed: The Problem of 'Houghed' Soldiers in Eighteenth-Century Ireland," a talk at the University of Notre Dame, 17 March 2015; Brown, *The Irish Enlightenment*, 309.

104. *Dublin Mercury* from 4 October 1770, cited in Martyn Powell, "Ireland's Urban Houghers: Moral Economy and Popular Protest in the Late Eighteenth Century," in *The Laws and Other Legalities of Ireland, 1689–1850*, edited by Michael Brown and Sean Patrick Donlan (Farnham, U.K., 2011), 242.

105. GT to "My Dear Lord," 13 September 1771; GT to Earl of Rochford, 11 March 1772, *Calendar of Home Office Papers*, vol. 3, 844, 1154; GT to Earl of Rochford, 18 March 1772, *Calendar of Home Office Papers*, vol. 3, 1165.

106. Morley, *Irish Opinion and the American Revolution,* 48–51. On the political angle, see Powell, "Ireland's Urban Houghers," in *The Laws and Other Legalities of Ireland, 1689–1850,* ed. Brown and Donlan, 253. On the "great fear," see Dickson, "Novel Spectacle? The Birth of the Whiteboys, 1761–1762," 73.

107. McBride, *Eighteenth-Century Ireland,* 319, 338–39.

108. The best statement on politicization in these years is Brown, *The Irish Enlightenment,* 308–9.

109. Gillen, "Ascendancy Ireland, 1660–1800," 63; Daniel Carey, "Intellectual History: William King to Edmund Burke," in *The Princeton History of Ireland,* edited by Richard Bourke and Ian McBride (Princeton, 2016), 204–5; Gillen, "Ascendancy Ireland, 1660–1800," 64; Bartlett, *The Fall and Rise of the Irish Nation,* 75.

110. Robert Burns, "The Catholic Relief Act in Ireland, 1778," *Church History* 32 (1963), 181–206.

111. Townshend to Shelburne, 17 May 1768, M 2446, Irish Correspondence, vol. 1, National Archives of Ireland. My thanks to Sam Fisher for alerting me to this source.

112. James Gisborne to GT, 25 March 1772, M715, National Archives of Ireland.

113. Lucas, *A Second Letter to the Free Holders and Tradesmen of the City of Dublin* (Dublin, 1768), 8.

114. Nash, *Unknown American Revolution,* 97; Pauline Maier, *The Old Revolutionaries: Political Lives in the Age of Samuel Adams* (New York, 1980), 3–18; Maier, *From Resistance to Revolution;* Patrick Griffin, "America's Changing Image in Ireland's Looking-Glass: Provincial Construction of an Eighteenth-Century British Atlantic World," *Journal of Imperial and Commonwealth History* 26 (1998), 28–49.

115. Bernard Bailyn and John Clive, "England's Cultural Provinces: Scotland and America," *William and Mary Quarterly,* 3rd ser., 11 (1954), 200–214.

116. Peter Berger quoted in Davis, *The Problem of Slavery in the Age of Revolution,* 279.

117. "Negro Conspiracy" represented more than a hypothetical worry in these years, and one scholar has even gone so far as to argue the decision to declare independence stemmed from such anxieties. That is overstating the case, but acknowledging the bind from which elites had to extricate themselves does not. See Horne, *The Counter-Revolution of 1776;* and for South Carolina, Frey, *Water from the Rock,* 52. On how improvement shaped relations in the eighteenth century, see Toby Barnard, *Improving Ireland? Projectors, Profits and Profiteers, 1641–1786* (Dublin, 2008), 179.

118. Duncan Macleod, "Toward Caste," in *Slavery and Freedom in the Age of the American Revolution*, edited by Ira Berlin and Ronald Hoffman (Charlottesville, 1983), 233. On growing confidence, even in South Carolina, see Matthew Mulcahy, *Hub of Empire: The Southeastern Lowcountry and British Caribbean* (Baltimore, 2014), 11–21; and Trevor Burnard, *Planters, Merchants, and Slaves: Plantation Societies in British America, 1650–1820* (Chicago, 2015), 237, 247.

119. On this dynamic, see Woody Holton, *Forced Founders: Indians, Debtors, Slaves, and the Making of the American Revolution in Virginia* (Chapel Hill, 1999). Robert Parkinson argues that the push for a Declaration of Independence, to a great measure, emerged from fears of slave insurrection and how some patriots made great use of such fears for propagandistic purposes. See *The Common Cause*, 247–49.

120. On the settlement of these years and how it did not change as much as is often suggested, see James Kelly, "The Politics of the Protestant Ascendancy," in *The Cambridge History of Ireland*, vol. 3, edited by James Kelly (forthcoming).

121. Dickson, *Dublin*, 194; Marshall, *The Making and Unmaking of Empire*, 340–41. My thanks to Tom Bartlett for enlightening me on this score.

122. On this, see McBride, *Eighteenth-Century Ireland*, 347–53. Grattan quote in James Kelly, "Patriot Politics, 1750–91," in *The Oxford Handbook of Modern Irish History*, edited by Alvin Jackson (Oxford, 2013).

123. GT to Harcourt, 26 February 1776, MS. Eng. d. 3837, Bodleian Library, 134.

124. GT to Edward Sexton Pery, 23 September 1775, PE 321, Huntington Library.

125. Aviezer Tucker, "Historiographical Counterfactuals and Historical Contingency," *History and Theory* 38 (1999), 264–76. For why this moment especially gives rise to the counterfactual, see John Shy, "The Spectrum of Imperial Possibilities: Henry Ellis and Thomas Pownall, 1763–1775," in *A People Numerous and Armed: Reflections on the Military Struggle for American Independence* (Ann Arbor, Mich., 1990). On path dependency, see Paul Pearson, "Increasing Returns, Path Dependence, and the Study of Politics," *American Political Science Review* 94 (2000), 251–67. My thanks to Sebastian Rosato on this point. Historians debate both the utility and the implications of the counterfactual. Some see it as a useful exercise, some deride it as entertainment. But in a carefully controlled setting, most agree that it can shed light on the necessary causes of what happened. For the debate, see two thought-provoking books: Richard Evans, *Altered Pasts:*

Counterfactuals in History (Waltham, Mass., 2013); and *Virtual History: Alternatives and Counterfactuals,* edited by Niall Ferguson (New York, 2000).

126. For a terrific study of the range of options, see Shy, "The Spectrum of Imperial Possibilities: Henry Ellis and Thomas Pownall, 1763–1775." On the careful use of the counterfactual, see John Murrin, "The French and Indian War, the American Revolution, and the Counterfactual Hypothesis: Reflections on Lawrence Henry Gipson and John Shy," *Reviews in American History* 1 (1973), 307–18.

127. On this theme, and its broad applicability throughout history, see Alistair Horne, *Hubris: The Tragedy of War in the Twentieth Century* (New York, 2015). For this idea I draw on O'Shaughnessy, *The Men Who Lost America*; and Ira Gruber, *The Howe Brothers and the American Revolution* (New York, 1972).

128. Lucius, *A Letter to a Great Man* (Dublin, 1770), 5–12. On ghosts and what-ifs, see the insightful essay by Breandán Mac Suibhne, "Spirit, Spectre, Shade: A True Story of an Irish Haunting; or, Troublesome Pasts in the Political Culture of North-west Ulster, 1786–1972," *Field Day Review* 9 (2013), 148–211.

129. Mercy Otis Warren, *The Adultateur: A Tragedy as It Is Now Acted in Upper Servia* (Boston, 1773); *Boston Gazette,* 11 February 1771; *Boston Evening-Post,* 11 March 1771; *New York Gazette,* 18 March 1771; *Boston Evening-Post,* 13 May 1771; *Pennsylvania Journal,* 4 January 1775; *Connecticut Courant,* 26 September 1774; *Norwich Packet,* 4–11 May 1775. Even the dead Montgomery appears. See *Pennsylvania Packet,* 19 February 1776; Caroline Wiginton, "Letters from a Woman in Pennsylvania, or Elizabeth Graeme Fergusson Dreams of John Dickinson," in *Community Without Consent: New Perspectives on the Stamp Act,* edited by Zachary McLeod Hutchins (Hanover, N.H., 2016), 91–92.

130. This would seem to fly in the face of recent interpretations like that of Nick Bunker, who argues that the tensions of empire—"fundamental flaws"— would inevitably lead to a bid for independence on the part of Americans. See his *An Empire on the Edge: How Britain Came to Fight America* (New York, 2014), 26–27.

131. *Hull Packet,* 20 October 1807; *Finns Leinster,* 9 October 1807; *Times,* 19 September 1807.

132. *Hull Packet,* 20 October 1807; *Finns Leinster,* 9 October 1807; *Times,* 19 September 1807.

133. *Charleston Courier,* 24 June 1807.

134. See Kerby A. Miller, " 'Scotch-Irish,' 'Black Irish' and 'Real Irish': Emigrants and Identities in the Old South," in *The Irish Diaspora*, edited by Andy Bielenberg (London, 2000), 111–38.

135. This honor stemmed, in part, from what he would go on to do for Irish trade. Nonetheless, it does speak to how sensibilities had shifted. On this, see Dr. Achmet to GT, 18 October 1779, Townshend Letterbook, M5040, 81, National Archives, Dublin. My thanks to Tom Bartlett for this reference.

136. Hill, *From Patriots to Unionists;* "List of those who attended banquet on Townshend's birthday, 11 March 1795, MS 394/16. My thanks to Tom Bartlett for this reference. *Freeman's Journal*, 10 March 1807.

137. *Freeman's Journal*, 25 September 1807; *Freeman's Journal*, 4 October 1807.

138. *Morning Post*, 30 September 1807.

139. *Morning Post*, 17 September 1807; *Hull Packet*, 29 September 1807. For the links between the Norfolk and American militias, see J. A. Holding, *Fit for Service: The Training of the British Army, 1715–1795* (Oxford, 1981), 207; and Gould, *The Persistence of Empire*, 101–2. My thanks to Lige Gould for this connection.

140. *Times*, 19 September 1807.

141. *Hull Packet*, 29 September 1807; *Morning Post*, 5 October 1807.

142. In 1778, for instance, as the French were threatening invasion, as his work in Ireland threatened to come undone with Chatham's passing, and with the American conundrum becoming unsolvable, he wrote of the "sad crisis." He declared many like him "perplexed," adding, "We feel and look as if we despair'd, nay if we dared not even be inform'd of our situation." He called again for "a system of measures." But such times had passed. Britain, in its dealings with the crises at hand, was led by "the red heel'd luxurious Rascals of this pamper'd, hermaphrodite Nation," which had pushed Britain "on the point of loosing" the whole. These "Hermaphrodites in Politics" were noted for "Charming Inconsistency, delightful half measures." They were "political Poltroons." George lived, trapped really, in a moment defined by "War and Peace, Supremacy and Submission, Chastisement and Negotiation, Execration and Embassy, and lastly, Provocation and Insult . . . followed by indiscretion and suspence." He sounded like the angry old man he had become. See GT to Edward Sexton Pery, 25 March 1772, 3 April 1778, PE 329, PE 330, Huntington Library.

143. Macartney to GT, 31 December 1771, M661, National Archives of Ireland; James Gisborne to GT, 7 March 1769, M707, National Archives of Ireland.

144. Lord Fitzgibbon to GT, 9 June 1772, M725, National Archives of Ireland.

145. Meyer, *The Furies;* Horne, *Hubris,* 1.

146. *Dialogues,* 106.

147. Charles and George thought they could manage the world, much like the men who surrounded President George W. Bush and believed they did not have to inhabit a "reality-based community." They thought they could act with certainty and could disregard "inconvenient facts" because, as one put it, "we're an empire now, and when we act, we create our own reality." While the rest of us were "studying that history—judiciously, as you will—we'll act again, creating other new realities, which you can study too." They saw themselves, like the brothers, as "history's actors . . . and you, all of you, will be left to just study what we do." See David Suskind's essay entitled "Faith, Certainty and the Presidency of George W. Bush," *New York Times Magazine,* 17 October 2004. My thanks to Brian Schoen for this reference.

148. For the patterns to this proclivity, seen throughout American imperial history, see David Milne, *Worldmaking: The Art and Science of American Diplomacy* (New York, 2015). Milne quotes Hume in the epigraph to the book.

149. For a study of how the so-called Arab Spring was transformed into anything but, see the enlightening study by Robert Worth entitled *A Rage for Order: The Middle East in Turmoil, from Tahrir Square to ISIS* (New York, 2016).

Index